Asia's New Multilateralism

Asia's New Multilateralism

COOPERATION, COMPETITION, AND THE SEARCH FOR COMMUNITY

Edited by Michael J. Green and Bates Gill

COLUMBIA UNIVERSITY PRESS

NEW YORK

Columbia University Press
Publishers Since 1893
New York   Chichester, West Sussex

Library of Congress Cataloging-in-Publication Data
Asia's new multilateralism : cooperation, competition, and the search for
community / edited by Michael J. Green and Bates Gill.
p.   cm.
Includes bibliographical references and index.
ISBN 978-0-231-14442-1 (cloth : alk. paper)
ISBN 978-0-231-14443-8 (pbk. : alk. paper)
ISBN 978-0-231-51341-8 (e-book)
1. Asian cooperation.   2. Asia—Foreign relations.   I. Green, Michael J.
II. Gill, Bates.
JZ1720.A75   2009
327.5—dc22   2008030820

Columbia University Press books are printed
on permanent and durable acid-free paper.

Printed in the United States of America

c 10 9 8 7 6 5 4 3 2 1
p 10 9 8 7 6 5 4 3 2 1

References to Internet Web sites (URLs) were accurate at the time of writing.
Neither the editors and contributors nor Columbia University Press is responsible
for URLs that may have expired or changed since the manuscript was prepared.

CONTENTS

PREFACE

Each of us has been grappling with the question of Asia's emerging multilateralism for well more than a decade as a matter of both policy and scholarship. In 2006, we decided it was time for a rigorous analysis of exactly what is happening in the region and what the prospects for multilateral cooperation really are. We approached the Stanley Foundation because of its previous work on multilateral security concepts and were fortunate to receive its full support for this project. We began by organizing a conference in St. Michaels, Maryland, in November 2006 with leading experts from the region. The chapter authors in this volume produced excellent first drafts for that meeting, and we also benefited from the insights of nine other practitioners and scholars: Ellen Frost, Kazumasa Kusaka, Evan Medeiros, Derek Mitchell, Dan Rosen, Susan Sim, Hitoshi Tanaka, and observers James Green and Sugio Takahashi. We appreciate the hard work our authors and all the participants did at St. Michaels and especially thank Michael Schiffer at the Stanley Foundation for his support and intellectual partnership, which made the early stages of this book possible. We also benefited from two detailed and encouraging outside reviews and thank the anonymous scholars who took the time to conduct their thorough critique for Columbia University Press. Thanks also are due to our wonderful editor at Columbia University Press, Anne Routon, and to Annie Barva for her meticulous editing of the final draft.

At the Center for Strategic and International Studies, this project was shepherded by research associate Yuko Nakano, without whom we would never have finished. Our research and logistics team also included Akiko Pace, David Fedman, Yuhei Komatsu, and Fujihiko Hayashi, as well as Ashley Calkins of the Stanley Foundation. We also thank Chin-hao Huang at the Stockholm International Peace Research Institute for his research assistance.

We do not expect Asia to arrive at a neat multilateral "architecture" anytime soon, but we believe this book will provide a framework for understanding the fluid and often competitive process of institution building in Asia as it unfolds in the years ahead.

ABBREVIATIONS

ABF	Asian Bond Fund
ABMI	Asian Bond Market Initiative
ACCORD	ASEAN and China Cooperative Operations in Response to Dangerous Drugs
AFTA	ASEAN Free Trade Area
APEC	Asia-Pacific Economic Cooperation
APPCDC	Asia-Pacific Partnership on Clean Development and Climate
APT	ASEAN Plus Three
ARF	ASEAN Regional Forum
ASEAN	Association of Southeast Asian Nations
BIMSTEC	Bay of Bengal Initiative for Multi-Sectoral Technical and Economic Cooperation
CEPEA	Comprehensive Economic Partnership in East Asia
CMI	Chiang Mai Initiative
CSCE	Conference on Security and Cooperation in Europe
EAEC	East Asia Economic Caucus
EAFTA	East Asian Free Trade Agreement

EAS	East Asia Summit
EAVG	East Asia Vision Group
EIDHR	European Initiative for the Development of Human Rights
EMEAP	Executives' Meeting of East Asia Pacific Central Banks
EPA	economic partnership agreement
EPG	Eminent Persons Group
ERIA	Economic Research Institute for ASEAN and East Asia
FTA	free-trade agreement
FTAAP	Free Trade Area of the Asia-Pacific
GATS	General Agreement on Trade in Services
GATT	General Agreement on Tariffs and Trade
ICC	International Criminal Court
IMF	International Monetary Fund
IPR	intellectual property rights
KEDO	Korean Energy Development Organization
MFN	most-favored nation
NAFTA	North American Free Trade Agreement
NATO	North Atlantic Treaty Organization
NGO	nongovernmental organization
NPT	Nuclear Non-Proliferation Treaty
NTS	nontraditional security
OSCE	Organization for Security and Cooperation in Europe
PBEC	Pacific Basin Economic Council
PECC	Pacific Economic Cooperation Council
PMC	Post-Ministerial Conference
PSI	Proliferation Security Initiative
SAARC	South Asian Association for Regional Cooperation
SARS	severe acute respiratory syndrome
SCO	Shanghai Cooperation Organization
SEATO	Southeast Asia Treaty Organization
TAC	Treaty of Amity and Cooperation
TSD	Trilateral Security Dialogue
UNSC	United Nations Security Council
USAID	U.S. Agency for International Development
WHO	World Health Organization

WMD	weapons of mass destruction
WTO	World Trade Organization
ZOPFAN	Zone of Peace, Friendship, and Neutrality

Asia's New Multilateralism

1. Unbundling Asia's New Multilateralism

Bates Gill and Michael J. Green

The sweeping arc of Asia—from the Indian Ocean to the Bering Straits and from Tashkent to Tasmania—stands out as the world's most dynamic region. Unprecedented economic and political forces powerfully shift the region's relationships large and small, from the rise of China and India to the emergence of new democracies. New transnational challenges—financial crises, environmental disasters, infectious disease outbreaks, the impact of globalization, terrorist networks—defy old notions of sovereignty. At the same time, traditional rivalries and emergent confrontations between regional powers raise the specter of past conflicts.

Whether Asia's future is characterized by cooperation or confrontation will be determined in large part by the region's ability to construct effective multilateral institutions for integration, collaboration, and cooperative problem solving—what is now being called the new Asian institutional "architecture." Over the past sixty years, Asia's stability has rested on the foundations of bilateral alliances between the United States and Japan, Australia, and South Korea principally, but also the Philippines and Thailand. However, in recent years the regional architecture has been reinforced with the long-standing Association of Southeast Asian Nations (ASEAN) and a more mature ASEAN Regional Forum (ARF), as well as with other multilateral mechanisms such as the

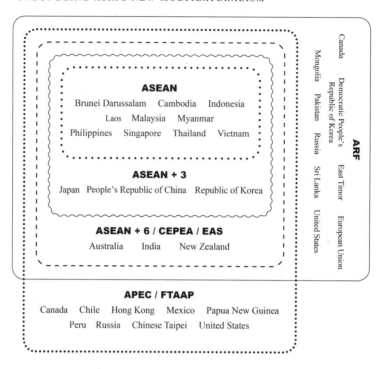

FIGURE 1.1 MULTILATERAL INSTITUTIONS IN ASIA.
Note: APEC, Asia-Pacific Economic Cooperation; ARF, ASEAN Regional Forum; ASEAN, Association of Southeast Asian Nations; CEPEA, Comprehensive Economic Partnership in East Asia; EAS, East Asia Summit; FTAAP, Free Trade Area of the Asia-Pacific; KEDO, Korean Energy Development Organization; PSI, Proliferation Security Initiative; TCOG, Trilateral Coordination and Oversight Group; TSD, Trilateral Security Dialogue.

Asia-Pacific Economic Cooperation (APEC) forum, the ASEAN Plus Three (APT) process, the Shanghai Cooperation Organization (SCO), the Six-Party Talks on Korean Peninsula stability, and the newly formed East Asia Summit (EAS) (figure 1.1). Reflective of the region itself, this new architecture is highly fluid and engenders both cooperation and competition among the region's powers. What is more, the future direction and success of these arrangements and the implications for global and regional security and prosperity remain unclear even as the elements of this dynamic regional architecture expand and become more complex. The financial crisis that struck in late 2008 quickly demonstrated the globalized interconnectedness of the world's economies and underscored the need for well-coordinated regional and global multilateral structures to implement an effective response. Yet across the region and beyond, con-

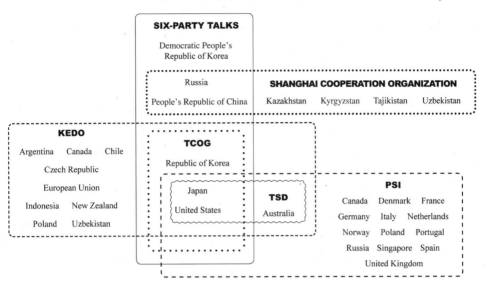

cerns persist whether the process is evolving toward less-inclusive, bloc-based "talking shops" rather than toward a more open, inclusive, and problem-solving regionalism.

Analysis of this evolving architecture has too often been trapped in the domain of liberal institutionalists who focus on the forums and institutions themselves (often with disappointment in comparative perspective with Europe) or of constructivists who are drawn to the region's seductive but misleading rhetoric about building an "East Asian community." The reality is that Asia's new multilateralism is still at a stage where it is best understood as an extension and intersection of national power and purpose rather than as an objective force in itself. But adopting such a perspective does not necessarily minimize the importance of new multilateral institutions forming in the region; indeed, it reinforces the idea that these institutions will be increasingly important in the dynamics of Asian international relations in the future.

The purpose of this book is to unbundle the myths and reality of "community building" in Asia. The volume employs a matrix approach for analyzing and understanding the emerging Asian architecture. Chapters 2 through 8 form the x axis and provide national strategic perspectives toward multilateralism and regional architecture. These chapters cover perspectives from the United States (Ralph Cossa), China (Wu Xinbo), Korea (Lim Wonhyuk), Japan (Akiko Fukushima), India (C. Raja Mohan), Australia (Greg Sheridan), and Southeast Asia (Amitav Acharya). In these chapters, the authors explain each country's traditional approach to regional institution building and integration; the internal, domestic debate about the emerging architecture in terms of function, inclusiveness, and rules; and views about the U.S. role in the region and in regional institutions. Each of these chapters concludes with a look ahead to the kinds of institutions that will be necessary to assure regional security and prosperity for the future.

Chapters 9 through 13 form the *y* axis of our matrix. Stepping entirely away from national strategies, the authors of these chapters explain the major transnational challenges in Asia that will require greater and more effective multilateral cooperation. These chapters examine trade and economic integration (Amy Searight); governance and democracy (William Cole and Erik Jensen); defense capabilities, regional security, and confidence building (Michael O'Hanlon); nontraditional security threats (Mely Caballero-Anthony); and the future challenges to building a multilateral "security architecture" in the region (Brendan Taylor and William Tow). In these chapters, the authors assess the nature of these emergent regional concerns, the ability of current multilateral forums and institutions in Asia to address these concerns effectively, and the prospects that existing institutions can be reconfigured or new institutions can emerge to meet and manage the array of common economic, political, and security challenges facing the region.

By cross-referencing national strategies and debates with regional challenges, we seek to demonstrate which patterns of multilateral cooperation offer the greatest prospect for moving from superficial rhetoric about "community building" toward substantive collaboration, convergence of norms, and strengthening of domestic institutions across the region that can effectively be engaged within multilateral problem-solving organizations. We also address whether the emerging architecture is likely to reinforce Asian states' integration with global norms and institutions, likely to increase exceptionalism and separation from the prevailing neoliberal international order, or possibly to have little effect at all. In addition, the book exposes how multilateral forums have become arenas for power rivalry and competition as much as for cooperation, pointing to the external balancing behavior in which states are engaged as the institutions are formed. And we consider how these developments complement and/or compete with the U.S. role and its bilateral alliances in the region.

In the remaining pages of this introductory chapter, we provide a brief overview of the history of Asian regionalism and multilateralism, consider the key theoretical and policy debates these developments pose to scholars and practitioners, and point to some of the principal policy conclusions we can draw for the years ahead.

THE RISE OF ASIAN REGIONALISM
AND MULTILATERALISM

Regional political, security, and economic arrangements and a search for an Asian community and identity are not at all new to the region. Trade linkages across the Asian "Silk Road" were an early form of regional economic integration. The spread of Buddhism from India and across Asia dating from the third century C.E. had an integrating cultural and religious effect that continues to this day. Chinese dynastic rulers had varying success in extending their dominion over parts of Asia under a system of military conquest combined with economic and political tribute. More recently, militarist Japan of the 1930s and 1940s attempted to integrate Asia within its "Greater East Asian Coprosperity Sphere." With the onset of the Cold War, rivalries within Asia sharply defined the political, economic, and military institutions that emerged at the time, many of which continue to the present. The United States established bilateral partnerships with Australia (1951), New Zealand (1951), the Philippines (1951), South Korea (1953), Japan (1954), Thailand (1954), and the Republic of China (Taiwan, 1954). In 1954, one of the original multilateral security arrangements in the region, the Southeast Asia Treaty Organization (SEATO), was formed, bringing together Australia, France, New Zealand, Pakistan, the Philippines, Thailand, the United Kingdom, and the United·States, aiming to stem the spread of communism in Southeast Asia; SEATO was dissolved in 1977. China and the Soviet Union formed their alliance in February 1950, and both formed their de facto alliance with North Korea at the onset of the Korean War later that year. South Korea initiated the formation of the Asian and Pacific Council with eight other member countries (Australia, Japan, Malaysia, the Philippines, New Zealand, Republic of China, South Vietnam, and Thailand) to focus on economic matters and solidarity in the face of Communist insurgencies in the region, but the group was disbanded in 1975.[1] In 1967, also in response to concerns about Communist encroachment, governments in Southeast Asia formed a looser political and economic organization, ASEAN, comprising Indonesia, Malaysia, the Philippines, Singapore, and Thailand as founding members. Three major Asian powers—China, India, and Indonesia—attempted early in the Cold War period to stand apart from the emerging bipolar system and instead build on their common colonial and postcolonial experience to seek relations based on nonalignment and the Five Principles of Peaceful Coexistence as declared at the Bandung Conference in 1955. That effort, although high on rhetoric, was short-lived in practice as the China-India rivalry erupted in a border war in 1962 and Beijing-Jakarta relations deteriorated in the mid-1960s over accusations of subversive Chinese Communist activities in Indonesia.

POST−COLD WAR DEVELOPMENTS

As the end of the Cold War neared, it was the Soviet Union that began floating new proposals for multilateral arrangements in Asia, beginning with Mikhail Gorbachev's proposal in Vladivostok in 1985 for a new regional security forum. Suspicious that Gorbachev was trying to weaken the reinvigorated U.S. security cooperation with Japan and South Korea in the wake of the Soviets' military buildup in the Far East over the previous decade, Washington, Tokyo, and Seoul quickly rejected the idea. However, when the intensity of Cold War divisions waned by the end of the 1980s and the appreciation of the Japanese yen fueled a first wave of regional growth and integration, the Asia-Pacific governments began exploring new arrangements commensurate with the political and economic dynamics of the time. Building on existing business forums such as the Pacific Basin Economic Council (PBEC, formed by Japan and Australia in 1968) and the Pacific Economic Cooperation Council (PECC, formed in 1980), Australia and Japan took the lead in initiating the intergovernmental APEC forum in 1989. The APEC forum—founded in the same month and year the Berlin Wall came down, November 1989—became the first major regionwide economic and trade organization. It started out as an informal dialogue group, growing from twelve members (Australia, Brunei, Canada, Indonesia, Japan, South Korea, Malaysia, New Zealand, the Philippines, Singapore, Thailand, and the United States) in 1989 to fifteen in 1991 with the addition of China, Hong Kong, and "Chinese Taipei," and then to its current strength of twenty-one with the addition of Mexico and Papua New Guinea (1993), Chile (1994), and Peru, Russia, and Vietnam (1997). Institutionalization began in February 1993, when the APEC Secretariat was established in Singapore.

APEC is first and foremost a "gathering of regional economies" (it is not referred to as a gathering of states or governments because of the presence of Hong Kong and Taiwan as members), with the members pledging to develop "a community of Asia-Pacific economies" committed to "openness and partnership."[2] Although aimed primarily at managing the effects of growing economic interdependence and seeking liberalized trade and economic relations in the region, APEC also became a forum for political and security discussions with the advent of the APEC Leaders' Meeting, initially convened by U.S. president Bill Clinton in Seattle in November 1993 and since then annually bringing together APEC member countries' heads of state. Following the September 11, 2001, terrorist attacks against the United States, the Shanghai APEC Summit placed a much stronger emphasis on counterterrorism cooperation (including combating terrorist-financing networks).

APEC has produced some meaningful cooperation through its system of working groups. Early on, however, it faced two problems: U.S. attempts to push it strongly in the direction of trade liberalization conflicted with the Japanese agenda of using it to promote economic development, and Malaysia challenged its legitimacy as a regional organization on the grounds that it was an Australian initiative.[3] Since the late 1990s, success in meeting the group's long-term economic goal of trade liberalization has been limited, and it has become apparent that APEC's ambitious "Bogor Goals" of liberalizing trade among industrialized members by 2010 and among all members by 2020 are off track. East Asian members have also raised questions about the relevance of Canada, Mexico, Chile, and Peru—and even of the United States—to East Asian integration. The George W. Bush administration added some new life to APEC in 2003 and 2004 by expanding the agenda to include cooperation on counterterrorism and other transnational threats, and these initiatives generated substantive cooperation across the region. However, the impression that APEC is not Asian enough has continued to grow on the western side of the Pacific.

Although APEC brought together the region's economies for the first time, it was not until the establishment of the ARF in 1994 that governments established a regionwide forum to address security issues. The ARF emerged from a luncheon discussion the previous year among members of ASEAN, its formal "dialogue partners" (including Australia, Canada, the European Union, Japan, and the United States), as well as China, Russia, and Vietnam, which were invited as outside observers to the 1993 meeting. Today, the ARF consists of twenty-six countries and is the largest Asia-Pacific forum dedicated to discussions on regional security and the creation of confidence-building measures. In addition to regularized working group meetings, the highlight of the ARF calendar is the annual gathering of foreign ministers.

ASEAN remains firmly in the driver's seat for the ARF, and the ARF operates strictly on the principle of consensus and all members' "comfort." Because the ARF includes members as diverse as North Korea, Cambodia, and the United States, this principle ensures that the output of the dialogue stays at a relatively low common denominator. Efforts to reform the organization by giving the chairperson greater powers, by allowing for supermajorities to implement decisions over the objections of a minority of members, or by establishing an effective secretariat for it have been stymied. The United States in particular appears frustrated by the slow progress in moving the organization beyond confidence-building discussions toward such activities as preventive diplomacy, and when Secretary of State Condoleezza Rice was faced with the choice of conducting Middle East diplomacy or attending the ARF meetings in 2005 and 2007, she quickly chose the former.

"ASIANIZATION" AND AN
"EAST ASIAN COMMUNITY"

Since the mid- to late 1990s, multilateralism in Asia has reflected two important new features. First, multilateralism in the region is increasingly characterized by its "Asianization" and the search for an "East Asian community." Put another way, more and more regional mechanisms have been established and run by countries located in Asia proper and do not always include members from the broader "Asia Pacific," such as Australia, Canada, New Zealand, and the United States. Several factors help explain this trend: the emergence or reemergence of new power centers in the region (such as China, India, and Japan); other important regional actors, such as ASEAN, seeking a greater voice in security and economic affairs, including the assertion of an elusive "Asian identity"; the growing importance of the European Union and the North American Free Trade Agreement; and a perception that the United States is not sufficiently focused on East Asian concerns, particularly in the wake of the slow U.S. response to the 1997 Asian financial crisis and its post-2001 preoccupation with counterterrorism.

For example, meetings convened in the early 1990s among China and four former Soviet republics—Kazakhstan, Kyrgyzstan, Russia, and Tajikistan—to settle long-standing border disputes and introduce confidence-building measures along their frontiers coalesced into the Shanghai Five in 1996 and later became a formal institution, the SCO, in 2001. The group added Uzbekistan as a member, established a secretariat and regional antiterrorism center, and now holds regular working- and summit-level exchanges on political, economic, and security issues. The group carries out joint military and counterterrorism exercises as well, which have raised suspicion in the United States and elsewhere in the region.

In another example, the APT process (the ten ASEAN countries plus China, Japan, and South Korea) began in December 1997 in the wake of the Asian financial crisis (and perceptions that Western countries had done little to assist those countries hardest hit by the disastrous fiscal downturn). In November 1999, the third APT Summit released a joint statement outlining principles, orientation, and areas for East Asian cooperation, marking a substantive step forward in the process. At the initiative of South Korean president Kim Dae-jung, a task force of scholars, the East Asia Vision Group (EAVG), was created to draft a report outlining APT cooperation for the future. The ultimate goal of East Asian regionalism, according to the EAVG, is to create a "bona fide regional community . . . for peace, prosperity and progress."[4] The EAVG's work was then taken up by an intergovernmental body, the East Asia Study Group, which recommended in their final report that the APT summit process should evolve into what would be called the "East Asian Summit."[5] Leaders attending the sixth APT Summit in November 2002 endorsed this concept and further agreed on the ambitious goals of building the East Asian Free Trade Agreement and creating an "East Asian community."

The EAS proposal was immediately a source of controversy. Which countries would be considered part of the EAS and hence part of the envisioned "East Asian community"? Should the new EAS replace existing mechanisms such as the APT process (as envisioned by the EAVG)? What would be the EAS's ultimate purpose? China preferred to keep the EAS centered on the APT grouping, a view shared by Malaysia. But others—such as Indonesia, Japan, and Singapore—favored an expansion of the EAS to include neighbors such as Australia, India, and New Zealand. Part of the motivation for an expanded EAS membership was to balance Chinese influence within the organization and to accommodate U.S. concerns that it was not to be included in the EAS process.

In consultation with its APT partners, ASEAN announced in April 2005 three criteria for membership in the EAS: members should have close relations with ASEAN, be full-dialogue partners with ASEAN, and be signatories of the ASEAN Treaty of Amity and Cooperation (TAC). Because Australia, India, and New Zealand fulfill these requirements, they were invited in July 2005 by the APT foreign ministers to join the EAS. The United States had not signed the TAC (though in 2007 Washington began reconsidering this position), which meant it would not be an EAS member. When the EAS held its first meeting in December 2005, it did not replace the APT process as originally proposed. As a result, the two groups have an uneasy coexistence, with Japan preferring the more open EAS process and China preferring the smaller APT grouping, where it can wield greater influence. The EAS held its second summit in January 2007.

At this stage, it remains too early to know what the EAS may become. Early indications suggest that it will fall short of forming an "East Asian community" and that this role—to the extent possible—will be assumed by the APT process. At the first EAS in Kuala Lumpur in 2005, the host, Malaysian prime minister Abdullah Badawi, made it abundantly clear that the ten ASEAN countries and their three partners constituted the core: "You are talking about a community of East Asians; I don't know how the Australians could regard themselves as East Asians, or the New Zealanders for that matter." He continued, "We are not talking about members of the community," even though Australia, New Zealand, and "our immediate neighbor" India have "common interests in what is happening in the region."[6] The architects of East Asian community building, he clearly implied, would all be Asians, with the APT participants providing the base. Although his comments indicate that, in his view, India might one day join the core group as an Asian nation, Australia and New Zealand (and presumably the United States) clearly would not. The EAS would provide a vehicle for outsiders to endorse the community-building effort; it "could play a significant role," but would not be an integral part of (much less drive) the process.[7] The chairperson's statement from the 2005 EAS underscored twice that ASEAN will be the "driving force" behind East Asian community building and that future meetings "will be hosted and chaired by an ASEAN Member Country . . . and be held back-to-back with the annual ASEAN Summit."[8] Beijing had suggested that it host the second round, but ASEAN rejected that proposal in order to remain squarely in the driver's seat for the community-building process.

AD HOC MULTILATERALISM AND "MINILATERALS"

In addition to "Asianization" and "community building," a second important feature of multilateralism in Asia in recent years has been the growth of "ad hoc" multilateralism and so-called minilaterals. In part a U.S. response to the slow pace and exclusionary tendencies seen in Asian multilateralism in recent years, the ad hoc or minilateral approach brings like-minded countries together to address and resolve specific, commonly faced challenges.

Perhaps the best example of this approach is how interested parties have joined together to address and roll back North Korean nuclear ambitions. From the onset of the first North Korean nuclear crisis in 1993, the United States and interested partners initiated a number of ad hoc processes, including the formation in 1995 of the Korean Energy Development Organization with Japan, South Korea, the European Union, and other contributing partners, and the creation of the Four-Party Talks involving China, the United States, North Korea, and South Korea, which convened between December 1997 and August 1999. As concern about North Korea's nuclear ambitions mounted during 2002 and 2003, a new set of minilateral talks were established at Washington's urging and hosted by Beijing. The Six-Party Talks on Korean security began in August 2003 with participation by China, Japan, North Korea, Russia, South Korea, and the United States. In September 2005, the parties issued a joint statement in which North Korea agreed to halt its nuclear weapons programs and to allow international inspections in exchange for economic cooperation, aid, and security assurances from the United States. With the North Korean test of a Tae-podong missile in July 2006 and a nuclear device in October of that year, however, these talks verged on failure. Nevertheless, additional rounds of the Six-Party Talks continued in early 2007 and appeared to be making progress toward some level of North Korean nuclear disarmament, at least with respect to Pyongyang's plutonium production at the Yongbyon complex, if not the highly enriched uranium program and existing nuclear weapons that North Korea is also suspected of hiding. Through the creation of various working groups, the six-party process has also taken up other divisive issues among the parties, including the problem of Japanese hostages taken by North Korea, economic assistance to North Korea, and normalization of diplomatic relations between the United States and North Korea. One of the working groups brought the parties together to explore a more permanent Northeast Asia security forum that would focus initially on issues associated with the Korean Peninsula, offering the prospect of broader confidence-building talks in the region as a whole. However, the prospects for such a forum cannot be explored fully without concrete progress on denuclearization by North Korea—the central problem that brought the countries together in the first place.

This ad hoc approach to problem solving is particularly appealing to the United States and other like-minded partners in the region. These efforts bring together "coalitions of the willing" (often, but not exclusively, U.S. friends and allies) and are action oriented, with the United States typically playing the lead role. Similar American motivations to see concrete results in Asia are behind the establishment of the Container Security Initiative and the Proliferation Security Initiative, both intended to prevent the transfer of sensitive technologies and weapons of mass destruction into terrorists' hands or reaching U.S. shores. Another example of this approach is the U.S.-initiated Asia-Pacific Partnership on Clean Development and Climate (APPCDC), bringing together Australia, Canada, China, India, Japan, South Korea, and the United States to focus on moderating the effects of climate change. The U.S.-led humanitarian response in the wake of the Indian Ocean tsunami of December 2004—a coordinated effort also involving Australia, India, and Japan—is often cited as another example of how effective ad hoc multilateralism can be in the absence of adequate responses from established mechanisms in the region, such as the ARF. Washington has also encouraged closer ties among its alliance partners and other friends—as in the U.S.-Australia-Japan and U.S.–Japan–South Korea trilateral security consultations—and has examined broader forums such as a quadrilateral U.S.-Japan-India-Australia dialogue proposed by Japan and a regional democracy caucus. China has criticized these developments as creating a Cold War structure in Asia and strengthening a U.S.-led cordon around the Asia mainland. The United States and its allies have maintained that coordination among allies on problems such as North Korea, counterterrorism, and humanitarian relief reinforces stability in the region and is not aimed at China. Washington has also made efforts to include China in key minilateral efforts such as the Six-Party Talks and the APPCDC.

A growing perception in the region that future challenges are likely to be transnational in nature also fuels a greater interest in the formation of ad hoc minilaterals that focus on specific, mutually shared problems. Such new transnational threats include financial instabilities; international crime syndicates; pandemics and other infectious diseases; pollutants and other environmental challenges; and illegal trafficking in weapons, narcotics, and people. As a result, even ASEAN members and other Asian countries are more actively promoting the establishment of minilateral groups (chapter 12 describes these groups in more detail).

FINDINGS AND IMPLICATIONS

This brief history of multilateralism within the Asia-Pacific region demonstrates continued underinstitutionalization compared with Europe and the Western Hemisphere, repeated moves and countermoves by states to initiate or manipulate multilateral institutions for balance-of-power purposes, and a heavy reliance on U.S. alliance networks to provide public goods. However, it also demonstrates a far more dynamic, ongoing, and uncertain debate about architecture in the region; a steadily growing desire within the region for Asian-led institutions; a significant increase in the sheer number of new multilateral mechanisms in the region (in contrast to the paucity of regional multilateral organizations in Asia during the Cold War, the region today hosts approximately one hundred new multilateral groupings);[9] rudimentary establishment of broad norms with respect to the use of force in settling territorial disputes; minimal defense transparency (publication of white papers); and, reminiscent of the European precedent, an appetite for focusing on economic integration before security cooperation.

Picking up the story in the second decade of the post–Cold War era, our matrix approach of contrasting national strategies (the x axis) with regional challenges (the y axis) demonstrates an intensification of both competition and cooperation in the region's multilateral arena, as well as a sometimes almost counterproductive proliferation of new forums and institutions as nations maneuver for competitive position and seek more advantageous ways to deepen cooperation. Rather than leading to a clearer picture of how Asia's multilateral architecture might look in the future, our empirical chapters demonstrate that the institution-building process is becoming increasingly fluid and in some cases redundant. The process will likely remain this way for some time to come for the simple reason that no state is prepared to bet its security or future on any neat single framework. There are too many uncertainties about the future of China and India, the Korean Peninsula, and the longer-term durability of U.S. strategic primacy. Moreover, developing multiple diplomatic outlets offers these states advantages in trying to shape the regional agenda. Nor does Asia enjoy a common set of values comparable to the European Union—as many others have frequently pointed out. As a result, both Hobbes and Kant are alive and well in Asia's multi-lateral process, and neither can claim dominance over the region's future.

It is precisely for this reason that it is important to unbundle the new multi-lateralism in Asia to discern broader trends in regional security. On the Hob-besian side of the equation, the chapters in this book (particularly the country chapters in part I) reveal that behind the language of "community building" there is intense rivalry and debate regarding the form, function, and norms of regional integration and institutionalization. These debates are not mere aca-demic discussions for the governments in the region, but reflect careful judg-ments of how very different sets of national interests and national values can be advanced or harmed by certain trajectories in the region's institutional architec-ture. These competitive instincts are reinforced by Asia's long tradition of ac-cepting a hierarchical regional order.[10] However, on the Kantian side of the ledger, the chapters in the book demonstrate that participation in regional mul-tilateral forums has affected state behavior in positive ways, leading to new ar-eas of cooperation not only on relatively "safe" transnational threats such as disease and terrorism, but also on more sensitive "hard" security threats such as the North Korean problem. Moreover, even the collision of different norms and national interests within a multilateral setting can engender cooperation over time, as we will see. These specific areas of dissonance and consonance are dis-cussed throughout the book, but deserve particular attention here.

DISSONANCE: FOUR CONTESTED AREAS

Competition in the process of regional integration and institution building is manifest in a struggle to resolve four key issues.

WHO IS IN ASIA?

The first issue is geographic in scope, centering on the question, Who actually is in Asia? Virtually the entire region has adopted the language of an "open and inclusive" regional architecture in the joint statements from APEC and the EAS. However, there is intense disagreement and competition about what states constitute the membership of emerging Asian institutions and which institu-tion can really claim to be "the" Asian institution. As Ralph Cossa explains in his chapter on U.S. approaches, Washington has a strong preference for trans-Pacific arrangements such as APEC. Wu Xinbo's chapter demonstrates China's readiness to participate in such trans-Pacific forums, but strong preference for narrower geographic definitions of Asia that increase China's relative weight and influence. Thus, Beijing actively participates in APEC, but tries to increase the importance of the SCO and the APT. Akiko Fukushima's chapter highlights Japan's efforts to balance this Chinese strategy by expanding the definition of Asia to include other democracies. Tokyo thus successfully maneuvered to include India, Australia, and New Zealand in the new EAS in 2005 and kept the door open for possible U.S. participation. Within ASEAN, Singapore takes a similar view, but as Amitav Acharya demonstrates, the general ASEAN preference is that as an organization it will retain leadership of regional institution building in order to mitigate against great-power rivalry in Northeast Asia. Thus, the ASEAN member states insisted that the new EAS be hosted by and the agenda set by their own members.

Although states continue to maneuver for a geographic definition and center of gravity in Asia that favors their own national interest, no state in this study has insisted on a single exclusive institutional architecture that would lock out any major player or provoke more direct zero-sum competition. China has been careful not to boycott or sabotage forums that include the United States, such as APEC and the Six-Party Talks, even though Beijing prefers to emphasize the narrower Asian forums where Washington is not present. Indeed, Sino-U.S. cooperation has probably intensified in APEC and the Six-Party Talks. Similarly, Japan has demonstrated a penchant for balancing Chinese influence in forums by expanding the membership of democratic states, but Amy Searight demonstrates in her chapter that Tokyo has simultaneously taken a leading role in pushing for studies of a regional currency through the Chiang Mai Initiative (CMI) that is consistent with the "Washington Consensus" but does not include the United States. And the United States and Australia, in spite of their leading roles as champions of an open and inclusive regional architecture, have joined with Japan in the Trilateral Security Dialogue since 2002 and in the APPCDC since 2004, both of which are by definition exclusive. This dynamic of both inclusivity and exclusivity ultimately helps to explain the proliferation of regional forums and institutions of late. The competition for position and leadership is intense, but it is sedentary rather than destructive because states still try to emphasize cooperation over competition. Thus, new layers of institutions are formed far more easily than old ones are improved or killed.

WHAT AGENDA? WHAT NORMS?

The second most important divergence within Asia is on the question of what norms or values are to guide regional integration and institution building. This is no trivial question; the process of regional integration in Europe depended on a common norm set. Wu's chapter captures accurately Beijing's focus on using multilateralism to preserve a diversity of norms and to create areas of value-neutral cooperation. Beijing is particularly attracted to the concept of "noninterference in internal affairs" that guided ASEAN's own formation three decades ago as well as that of the ARF in the 1990s. Fukushima's chapter is equally accurate in conveying the Japanese government's increasing emphasis on "values-oriented diplomacy" and the use of "principled" multilateralism to narrow the normative gaps among countries on key issues such as democracy, human rights, and the rule of law. Japan has moved away from its own earlier emphasis on preserving "Asian" values in regional organizations, but China has filled that ideational space now that it is Beijing that feels the greatest pressure from the American-led neoliberal order. These issues are not just matters of ideology or branding, of course. As Fukushima explains, Japan has always sought a leadership role in rule making in Asia for the pragmatic purpose of shaping the regional environment in ways that preserve Japanese economic and security interests.

The other chapters in this volume reflect the view of the rest of the region on this ideational contest, which is centered on Japan and China. As C. Raja Mohan's chapter indicates, India clearly shares a sense of common democratic values with Japan and relied on that particular hook to win membership in the EAS. But India is also cautious about appearing to "impose" its values on regional states and retains some of the resentment of the Anglo-American neoliberal order that characterized its more pronounced nonaligned positions during the Cold War.[11] Lim's chapter on South Korea reveals Seoul's preoccupation with unification in its overall multilateral diplomacy and a caution about being caught between Sino-Japanese rivalry, but at the same time Seoul has also been active on multilateral cooperative efforts aimed at advancing democracy and the rule of law, hosting both anticorruption and Community of Democracy summits in Seoul. The most rapidly shifting views of the regional normative agenda are in Southeast Asia, as William Cole and Erik Jensen demonstrate. They explain that the draft ASEAN Charter, released in January 2007, emphasized democracy, human rights and the rule of law in ways that defy ASEAN's original embrace of "noninterference in internal affairs" and preference for the ASEAN way (although these norms were ultimately whittled down to some extent in the charter's final version, which appeared at the end of 2007). As Cole and Jensen note, the future of this ideational debate that is now centered on Japan and China may be decided by what is happening in Southeast Asia. And, of course, all of this resonates with long-standing principles of U.S. foreign policy, though it is not clear how far the United States can lead in this debate or organize the region's democracies without inadvertently causing a backlash from within the region. It nevertheless serves longer-term U.S. interests that the debate is among Asians and not between Asia and the West. As Brendan Taylor and William Tow aptly point out in their chapter, even the concept of "security architecture" is not without normative debate, which is then reflected in the competing frameworks put forward by different regional "architects."

WHAT KIND OF ECONOMIC INTEGRATION?

Searight's chapter demonstrates that although all Asia-Pacific nations favor further economic integration, there are differing perspectives on how quickly, how inclusively, and how systematically governments should reduce barriers to trade and investment and how deeply the United States should be involved in the process. Greg Sheridan's chapter notes that Australia (and we would add New Zealand) are probably the most enthusiastic about reducing tariff and nontariff barriers, especially on agriculture. This stance reflects the Hawke and Keating government's revolutionary decision several decades ago unilaterally to eliminate barriers to trade at home and rely on international market forces to strengthen Australia's competitiveness and grow the Australian economy. The United States maintains an emphasis on global liberalization in trade and services, centered on the Doha Round, but Washington has also energized the trade debate in Asia with the November 2006 Free Trade Area of Asia-Pacific (FTAAP) proposal. Japan has endorsed the FTAAP idea, but has advocated beginning with an "ASEAN Plus Three (APT)" process centered on EAS members. China has energetically pursued a narrower free-trade agreement (FTA) with ASEAN and prefers to expand to an APT FTA before considering the broader APT Plus Three or the FTAAP. ASEAN has generally preferred its "ASEAN Plus One" negotiations with Japan, South Korea, China, India, and others so as not to be squashed between the larger economies (any one of which is larger than all ten ASEAN gross domestic products combined).

With global trade liberalization stalled over the disputes on agriculture and services and the probable lapse of the original APEC Bogor Goals of region-wide trade liberalization among advanced economies by 2010 and for all APEC members by 2020, bilateral FTAs have become all the rage in Asia. Economists continue to debate whether this proliferation of FTAs will create a "noodle bowl" effect that complicates regional business transactions and actually undermines economic integration. For the most part, FTA negotiations in the region are leading to "low-quality" agreements with numerous loopholes and exemptions, all possibly in violation of World Trade Organization rules requiring liberalization in substantially all areas of trade. The exceptions are the U.S. FTAs negotiated with Australia, Singapore, and South Korea, which set a higher standard for liberalization across all sectors, though some economists also criticize these FTAs as particularly unhelpful because they take U.S. attention away from the more important leadership role of completing global trade talks.[12]

As Searight explains, the FTA process in Asia is for the most part political and strategic, following trade and investment flows rather than creating them. It is not yet like the European Common Market, where trade policies by governments cause a profound shift in economic relations for the member states. Although intraregional trade may now approach 50 percent of all trade, the region still relies on external demand and sources of capital. Even with the growth of regional production networks, the United States will remain for some time the largest single market for final products. The region also depends on foreign direct investment and external sources for approximately half of the inward capital. One thing not yet clear is whether the continuing shift in regional trade patterns with the growth of China and India will change this larger global flow of goods, money, and investment in ways that will intensify narrower Asian trade and investment liberalization at the expense of the United States and Europe (i.e., that FTAs within the region will move to "high-quality" FTAs or a common market).

Searight's chapter also draws our focus to the important area of monetary cooperation. When Japan proposed an Asian monetary fund at the height of the financial crisis of 1997, the fund appeared to be a counterforce to the International Monetary Fund (IMF), reflecting regional resentment at Washington's heavy-handed conditionality at the time. However, the proposal has morphed into an APT CMI process of debt and bond swaps within the region consistent with IMF terms rather than being revisionist or hostile to the Washington Consensus (Japan, after all, would face its own moral hazard within Asia if it took on the role of the IMF without the help of the global body). As Searight notes, Tokyo has been pushing the idea of a common currency, but the notion still has little resonance in the region and particularly in Beijing. For the most part, the CMI appears to be raising standards and transparency rather than causing a divergence from the global rules.

WHO PROVIDES PUBLIC GOODS?

As Michael O'Hanlon notes at the beginning of his chapter, Asia faces three specific kinds of military problems: war or collapse on the Korean Peninsula, conflict with a rising China, or state failure. Multilateral cooperation can inherently build confidence and help reduce the threat of war at the margin in the first two cases, but stability ultimately rests on deterrence and the U.S. network of alliances in the region. Despite hundreds of hours spent in the ARF trying to reach a common lexicon on the definition of "preventive defense" in a crisis, no major regional capital is going to call the ARF asking for help. They will call Washington. In the case of state failure, there is more potential for multilateral cooperation, but the capacity for responding with deployable and sustainable ground forces still rests almost entirely with the United States and its allies. This point was demonstrated in the case of the 2004 tsunami, after which the United States, India, Japan, and Australia formed the Regional Core Group to provide relief supplies in ways that only these four naval powers could (and almost all of it centered on the U.S. Seventh Fleet). Other cases of response to humanitarian crises or state failure also rely heavily on U.S. military capabilities and alliances—in 1999 in East Timor, for example, where Australia took the lead but depended heavily on U.S. strategic assets of intelligence, lift, and logistics. Japan, even with its new rules of engagement and activism, caps its overseas deployments at two thousand military personnel.

The U.S. Pacific Command has a clear interest in strengthening interoperability and coalition operations to share the burden in providing these public goods and simultaneously to promote confidence and transparency. However, as the secretary of the navy learned when he described this idea as the "1,000-ship Navy" (i.e., developing a capacity to integrate other navies to deal with challenges), many governments in the region continue to resist collective security types of arrangements even against nonstate threats such as piracy, terrorism, and natural disasters.[13] There is still a lingering adherence to noninterference in internal affairs, a fear of entrapment in U.S. strategies, and a strong apprehension about creating a cooperative collective response capability.

This debate will not be resolved any time soon. The United States and perhaps Australia, New Zealand, and, to a lesser extent, Singapore, Japan, and South Korea favor more collective interoperability and collective capacity in the region to deal with crises other than state war. China has stepped out as a far more active player in military diplomacy and in United Nations peacekeeping operations, but remains resistant to anything even approaching the "one-thousand-ship navy" concept. Individual ASEAN militaries (especially U.S. treaty allies Thailand and the Philippines) have good working relations and interoperability with the U.S. military, but on the whole ASEAN member states have a preference for developing problem-solving capacity within their own region. Thus, as Mely Caballero-Anthony's chapter on transnational threats notes, within ASEAN there is a great deal of activity and promotion of cooperation on avian influenza and terrorism, but not much development of interoperability or coalition capacity within the region. Indeed, there is significantly more bilateral military cooperation by ASEAN states with the United States than there is internally among the members of ASEAN.

CONSONANCE: WHEN MULTILATERALISM
HAS WORKED

Despite these four areas of discord and competition, the chapters in this book also reveal that new patterns of multilateral cooperation are taking form from within the region's institutions. On balance, the emerging architecture is shaping state behavior for the better.

These positive trends are not as clear when Asian multilateral institution building is set against the higher standard set by Europe. The standard academic definitions of multilateralism are also often too broad or too stringent to be applied to what is now happening in Asia. Robert Keohane has written that cooperation or coordination of three or more nations in any form is by definition "multilateralism." In that sense, Asia easily passes the test, but probably always has. John Ruggie sets the bar higher by putting weight on the institutionalization of that cooperation through common rules and norms within the multilateral forum. James Caporaso sets the bar even higher, describing multilateral cooperation as being regulated by certain general norms and indivisibility of values.[14] John Duffield has noted that the highest form of multilateral institutionalization involves clear rules, compliance, commitment, and an institutionalized third-party mediator.[15] Although that level of institutionalization exists in bilateral alliances in Asia, the region's multilateral architecture clearly does not reach it.

The problem with many traditional studies of multilateralism is that they tend to focus on the efficacy of the multilateral institution or organization itself rather than on the effect of participation in multilateral cooperation on state behavior. In Asia, the nation-state still rules supreme, and the focus of international-relations studies should be weighted heavily toward state behavior. More advanced multilateral institutions affect state behavior by setting external rewards and punishments or by empowering internal interest groups in a way that changes the domestic balance of power. Asian institutions have not reached that level. However, as Alastair Iain Johnston has noted, the region's burgeoning institutions can still "socialize" states to take on certain regional norms.[16] This socialization effect can happen when nations are persuaded to follow certain uninstitutionalized but broadly accepted patterns of behavior. Alternately, it can occur because the states gravitate to a group identity, such as being "Asian," that is useful politically at home and abroad. In addition, socialization can occur because participation in multilateral forums and institutions leads to a common lexicon or discourse about state-to-state relations that shapes a nation's overall foreign policy.

Throughout the chapters in this volume, there is clear evidence of socialization occurring across the new regional architecture in Asia. Every state is eager to be identified with the emerging multilateral institutions and Asian identity. Japan and Australia were early enthusiasts of the PECC, PBEC, and APEC processes toward the end of the Cold War, and ASEAN also took the lead in creating the ARF. In spite of frequent charges that the United States is stuck in the old "hub and spokes" approach to the region, Ralph Cossa's chapter clearly demonstrates that the Clinton and George W. Bush administrations moved well beyond the more cautious approach advanced by Secretary of State Jim Baker in the George H. W. Bush administration. Wu's chapter notes China's cautious move into multilateralism in the ARF and APEC and subsequent enthusiastic embrace of multilateral diplomacy as part of its new strategy after 1999. China has also moved quietly beyond its own principle of noninterference in other states' internal affairs in order to pressure North Korea to stay on track in the Six-Party Talks and to urge Burma's (Myanmar's) leaders to open a more productive dialogue with opposition groups and accept United Nations mediation—roles Beijing was unlikely to have played without the regional expectations created by China's hosting that forum. India is clamoring to be part of "Asia." With the possible exception of Burma and North Korea, none of the region's powers want to be left out of the multilateral game.

It is also clear from the chapters that there is increasing use of a common lexicon, with oft-repeated phrases such as "East Asian community" and "open and inclusive regionalism," while the joint statements in the Six-Party Talks have increasingly noted that the North Korean nuclear problem is a regional problem rather than being just between the United States and North Korea, and the parties have embraced the concept of a Northeast Asian forum. Moreover, in many cases the patterns of shared behavior go beyond rhetoric. In the Six-Party Talks, the five major powers are developing patterns of cooperation and coordination that will transcend the nuclear problem and perhaps North Korea's existence itself. Through APEC and the CMI, rules for transparency and capacity are being steadily entrenched. Drawing from concepts developed by the Organization for Security and Cooperation in Europe (OSCE) in the 1970s and 1980s, SCO members have demarcated borders, settled border disputes, and introduced an array of security and confidence-building measures to these once tense frontiers (although in noted contrast to the OSCE or the Helsinki process, the promotion of human rights is not on the SCO agenda).

This socialization effect is important and positive, but it goes only so far. As we have noted, there is not yet a common definition of what it is to be "Asian," which remains a source of contention as much as a unifying theme. In addition, although China and Japan may use an increasingly common lexicon about community building, they are also engaged in a parallel battle over what terms should describe the values behind that community. Finally, patterns of behavior are forming in the SCO, APEC, Six-Party Talks, and elsewhere, but a distinction must be drawn between behavior based on mutual constraint (i.e., agreeing on border demarcation in the SCO or agreeing that consensus will define all agreements in the ARF) and actual collective action against common problems and threats. In their chapter, Taylor and Tow caution against an overly "euphoric sense" about regional community building, which needs to be balanced against "a clearheaded and candid recognition of the substantial challenges to building an effective and sustainable Asia-Pacific architecture."

Interestingly, the chapters in this book do provide ample evidence that collective action against common problems is becoming a more common norm in Asia in certain areas. The Six-Party Talks are disguised as an equal-opportunity multilateral process, but the reality is that the dynamic is overwhelmingly five against one (North Korea), particularly since Pyongyang's missile and nuclear tests in 2006. Within APEC and ASEAN, there is increasing cooperation and coordination on counterterrorism since September 11, 2001, as well. Moreover, after Beijing's initial stumble on severe acute respiratory syndrome (SARS), there has been a strong pattern of multilateral cooperation on infectious diseases in both APEC and ASEAN.

What is striking about all these cases is that nations are ceding certain aspects of sovereignty and freedom of action, at least at the margins. In the Six-Party Talks, the United States is withholding coercive options in order to maintain consensus with South Korea and China, and Beijing is signaling a clear shift away from its historic "lips and teeth" alliance with Pyongyang. China, Japan, Russia, South Korea, and the United States are coordinating their actions vis-à-vis North Korea in ways never demonstrated before. As Caballero-Anthony explains, ASEAN states are establishing common practices, sharing information, pooling resources, and coordinating policies on transnational threats such as terrorism and infectious disease. This pattern is also playing out in APEC as well, of course.

Energy is also an area where Asian states might potentially use multilateral arrangements to shift the dynamic from resource competition and nationalism toward greater cooperation. So far the record is mixed at best. The increase in demand for energy in Asia is rapidly outpacing the rest of the world. Total primary energy demand has increased in Northeast Asia[17] from 421.8 megatons in 1980 to 812.4 in 2002 and is projected to increase to 1,151.9 by 2030.[18] Southeast Asia (excluding Burma, Laos, and Cambodia) used 130.6 megatons in 1980 and are projected to use 1,065.6 by 2030,[19] turning many of the ASEAN energy exporters into net importers. Petroleum products will account for 21 percent of China's energy demand in 2030, and 70 percent of those products will be sourced from abroad.[20] An expanding need for natural resources has driven territorial disputes between China and Japan over the Senakaku/Diaoyutai Islands; between Japan and South Korea over the Tokdo/Takeshima Islands; between China and Vietnam and other Southeast Asian states over the Paracels; and between China and India for influence in Burma. China and India have already surpassed the United States as the world's largest emitters of carbon, and demand for nuclear energy in these two nations and elsewhere in the region is expected to increase greatly by 2030.[21]

Given the potential for energy and resource demand to become a driver for regional tension, Asia can certainly use the kind of multilateral cooperation that Europe pioneered with the European Coal and Steel Union. So far, however, the energy issue has generated more meetings and data sharing across the region than actual rules for joint exploration, shared power grids and reserves, and safe use of atomic energy. Nevertheless, the energy dialogue that has developed in Asia has been intense. Forums on energy include APEC and the APEC Energy Ministers' Meeting, the EAS and EAS Energy Ministers' Meeting, activities within ASEAN, the Six-Party Talks, and the APPCDC (Australia, Canada, China, India, Japan, South Korea, United States). Nevertheless, the question remains whether the willingness to talk about energy can be translated into a readiness to cede some national claims and freedom of action for the collective good in the region.

In general, although these specific patterns of proactive collective action probably result in part from the socialization effect, they have much more to do with the nature of the threat or challenge being addressed. Beijing learned from its unfortunate experience with SARS that a failure to cooperate internationally hurt China's position in the world and hampered its ability to manage the problem at home. When avian influenza appeared, Beijing took a notably more proactive posture in multilateral settings. ASEAN was initially reluctant to pool efforts against terrorism after the September 11, 2001, attacks against the United States, but when it became clear that groups such as Jemaah Islamiya were operating across borders, the member states were more prepared to work collectively. As realists would expect, external threats led to security cooperation. The Six-Party Talks are a more complicated example because the process addresses a threat from one of the participants, but the cooperation has become more intense as recognition of that threat has deepened among the other five members.

These drivers for multilateral cooperation in Asia yield important clues about how the regional architecture will likely unfold in the future. Many observers of institution building in Asia would agree with John Duffield that "the choice of institutional arrangements at one point in time can have an important bearing on institutional (and other) possibilities and outcomes at subsequent junctures."[22] Certainly, this institutional path dependence occurred in Europe and drove Bush administration officials' concerns about whether the formation of the EAS in 2005 might set a precedent for excluding the United States from Asian regional diplomacy in the future.

However, the chapters in this volume point to another dynamic in the region's emerging architecture, one in which patterns of multilateral cooperation and institution building are often most pronounced at points of discontinuity or crisis. Thus, APEC's mission was expanded and revitalized in the wake of September 11, 2001, to address terrorism and transnational security threats, an area of cooperation that China and many ASEAN states had vehemently opposed before the terrorism crisis struck. The Six-Party Talks, which will likely form a lasting institution in Northeast Asia, were born out of a crisis. ASEAN's growing cooperation against terrorism and avian influenza followed explosions in Bali and Jakarta, plots for more attacks in Singapore, and the near pandemic caused when Vietnam tried to cover up its bird flu problem. The precursor to the SCO was initially formed out of concern to avoid unnecessary conflicts across borders in Central Asia in the potentially volatile period following the collapse of the Soviet Union, and the organization now claims it is principally concerned with combating the "three evils" of terrorism, separatism, and religious extremism. Nations in this hierarchical and power-sensitive region appear to have moved beyond talk shops and have ceded certain degrees of sovereignty, but only when confronted with a new threat or questions about the reliability of old allies and institutions.

The importance of crisis and discontinuity in shaping the region's multilateral architecture means that the greatest provider of public goods will likely remain central to the process. When the United States appeared to abdicate its leadership responsibilities—for example, after the 1997 financial crisis—alternate institutions such as APT began to take form. When the United States led in responding to crises—as in counterterrorism, the North Korean nuclear problem, and avian influenza—that initiative shaped the agenda in existing forums such as APEC or led to the creation of new forums such as the Six-Party Talks. Through a comparison of the O'Hanlon and Anthony-Caballero chapters, it is evident that intraregional cooperation is more likely against transnational threats and that U.S. initiative is still indispensable for major operational challenges such as the 2004 tsunami or for state threats such as North Korea's nuclear program. The ability of actors within the region to provide these public goods in the future will determine how much initiative there is on the Western side of the Pacific in forming substantive multilateral institutions compared to how trans-Pacific these institutions remain. In any case, as we have noted, the process will remain highly fluid and overlapping. Given the diversity in the region, it is impossible to say which of its many forums will become the equivalent of the European Coal and Steel Union, which laid the foundation for the European Union half a century ago. But the history of Asia's multilateralism to date suggests that the different elements of the region's architecture will be tested by economic, security, and transnational crises and that the most effective elements will prevail in this Darwinian process.

CONCLUSIONS AND A LOOK AHEAD

Readers of the volume will recognize that the debate over the relevance of multilateral diplomacy to Asian security is now long over. The "hub and spokes" logic of prioritizing the U.S. alliance network and downplaying multilateralism that characterized neorealist thinking in the early 1990s cannot be sustained today. China has engaged in a more active and assertive multilateral diplomacy in Asia since the early 2000s. Japan, South Korea, and Australia have engaged for many years in multilateral security diplomacy in the region and embraced the concept of an East Asian summit, all without moving away from close alliance ties with the United States. ASEAN has scrambled to stay in the driver's seat as new institutions attract the attention of these larger powers.

Yet although most of the region now embraces the goal of strengthening regional institutions, the multilateral diplomatic game in Asia remains highly fluid and contested, particularly in the four areas we flagged earlier: the norms that guide integration, the membership, the economic rules, and the question of who provides public goods. As noted in O'Hanlon's contribution to this volume, Winston Churchill's maxim that "jaw, jaw, jaw is better than war, war, war" is no doubt true. But as Taylor and Tow point out in their chapter, it is critical to resolve these contested areas, or else the dynamics of multilateral diplomacy in Asia may end up causing more harm than good.

Three risks to the current generally positive dynamic will demand close scrutiny in the future.

First, there is the danger that the region's zeal for creating new forums and institutions will lead to a redundancy and a continued reinforcement of form over substance—particularly because many governments have found that declaring a new forum grabs more headlines than hammering out consensus and results in one of the existing forums. The outcome would be more talk but no more action.

A second danger is that Asian governments might begin to believe their own rhetoric about a common East Asian community and lose sight of the underlying pillars of stability in the region. Although most governments today are happily employing the harmonious language of "community" while balancing and hedging against those neighbors they trust least, there is no evidence that naive idealism has trumped hard-headed realism. Nevertheless, Asia's history suggests a cultural predisposition to pretend that a broader regional framework is keeping the peace when in fact it is not. The relic of the Chinese tributary system continued even after imperial encroachment and Japanese modernization shifted the fundamental balance of power. And the multilateral treaties of the 1920s and 1930s created the illusion of arms control and common security norms that Japan defied and the United States and Great Britain failed to enforce. Failure to tend to alliances and recognize that balance of power matters to stability in Asia may lead to a dangerous repeat of that history.

Third, there is the opposite danger that competition in the multilateral realm—particularly between opposing minilateral arrangements—may create new security dilemmas if not managed carefully. Security minilateral groupings such as the Trilateral Security Dialogue have contributed to regional stability by enhancing more effective cooperation among major providers of public goods, and the SCO's main focus has been on strengthening common efforts against terrorism and transnational threats in Central Asia, although the SCO has also raised concerns with respect to norm setting on governance and other issues, as Cole and Jensen note. However, if these kinds of minilateral security arrangements begin to view one another as "containment" mechanisms, "exclusionary blocs," or potential rivals, the result will not be positive for regional security. For now, the plurality of regional forums and arrangements, most of which bring the United States and China together, have mitigated against this scenario. But this trend is one to watch.

This downside risk of competitive minilateralism is true in the world of trade and finance as well. For now, the U.S. strategy of competitive trade liberalization has aimed at keeping bilateral and subregional FTAs on track with broader trans-Pacific liberalization and global trade negotiations. However, with a collapse of global or even trans-Pacific trade liberalization, smaller bilateral or subregional FTAs may lead to harmful trade and investment diversion, ultimately moving from building blocks to trading blocs.

Likewise, financial regionalism has advanced in ways that promote openness and transparency in Asian financial markets. Arrangements such as the CMI and the Asian monetary fund initiative remain anchored in multilateral principles and involve close work with global institutions such as the IMF, the Bank for International Settlements, and the Asian Development Bank. However, if APT countries decide to move away from these linkages to the global financial system, it may lead to regional rivalry in finance and the possibility that trade blocs may also become currency blocs. In the near to medium term, in the wake of the global financial devastation emanating from the United States in late 2008, Asian financial markets and political leaders will be wary at best of financial liberalization and connectedness, and could be further tempted to pursue a more insulated, bloc-based approach in the region.

Although the fissures and potential conflicts of Asian international relations are apparent in the current dynamics of the region's multilateral diplomacy, so too are the prospects for building lasting patterns of cooperation. The Six-Party Talks have established working groups on regional security dialogue and peace mechanisms on the Korean Peninsula that may evolve into forums that surpass the OSCE in effectiveness, contributing to a reduction of mistrust among the major powers in Northeast Asia. The various proposals for trade liberalization may fuse into a broad trans-Pacific arrangement that adds new impetus to global free-trade talks. ASEAN's steady approach to community building can now look forward to an unprecedented era of interstate peace and stability in Southeast Asia, and ASEAN's new charter may set the example for using multilateral forums to narrow gradually the normative differences that divide Asia's different political systems. The ARF may further entrench broad norms against the use of force. ASEAN, APEC, and groupings such as the tsunami-originated Regional Core Group may establish regular procedures and planning for regional responses to transnational threats.

These developments are more likely if the United States and its partners in Asia work together toward an open and inclusive regional architecture. This task will require

- Investment in U.S. alliances with Japan, South Korea, and Australia, which for the foreseeable future will remain the irreplaceable underpinnings of regional stability
- Cooperation among like-minded states to work for a steady improvement in regional norms and rule making, rather than settling for incremental or lowest-common-denominator approaches that many states prefer
- Active and consistent U.S. participation and visibility in APEC, the ARF, and other forums, but a readiness to let Asian powers take the lead in advancing initiatives consistent with U.S. interests
- Engagement of ASEAN as an institution, perhaps through formalized U.S.-ASEAN summits
- Resistance to protectionist impulses in the United States and active promotion of bilateral and trans-Pacific trade liberalization
- Increased cooperation among regional governments and militaries to improve the capacity for responding collectively to transnational threats such as piracy, disease, and terrorism
- Efforts to promote trans-Pacific regional economic integration in ways that support the multilateral trading system, including active promotion of bilateral and regional FTAs

- Support for initiatives to strengthen and deepen financial markets in the region, while encouraging close linkages with the IMF and other global financial institutions
- Further development of the six-party framework for confidence building and cooperation in Northeast Asia, but not at the expense of not completing the denuclearization of the Korean Peninsula
- Increased willingness and capacity among like-minded states to join together in "ad hoc coalitions of the willing" to tackle and resolve shared, immediate challenges
- Readiness to turn crises and discontinuities into opportunities for substantive regional cooperation among both like-minded states and potential adversaries

In sum, this volume points us to a future in which peace, prosperity, and stability in Asia can be enhanced by the region's new multilateralism, but the underlying security and well-being provided by an attentive and attuned United States, in dynamic concert with friends and allies in the region, will remain indispensable for decades to come. Above all, scholars and policymakers must understand that multilateral diplomacy is a means of statecraft and not an end in itself. As such, it can be an arena for both cooperation and competition. True statecraft will require a readiness to compete where necessary *and* to cooperate where possible.

NOTES

1. "A New Alliance, and More Help for Viet Nam," *Time*, June 24, 1966, http://www.time.com/time/magazine/article/0,9171,835789,00.html.

2. U.S. Office of the Historian, Bureau of Public Affairs, "History of the Department of State During the Clinton Presidency (1993–2001)," http://www.state.gov/r/pa/ho/pubs/8535.htm. Background materials and key documents for APEC can be found on the APEC Secretariat Web site at http://www.apecsec.org.sg.

3. Richard Higgott and Richard Stubbs, "Competing Conceptions of Regionalism: APEC Versus EAEC in the Asia Pacific," *Review of International Political Economy* 2, no. 3 (1995): 516–35.

4. East Asia Vision Group, *Towards an East Asian Community: Region of Peace, Prosperity, and Progress*, report (Jakarta, Indonesia: ASEAN, 2001).

5. ASEAN Secretariat, *Final Report of the East Asia Study Group* (Jakarta, Indonesia: ASEAN, 2002), presented at the APT Summit, Phnom Penh, Cambodia, November 4, 2002, 4, http://www.aseansec.org/viewpdf.asp?file=/pdf/easg.pdf.

6. Quoted in Connie Levett, "Malaysia Delivers Blow to Australia," *Sydney Morning Herald*, December 15, 2005, http://www.smh.com.au/news/world/malaysia-delivers-blow-to-australia/2005/12/14/1134500916425.html.

7. ASEAN Secretariat, "Chairman's Statement of the First East Asia Summit," Kuala Lumpur, Malaysia, December 14, 2005, http://www.aseansec.org/18104.htm.

8. ASEAN Secretariat, "Kuala Lumpur Declaration on the East Asia Summit," Kuala Lumpur, Malaysia, December 14, 2005, http://www.aseansec.org/18098.htm.

9. William T. Tow and Brendan Taylor, "Asia-Pacific Security Architecture: Clothing the Emperor," working manuscript provided to the editors, August 2007, 16, citing Center for International Exchange, *Towards Community Building in East Asia*, Dialogue and Research Monitor Overview Report (Tokyo: Center for International Exchange, 2005).

10. For a history of the hierarchical system in Asia, see, for example, David Kang, "Hierarchy, Balancing, and Empirical Puzzles in Asian International Relations," *International Security* 28, no. 3 (2004): 165–87; Muthiah Alagappa, "International Politics in Asia: The Historic Context," in *Asian Security Practice: Material and Ideational Influences*, ed. Muthiah Alagappa (Stanford, Calif.: Stanford University Press, 1998), 65–114.

11. See also C. Raja Mohan, "India's Struggle with Democracy Promotion," *Washington Quarterly* 30, no. 3 (2007): 99–116.

12. Jagdish Baghwati, "From Seattle to Hong Kong," *Foreign Affairs* 84, no. 7 (2005): 2–14; I. M. Destler and Marcus Noland, "Constant Ends: Flexible Means: C. Fred Bergsten and the Quest for Open Trade," in *C. Fred Bergsten and the World Economy*, ed. Michael Mussa (Washington, D.C.: Peterson Institute, 2006), 15–37.

13. Donald C. Winter, secretary of the navy, remarks at the Current Strategy Forum, Naval War College, June 13, 2006, http://www.navy.mil/navydata/people/secnav/winter/SECNAV_Remarks_NWC_Current_Strategy_Forum.pdf.

14. Robert Keohane, "Multilateralism: An Agenda for Research," *International Journal* 45 (1990): 731–64; John G. Ruggie, *Constructing the World Polity: Essays on International Institutionalization* (New York: Routledge, 1988), 109; James A. Caporaso, "International Relations Theory and Multilateralism: The Search for Foundations," in *Multilateralism Matters: The Theory and Practice of an Institutional Form*, ed. John G. Ruggie (New York: Columbia University Press, 1993), 53. Also noted in Shin-wha Lee, "Northeast Asian Security Communities: From Concepts to Practice," paper presented at the German Institute for International and Security Affairs, Ebenhausen (Munich), September 2006.

15. John Duffield, "Asia Pacific Security Institutions in Comparative Perspective," in *Asian Security Practice: Material and Ideational Influences*, ed. Muthiah Alagappa (Stanford, Calif.: Stanford University Press, 1998), 243–70.

16. Alastair Iain Johnston, "Socialization in International Institutions: The ASEAN Way and International Relations Theory," in *International Relations Theory and the*

Asia Pacific, ed. G. John Ikenberry and Michael Mastanduno (New York: Columbia University Press, 2003), 123–44; "Conclusions and Extensions: Toward Mid-range Theorizing and Beyond Europe," *International Organization* 59, no. 4 (2005): 1013–44.

17. Japan, China, South Korea, and Taiwan.

18. Asia Pacific Energy Research Center, *APEC Energy Demand and Supply Outlook 2006* (Tokyo: Asia Pacific Energy Research Center), 206, http://www.ieej.or.jp/aperc/2006pdf/Outlook2006/Whole_Report.pdf.

19. Ibid., 210.

20. Ibid., 25.

21. On trends in energy demand in China and India, see International Energy Agency, "World Energy Outlook 2007," executive summary available at http://www.iea.org/Textbase/npsum/WEO2007SUM.pdf.

22. John S. Duffield, "Asia Pacific Security Institutions," in *International Relations Theory and the Asia Pacific*, ed. G. John Ikenberry and Michael Mastanduno (New York: Columbia University Press, 2003), 256.

PART I

National Strategies for Regionalism

2. Evolving U.S. Views on Asia's Future Institutional Architecture

Ralph A. Cossa

The views held by the United States toward the ongoing development of a future institutional architecture for Asia are still evolving. They ultimately will be determined by the outcome of several simultaneous debates both in the United States and in Asia. First, there is the debate between Asia-Pacific (or trans-Pacific) regionalism and Asian regionalism and how (or if) the two can coexist. A second debate involves the future role of Washington's traditional alliance-oriented strategy in Asia and how it coincides or conflicts with Asian multilateralism. A third debate concerns institutionalized versus ad hoc multilateralism, and it plays out both throughout the world and within Asia. These three debates interrelate and are made more difficult by the current uncertain nature of organizing principles and objectives behind East Asian community-building efforts and the desired or anticipated U.S. role in this process.

Washington's preferences today are fairly clear, but in each case tentative and subject to change or revision. In addition, its continuing preoccupation with developments in other parts of the world—the Middle East, Iraq, and Afghanistan—will likely constrain its ability to focus clearly on the evolving debates on Asian regionalism. The George W. Bush administration made it very clear that it prefers the more inclusive trans-Pacific format to the narrower Asian regionalism; the former involves the United States as an active player, whereas the U.S. role in the latter remains unclear and is subject to caveats that Washington views with suspicion. This debate potentially—although not automatically or inevitably—pits institutions such as the Asia-Pacific Economic Cooperation (APEC) "gathering of economies," the Association of Southeast Asian Nations (ASEAN), and the ASEAN Regional Forum (ARF) against more exclusive Asian community-building exercises such as the well-established ASEAN Plus Three (APT) effort or the embryonic East Asia Summit (EAS).

Washington's view on the second debate has historically been clear, consistent, and bipartisan. Alliances come first. But Democratic and Republican administrations alike have argued that it is not an "either-or" choice: bilateral alliances and multilateral cooperation are (or should be) mutually supportive, not mutually exclusive. This view may be changing, especially in Asia, but it is being challenged in Washington as well, at least in unofficial circles. Some Asian states, China foremost among them, appear to view U.S. alliances as reflective of a "Cold War mentality" or debate their future relevance, arguing for cooperative or collective security arrangements instead. Although U.S. leaders have consistently maintained the primacy of America's alliances, in recent years Washington seems more inclined to lean toward ad hoc arrangements where "the mission defines the alliance" rather than the reverse.[1] The perceived "requirement" for allies to support ad hoc efforts also adds new strains to both structures and has been particularly challenging for Japan and South Korea. Both Tokyo and Seoul faced significant public resistance to participation in the global war on terrorism, but proceeded in the name of being a "good ally." (Nonetheless, the U.S.-Japan alliance remains strong and the U.S.–South Korea alliance appears destined for better days following the election of a more conservative, pro-alliance administration in South Korea.)

On the third debate, there has been a growing preference in Washington since the mid-1990s for ad hoc multilateralism over more institutionalized mechanisms. But here again the two are not seen as mutually exclusive. Arguably, there would be less need for the former if the latter were more functional: the lack of effective institutions (globally as well as regionally) has prompted the ad hoc approach.

This chapter presents a perspective on the evolving U.S. views of Asian multilateralism and community building, and examines the perceived pros and cons of multilateralism in relation to U.S. national-security objectives. It focuses in particular on continued Asian community-building efforts and the anticipated role that the EAS and APT will play in that effort, while examining current U.S. views on the "Pan-Pacificism versus Pan-Asianism" debate.[2] The chapter also looks at the current and potential future role of U.S. alliances and closes with some speculation on the type of regional institutional architecture Washington would or should prefer.

U.S. APPROACHES TO
ASIAN MULTILATERALISM:
A HISTORICAL OVERVIEW

During the Cold War and immediate post–Cold War era, Washington's leaders viewed the idea of institutionalized East Asian multilateral security cooperation with a great deal of apprehension and suspicion. They often saw—usually with good justification—proposals by others (most notably the Soviet Union) for East Asian or Asia-Pacific multilateral cooperation as an attempt to undercut Washington's bilateral alliance structure or to create exclusionary blocs. Meanwhile, U.S. attempts to create its own multilateral security structures—the Southeast Asia Treaty Organization (SEATO), the Central Treaty Organization, and even the Australia–New Zealand–U.S. trilateral alliance—were less than successful, surviving, if at all, only in a bilateral context: the United States and the Philippines, the United States and Thailand after SEATO's demise, and the United States and Australia after New Zealand came down with a severe case of "nuclear allergy."[3]

Even as late as 1991, when Japanese foreign minister Nakayama Taro suggested at an ASEAN Post-Ministerial Conference (PMC) gathering that a forum be established to discuss regional security issues, his remarks were not well received.[4] The United States, under President George H. W. Bush, was particularly cool to such an idea. More comfortable with a one-on-one approach to security issues in Asia, U.S. officials at the time were hesitant to embrace multilateral approaches. Washington's motto was, "If it ain't broke, don't fix it."[5]

As the Cold War faded, however, there was a decided shift in regional attitudes toward and U.S. support for multinational security initiatives in Asia. On the U.S. side, the first clear signal of this shift came in 1993 when Assistant Secretary of State for East Asian and Pacific Affairs Winston Lord identified "a commitment to enhanced multilateral security dialogue" as one of the incoming Clinton administration's ten priority policy goals for Asia.[6] President Bill Clinton formalized this approach in July 1993 with his embrace of multilateral security dialogue in Asia, calling it one of the four pillars of his vision for a "new Pacific community."[7] This shift was solidified at the 1993 ASEAN PMC meeting when the PMC dialogue partners met informally over lunch with representatives from China, Russia, and Vietnam (which was not yet a member of ASEAN) and with other PMC observers to talk about security matters. The group decided that they would reconvene the following year to form the precedent-setting ARF.[8]

President Clinton also proposed and then in the fall of 1993 served as the first host of what has now become an annual APEC Leaders' Meeting. Although focused on broader regional trade issues, this gathering of trans-Pacific heads of state quickly took on a political and at least quasi-security role just by its mere existence. This addition was then followed by the July 1994 inaugural ARF meeting in Bangkok, which again provided a clear signal that attitudes regarding multilateral security dialogue were changing, both in the United States and throughout Asia.[9]

Although instituted during the Clinton era, both the ARF and the APEC Leaders' Meeting have enjoyed strong support from the George W. Bush administration as well; witness Bush's willingness to attend the October 2001 Shanghai APEC meeting in the immediate wake of the September 11, 2001, terrorist attacks (and every APEC Leaders' Meeting since then) and the presence of Secretary of State Colin Powell at all four ARF meetings held during his tenure in office (something neither of his predecessors could claim).[10] Secretary of State Condoleezza Rice received widespread criticism for missing her first ARF meeting in July 2005,[11] although she was ably represented by her Asia-oriented deputy Robert Zoellick. She sent a positive signal of U.S. commitment to the ARF the next year by attending the 2006 meeting in Malaysia despite multiple crises in the Middle East that might have otherwise excused her absence.

The Bush administration's early support for Asian multilateralism was reinforced in the White House's September 2002 *National Security Strategy for the United States of America*, which expressed the conviction that "multilateral institutions can multiply the strength of freedom-loving nations" and further stated that the United States would build on the stability provided by institutions such as ASEAN and APEC "to develop a mix of regional and bilateral strategies to manage change in this dynamic region."[12] This emphasis was further reinforced in the 2006 *National Security Strategy*, which noted that existing institutions such as the ARF and APEC can play a "vital role" when it comes to "the spread of freedom, prosperity, and regional security." It also noted that "new arrangements, such as the United States–ASEAN Enhanced Partnership, or others that are focused on problem-solving and action, like the Six-Party Talks and the PSI [Proliferation Security Initiative], can likewise bring together Asian nations to address common challenges."[13]

In short, the Bush administration, despite its (sometimes deserved) reputation for unilateralism elsewhere, was particularly supportive of Asian and broader Asia-Pacific multilateralism. It has renewed and reinvigorated U.S. interest in the ARF and APEC and, against some initial regional resistance and criticism, insisted on a multilateral approach under the Six-Party Talks, for dealing with the North Korean nuclear problem. On a somewhat more contentious note, it has also placed a great deal of importance on "ad hoc multilateralism"—through the PSI, for example, which serves as a primary vehicle in the U.S.-led global effort to counter the proliferation of weapons of mass destruction—although Washington continues to believe that both ad hoc and institutionalized multilateral forums have value and stresses that its "coalitions of the willing" are open to all who share coalition goals.

EVOLVING U.S. APPROACHES TO EAST ASIAN COMMUNITY BUILDING

A number of serious debates have arisen in the United States regarding the nature, intent, and future direction of Asian community building and the motivation of some of its key proponents. One lingering question concerns the extent of U.S. involvement in Asian community building: Should Washington be included as a member, as an observer, or not at all in this evolving Asian community? How and why the United States is excluded can be as important as whether it is invited to participate.

When it comes to the EAS in particular, it is not clear if Washington even desires a seat at the table—getting the U.S. president to two Asian summits in any given year, especially if scheduled only a few months apart, would be no mean feat, not to mention the problem of bringing the U.S. president into direct contact with the leader of Myanmar (Burma) or any other Asian leader whose legitimacy Washington does not recognize. Nonetheless, the United States has made it clear that it is interested in learning more about the composition of the EAS, the criteria for membership, and, most important, its mission, objectives, and priorities.

Much will depend on who leads the Asian community. Will ASEAN remain in the driver's seat? If so, can ten drivers steer a steady course, and will ASEAN's failure to achieve a more robust charter undermine its credibility in Washington? If not ASEAN, then who will emerge as leader? One may argue that leadership should go to Japan as the real economic giant in the region. Ironically, a decade ago, when others in the region seemed prepared to accept Japan as the so-called lead goose, Japan itself was hesitant to assume this role. Today, Tokyo is apparently more willing to do so. However, "history" issues, many self-inflicted, have made it difficult for Japan to emerge from the shadow of its own past, even as it seems to be covered by the shadow of the region's emerging new giant, China. Will China be the presumptive or de facto leader of a new Asian community? If so, will that leadership be benign, or will it be aimed—or be perceived by the United States as being aimed—at limiting or replacing Washington's (and Tokyo's) influence in the region?

Most important from a U.S. perspective will be how an emergent and much trumpeted East Asian community relates to the region's other multilateral organizations and initiatives—both institutionalized (such as the ARF and APEC) and ad hoc (such as the Six-Party Talks and PSI). As Deputy Assistant Secretary of State for East Asia Eric John observed, "[T]he EAS has focused our attention on the longer-term questions of regional architecture in East Asia." Speaking directly about pan-Asian community-building efforts such as the EAS and APT, he asked: "Do their overlapping agendas make sense or do they duplicate or undermine existing forums such as APEC and ARF?"[14]

Another key factor affecting Washington's attitude will be emerging Asian mechanisms' willingness (or lack thereof) to adopt global norms, especially in the areas of counterterrorism, counterproliferation, and the promotion of free and open markets. Will emerging regional community building reinforce or dilute existing multilateral efforts to accomplish these goals? Will it help the region's states to address more effectively the growing transnational challenges or provide another excuse for avoiding such efforts? I explore these questions and some preliminary answers from an American perspective in the next few sections.

PRO-MULTILATERALISM, WITH CAVEATS

As a general rule, Washington has historically viewed Asia-Pacific multilateral organizations as useful vehicles for promoting greater political and economic cooperation, enhancing regional security, and supporting U.S. interests. This support for multilateral institutions—in the Asia Pacific and throughout the world—has one important caveat, however: no U.S. administration will likely allow such mechanisms to substitute for or threaten U.S. bilateral alliances and other U.S.-led security arrangements. This stance was clearly spelled out in the 2006 *National Security Strategy:* "Asian nations that share our values can join us in partnership to strengthen new democracies and promote democratic reforms throughout the region. This institutional framework, however, must be built upon a foundation of sound bilateral relations with key states in the region."[15]

During its first term in office, the George W. Bush administration was also cautiously supportive of multilateral organizations, such as APT and the Shanghai Cooperation Organization (SCO), which do not include the United States. In its second term, however, the Bush administration started to cast a more watchful eye on those organizations established and/or dominated by China to see if they might be efforts to diminish Washington's (or Tokyo's) involvement or interests in the region. Beginning in July 2005, it was especially concerned when the Beijing- and Moscow-driven SCO (which also involves four Central Asian states: Kazakhstan, Kyrgyzstan, Tajikistan, and Uzbekistan) called for the United States and its allies—although not naming them—to set a date for the withdrawal of their forces from Central Asia given "the positive dynamics of [the] stabilizing internal political situation in Afghanistan."[16]

The SCO proclamation continued: "Considering the completion of the active military stage of antiterrorist operation in Afghanistan, the member states of the Shanghai Cooperation Organization consider it necessary, that respective members of the antiterrorist coalition set a final time line for their temporary use of the above-mentioned objects of infrastructure and stay of their military contingents on the territories of the SCO member states."[17]

At the time of this pronouncement, the United States had roughly one thousand troops at each of the airfields in Karshi-Khanabad in Uzbekistan and Manas in Kyrgyzstan. By the end of that month, it became obvious that one of the hosts, Uzbekistan—which had come under increasing criticism from the United States and the international community in general for its harsh repression of protestors in Andijan in May—would not wait for the United States to set its own deadline: on July 29, Uzbekistan gave Washington 180 days to vacate Karshi-Khanabad.[18] Although this demand no doubt reflected Uzbek president Islam Karimov's displeasure over Washington's criticism of his dismal human rights record, it is doubtful it could have been made without Moscow and Beijing's consent, if not active encouragement and support. As a result, this action has raised serious questions about Beijing and Moscow's motives and has resulted in a more watchful U.S. eye being cast on exclusionary Asian multilateralism.[19]

Although the United States is still not attempting to block or interfere with regionalism efforts such as the APT and SCO that exclude the United States, it is closely monitoring their future direction and carefully examining the motives of those who seek to guide them. Meanwhile, the Bush administration continues to state its clear preference for "inclusive" Asia-Pacific regional efforts, despite some of the inherent perceived weaknesses in them.[20]

MULTILATERALISM WITH CAVEATS

The United States has been circumspect regarding Asian community building in general, but it has increasingly made clear its support for ASEAN in general and for more "inclusive" multilateral approaches in particular. During a visit to Singapore in May 2006, Assistant Secretary of State for East Asian and Pacific Affairs Christopher Hill noted that U.S. "engagement with Southeast Asia continues to broaden and deepen."[21] Washington had no intention of abandoning or turning its back on a region it had dubbed the "second front in the war on terrorism."[22]

But Hill fired a warning shot regarding "inclusivity," noting that "the dynamism of the region means that our relationship is in a constant state of evolution, which has given rise to renewed debate and discussion about regional fora, and whether they should be inclusive or exclusive." Hill characterized the debate as being between "Pan-Asianism" and "Pan-Pacificism."

The United States has no objection to Asian regionalism per se and in fact "welcomes it," according to Hill. As Hill's deputy Eric John noted at Georgetown, "[E]very region in the world has developed its own institutions. . . . [T]he United States cannot take the position that Asia should be an exception."[23] It is not East Asian community building per se that bothers Washington, but whether the welcome mat will remain out for pan-Pacific institutions as well. Warning of the danger of "meeting fatigue" and the "proliferation" of multilateral initiatives, Hill argued: "We need to think hard and clearly about the question of how we can integrate pan-Asian and trans-Pacific fora. We have heard much debate about the East Asian Summit. Before coming to any conclusions, we need to look at the whole landscape—and indeed the seascape—of proliferating regional fora—ASEAN + 3, APEC, ARF, and the EAS—to determine how the pieces can fit better together. The goal should be to achieve synergy and avoid redundancy and duplication."

Even after several EAS meetings, the fundamental objectives of this emerging community-building effort remain unclear. Nonetheless, Washington has been careful not to object publicly to or discourage this initiative. As one senior official noted in an off-the-record, not-for-attribution comment when pressed by Southeast Asia interlocutors at a Honolulu conference to make a more definitive statement, "[T]ell me what it is—what it plans to achieve—and then I'll tell you what we think of it!"[24] Until then, the United States will continue to "watch with interest" how these pan-Asian efforts develop and, according to Hill, will continue to work closely with ASEAN to ensure these new mechanisms "don't dilute the effectiveness of [APEC and the ARF] and the important cooperation they foster."

THE ARF: A USEFUL BUT LIMITED FORUM

Given Washington's clearly stated preference for these two more broadly based pan-Pacific gatherings, this section and the next offer a brief examination of U.S. approaches toward the ARF and APEC. Various ARF study groups (called intersessional support groups) have provided a vehicle for the United States to move the multilateral process along in areas important to Washington, such as preventive diplomacy, enhanced confidence building, counterproliferation, and maritime (including search and rescue) cooperation, all of which help promote greater transparency and military-to-military cooperation. Most important, since September 11, 2001, the ARF has helped generate regional attention on and some practical cooperation in fighting terrorism and in countering the proliferation of weapons of mass destruction (WMD).[25]

In general, the ARF seems well suited to serve as the consolidating and validating instrument behind many security initiatives proposed by governments and at nonofficial gatherings and has become a useful vehicle in the war on terrorism. From a U.S. perspective, however, its contribution to regional security remains somewhat constrained. For example, Taiwan has not been permitted to participate, and Beijing has insisted that "internal Chinese affairs" not be on the agenda, effectively blocking ARF discussion of cross-Strait tensions despite their obvious regional implications. The Chinese have even been reluctant to address conflicting claims in the South China Sea at the ARF, insisting instead on separate talks with ASEAN or with the other claimants on an individual basis.

Few expect the ARF to solve the region's problems or even to move rapidly or proactively to undertake that mission. The agreement to "move at a pace comfortable to all participants" was aimed at tempering the desire of more Western-oriented members for immediate results in favor of the "evolutionary" approach preferred by the ASEAN states, which all too often seems to see the process as being as important as or even more important than its eventual substantive products.[26] The Asian preference for "noninterference in internal affairs" also has traditionally placed some important topics essentially off limits, although this approach may be changing (witness ASEAN's increased willingness to comment on Myanmar's domestic politics). Nonetheless, U.S. officials assume that the evolution of the ARF from a confidence-building measures "talk shop" to a true preventive diplomacy mechanism (as called for in its 1995 concept paper) will be a long and difficult one.[27]

In addition, the absence of Taiwan from this gathering (and from most others, especially if the subject is security related) and Beijing's refusal to allow the Taiwan issue to be placed on the multilateral security or dialogue agenda limits the ARF's utility in dealing with one of the region's most significant and sensitive security issues.

APEC: CAUTIOUSLY TESTING THE SECURITY WATERS

President Bush used APEC 2001 as an important vehicle to explain Washington's war on terrorism to his Asian colleagues and to garner their support. In addition to the usual annual APEC Leaders' Declaration, the assembled leaders also issued the "APEC Leaders' Statement on Counter-terrorism"—the first political document to be issued in APEC's thirteen-year history—which unequivocally condemned the September 11 attack and deemed it "imperative to strengthen international cooperation at all levels in combating terrorism in a comprehensive manner."[28] This statement was considered a real victory for President Bush and no doubt helped to increase APEC's relevance in his eyes.

The APEC Shanghai meeting also provided President Bush with his first opportunity to meet directly with Chinese president Jiang Zemin, which helped to end the downward slide in Sino-U.S. relations under way since Bush's inauguration (and especially after the collision between a U.S. reconnaissance plane and a Chinese jet fighter over the South China Sea in April 2001). The two leaders were able to put the relationship back on track, aided by China's willingness to cooperate in the battle against terrorism.[29]

Security matters continue to be discussed at the Leaders' Meeting, not to mention at the numerous side summits that normally accompany this gathering. For example, at the October 2003 Leaders' Meeting in Bangkok, the final communiqué referred to cooperation on combating WMD proliferation, while President Bush used the occasion and his side meetings with the leaders of South Korea, Japan, and China to call on North Korea to abandon its nuclear weapons aspirations, while repeating his offer to provide Pyongyang with written assurances that the United States does not intend to attack North Korea.[30]

President Bush met jointly with the seven ASEAN members of APEC at the sidelines of the 2005 APEC Leaders' Meeting in what constituted his first-ever U.S.-ASEAN Summit. Both sides expressed a desire to make this summit a regular event, and President Bush met with the "ASEAN Seven" again in November 2007 at the sidelines of the Hanoi APEC Leaders' Meeting.[31] The setting is particularly attractive to Washington because Myanmar is not an APEC member.

Some have speculated that concern over growing Chinese influence in Southeast Asia helped prompt this summit series. U.S. State Department officials publicly deny this argument, stating that "this is not necessarily a zero sum game" and that "China's re-emergence does not mean the U.S. is any less involved or less of a critical actor in the Asia-Pacific."[32] Privately, however, many U.S. officials acknowledge that Washington is paying attention to Chinese inroads to make sure they do not work to America's detriment. Regardless of the motives involved, the APEC gathering provides a good opportunity for the U.S. president to focus on Asia and to meet with Asia's leaders (even when the meetings are hosted by APEC's Latin American members).

Politics and security issues aside, APEC still is, first and foremost, aimed at promoting free trade and economic cooperation. The United States (among other nations) has used the annual gathering to push its global free-trade agenda. At Washington's urging, the assembled leaders issued a statement aimed at reviving the stalled round of Doha global trade talks at the November

2006 Hanoi Leaders' Meeting.[33] As in previous years, the leaders also pledged to fight terrorism, WMD proliferation, and other threats to regional security and stability, such as pandemic disease, natural disasters, and dwindling reliable supplies of energy.

President Bush also encouraged the leaders to consider a free-trade area for the Asia-Pacific region. This proposal seemed intended, in part, to restore some momentum to stalled global-trade talks by hinting that a regional alternative might be in the works, but it can also be interpreted as an alternative (or at least an adjunct) to more restrictive EAS or APT initiatives. In their final declaration, the leaders agreed to "undertake further studies on ways and means to promote regional economic integration," including a Free Trade Area of the Asia-Pacific as a long-term prospect, but only to study whether it is a "reasonable long-term objective for APEC."[34] Nonetheless, Washington seemed most pleased with the results.[35]

As long as APEC provides a useful venue not only for the promotion of free trade but also for fighting the war on terrorism, Washington will likely continue to be an active player in it. However, as with the ARF, APEC will remain more suited to talking about security problems than to helping to implement solutions. In addition to the usual drawbacks associated with Asian multilateralism, APEC has the added "problem" of including Taiwan. Rather than using this venue as a vehicle for incorporating Taiwanese views and concerns into the regional security debate in a quasi-nongovernmental setting, Beijing has tried to block any substantive security-oriented activities and to isolate Taiwan further from the dialogue process.

AD HOC MULTILATERALISM: THE PSI AND SIX-PARTY TALKS

If Washington has only limited confidence in institutionalized multilateral mechanisms, it is developing a clear preference for ad hoc or tailored multilateralism aimed at a specific task or objective and composed of a "coalition of the willing." The multinational force assembled for the war in Iraq provides one example, as does the aforementioned PSI.

The PSI was first laid out in a speech by President Bush in May 2003 and formalized at an eleven-nation meeting (involving Australia, France, Germany, Italy, Japan, the Netherlands, Poland, Portugal, Spain, the United Kingdom, and the United States) in Madrid a month later.[36] It is "a global initiative with global reach," under which coalition members have agreed "to move quickly on direct, practical measures to impede the trafficking in WMD, missiles, and related items."[37] As such, it is clearly "task oriented." It represents cooperation for a specific, clearly defined purpose as opposed to dialogue for dialogue's sake or in support of more generic objectives. In September 2003 in Paris, the eleven core participants agreed on the Statement of Interdiction Principles "to establish a more coordinated and effective basis through which to impede and stop [WMD] shipments . . . consistent with national legal authorities and relevant international law and frameworks, including the UN Security Council." More than seventy nations have expressed support for these principles.[38]

Other major Asia-Pacific participants beyond the initial PSI core group include Canada, the Philippines, Russia, and Singapore. Others, such as China and South Korea, claim they support the PSI's objectives but have refrained from directly participating, in part due to objections from North Korea.[39] PSI participants have conducted numerous air, ground, and (mostly) sea interdiction exercises to develop and demonstrate its capability to prevent illicit trafficking in nuclear weapons and fissile material. The PSI's most widely acknowledged success was the interception of the *BBC China* en route to Libya with a shipment of centrifuges—an action that reportedly convinced Libyan leader Mu'ammar Qaddafy to come clean about his clandestine nuclear weapons programs.[40]

The best example of task-oriented ad hoc multilateral cooperation in Northeast Asia is the Six-Party Talks, established by Washington to deal with the specific issue of denuclearization of the Korean Peninsula. The talks were also intended and served to multilateralize what many initially viewed as a bilateral U.S.–North Korea problem. Although the ultimate outcome of the six-party process remains uncertain at present, the creation of this mechanism may represent one of the Bush administration's finest diplomatic hours. This initiative draws from the lessons learned during the 1993/1994 North Korea nuclear crisis, where—despite close coordination and consultation—Washington was widely perceived as unilaterally cutting a deal with Pyongyang before sticking Seoul and Tokyo with the bill. Pyongyang argued for bilateral consultations (and a separate U.S.–North Korea nonaggression pact), but Washington rightfully insisted this time that participation by Seoul and Tokyo was "essential." It also acknowledged the important role that China and to a lesser extent Russia must play if multilateral security guarantees are to be part of the final solution. Finally, the Bush administration recognized and tried to work around Pyongyang's strategy of playing all sides against one another by presenting different, conflicting messages depending on the audience.

The creation of the Six-Party Talks mechanism provides a framework for broader Northeast Asia multilateral cooperation in the future. If these talks eventually succeed, most parties agree that a more formalized mechanism must evolve in order to implement the agreement, provide necessary security assurances, monitor compliance, and facilitate whatever aid packages are associated with the final accord. Some analysts (myself included) argue that if the talks fail, there will be an even greater need for some form of institutionalized cooperation in order to manage the danger posed by a presumed (and self-confessed) nuclear-armed North Korea. If and how the six-party mechanism transitions from a form of ad hoc multilateralism into a more institutionalized Northeast Asia forum will help determine the degree of future security cooperation in this East Asia subregion and Washington's involvement in it.

In Asia, one of the most effective and impressive ad hoc multilateral efforts took place in the wake of the horrific December 2004 earthquake and tsunami that left some three hundred thousand people dead or missing, with upwards of a million more displaced in eleven South Asian and Southeast Asian nations. As devastating as the damage was, it could have been much worse if it had not been for the rapid response by the international community led by the U.S. Pacific Command.[41] At the height of the relief effort, some sixteen thousand U.S. military personnel were deployed throughout the areas most affected by the tragedy; more than two dozen U.S. ships (including an aircraft carrier battle group, a Marine amphibious group, and a hospital ship) and more than one hundred aircraft were dedicated to the disaster-relief effort, along with forces from Australia, Canada, Japan, India, and the affected countries. They all operated under a joint command post created by the quickly established Regional Core Group to coordinate the first stages of the international relief effort, identify and fill gaps, and avoid or break logistical bottlenecks until the United Nations was able to mobilize and play a more central role in the relief response.[42]

Not all coalitions are military or security oriented, of course. Numerous other examples of mission-oriented or single-task-oriented ad hoc multilateral efforts abound, including the Asia-Pacific Partnership on Clean Development and Climate (also called the Asia-Pacific Energy Partnership) involving Australia, China, India, Japan, South Korea, and the United States. This ministerial-level initiative is aimed at meeting energy needs while protecting the environment by "combining the ingenuity of the private sector, the efficiency of markets, and the strength of the public sector."[43] It was aimed at putting the United States back on the environmental high road after its rejection of the Kyoto Protocol and is deemed much more appropriate by Washington because it involves the private sector more directly and, unlike Kyoto, directly involves both China and India in the effort.

APT AND THE EAS

Whereas Washington focuses on ad hoc initiatives and Asia-Pacific regionalism, Asian states have continued their community-building efforts. In December 2005, Malaysia convened the first EAS. It should be noted that the EAS was not the only summit taking place in Kuala Lumpur at that time. ASEAN leaders also met among themselves, with their "plus three" partners, and in individual "plus one" meetings with their Australian, New Zealand, and Indian counterparts. This was the second time that Canberra and Wellington and the third time that New Delhi participated in this conclave. Russian president Vladimir Putin also appeared on the ASEAN Summit scene for the first time, conducting his first ASEAN Plus One dialogue.[44] He was also invited to meet with, but not officially to join the other sixteen assembled leaders at this inaugural EAS.[45] The second so-called ASEAN Plus Three EAS meeting took place in January 2007 in Cebu, Philippines, with the sixteen core members (sans the Russians).[46]

However, although the EAS appears to accept the participation of "non-Asian" states such has Australia and New Zealand, it is also clear that ASEAN intends to form the core of the EAS and that U.S. involvement remains in question. ASEAN's driving role was reinforced at the January 2007 ASEAN, APT, and EAS heads-of-state meetings.[47] The chairman's statement from the ASEAN Summit meeting reaffirmed that "ASEAN should consolidate its leading and central role in the evolving regional architecture" and that "the ASEAN Plus Three process would be the main vehicle towards achieving an East Asia Community."[48] Likewise, the chairman's statement from the APT Summit put ASEAN "at the center of our long-term pursuit of an East Asia community," further noting that the APT process "could make positive contributions" and was "an essential part of the evolving regional architecture, complementary to the East Asia Summit and other regional fora."[49] The EAS chairman's statement further reinforced this point, expressing "our conviction that the EAS should remain outward looking, with ASEAN as the driving force working in close partnership with other participants of the East Asia Summit."[50]

Despite being "outward looking," the chairmen said nothing about new members or about any changes to the membership criteria. At the end of 2007, Washington's full membership in the EAS would still require it to accede to the ASEAN Treaty of Amity and Cooperation (TAC), something the Bush administration (like its predecessors) has been reluctant to do. Observer status appears possible, however, and is more likely to be sought by Washington if and when the EAS establishes such a membership category. In an apparent attempt to address one of Washington's potential concerns, the 2005 Kuala Lumpur Declaration noted that the EAS would be "an open, inclusive, transparent, and outward-looking forum in which we strive to strengthen global norms and universally recognized values," and that building an East Asia community is "a long-term goal." The first priority would be building "a strong ASEAN Community which will serve as a solid foundation for our common peace and prosperity."[51]

Still undefined after two meetings is how the EAS (or APT, for that matter) will interact with broader regional organizations such as APEC or the ARF. To its credit, the chairman's statement from the second EAS claimed "that the EAS complements other existing regional mechanisms, including the ASEAN dialogue process, the ASEAN Plus Three process, the ARF, and APEC in community building efforts." Details as to how these various efforts will mesh or work together is still lacking. The chairman's statement did note that "our officials and the ASEAN Secretariat will use existing mechanisms to facilitate the implementation of [priority] projects," again underscoring that the EAS was not going to develop a life of its own, but would remain under ASEAN and APT.[52]

As noted at the onset of this chapter, how the EAS relates to the region's other multilateral organizations and initiatives—both institutionalized (such as the ARF and APEC) and ad hoc (such as the Six-Party Talks and the PSI)—will also be a key factor affecting Washington's attitude, as will its adoption of global norms, especially in the areas of counterterrorism and counterproliferation. Will the EAS (or APT, for that matter) reinforce or dilute these efforts? Will it help regional states more effectively address growing transnational challenges, or will it provide another excuse for avoiding such efforts? The answers to these questions will help determine Washington's attitude toward the EAS and any subsequent East Asian community.

MULTILATERAL PLUSES AND MINUSES

In short, U.S. policymakers generally believe that Asia-Pacific multilateral organizations such as the ARF and APEC are useful vehicles both for promoting greater political and economic cooperation and for enhancing regional security. Although such organizations hold many promises for Asia, it is important to understand their limits and the opportunities they present. A comprehensive security arrangement or North Atlantic Treaty Organization–type alliance aimed at containing or responding to a specified threat simply does not apply to a post–Cold War Asia. Rather, Asian multilateral security mechanisms should be viewed more as confidence-building measures aimed at avoiding or dampening the possibilities of (rather than reacting to) crises or aggression. Peacekeeping and disaster-relief operations and nontraditional security issues (such as refugee problems, maritime safety, pollution, and other environmental and safety issues) also seem well suited to a multilateral approach. In many instances, the process is as important as the product. Efforts that build upon and seek to complement, rather than replace, existing bilateral and ad hoc relationships that already exist in Asia are of particular value from a U.S. perspective. Both today and in the future, Washington is sure to reject any efforts perceived as undermining U.S. bilateral dealings, especially those that seek to diminish or replace key U.S. bilateral security alliances.

Asian multilateral security mechanisms can more generally serve as important vehicles for promoting long-term peace and stability. They provide a framework for continued direct U.S. involvement in regional security matters. They offer a means for Japan, China, and Russia, among others, to become more actively involved in regional security affairs in a manner that is nonthreatening to their neighbors. They also provide a forum for exposing North Korea to regional realities while facilitating bilateral dialogue between North Korea and South Korea or Japan or the United States. They also provide a mechanism for other regional actors to be heard, while contributing to a sense of regional identity and a spirit of cooperation and confidence building. Since September 11, 2001, they have also become increasingly relevant for coordinating regional views and efforts in the war on terrorism.

Nonetheless, these mechanisms' utility remains limited, especially in the security arena, for two primary reasons. First, although steps have been taken to put some operational substance behind cooperative efforts, these organizations still largely remain dialogue mechanisms that talk about rather than respond to or deal effectively with emerging security challenges. Second, Taiwan has been systematically excluded from many of these mechanisms, so that one of the region's greatest security challenges—cross-strait relations—has been purposefully kept off the security dialogue agenda at Beijing's insistence. As long as these characteristics prevail, the prospects and promises of multilateral security cooperation in the Asia-Pacific region, at least from a U.S. perspective, will necessarily be limited.

FUTURE INSTITUTIONAL ARCHITECTURE

From the previous discussion, it is possible to develop at least a tentative outline of Washington's preferred future institutional architecture for Asia. It prefers that pride of place go to pan-Pacific institution building, which would create mechanisms for cooperation that include the United States as an active partner. Clearly, APEC and the ARF should have priority over—or, at a minimum, not be overshadowed or diminished by—pan-Asian community building. This attitude is shared by other Asian "outsiders," such as Australia, and even by some insiders, such as Japan.

To the extent that Asian community building continues in parallel with the broader institution-building effort, Washington's main concerns will be related to the establishment of (and the subsequent willingness to honor and enforce) norms and objectives consistent with international (read: Washington's) standards. Washington is likely to prefer continued ASEAN leadership and, within

ASEAN, sees Indonesia as the most logical driver of the train, both because it is the largest member and because it is currently committed to promoting democratic values. Indonesia's proposed ASEAN security community, for example, stresses the role of democracy and human rights, which is no doubt music to Washington's ears (even if many of Indonesia's ASEAN partners object to this focus).

Within Asia, the APT appears destined to be the primary vehicle for community building, with the EAS as window dressing, aimed at endorsing the internal East Asian effort. It is doubtful that Washington will push for full membership in the EAS, but it may seek observer status, depending on the admission requirements. In this regard, Washington should be asking itself why it continues to resist acceding to the TAC. The oft-stated contention that joining this treaty would somehow undercut U.S.-Asian alliances appears unfounded: two of Washington's Asian allies—Thailand and the Philippines—are charter members of ASEAN, and the other three—Australia, Japan, and South Korea—have now acceded to the TAC without any perceptible impact on Washington's network of bilateral alliances. As a member of the ARF, the United States has already endorsed the purpose and principles of the TAC "as a code of conduct governing relations between states and a unique diplomatic instrument for regional confidence-building, preventive diplomacy, and political and security cooperation."[53] Perhaps it is time for the United States to take the next step in demonstrating its commitment to regional prosperity and stability and in underscoring its support for Asian community building.

To the extent that Asian community-building efforts signal a willingness to coexist with Washington and are not seen as threatening or attempting to undermine Washington's bilateral alliances, its own central role in Asian security affairs, or the broader Asia-Pacific regional institutions in which it participates, there is little reason to expect objections from Washington or a serious effort to discourage or derail such regional efforts. Washington will likely continue to "wait and see" if Asian community building continues on such a path. Even with new leadership in the White House in 2009, this approach is unlikely to change significantly. In fact, an embrace of regional community building that includes a willingness to sign the TAC and to participate in the EAS is one way in which a new U.S. administration, regardless of party, can distinguish itself from its predecessor, as all are inclined to do.

NOTES

1. This theme was common for Bush's first defense secretary Donald Rumsfeld, who talked about the need for "flexible" coalitions so as not to "dumb down" the

mission. See, for example, Jim Garamone, "NATO Must Address Asymmetric Threats," *American Forces Press Service*, December 18, 2001, http://www.defenselink .mil/news/Dec2001/n12182001_200112181.html. Rumsfeld emphasized this point to an Asian audience at the 2006 Shangri-La defense ministers meeting in Singapore. For an assessment of his Shangri-La remarks, see Ralph A. Cossa, "Demystifying China," *PacNet*, no. 24 (June 5, 2006), http://www.csis.org/media/csis/pubs/pac0624. pdf.

2. For a comprehensive overview of the debate, see Christopher Hill, "The U.S. and Southeast Asia," remarks at the Lee Kuan Yew School of Public Policy, Singapore, May 22, 2006, http://www.state.gov/p/eap/rls/rm/66646.htm.

3. For a concise summation of these Cold War alliances, see Denis McLean, "The United States and Global Security at the Turn of the Century," *American Diplomacy* 5, no. 2 (2000), http://www.unc.edu/depts/diplomat/AD_Issues/amdipl_15/mclean_15. html.

4. Foreign Minister Nakayama Taro, statement at the General Session of the ASEAN Post Ministerial Conference, Kuala Lumpur, Malaysia, July 22, 1991, http:// www.mofa.go.jp/policy/other/bluebook/1991/1991-appendix-2.htm.

5. For a review of U.S. attitudes at that time, see Secretary of State James A. Baker III, "America in Asia: Emerging Architecture for a Pacific Community," *Foreign Affairs* 70, no. 5 (1991–1992): 1–18.

6. Assistant Secretary of State Winston Lord, comments in the Joint Press Statement, Meeting of the ASEAN-U.S. Dialogue, Bandar Seri Begawan, Brunei Darussalam, May 16, 1993, http://www.aseansec.org/2053.htm.

7. This term was first introduced by President Bill Clinton during his address to the Republic of Korea National Assembly in July 1993.

8. For background on the creation of the ARF, see U.S. Department of State, "Fact Sheet: Association of Southeast Asian Nations," *Dispatch* 6, no. 31 (July 31, 1995), http://dosfan.lib.uic.edu/ERC/briefing/dispatch/1995/html/Dispatchv6no31.html.

9. ASEAN Secretariat, "Chairman's Statement: The First Meeting of the ASEAN Regional Forum," Bangkok, Thailand, July 25, 1994, http://www.aseansec.org/2105. htm.

10. Secretary Powell attended the 2001 Shanghai meeting, the 2002 Bandar Seri Begawan meeting, the 2003 Phnom Penh meeting, and the 2004 Jakarta meeting. By contrast, each of his predecessors, Warren Christopher and Madeleine Albright, missed one meeting, with Albright departing a second one early.

11. See, for example, Ralph A. Cossa, "Rice's Unfortunate Choice," *Asia Times*, July 28, 2005.

12. White House, *The National Security Strategy of the United States of America* (Washington, D.C.: Government Printing Office, 2002), 5, 29.

13. White House, *The National Security Strategy of the United States of America* (Washington, D.C.: Government Printing Office, 2006), 40.

14. Eric John, "The Promise of Regional Architecture in Asia," remarks at the Georgetown Conference on Korean Society, Georgetown University, Washington, D.C., December 15, 2006.

15. White House, *National Security Strategy* (2006), 40.

16. Shanghai Cooperation Organization Secretariat, "Declaration of Heads of Member States of Shanghai Cooperation Organization," Astana, Kazakhstan, July 6, 2005. This "positive dynamics" assertion came at a time when a resurgent Taliban was beginning to make the security situation in Afghanistan demonstrably worse.

17. Ibid. What follows is a U.S. interpretation of events. For an alternative view, see Pan Guang, "The Chinese Perspective on the Recent Astana Summit," *China Brief* 5, no. 18 (August 16, 2005), http://jamestown.org/china_brief/article.php?articleid = 2373127.

18. Jim Garamore, "Uzbeks Ask U.S. to Leave Karshi-Khanabad," *American Forces Press Service*, August 1, 2005, http://www.defenselink.mil/news/newsarticle.aspx?id = 16994.

19. See, for example, "Central Asian Alliance Calls for U.S. Pullout Date: Russia, China Among Those Seeking Firm Date for Withdrawal from Region," Associated Press, July 5, 2006. For recurring comprehensive coverage and analysis of Sino-Russian relations and their impact on the United States, see Yu Bin, "China-Russia," *Comparative Connections* (online journal), http://www.csis.org/pacfor/ccejournal.html.

20. For examples of this preference for "inclusive" Asia-Pacific regional efforts, see Office of the Press Secretary, White House, "Joint Statement Between the United States of America and the Republic of Indonesia," May 25, 2005; "Joint Statement Between President Bush and Prime Minister Lee of Singapore," July 12, 2005.

21. All quotes in this section attributed to Assistant Secretary Hill derive from "U.S. and Southeast Asia."

22. See, for example, Paul Wolfowitz, interview by Michael Dwyer, Australian Broadcasting, May 31, 2007, http://www.defenselink.mil/transcripts/transcript.aspx ?transcriptid = 2700, in which Wolfowitz describes the Bush administration derivation of this phrase.

23. John, "Promise of Regional Architecture in Asia."

24. This particular exchange took place in the summer of 2006, after the first EAS meeting. However, at another not-for-attribution session held in Jakarta after the second EAS meeting, another senior U.S. official made essentially the same response.

25. See, for example, ASEAN Secretariat, "Statement by the Chairman of the ASEAN Regional Forum (ARF) on the Terrorist Acts of the 11th September 2001," Bandar Seri Begawan, Brunei Darussalam, October 4, 2001; "ASEAN Regional Forum Statement on Strengthening Transport Security Against International Terrorism" and "ASEAN Regional Forum Statement on Non-Proliferation," Jakarta, Indonesia, July 2, 2004. Such statements have become regular attachments to ARF chairman statements and are frequently echoed at ASEAN summits.

26. ASEAN Secretariat, "Chairman's Statement: The First Meeting of the ASEAN Regional Forum," Bangkok, Thailand, July 25, 1994, http://www.aseansec.org/2105.htm.

27. U.S. Department of State, Bureau of Political-Military Affairs, *The ASEAN Regional Forum: A Concept Paper* (Washington, D.C.: Department of State, July 15, 2002), http://www.state.gov/t/pm/rls/fs/2002/12052.htm.

28. APEC Secretariat, "APEC Leaders' Statement on Counter-terrorism," ninth APEC Economic Leaders' Meeting, Shanghai, China, October 21, 2001, http://www.apec.org/apec/leaders__declarations/2001/statement_on_counter-terrorism.html.

29. The Sino-U.S. interaction and cooperation can be seen in a press release made by President George W. Bush and President Jiang Zemin, "U.S., China Stand Against Terrorism," October 19, 2001, Shanghai, China, http://www.state.gov/s/ct/rls/rm/2001/5461.htm.

30. APEC Secretariat, "Declaration on Partnership for the Future," eleventh APEC Economic Leaders' Meeting, Bangkok, Thailand, October 21, 2003, http://www.apec.org/apec/leaders__declarations/2003.html. APEC leaders have consistently sent a message to Pyongyang to return to six-party negotiations and were especially critical of Pyongyang after its October 2006 nuclear weapons test.

31. There were some concerns that the 2006 ASEAN-U.S. Summit would be canceled due to apprehensions in Washington about President Bush's meeting with Thailand's coup-installed prime minister General Surayud Chulanont, but (wisely, in my opinion) it went ahead as scheduled.

32. John, "Promise of Regional Architecture in Asia."

33. APEC Secretariat, "Ha Noi Declaration," fourteenth APEC Economic Leaders' Meeting, Ha Noi, Vietnam, November 18–19, 2006, http://www.apec.org/apec/leaders__declarations/2006.html. For U.S. coverage of the event, see Melody Merin, "Asia-Pacific Leaders Commit to Free Trade, Security, Community: APEC Hanoi Declaration Affirms Support for Doha Development Round," USINFO (U.S. Department of State), November 19, 2006, at http://usinfo.state.gov/xarchives/display.html?p = washfile-english&y = 2006&m = November&x = 20061119164659niremydolemo.3842432.

34. The Ha Noi Declaration did, however, also note that "there are practical difficulties" in negotiating an Asia-Pacific free-trade agreement "at this time."

35. Office of the Press Secretary, White House, *Fact Sheet: Asia-Pacific Economic Cooperation (APEC) 2006* (Washington, D.C.: Government Printing Office, November 19, 2006), http://www.whitehouse.gov/news/releases/2006/11/20061119-2.html. For a somewhat less enthusiastic assessment, see Denis Hew, "Hurdles Ahead for Asia-Pacific FTA," *Singapore Straits Times*, March 8, 2007, http://www.iseas.edu.sg/viewpoint/dh8mar07.pdf.

36. Office of the Press Secretary, White House, "Remarks by President Bush to the People of Poland," Wawel Royal Castle, Krakow, Poland, May 31, 2003, http://www

.whitehouse.gov/news/releases/2003/05/20030531–3.html. The first PSI meeting was held on June 12, 2003, in Madrid, Spain, with representatives from all eleven core participants in attendance.

37. Department of Foreign Affairs and Trade, Australia, "Proliferation Security Initiative: Chairman's Statement at the Second Meeting," Brisbane, Australia, July 10, 2003, http://www.dfat.gov.au/globalissues/psi/chair&_statement_0603.html.

38. For more information on the PSI, please refer to the U.S. Department of State Web site and, in particular, to John R. Bolton, "Proliferation Security Initiative: Statement of Interdiction Principles," remarks at the PSI Meeting, Paris, September 4, 2003, http://www.state.gov/t/us/rm/23801.htm.

39. For a review of the PSI and East Asian attitudes toward it, see *Countering the Spread of Weapons of Mass Destruction: The Role of the Proliferation Security Initiative (A Review of the Work of the Council for Security Cooperation in the Asia Pacific International Working Group on Confidence and Security Building Measures)* (Honolulu: Pacific Forum, Center for Strategic and International Studies, 2004), http://www.csis.org/media/csis/pubs/issuesinsights_v04n05.pdf.

40. Andrew C. Winner, "The Proliferation Security Initiative: The New Face of Interdiction," *Washington Quarterly* 28, no. 2 (2005): 137.

41. For details on this operation, see the tsunami relief page on the U.S. Pacific Command Web site, http://www.pacom.mil/special/0412asia/.

42. For another perspective on this massive relief effort, see Ralph A. Cossa, "South Asian Tsunami: U.S. Military Provides 'Logistical Backbone' for Relief Operation," *USA: Foreign Policy Agenda* (e-journal) 9, no. 4 (2004), http://usinfo.state.gov/journals/itps/1104/ijpe/update.pdf, under "Improving Lives: Military Humanitarian and Assistance Programs."

43. Andrew Zwaniecki, "Bush to Request $52 Million for Asia-Pacific Energy Partnership: Promoting Clean Development One of Group's Goals, Energy Secretary Says," USINDO, January 12, 2006.

44. ASEAN Secretariat, "Chairman's Statement of the First ASEAN-Russian Federation Summit," Kuala Lumpur, Malaysia, December 13, 2005, http://www.aseansec.org/18085.htm.

45. ASEAN Secretariat, "Chairman's Statement of the First East Asia Summit," Kuala Lumpur, Malaysia, December 14, 2005, http://www.aseansec.org/18104.htm.

46. The EAS was originally scheduled for December 2006 in Cebu, Philippines, but was postponed, ostensibly due to an incoming typhoon, although there were also press reports about concerns of a terrorist attack against the assembled leaders. The January 2007 meeting took place under heightened security.

47. As was the case in 2005, the EAS meeting was preceded by an ASEAN summit, an APT summit, and various ten-plus-one summit meetings.

48. ASEAN Secretariat, "Chairperson's Statement of the 12th ASEAN Summit," Cebu, Philippines, January 13, 2007, http://www.aseansec.org/19280.htm.

49. ASEAN Secretariat, "Chairman's Statement of the Tenth ASEAN Plus Three Summit," Cebu, Philippines, January 14, 2007, http://www.aseansec.org/19315.htm.

50. ASEAN Secretariat, "Chairman's Statement of the Second East Asia Summit," Cebu, Philippines, January 15, 2007, http://www.aseansec.org/19303.htm.

51. ASEAN Secretariat, "Kuala Lumpur Declaration on the ASEAN Plus Three Summit," Kuala Lumpur, Malaysia, December 12, 2005, http://www.aseansec.org/18036.htm.

52. The quotations are from ASEAN Secretariat, "Chairman's Statement of the Second East Asia Summit."

53. ASEAN Secretariat, "Chairman's Statement of the First East Asia Summit," Kuala Lumpur, Malaysia, December 14, 2005, http://www.aseansec.org/18104.htm.

3. Chinese Perspectives on Building an East Asian Community in the Twenty-first Century

Wu Xinbo

The closing years of the twentieth century and the opening ones of the twenty-first have witnessed a significant development in the history of Asia. A region long plagued by war, chaos, division, and mutual suspicion began moving toward integration. To be sure, Asian integration is a nascent undertaking, and its future is unclear. Different countries in the region have quite different visions and expectations, and outcomes will result at least in part from currently unforeseen interactions of various players with various preferences. China, as a major power with growing political and economic influence in the region, will certainly have a significant impact on the process.

This chapter presents a Chinese perspective on some major questions regarding Asian integration. How has the Chinese perspective on regional multilateralism evolved, and what are the dynamics behind it? How should an Asian community be constructed? What are the roles of other regional mechanisms such as the Asia-Pacific Economic Cooperation (APEC) forum, the Association of Southeast Asian Nations (ASEAN), the ASEAN Regional Forum (ARF), the Six-Party Talks, and the Shanghai Cooperation Organization (SCO)? What are the Chinese views regarding the U.S. role and its alliance system in the region? What kind of norms and principles should guide Asian regionalism? And finally, what should the Asian security architecture look like in the future in order to address regional challenges?

THE EVOLUTION OF CHINA'S ATTITUDE TOWARD REGIONAL MULTILATERALISM

In the post–Cold War era, China's perspective on regional multilateralism has evolved substantially. Its participation in regional multilateral mechanisms started with its membership in APEC in 1991. APEC was founded in 1989 with a mandate to promote the liberalization of trade and investment in the Asia-Pacific region, and after three years of observation Beijing decided to jump aboard because APEC was perceived to serve China's economic development agenda. China's role was designed as "active participation and adroit guidance of its development."[1] Involvement in APEC helped foster among the Chinese a sense of belonging to a broader Asia-Pacific region, as well as a sense of participating in regional economic cooperation. Throughout the 1990s, the terms *Asia Pacific* and *regional economic cooperation* appeared frequently in Chinese media reports, academic discourse, and official documents, giving rise to a sense that China should conduct its economic relations with the outside world not only on a bilateral basis, but also in a regional context. To some extent, China's experience with regionalism originated with APEC, although the regionalism represented by APEC is actually a transregionalism given its geographical scope.

The tougher test for China's approach to regional multilateralism came with the establishment of the ARF in 1994. Unlike APEC's original mandate, the ARF is a mechanism aimed at promoting regional security cooperation. When China joined the ARF in 1994, it harbored serious concerns for two principal reasons. One was that against the background of China's rise and the notion of a "China threat" in the Asia Pacific, the United States, Japan, and even Southeast Asian countries might employ the ARF to check and contain a stronger China. Given that Washington did forge a regional mechanism in the mid-1950s—the Southeast Asia Treaty Organization—to contain China, Beijing's concern was not entirely groundless. The other concern was that the ARF might lead to the internationalization of disputed territorial issues in the South China Sea, which Beijing preferred to deal with on a bilateral basis with various Southeast Asian claimants. If the ARF was going to put the South China issue on its agenda, then disputants such as Malaysia, the Philippines, and Vietnam might form a united front against China with the support of other Southeast Asian countries and possibly the United States and Japan.

As it turned out, neither scenario emerged. ASEAN has been in the ARF driver's seat and precludes others—including Washington—from setting the agenda. Rather than being a tool employed by the United States to check or contain China, the ARF has proved to be a useful forum to promote security dialogue and cooperation among member countries. Meanwhile, the South China Sea issue was not brought to the ARF agenda and was dealt with largely in a bilateral context. As a result, the ARF experience made Beijing feel more comfortable with regional security cooperation.

Subsequently, the Asian financial crisis of 1997/1998 had a defining impact on China's attitude toward Asian regionalism. As the crisis exposed, Asian economies had become so intertwined that a crisis in one place easily spread to another, causing chain reactions throughout the region. Under these circumstances, concerted efforts based on substantive economic cooperation among regional members stand as the best way to deal with future challenges. Moreover, by lending money to crisis-stricken countries such as Thailand and Indonesia and by refraining from depreciating its currency as a way to offset the pressure resulting from the crisis, Beijing made an important contribution to stabilizing the situation and was widely applauded. For the first time, many of its neighbors regarded China as a "responsible power" rather than as a threat. Not surprisingly, such positive appraisals encouraged a more receptive posture in Beijing toward regional economic cooperation. In the years following the financial crisis, China began to play an active role in the ASEAN Plus Three (APT) and ASEAN Plus China mechanisms.

These trends were further reinforced with subtle but steady adjustments in China's diplomacy. Compared with the 1990s, when relations with the major powers, in particular the United States, took the center stage of China's diplomatic efforts, ties with neighboring countries gained increasing importance in the late 1990s and early 2000s. As a result, China's diplomacy around its periphery expanded from the traditional *mu lin you hao* (good neighbor and friendliness) approach to the *you lin, an lin, fu lin* (amicable, peaceful, and prosperous neighborhood) approach. This shift can be attributed to two causes. One is China's concern for security and stability on its periphery. Since the 1990s, the so-called three evil forces in Central Asia—terrorism, separatism, and extremism—posed growing threats to security in China's northwestern region,[2] and actions taken by the United States since the late 1990s to forge closer political and security ties with some of China's neighbors—as part of its hedging strategy in Asia—also jangled China's security-related nerves. Such developments required China to devote more attention to relations with its neighbors so as to stabilize its periphery. It was against this background that the SCO was founded in June 2001. The SCO stands out as the first multilateral institution that China ever sponsored. Meanwhile, as China joined the World Trade Organization in 2001, Southeast Asian countries were commonly concerned that China might become a formidable rival in competing for foreign direct investment and export-market share. Aware of the anxiety in Southeast Asia, Beijing began to view expanded economic cooperation as a way to mitigate ASEAN's concern and create a win-win situation. This change in outlook gave rise to the idea of a China-ASEAN free-trade agreement (FTA). Building on this momentum, China became more active in promoting regionalism in Asia.

On another front, China's involvement in Korean Peninsula affairs since the late 1990s also coincided with its growing interest in multilateralism. From December 1997 to August 1998, it joined with the United States and the two Koreas in four-party talks on the Korean Peninsula issues, aimed at building a peace mechanism on the peninsula. Although the talks ended without any concrete progress, they did contribute to the improvement of U.S.–North Korea and North-South relations. China, participating in a multilateral diplomatic approach to the Korean issue for the first time, won appreciation from both Washington and Seoul for the constructive role it played. After North Korean nuclear ambitions were once again revealed in October 2002, China brokered three-party talks along with the United States and North Korea in April 2003. These talks later expanded to include South Korea, Japan, and Russia and became known as the Six-Party Talks. As the Six-Party Talks proceeded, China became indispensable to their success, serving as a considerate host, active convener, and a skillful consensus maker. The evolving Chinese role in the process attests to Beijing's new diplomatic thinking, which takes a more favorable view of multilateralism.

As these processes unfolded, Beijing came to see regional multilateralism as a useful instrument to enhance China's economic, political, and security interests. On the economic front, it is generally held that globalization and regionalization are the two preeminent trends in the world economy. As the North American Free Trade Agreement and the Europe Union suggest, regional integration is a natural choice as countries seek to benefit from creating a larger economic platform for themselves. To some extent, regionalization is the stepping-stone toward globalization. So far as China is concerned, as its economic links with other parts of Asia grow, it should seek more formalized arrangements to expand and consolidate cooperation with its regional neighbors. On the political front, as multilateralism is hailed as the new norm of international politics in the era of globalization, China's embrace of it will demonstrate progressiveness and responsibility in its diplomacy. Beijing hopes that deepened regional multilateralism and cooperation will help forge stronger ties with its neighbors and promote China's influence in regional affairs. On the security front, Beijing recognizes that multilateral cooperation is necessary to address the many nontraditional security challenges in the region, from terrorism to drug trafficking. It also calculates that by promoting regional cooperation, it can help create a friendlier and more stable security environment around China's periphery, offsetting security pressures emanating from the U.S. pursuit of a hedging strategy vis-à-vis China.[3] Finally, it recognizes that the overall trend in the post–Cold War Asian regional order is one of transformation toward greater multilateral cooperation. China needs to be an active part of this trend and contribute to a more desirable regional order.[4]

CHINESE VIEWS ON EAST ASIAN COMMUNITY BUILDING

As the previous section explains, from the early 1990s to the early 2000s China's attitude toward regionalism evolved from passivity to proactivity, and its multilateral behavior moved from participation to creation. The process was not just driven by specific events, however; it was also informed by intellectual debate in China. From the late 1990s in particular, Chinese academic and policy analysts debated a range of questions concerning China's diplomatic strategy: How should China behave as a responsible power as its material power grows? What should China's regional strategy look like? How should China define and pursue its interests in Asia? How should China deal with regionalism, multilateralism, and international regimes?[5] Such discussions reflected the ongoing changes in the regional economic, political, and security landscape and provided useful intellectual guidance for policymakers to deal with the challenges confronting China. The evolution in China's multilateral behavior is not just an adjustment in policy practice, but also the outcome of a significant debate and learning process.

In China, the mainstream opinion is that if an East Asian community is to be realized, it should be a comprehensive cooperation mechanism that comes out of a gradual process of regional economic, political, and security cooperation. The process would start with an economic community; expand to political, security, social, and cultural areas; and finally end up with a regional community that covers cooperation among regional members on all major dimensions. However, there exist both optimistic and pessimistic views about this process. The optimists believe that the deepening interdependence among East Asian members, the growing sense of shared destiny, and emerging common norms are conducive to the establishment of a regional community. The pessimists argue that differing opinions among countries about the future regional community—for example, regarding the participation of non-Asian countries such as Australia and New Zealand and the perceived U.S. opposition to East Asian community building—will complicate and possibly freeze the process.

From the very beginning, China expected the East Asia Summit (EAS) to be a major venue in building an East Asian community. Some analysts hailed the

evolution from the APT Summit to the first EAS and believed it marked a substantive step forward in East Asian cooperation and a new stage in the development of East Asian regionalism because stress was now being placed on the entire
region rather than just on ASEAN.[6] However, Beijing felt somewhat frustrated
that non–East Asian countries such as Australia, India, and New Zealand were
invited to participate in the EAS. What dismayed it even more was the decision
that the EAS would be hosted only by ASEAN countries, thus not including
China, which was initially enthusiastic about hosting the second meeting. From
the Chinese perspective, the purpose of including non–East Asian countries was
to dilute a perceived predominant Chinese influence within the mechanism.
There was a widespread suspicion in China that the United States, concerned
with possible Chinese dominance in the EAS, was actually behind the idea of
bringing in non–East Asian members. The Kuala Lumpur Declaration signed at
the first EAS suggested that "the East Asia Summit could play a significant role in
community building in this region," but China made it clear that the EAS can be
a useful supplement only to the process of East Asian community building. In
fact, due to China's insistence, the declaration did not even use the term *East
Asian community* in the text.[7] Some Chinese scholars openly complained that the
EAS was simply another APEC-style organization and not a tool tailored to the
needs of East Asia community building: APEC had so far failed to promote regional integration, so another APEC-like group would not make a difference.[8]

Under such circumstances, China expects APT to be the main venue for
the building of an East Asian community. First and foremost, APT provides an
important framework to promote regional economic cooperation at multiple
levels. Within this framework, the thirteen East Asian countries can jointly
plan and promote regionwide economic cooperation and regional integration.
Meanwhile, the three Northeast Asian countries—China, Japan, and South
Korea—can sit together to explore the possibility of cooperation among themselves. In addition, they can separately pursue their respective economic cooperation with ASEAN. Moreover, APT promises to be a useful instrument to integrate all kinds of subregional economic cooperation initiatives in East Asia. In
fact, various cooperation projects and mechanisms established within APT
have contributed greatly to its substantive growth. Second, not only does APT
drive economic cooperation, but it also helps improve political relations among
regional members. Given the many existing differences and disputes among
East Asian countries, building trust is a precondition to greater economic cooperation, regional integration, and the establishment of true East Asian community. By providing a platform for dialogue and interaction, APT has proven to
be a valuable channel for promoting mutual understanding and improving bilateral relations. Finally, building a community encompassing thirteen East
Asian countries is definitely a daunting task, but creating a community that in-

cludes non–East Asian countries such as India, Australia, and New Zealand will be even more difficult. As T. J. Pempel correctly notes, "[T]he wider the geographic area across which coordination is sought, the more complicated it becomes to generate comprehensive and meaningful agreement."[9] Therefore, it is more pragmatic and viable to pursue an East Asian community based on the APT framework.

To be sure, this emergent community will not be created in a vacuum, and various existing mechanisms will have different impacts on the process. One such mechanism is APEC. It is worth noting that it was due to declining interest in APEC that East Asian countries began to attempt to deepen economic cooperation among themselves through other means. During the financial crisis of 1997/1998, APEC was not able to take any concrete measures to help mitigate the crisis, thus disappointing the stricken countries and dampening their enthusiasm for the mechanism. Moreover, in the Kuala Lumpur Summit Meeting in 1998, APEC failed to launch the Early Voluntary Sectoral Liberalization initiative, a major setback and loss of momentum in promoting further trade liberalization. At the Shanghai Summit Meeting in 2001, APEC members vowed to turn APEC into a mechanism for closer regional economic cooperation. Nonetheless, against a background of deepening economic cooperation within East Asia and with an increasing focus on security issues such as terrorism and North Korean nuclear ambitions, APEC has gone adrift.

These developments do not mean that APEC is totally irrelevant to East Asian integration, however. For one thing, APEC's timetable for the realization of free trade and investment among its members by 2020 will give impetus to cooperation among East Asian countries because they certainly want to achieve more than APEC by that time. For instance, ASEAN has announced that it will finish building the ASEAN Free Trade Area by 2015, five years ahead of the APEC goal. China, Japan, and South Korea also bear in mind the APEC timetable when pursuing FTAs with ASEAN as well as among themselves. Looking into the future, if APEC can regain its vigor and make substantive achievements in promoting trans-Pacific economic cooperation, it can further enhance East Asian cooperation because most East Asian countries are APEC members. In this sense, a vigorous APEC can contribute to the development of an East Asian community. However, APEC is unlikely to turn itself into an institutional structure that accommodates regional economic, political, and security cooperation and thus take away the rationale for building an East Asian community. After all, ASEAN does not want to be marginalized in an Asia-Pacific community, and China would be concerned with a predominant U.S. influence in such a transregional structure.

The ARF is another regional mechanism that may have some impact on the growth of East Asian community building. As a forum aimed at promoting cooperative security in the Asia-Pacific region, the ARF seeks to pursue confidence building, preventive diplomacy, and conflict resolution. Since its inception, it has pushed its participants to hold security dialogues, increase defense transparency, adopt confidence-building measures, and conduct cooperation in nontraditional security fields. Although it is unlikely to become a regional security institution because it includes too many members from different regions, it has helped enhance mutual trust among Asian countries and fostered habits of security cooperation. These positive developments are conducive to security dialogue and cooperation among APT members as they move to turn the framework into a comprehensive cooperation mechanism. As a result, the East Asian Study Group recommended in its study that ARF be strengthened, noting that "[t]he ARF helps provide channels of communications to enhance mutual understanding. It is, therefore, desirable to strengthen the role of the ARF to encourage the dialogue."[10]

Although ASEAN launched the ARF as a means of cooperative security, the Six-Party Talks on Korea Peninsula security represent a nontraditional approach to a traditional security challenge in Northeast Asia. The North Korean nuclear issue is largely a lingering Cold War legacy: the long-standing antagonism between North Korea and the United States. However, due to changes in Northeast Asian international politics as well as to the common aim of all the related major powers—China, Japan, Russia, and the United States—to achieve the denuclearization of the Korean Peninsula, it was possible to put into place a multilateral mechanism to address the problem. Although Pyongyang's apparent test of a nuclear device in October 2006 cast doubt on the Six-Party Talks' effectiveness and viability, the North Korean nuclear challenge and the security of the Korean Peninsula more broadly must be addressed in a multilateral diplomatic process rather than with the traditional approach of deterrence and containment. The resumption of the Six-Party Talks in the wake of the North Korean nuclear test and the agreement reached in February 2007 on the initial actions for the implementation of the joint statement of September 19, 2005, attest to this point.

In the longer run, the Six-Party Talks may turn into an institutionalized security mechanism to address Northeast Asian issues.[11] In broad terms, such a mechanism will serve three main purposes. First, it will help build and maintain a permanent peace on the Korean Peninsula as it undergoes tremendous and complicated transformation in the decades ahead. Second, it will enhance confidence building and mutual trust among all the parties concerned. And third, it will promote cooperation on nontraditional security issues in Northeast Asia.

Meanwhile, the Six-Party Talks may have a positive impact on the process of East Asian community building as well. The talks succeeded not only in bringing North Korea into a multilateral mechanism, but also in enhancing cooperation among China, Japan, and South Korea, countries that will play important roles in forging an East Asian community. However, the six-party approach also reminds the region that an East Asian community should maintain its openness because it cannot address all issues on its own, and arrangements involving outside countries, in particular the United States, in regional affairs are necessary to supplement the regional architecture.

The SCO will also likely have both normative and practical impacts on East Asian community building. Initially created to promote cooperation in dealing with challenges posed by terrorism, separatism, and extremism in Central Asia, the SCO broadened its agenda to develop effective cooperation in political, economic, energy, environmental, and other areas. The SCO stands for a new security concept anchored by mutual trust, disarmament, and cooperative security; a new state-to-state relationship with partnership instead of alignment at its core; and a new model of regional cooperation featuring the concerted efforts of countries of all sizes. Over time, the SCO has characterized its norms, labeled "Shanghai Spirit," as mutual trust, mutual benefit, equality, cooperation, respect for diverse civilizations, and common development.[12] Reflecting the common aspirations of as well as the diversity among SCO members, Shanghai Spirit is likely to appeal to most East Asian countries and may help shape the norms of East Asian community building. Moreover, the SCO practice of emphasizing cooperation in nontraditional security fields and of underscoring economic cooperation will also likely affect the agenda of cooperation within the East Asian community.

Although two kinds of multilateralism generally exist in the region, ad hoc and institutionalized, and each operates in somewhat different ways, the Chinese suggest that each mechanism has its own merits and that there is no need to push for a unitary platform. In their opinion, it is necessary to enhance the coordination among various mechanisms and make the best use of their capacity, with the aim of gradually creating a vibrant, multifaceted, and complex pattern of regional cooperation.[13] Meanwhile, some in China believe that gradual institutionalization of regional cooperation is desirable because such institutionalization can legitimize regional cooperation while making it more effective.[14]

With regard to ASEAN remaining in the "driver's seat" in regional cooperation, there seem to be different attitudes in China. Some still believe that ASEAN is a realistic choice for leader because neither China nor Japan can single-handedly play that role, but the skeptics question both ASEAN's willingness and its capability. Some suggest that due to the concern over becoming a "subregion of East Asia," ASEAN really wants not an East Asian community, but an ASEAN community, so it is not going to make whole-hearted efforts to push East Asian cooperation.[15] Others argue that although ASEAN helped kick off the process of regional cooperation, it simply lacks both political and economic might to bring regional cooperation to a new level.[16] Some suggest that China-ASEAN joint efforts can generate the driving force for regional cooperation, whereas others believe that China, Japan, and the United States should provide the leadership.[17]

A rising India is going to be a major player in the Asian security architecture of the future. In recent years, it has been trying to promote its influence in regional security by pursuing security cooperation with the United States and Japan and by participating in East Asian cooperation. According to the Chinese perspective, the United States and Japan want to use India to balance China by taking advantage of India's concern over China's growing capability, which will certainly complicate the regional security landscape. However, given India's tradition of nonalignment and the importance it attaches to its relations with China, New Delhi is more likely to pursue the diplomacy of equidistance from the major powers. India's lukewarm attitude toward the Japanese proposal of creating a four-nation coalition that includes Australia, India, Japan, and the United States indicates that it is unlikely to be actively involved in any regional security mechanism aimed at containing China. China thus should not worry too much about India's growing but still moderate role in regional security.[18]

CHINESE VIEWS ON THE U.S. ROLE IN ASIA

The United States is certainly the single most important external factor affecting Asian integration. Although geographically not an Asian country, the United States has significant interests and influence in the region. As such, the posture Washington adopts toward East Asian cooperation and community building will have a crucial impact on the process. Chinese analysts understand that the United States will watch the process closely, giving particular attention to the impact it has on U.S. interests in the region. Chinese analysts consider Washington's concern to be focused specifically in two areas: first, U.S. exclusion from APT and the EAS and possible marginalization by East Asian integration; and second, the strengthening of China's hand in East Asia to Washington's detriment.[19] They believe that as a result of these two factors, Washington will try to exert influence on the process directly or indirectly. Such efforts may include promoting ASEAN's leading role; encouraging India, Australia, and New Zealand to play a stronger role in the EAS; turning the Six-Party Talks on the North Korean nuclear issue into a forum for a Northeast Asian security dialogue; and possibly signing on to the EAS process (these possibilities are discussed in chapter 2 of this volume).[20]

As a matter of fact, Chinese experts have many different interpretations and expectations regarding the U.S. role in the process of East Asian integration.[21] Some would urge Washington to realize that this process is an inevitable trend, to abandon its traditional thinking that puts politics and security ahead of economics, and to play a constructive role in regional integration. They hope that the United States will encourage countries in the region to pursue community building in the East Asian way, see the APEC and ARF processes as supplements to East Asian community building, and support a leadership role for ASEAN in the process. Others, however, are very negative about the U.S. role. They argue that Washington is very much concerned with the rise of East Asia in particular and would oppose the efforts aimed at solidifying community building in the region. Although the actual U.S. role remains uncertain, mainstream opinion in Chinese academic and policy circles holds that in pursuing East Asian integration, U.S. influence and legitimate concerns in the region must be taken into account; otherwise, regional integration cannot proceed smoothly. Beijing also understands that the U.S. factor must be handled very carefully because there is always a suspicion in Washington that an increasingly strong China may seek to push the United States out of East Asia. As a result, Beijing tries hard to assure Washington that it does not advocate an "exclusive" form of regionalism. Instead, as Chinese premier Wen Jiabao stressed at the first EAS, China supports transparent and open East Asian cooperation and is opposed to self-contained or exclusive East Asian cooperation or cooperation targeted at any particular party. He also suggested that East Asian countries should take into full consideration non–East Asian countries' reasonable interests in the region in order to enhance these countries' understanding and support for East Asian cooperation.[22]

At the end of the day, the U.S. role will depend very much on the policy debate within the United States. From a Chinese perspective, Washington has to think through certain issues. First is the concern over the prospect of U.S. marginalization in regional affairs. It is true that as a non-Asian country, the United States will not necessarily be included in East Asian regional community building. However, given the profound political, economic, and security linkages between the United States and East Asia, Washington will definitely remain an indispensable partner to the region, and its involvement will remain crucial to the management of a wide range of regional affairs, particularly on the security front. The fact that an East Asian community is not going to be an exclusive regional bloc further suggests that U.S. influence in the region will not be diluted.

The second issue is how to view the possible expansion of Chinese influence as brought about by East Asian community building and multilateralism. Here it is important to put a rising China in the context of East Asian integration rather than place East Asian integration under the shadow of a rising China. Although China's active participation in regional integration may enhance its influence on regional affairs, it will also make China more reliant on cooperation with others given the growing complex interdependence in East Asia. In the end, this web of interdependence will likely make growing Chinese power an integral part of regional strength. Will China be tempted to take advantage of regional integration to create a Sino-centric order in East Asia? Beijing appears smart enough not to undertake such a mission impossible. Even if it does, the growing interdependence and the pluralistic power structure in East Asia—where the India, Japan, Russia, and the United States are major players— would create formidable obstacles to Beijing's ambition.

Finally, the third issue involves the question, Will East Asian integration undermine the Asia-Pacific economic cooperation espoused by APEC? It is true that many East Asian countries turned their interest to promoting cooperation among themselves in the wake of the Asian financial crisis and APEC's failure to reach consensus on its future path. However, this does not mean the end of APEC or its vision. If a more realistic agenda can be set for APEC, it can certainly regain its vigor in the future. In fact, it is better to view East Asian community building and APEC as two partly overlapping circles with both divergent and convergent missions rather than as two separate spheres with entirely different trajectories. For instance, some East Asian cooperation might be expanded to APEC at a later stage. Likewise, a revitalized APEC can stimulate the East Asian community-building process.

As economic interdependence has reached a new stage, Asian integration is an inevitable trend. It is transforming both the East Asian landscape and U.S.– East Asian relations. Confronted with this development, the United States should stay actively involved in regional affairs, put its relations with all the major indigenous players on a solid basis, and encourage China's participation in regional cooperation. Meanwhile, it should also continue to promote Asia-Pacific economic cooperation and work with others to set a more realistic agenda for APEC.

The U.S. alliance system in East Asia is another important factor affecting East Asian community building. Forged during the Cold War, this system has undergone significant transformation. U.S. alliances with Thailand and the Philippines have lost much momentum due to the improvement in these two countries' respective security environments, and U.S.–South Korea security ties have also begun to loosen in recent years owing in part to Seoul's effort to shift its policy toward the North from one of antagonism to one of peaceful coexistence. An exception to this trend is the U.S.-Japan alliance, which has been redefined and strengthened since the mid-1990s. Both Tokyo and Washington see benefits in a rejuvenation of the alliance. For Japan, renewed alliance will allow it to play a larger and more active security role in the region and balance the rising Chinese power; for the United States, enhanced security ties with Japan will help consolidate U.S. preponderance in the Asia Pacific and hedge against a stronger China. However, a strengthened U.S.-Japan alliance, if aiming at China as its major target, will run the risk of throwing the region back into a bipolar structure featuring strategic competition, antagonism, and even confrontation—a scenario that will seriously impede community building in Asia, especially East Asia.[23] In a nutshell, the impact of a strengthened U.S.-Japan alliance on East Asian community building and multilateralism will depend largely on the state of two sets of bilateral relations—those between China and the United States, and those between China and Japan. As those relationships develop, however, it seems clear that East Asian community building will not lead to the establishment of an overarching, unified security mechanism: for the foreseeable future and probably beyond it, the U.S. alliance system will continue to exist as part of the pluralistic security arrangements in the region.

LOOKING AHEAD: THE FUTURE SECURITY ARCHITECTURE IN ASIA

Certain mainstream principles have emerged in China in debates about East Asian community building for the future, drawing on Beijing's understanding of the political, economic, and security realities in East Asia, its own preferred approach to East Asian integration, and its experiences of regional cooperation. Under the rubric of "neo–East Asian regionalism," China expects these principles to guide the construction of regional architecture in the years ahead.[24] They will form the foundation of future mechanisms to meet the regional security challenges of tomorrow effectively.

KEY PRINCIPLES FOR THE FUTURE

First, the APT process should serve as the main vehicle for East Asian cooperation, and ASEAN should play a leadership role. Meanwhile, the three "ten plus one" arrangements (ASEAN plus China or Japan or South Korea) will constitute the foundation for the APT framework, and the EAS will serve as an important outside stimulus. China prefers the APT process to the EAS process as the main vehicle for East Asian community building mainly because it believes that the APT framework, with fewer members and more substantive cooperation than the EAS, is more viable. Meanwhile, it encourages ASEAN leadership because the complicated nature of East Asian politics makes unrealistic either China's or Japan's lead in building an emergent East Asian community. That said, however, different countries, drawing on their respective comparative advantages, can take the lead in cooperation in different functional areas.

Second, the future process of regional integration will continue to emphasize participating countries' sovereignty. In recent years, China has become more liberal in promoting regional cooperation, but has remained conservative on the issue of sovereignty. The same can be said of most East Asian countries. In the European experience of regional integration, member states' sovereignty has been slowly transferred to the regional institution, work that is still in progress. In Asia, state sovereignty and nationalism remain very strong concepts, and most, if not all, Asian countries wish to pursue cooperation as independent and sovereign nation-states. As such, the emerging regional architecture will need to be constructed in a way that promotes cooperation and mutual security among regional members without intruding too much into their domestic affairs. Some degree of compromise on sovereignty will be inevitable. As the East Asia Vision Group (EAVG) report noted, "While respecting the principle of national sovereignty, the overall mechanism for regional cooperation should be based on regional thinking and the welfare of all East Asians."[25] The challenge will be how to institutionalize substantive cooperation while at the same time accommodating the sensitivity to sovereignty.

Third, the future of a regional East Asian institution will demand accommodation for diversity. East Asia is widely diverse in terms of social, political, economic, and security conditions. Although modernization will bring about social, economic, and political changes and narrow the gap among East Asian countries, differences will remain on many fronts. Because the regional institution will be built well before these differences are removed, long-term success will require in the early stages the capacity to accommodate diversity while institutionalizing cooperation among countries. China, with a developing economy and a political system different from that adopted by many East Asian countries, pays particular attention to the need for accommodating diversity. As Premier Wen Jiabao stressed at the second EAS, "East Asia Cooperation should respect diversified development of social systems and cultures. We should bear in mind the particular national conditions of and uneven development in East Asian countries, respect each other and accommodate the needs and capabilities of different countries."[26]

Fourth, the future success of East Asian community building will hinge on common development goals. Reflecting on the criticism of APEC that it was more interested in pushing a trade liberalization agenda—which most serves the interests of the United States and other developed economies—rather than in promoting the economic and technological cooperation desired by APEC's developing economies, China suggested that cooperation in East Asia should give priority to areas in which there exists extensive common economic interest. According to Premier Wen, "We should ensure that East Asia cooperation grows in a balanced way and brings benefits to all, so that we can, through practical cooperation at bilateral and multilateral levels, build strong economic and trade linkages and put in place a cooperation framework based on mutual benefit and drawing on mutual strength."[27] Because East Asia comprises both developed and developing economies, China calls for more attention to the latter group's needs.

Fifth, a successful regional architecture in the years ahead will need to stress openness. Given the fact that some regional members maintain important political, economic, and security ties with outside countries, in particular the United States, it is necessary for future regional institutions to be nonexclusive. Even as the regional architecture promotes cooperation among regional members, it should also allow for and encourage cooperation with outside countries as well. For instance, a member of an East Asian FTA can also enter agreements with outside countries. Such openness will be even more obvious on the security front. Given the fact that the United States will continue to play an important role in regional security affairs, certain security institutions will have to respect the ties that some regional members have forged with Washington. Beijing's emphasis on openness in regional integration recognizes the interconnectedness between Asia and other parts of the world. It is also intended to mitigate Washington's concern that the United States may be marginalized from Asian affairs.

Sixth, a successful regional architecture in the future will need to place more emphasis on economic cooperation and nontraditional security than on security cooperation and traditional security. East Asian integration started with economics, and that impetus will continue to drive the process and to inform community and institution building. Strong ties will be forged to promote economic cooperation among regional actors. However, given the diverse security interests within the region, it is unlikely that arrangements for security cooperation will be as strong as, let alone stronger than, economic cooperation. Moreover, because some regional members maintain closer security ties with the United States than with their neighbors, it is understandable that security cooperation, as part of the overall community-building effort, will focus more on nontraditional issues than on traditional ones. China, for instance, proposed at the fifth APT Summit that greater cooperation be initiated on nontraditional security issues such as terrorism, drug trafficking, and illegal immigration. Such cooperation in its initial stages will not reflect traditional alliance and other security ties, which are typically tighter and more institutionalized. Cooperation on nontraditional issues will take on a much looser format, at least initially.

Although other APT members do share some of the norms and principles described here, they also have differences with China. For instance, Japan would prefer the EAS rather than APT to serve as the main venue for Asian community building. Moreover, whereas China and some other countries stress respect for sovereignty and diversity, others emphasize respect for democracy, human rights, and certain universal values, and ASEAN has shown an increased willingness to comment on Myanmar's (Burma's) domestic politics. As preferred norms and principles in the region are both diverging and evolving, East Asian countries have to keep building consensus so as to move ahead.

FUTURE REGIONAL ARCHITECTURE

The EAVG saw that the creation of a community in East Asia would help turn the region into one of peace, prosperity, and progress. But what challenges must such a community meet, and how will it do so effectively? In general, an East Asian community will be in a better position to address the following challenges. Such a community must be able to meet the region's number one challenge—economic development—by promoting closer economic cooperation and deeper integration among East Asian countries. Regional integration is important both internally and externally. Arrangements such as an East Asia FTA will internally help "expand trade and investment opportunities, promote economic growth and sustainable development, and catalyze other forms of cooperation among countries of the region."[28] Stronger economic integration and cooperation in East Asia will help improve the region's economic stability and resilience as individual countries become more vulnerable to global economic forces, a lesson drawn from the Asian financial crisis. Moreover, they will help raise the standing of the East Asian economy, the third largest in the world. Compared with the European Union and North America, where regionalization and integration have made remarkable progress, East Asia is lagging far behind. It must meet this challenge by forming a more integrated mechanism of economic cooperation and by avoiding falling into a disadvantageous position in world economic competition. The fact that intraregional trade in East Asia in 2005 represented 55 percent of its total trade suggests that deepening East Asian economic cooperation already has a solid foundation.[29]

A successful regional architecture will also need to build trust and improve political relations among its members. All kinds of problems persist in relations among East Asian countries. One typical case is China-Japan relations, which are constantly strained by entanglements over historical issues, territorial disputes, and nascent geopolitical competition. Although such problems are usually difficult to address in a bilateral context, regional cooperation mechanisms can provide a framework in which disputants develop common interests and in the end gain a different and more positive perspective on their relationship.[30] As the experience of the European Union indicates, regional cooperation can turn past enemies into close partners, which is exactly what East Asian nations need to expect and create in the process of community building.

The future regional architecture will help turn East Asia into a regional entity and contribute to a more balanced and reasonable international political and economic order. Despite the fact that East Asia is already the third pole in the world economy, its international clout does not match that position. As some U.S. scholars have observed, "[T]he countries of the region have not been major actors in shaping the institutions and rules of the international system. They often lack the weight and status in international organizations they should have based on population or economic size."[31] To redress this imbalance, East Asian community building must facilitate an "[a]mplification of the East Asia voice in international affairs and expansion of the region's contribution to the process of creating and evolving a new global order."[32] For instance, an integrated East Asia will need to place the framework of the East Asia–North America relationship on a more balanced foundation and begin to play a larger role in world affairs in general. It will gain a more advantageous economic position vis-à-vis the European Union and North America in helping to establish the rules of the game.

To be sure, the achievement of East Asian integration and community building is still in its infancy, and obstacles abound. However, viewed from a broader historical perspective, East Asia as a whole has come a long way since World War II. From the end of World War II to the end of the Vietnam War, most East Asian countries wrestled with the task of nation and state building. From the mid-1970s to the mid-1990s, the dominant agenda in East Asia was economic development, and it witnessed the so-called East Asian Miracle. In the wake of the Asian financial crisis, East Asia attempted to deepen regional economic cooperation and integration while also seeking to build a regional identity—part of which means building a regional architecture. Aspiring to create "a new community of common destiny whose members enjoy common development in times of peace and meet challenges together in times of crisis,"[33] members in East Asian institutions are making serious, concerted efforts toward that goal. Ten years after the kick-off of the APT process, the achievements are remarkable. As Premier Wen noted at the tenth APT Summit in January 2007, "The growth of 10 + 3 cooperation has increased our mutual understanding and trust, boosted economic growth and social progress, promoted stability and development and enhanced the international standing of East Asia."[34] Building on the efforts of the past decade, East Asian countries today have a clearer vision of what they want to accomplish in the future. The second Joint Statement on East Asia Cooperation, released at the eleventh APT Summit held on November 20, 2007, drew a blueprint for East Asian cooperation and integration in the coming decade.[35] Compared with the first decade of growth and expansion in regional cooperation, the second decade has been defined as one of consolidation and closer integration. The summit also approved a work plan for cooperation among the "ten plus three" countries from 2007 to 2017. Regional actors' shared aspirations and joint efforts will bring the dream of an East Asia community much closer to reality.

Overall, this community will likely be built on three principal pillars. The first is the deepening of economic cooperation, the core of which will be an East Asian FTA. Although it is not yet entirely clear how such an agreement will come about, certain efforts will contribute to its birth: the establishment of an ASEAN economic community; FTAs with ASEAN pursued separately by China, Japan, and South Korea; a possible FTA among China, Japan, and South Korea; and the realization of freer trade and investment within the APEC framework.

The second pillar is the broadening of the cooperation agenda to include political and security issues. At the fifth APT meeting, China proposed to conduct political and security dialogues and to initiate cooperation within the APT framework. It suggested that dialogue and cooperation might start with such nontraditional security issues as terrorism, drug trafficking, and illegal immigration, and then gradually expand the agenda.[36] At the tenth APT Summit, Beijing urged ASEAN members to take bigger steps toward cooperation in the security field. It proposed to make full use of existing cooperation mechanisms to strengthen dialogue and cooperation on major regional security issues.[37]

However, as noted earlier, the APT process is unlikely to come up with substantive cooperation on traditional security issues in the near to medium term. Rather, two traditional approaches will remain at play in the absence of an overarching regional security architecture. One is the "concert of powers," such as ad hoc cooperation among China, the United States, Japan, and Russia on the North Korean nuclear issue. The other is the U.S. alliance system, which, although having become less important than it was during the Cold War era, will stand as a major security instrument for some countries and for some years to come.

The third pillar is that the future regional architecture will need to become more institutionalized. As cooperation deepens and expands, the APT framework should be institutionalized and move toward a structured regional organization. Although some scholars doubt that East Asia cooperation will lead to the creation of formal and rule-based institutions, the fact that the SCO evolved out of a previous security mechanism—the Shanghai Five—demonstrates that when there is a need, formal institutions can be created for Asia regional cooperation. In fact, the need for institution building in the APT process has been recognized. The EAVG, for instance, proposed "progressive institutionalization" and stressed that "organizational capacity is crucial for effective formulation and implementation of programs." Meanwhile, the ninth APT Summit held in December 2005 also pledged to "enhance and strengthen the various mechanisms crucial for the development of ASEAN Plus Three cooperation" and agreed to set up the APT Unit in the ASEAN Secretariat.[38]

Overall, the institutionalization of East Asia cooperation should occur at two levels. At the structural level, a secretariat in the place of the APT Unit embedded in the ASEAN Secretariat should be set up for the APT process to better manage the annual summit as well as the ministerial meetings. At a functional level, an administrative office should be created to coordinate, implement, and supervise various programs in functional areas such as trade, finance, and agriculture. Given East Asians' preference for loose and informal arrangements over strong and formal ones, such institutionalization should proceed gradually, responding to the needs of cooperation and taking advantage of the progress in East Asia community building.

The year 2020 is a useful goal to keep in mind with regard to the prospects of an East Asian community. By that time, all the APEC members are supposed to be open to free trade and investment, a goal set by the APEC Bogor Summit in 1994. Even more important, Southeast Asia will have built an ASEAN community by 2020, a prospect that will certainly have a significant impact on East Asian community building.[39] What will East Asian integration look like by 2020? It is very likely that an East Asian FTA will come into being, marking a major achievement in regional economic cooperation.[40] Meanwhile, the prospective establishment of an ASEAN community by that time will serve as both a blueprint for and an impetus to the building of a broader East Asia community. The agenda of cooperation within the APT framework should have expanded by then to include political and security issues, with far closer political and security ties forged among East Asian countries. The state of institution building, however, is uncertain, because it is likely to remain a work in progress. To be sure, the APT organizational structure will be more institutionalized than its current framework, but probably still fall short of being a formal regional entity, like the SCO. All in all, by 2020 East Asia will look quite different from what it does today, with intraregional ties greatly deepened and external influence much expanded. This change will place the region in a far better position that it is in today to meet the many economic, trade, environmental, and employment challenges facing East Asia.

NOTES

1. Han Zhiqiang, "Dui APEC de jidian renshi yu sikao" [Some thoughts on APEC], *Guoji Wenti Yanjiu* [*International Studies*] 2 (2003): 32.

2. According to the Chinese government, from 1990 to 2001 the eastern Turkistan terrorist forces were responsible for more than 200 terrorist incidents in Xinjiang, which resulted in 162 deaths and more than 440 injuries. Moreover, these forces are believed to have close connections with Al Qaeda. Information Office of the State Council, People's Republic of China, "'East Turkistan' Terrorist Forces Cannot Get Away with Impunity," *Beijing Review*, January 31, 2002, 14–15.

3. The report on U.S. national-security strategy released by the Bush administration in March 2006 noted that "[o]ur strategy seeks to encourage China to make the right strategic choices for its people, while we hedge against other possibilities" (White House, *The National Security Strategy of the United States of America* [Washington, D.C.: Government Printing Office, 2006], http://www.whitehouse.gov/nsc/nss/2006/sectionVIII.html).

4. Wang Yi, "Quanqiuhua jincheng zhong de Yazhou quyu hezuo" [Regional cooperation of Asia in the process of globalization], *Waijiao Xueyuan Xuebao* [*Journal of China Foreign Affairs University*] 76 (2004): 19–21.

5. See, for instance, Pang Zhongying, "Zhongguo de Yazhou zhanlue: linghuo de duobian zhuyi" [China's Asian strategy: Flexible multilateralism], *Shijie Jingji Yu Zhengzhi* [*World Economics and Politics*] 10 (2001): 30–35; Deng Xianchao and Xu Derong, "Lun Zhongguo Yazhou diqu zhuyi zhanlue de goujian ji yingxiang yinsu" [China's strategy of Asian regionalism], *Dongnanya Yanjiu* [*Southeast Asian Studies*] 5 (2005): 7–8.

6. "Dongya Fenghui yu quyu zhenghe de shenghua" [East Asian Summit and the deepening of regional integration], *Xiandai Guoji Guanxi* [*Contemporary International Relations*] 3 (2005): 40–41.

7. ASEAN Secretariat, "Kuala Lumpur Declaration on the East Asia Summit," Kuala Lumpur, Malaysia, December 14, 2005, http://www.aseansec.org/18098.htm.

8. Pang Zhongying, "Dongya Fenghui yu Dongya gongtongti" [East Asian Summit and "East Asian community"], *Shijie Zhishi* [*World Affairs*] 21 (2005): 67.

9. T. J. Pempel, "The Race to Connect East Asia: An Unending Steeplechase," *Asian Economic Policy Review* 1, no. 2 (2006): 241.

10. ASEAN Secretariat, *Final Report of the East Asia Study Group* (Jakarta, Indonesia: ASEAN, 2002), 15, submitted to the APT Summit, Phnom Penh, Cambodia, November 4, 2002, http://www.aseansec.org/viewpdf.asp?file = /pdf/easg.pdf.

11. Ren Xiao, "Liufang Huitan yu Dongbeiya duobian anquan jizhi de kenengxing" [Six-Party Talks and the possibility of building a multilateral security mechanism in Northeast Asia], *Guoji Wenti Yanjiu* [*International Studies*] 1 (2005): 41.

12. Ministry of Foreign Affairs, People's Republic of China, *Shanghai Cooperation Organization* (Beijing: Ministry of Foreign Affairs, January 7, 2004), http://www.fmprc.gov.cn/eng/topics/sco/t57970.htm.

13. Wang Yi, "Sikao Ershiyi Shiji de xin Yazhou zhuyi" [Neo-Asianism in the twenty-first century], *Waijiao Pinglun [Foreign Affairs Review]* 89 (2006): 6–10.

14. Zhang Yunling, "Tanqiu Dongya de quyu zhuyi" [A probe into East Asian regionalism], *Dangdai Yatai [Contemporary Asia-Pacific Studies]* 12 (2004): 3–7.

15. Pang, "East Asian Summit and 'East Asian Community,'" 67.

16. See, for instance, Wei Hong, "Zhongguo Dongmeng hezuo yu Dongya yitihua" [China-ASEAN cooperation and East Asian integration], *Xiandai Guoji Guanxi [Contemporary International Relations]* 9 (2005): 21–23; Tang Xiaosong, "Sanqiang gongzhi: Dongya quyu yitihua de biran xuanze" [Three-power governance: The only way for East Asian integration], *Xiandai Guoji Guanxi [Contemporary International Relations]* 29 (2008): 10–15.

17. Wei, "China-ASEAN Cooperation"; Tang, "Three-Power Governance."

18. Zhao Gancheng, "Yindu dongxiang zhengce de fazhan ji yiyi" [India's Look East policy: Development and significance], *Dangdai Yatai [Contemporary Asia-Pacific Studies]* 8 (2007): 10–16, 64; Wei Ling, "Xi Meiyin guanxi jiqi duihua yingxiang" [An analysis of the American-Indian relations and their influence on China], *Jiaoxue Yu Yanjiu [Teaching and Research]* 5 (2007): 67–71.

19. Morton Abramowitz and Stephen Bosworth make this point in *Chasing the Sun: Rethinking East Asian Policy* (New York: Century Foundation Press, 2006), 30.

20. Dao Shulin, Lin Limin, Liu Junhong, and Yang Wenjing, "Dongya Fenghui yu quyu zhenghe de shenghua" [East Asia Summit and deepening of regional integration], *Xiandai Guoji Guanxi [Contemporary International Relations]* 3 (2005): 44–46.

21. See, for instance, ibid.; Qin Yaqing, "Dongya Gongtongti jianshe jincheng he Meiguo de zuoyong" [East Asian community-building process and the U.S. role], *Waijiao Pinglun [Foreign Affairs Review]* 6 (2005): 27–28; Xiao Gang, "Duobian zhuyi yu Dongya gaozhengzhi hezuo" [Multilateralism and high political cooperation in East Asia], *Dongnanya Yanjiu [Southeast Asian Studies]* 5 (2005): 9; Pang, "East Asian Summit and 'East Asian Community,'" 67; Han Zhiqiang, "Dongya quyu hezuo zhong de Meiguo yinsu" [The U.S. factor in East Asian regional cooperation], *Guoji Wenti Yanjiu [International Studies]* 3 (2004): 36–39.

22. Ministry of Foreign Affairs, People's Republic of China, "Wen Jiabao Delivers a Speech at the East Asia Summit," Kuala Lumpur, Malaysia, December 14, 2005, http://www.fmprc.gov.cn/eng/zxxx/t226715.htm.

23. This point is explored more deeply in Wu Xinbo, "The End of the Silver Lining: A Chinese View of the U.S.-Japanese Alliance," *Washington Quarterly* 29, no. 1 (2005–2006): 119–30.

24. Zhang Yunling, "A Probe into East Asian Regionalism," *Contemporary Asia-Pacific Studies* 12 (2004): 3–7.

25. East Asia Vision Group (EAVG), *Towards an East Asian Community: Region of Peace, Prosperity, and Progress* (Jakarta, Indonesia: ASEAN, 2001), report submitted to the APT Summit, Bandar Seri Begawan, Brunei Darussalam, October 31, 2001, 8, http://www.mofa.go.jp/region/asia-paci/report2001.pdf.

26. Wen Jiabao, "Work in Partnership to Promote Win-Win Cooperation," address to the second East Asia Summit, Cebu, Philippines, January 15, 2007, http://www.fmprc.gov.cn/eng/wjdt/zyjh/t290183.htm.

27. Ibid.

28. ASEAN Secretariat, *Final Report of the East Asia Study Group*, 43.

29. He Peng, "Duiwai touzi chengwei woguo xinyilun duiwai hezuo zhongdian" [Investment in overseas has become the focus of the next round of China's international cooperation], *Shanghai Securities News*, July 16, 2007, http://paper.cnstock.com/paper_new/html/2007–07/16/content_57354978.htm.

30. Zhang, "Probe into East Asian Regionalism."

31. Trilateral Commission, *East Asia and the International System: Report of a Special Study Group to the Trilateral Commission* (New York: Trilateral Commission, 2001), 1.

32. EAVG, *Towards an East Asian Community*, 12.

33. Ibid.

34. Wen Jiabao, "Work Together to Build an East Asia of Peace, Prosperity, and Harmony," speech at the tenth APT Summit, Cebu, Philippines, January 14, 2007, http://www.fmprc.gov.cn/eng/wjdt/zyjh/t290180.htm.

35. "Second Joint Statement on East Asian Cooperation," Singapore, November 20, 2007, http://www.aseansec.org/21100.htm.

36. Hu Zhaoming, "Dongya hezuo de xianzhuang yu weilai" [East Asian cooperation: Current and prospective], *Guoji Wenti Yanjiu* [*International Studies*] 87 (2002): 21–25.

37. Wen, "Work Together."

38. EAVG, *Towards an East Asian Community*, 18; ASEAN Secretariat, "Kuala Lumpur Declaration on the ASEAN Plus Three Summit," Kuala Lumpur, Malaysia, December 12, 2005, http://www.aseansec.org/18036.htm.

39. In December 1997, ASEAN released *ASEAN Vision 2020* (Jakarta, Indonesia: ASEAN, 1997), http://www.aseansec.org/1814.htm, envisioning "the entire Southeast Asia to be, by 2020, an ASEAN community conscious of its ties of history, aware of its cultural heritage and bound by a common regional identity." In October 2003, at the ninth ASEAN Summit, leaders from ASEAN countries signed the Declaration of ASEAN Concord II, noting that "an ASEAN Community shall be established comprising three pillars, namely political and security cooperation, economic cooperation, and socio-cultural cooperation that are closely intertwined and mutually rein-

forcing for the purpose of ensuring durable peace, stability and shared prosperity in the region" (http://www.aseansec.org/15159.htm).

40. The EAVG suggested the establishment of the East Asian Free Trade Agreement and liberalization of trade well ahead of the APEC Bogor Goal. On the other front, ASEAN decided in January 2007 to hasten the establishment of the ASEAN Economic Community by 2015, five years ahead of the original schedule.

4. Regional Multilateralism in Asia and the Korean Question

Lim Wonhyuk

The partition of Asia along ideological lines after World War II brought great suffering to the Korean people. The nation was divided along the thirty-eighth parallel in 1945 and became the battleground for an internationalized civil war from 1950 to 1953, pitting South Korea and the United States against North Korea and China, with the Soviet Union in the background. Although the Cold War has since ended, the Korean question remains unresolved.

Will a reunified nation-state become a reality for the Korean people? This question has internal, inter-Korean, and international dimensions: What kind of political and economic system should a reunified Korea have? How should Koreans overcome national division and move toward unification? How should the Korean nation position itself as an international player? For the first two dimensions, the broad consensus in South Korea is that a democratic market economy should be the objective and that "change through rapprochement"—rather than transplantation of democracy through regime change—would provide the best chance to realize this vision. As for the international dimension, placing Korean unification within the broader context of regional integration may be an effective geopolitical strategy for the Korean nation.

Just as Germans and their neighbors agreed to make reunified Germany an integral part of Europe rather than risk the emergence of an unhinged revisionist power, Koreans and their neighbors may come to see regional integration as a critical component of the solution to the Korean question. As a divided land bridge in Asia, Korea has much to benefit from regional integration. By contrast, a maritime-continental confrontation in Asia is not in the interest of the Korean people because it would perpetuate national division and increase the risks of military conflict on the Korean Peninsula. This line of geopolitical thinking has tended to guide South Korea's perspective on regional multilateralism in Asia, especially since the end of the Cold War and the restoration of democracy in the late 1980s. Increasingly, Korean strategists are exploring how to maintain a strong U.S.–South Korea alliance, while building regional forums and patterns of cooperation that provide a big picture for cooperation among the major powers of Northeast Asia and for engagement with North Korea, without ceding the initiative on the peninsula to outside powers.

This chapter explores these questions and their impact on Korean views of community building in Asia. The first section looks at South Korea's evolving perspective on regional multilateralism in Asia since the inception of the republic in 1948. The second section covers current approaches and attitudes toward regional multilateralism. It compares U.S.-centric, Asia-centric, and U.S.-in-Asia approaches and analyzes recent trends in South Korea's foreign policy. The concluding section looks at South Korea's geopolitical choices for the future.

SOUTH KOREA'S EVOLVING PERSPECTIVE ON REGIONAL MULTILATERALISM

In the early days of the Cold War, South Korea could care less about improving relations with Japan and Communist China, to say nothing of promoting Sino-Japanese rapprochement. Harsh Japanese colonial rule in Korea from 1910 to 1945 had left a bitter memory; in fact, not until 1965 would South Korea establish diplomatic relations with Japan. South Korea's strong anti-Communist stance also precluded dialogue with the People's Republic of China. To the extent that regional multilateralism was discussed in those days in South Korea, it had mostly to do with establishing an anti-Communist bloc.

When in March 1949 Elpidio Quirino of the Philippines called for the creation of a Pacific alliance along the lines of the North Atlantic Treaty Organization (NATO), Syngman Rhee, leader of the Republic of Korea from 1948 to 1960, welcomed the proposal because he saw it as guaranteeing automatic intervention by U.S. military forces in the event of attack from Communist North Korea. On May 6, 1949, when Rhee could not obtain a bilateral security assurance from the United States, he pressed for a Pacific security pact under U.S.

leadership, with Nationalist China and the Philippines as the other founding members.[1]

However, with the Nationalist Chinese on the verge of defeat in China and U.S. policy toward Asia under review, Washington was unwilling to support overtly such an anti-Communist military alliance. Moreover, for various reasons, the United States preferred to deal with Asian nations on a bilateral basis and to form a hub-and-spoke alliance system. Although it supported the creation of the Southeast Asia Treaty Organization in 1954, it noted that this organization had no joint command with standing forces, lacked "all for one, one for all" collective defense provisions, and was limited in geographical scope to Southeast Asia. No similar multilateral structure was created in Northeast Asia or East Asia as a whole. Even after the signing of the South Korea–U.S. Mutual Defense Treaty in 1953, Rhee continued to push for a U.S.-supported anti-Communist security alliance in Asia—but again to little avail.[2]

Rhee's anti-Communist stance shaped his unification policy as well. This policy precluded dialogue with the Communist regime in North Korea and called for free general elections in all of North and South Korea under the auspices of the United Nations. Whether it was realistic to hold free general elections in North Korea was a moot point. In the ideologically charged atmosphere of the early Cold War period, Rhee's priority was on diplomatically isolating North Korea and creating an advantage for South Korea in the international legitimacy game. His policy was similar in spirit to West Germany's tough stance toward East Germany under the Hallstein Doctrine.[3]

Although the thawing of the Cold War, or détente, in the late 1960s and 1970s changed the international context of policy discussions on regional multilateralism and national unification, the bitter memory of the Korean War as well as Communist advances in Southeast Asia made most South Koreans cautious, if not skeptical, about any proposal to improve relations with Communist regimes. In fact, those who promoted the idea of obtaining security guarantees from the United States, Soviet Union, China, and Japan for peace on the Korean Peninsula were regarded as dangerous radicals out of touch with reality.[4] Kim Dae-jung, who later became the president of South Korea from 1998 to 2003, was portrayed as such during his first presidential campaign in 1971.[5] The thawing of the Cold War also created strains in the South Korea–U.S. alliance because of the two allies' diverging threat perceptions and domestic political considerations. Whereas the United States pursued détente and reduced its military presence in Asia, South Korea felt more vulnerable to a North Korean attack and launched an ambitious campaign to build up its military capability, including a covert nuclear program. Richard Nixon's visit to Beijing in 1972 and the withdrawal of one of the two U.S. infantry divisions stationed in South Korea marked the beginning of the strained alliance relationship in the 1970s.[6]

To the authoritarian governments of Park Chung Hee (1961–1979) and Chun Doo-hwan (1980–1988), an uncompromising anti-Communist stance was not only a prudent security strategy, but a politically expedient one as well, for they could take advantage of popular fears and anxieties about a Communist takeover to justify their authoritarian rule. Due in part to these domestic political considerations, South Korea made few comparable moves even after the United States and Japan took steps to normalize relations with China in the 1970s. Although a high-level inter-Korean meeting was held for the first time in July 1972, it did not usher in a new era of cooperation between the two sides. On the contrary, citing threats to national security, Park declared a state of national emergency in October of the same year and adopted a new constitution that gave dictatorial powers to the president, eliminated term limits, and abolished direct presidential elections. No serious attempt was made to normalize relations with Communist regimes during the authoritarian period.

However, the end of military rule in 1987 and ensuing democratization made it possible to expand the scope of public discussions on issues pertaining to unification and regional multilateralism. Furthermore, the end of the Cold War and economic reform in transition countries such as China and Vietnam changed the prospects for regional multilateralism in Asia, and advocacy of regional multilateralism became an intellectually and politically respectable position in South Korea. These changes in domestic and international politics encouraged both academics and practitioners to take a look at South Korea's geopolitical challenges from a more strategic perspective.

In his speech at the United Nations on October 18, 1988, President Roh Tae-woo (1988–1993) called for the creation of a six-party consultative conference for peace in Northeast Asia with a view toward commencing "an era of Pacific prosperity." He proposed that this conference address regional security issues so as to ease U.S.-Soviet tensions, resolve Japan-Soviet territorial disputes, promote China-Soviet rapprochement, and secure peace on the Korea Peninsula.[7] The idea was in part a response to Mikhail Gorbachev's September 1988 proposal for multilateral security cooperation in the region.[8] The Soviet Union and Japan welcomed Roh's proposal, but it failed to produce a substantive outcome due to lukewarm response from the United States and China and to opposition from North Korea, which wanted to normalize bilateral relations with the United States and Japan first. Nevertheless, with the subsequent normalization of relations with the Soviet Union in 1990 and with China in 1992, multilateral security cooperation became an increasingly important objective in South Korea's foreign policy. Under *nordpolitik*, Roh Tae-woo also sought to bring North Korea out of the cold and change its behavior through engagement. These efforts led to the signing of the Agreement of Reconciliation,

Nonaggression, and Exchanges and Cooperation Between South and North Korea ("Basic Agreement") in December 1991.[9]

Maintaining a strong bilateral alliance with the United States *and* developing good relations with former adversaries in Northeast Asia became the central policy challenge for South Korea in this period. In his keynote speech at the twenty-sixth Pacific Basin Economic Council meeting in May 1993, President Kim Young-sam (1993–1998) declared that South Korea would push for a multilateral security dialogue while deepening and further developing a bilateral security consultation mechanism with the United States.[10] As for the geographical scope of this multilateral security dialogue, South Korea preferred the subregion of Northeast Asia to the Asia Pacific as a whole and sought to create "a mini–Conference on Security and Cooperation in Europe (CSCE)" in Northeast Asia.[11] At the first Association of Southeast Asian Nations (ASEAN) Regional Forum (ARF) in May 1994, South Korea made a proposal for a Northeast Asia security dialogue that would address such security issues as threats to peace on the Korean Peninsula, tensions across the Taiwan Strait, and arms buildups in the region. In promoting multilateral security cooperation in Northeast Asia, South Korea drew inspiration from the European experience and put forth the following six principles: (1) respect for sovereignty and territorial integrity, (2) nonaggression and nonuse of force, (3) nonintervention in domestic affairs, (4) peaceful resolution of disputes, (5) peaceful coexistence, and (6) respect for democracy and human dignity.[12]

North Korea's nuclear brinkmanship and precipitous economic decline in the mid-1990s prompted further discussion on multilateral security cooperation. Although the Geneva Agreed Framework of 1994 was officially a bilateral agreement between the United States and North Korea, its implementation required multilateral security and energy cooperation. To bring a formal end to the Korean armistice regime, North Korea, South Korea, China, and the United States launched four-party talks. The ostensible objective of the process was to create a new peace regime on the Korean Peninsula, but some policymakers in South Korea believed that it could also provide a framework for dealing with North Korea's collapse.[13]

In addition to security cooperation, economic cooperation in Northeast Asia and East Asia also began to attract a great deal of interest in the 1990s. A number of academics and practitioners in South Korea called for tighter economic integration in the region, including the construction of energy and transportation networks that would connect formerly hostile nations and facilitate economic development. They argued that such regional efforts would support the economic integration and eventual unification of the Korean Peninsula.[14] Furthermore, the signing of the North American Free Trade Agreement and the formation of the European Union spurred exploratory discussions on "defensive" responses from Asia.

The 1997 Asian economic crisis highlighted the need to create transnational institutions such as an Asian monetary fund to protect the common interests of the countries in the region. In fact, a collective sense of humiliation stemming from the crisis helped to produce a new impetus for regional cooperation and led to the establishment of the ASEAN Plus Three (APT) process at the end of 1997.[15] In addition, the resurgence of China prompted a search for an international arrangement designed to minimize the risks associated with a shifting balance of power in Asia. These developments in the late 1990s led South Korea to engage in middle-power diplomacy to promote regional cooperation. Kim Dae-jung sought to improve South Korea's bilateral relations with its "close but distant" neighbor Japan[16] and with other nations in East Asia, while maintaining a strong alliance with the United States. Building on improved bilateral relations with South Korea's neighbors, he supported the APT process and other multilateral efforts to address economic and security concerns in the region. These diplomatic efforts helped to set the stage for the historic inter-Korean summit in 2000. Kim believed that an integrated approach was essential to the success of South Korea's inter-Korean and foreign policy.[17]

In a sense, the Northeast Asian Cooperation Initiative for Peace and Prosperity by President Roh Moo-hyun (2003–2008) represented the culmination of South Korea's efforts to promote regional cooperation and to facilitate Korean unification since the end of the Cold War.[18] At his inauguration in February 2003, Roh declared that although the geopolitical characteristic of the Korean Peninsula as "a bridge between China and Japan, linking the continent and the ocean" had caused pain and suffering in the past, this same feature demanded that the Korean people play "a pivotal role in the Age of Northeast Asia in the 21st century," to realize "a dream of seeing a regional community of peace and prosperity in Northeast Asia like the European Union." However, subsequent strains in South Korea's bilateral relations with Japan and the United States made it difficult for Roh to play a facilitating role in promoting regional cooperation. The intensifying rivalry between China and Japan in recent years has made his task even tougher. Although the Six-Party Talks may evolve into a regional security cooperation organization in the future, Roh's Northeast Asian Cooperation Initiative achieved only uneven progress.

In sum, geopolitical logic in combination with international and domestic politics has influenced South Korea's perspective on regional multilateralism in Asia. Applied to the Korean Peninsula as a divided land bridge in Asia, geopolitical logic seems to dictate that South Korea promote regional cooperation, especially between continental and maritime powers, so as to minimize the risks of conflict on the peninsula and to facilitate unification. However, during the years of the Cold War and authoritarian rule, international and domestic political considerations placed important restrictions on South Korea's diplomatic efforts and intellectual discussions. In fact, only with the end of the Cold War and authoritarian rule could the geopolitical logic of promoting regional cooperation work in concert with international and domestic political considerations.

DEBATES IN SOUTH KOREA ABOUT REGIONAL MULTILATERALISM

DRIVERS FOR REGIONAL MULTILATERALISM: SECURITY, ECONOMY, AND IDENTITY

In South Korea's case, support for Asian regionalism is driven mostly by security and economic considerations and far less by identity politics. Most South Koreans believe that Asian nations, along with extraregional powers such as the United States, can reduce the security dilemma and realize mutual economic gains through regional multilateralism. By contrast, they tend to have a somewhat skeptical view of identity politics. In theory, regionalism can reflect and amplify a shared identity through either positive values or a negative sense of humiliation and victimization; in practice, however, with nations in the region at different stages of development and historical issues still affecting relations among them, identity politics has significant limitations as a catalyst for Asian regionalism, at least in the eyes of most South Koreans.

The primary driver for promoting regional multilateralism in South Korea's case is security concerns. First and foremost, to resolve North Korea's nuclear problem and to promote peace and security in Asia, South Korea not only supports the six-party process but is also interested in making it into a more permanent multilateral security arrangement. As South Korea's leaders have made clear on a number of occasions since Roh Tae-woo's speech at the United Nations in 1988, South Korea believes that multilateral security cooperation is critical to securing peace not only on the Korea Peninsula, but also in the broader region. And Seoul has welcomed the inclusion of talks on a peace regime and regional dialogue in the six-party process.

However, South Korea's embrace of the Six-Party Talks was not a foregone conclusion when U.S. secretary of state Colin Powell broached the idea for a multilateral approach in February 2003. Washington had pushed the multilateral negotiating process with the goal of enlisting the region's other powers to keep pressure on Pyongyang after North Korean officials acknowledged during U.S.–North Korea bilateral talks in October 2002 a clandestine uranium program in violation of the Geneva Agreed Framework. Although the Roh government's interest was not necessarily in increasing pressure on the North, there was an interest in multilateralizing the approach to the North to ensure that diplomacy remained the primary tool for convincing Pyongyang to abandon its nuclear weapons program.

Over time, the United States, South Korea, Japan, Russia, and China began to see the utility of the six-party process in terms of establishing a lasting mechanism for peace in security in Northeast Asia, not unlike the vision put forward by Roh Tae-woo two decades earlier. In the September 2005 joint statement of the Six-Party Talks[19] and a subsequent implementation statement on February 13, 2007,[20] the parties agreed to establish six working groups. One of the groups focuses on establishing a peace mechanism on the peninsula, essentially reviving the stalled Four-Party Talks from the mid-1990s. Another group focuses on promoting security cooperation in Northeast Asia. Although the linkage of progress in these working groups to actual denuclearization by the North remains challenging, and Pyongyang's stance toward regionalism is still highly situational and opportunistic, there is no question that security and confidence-building talks are now entrenched in the diplomacy of Northeast Asia. The focus of that dialogue is still on security issues related to the Korea Peninsula, but if success is achieved there, it is possible the talks might be broadened to address other security problems of the major powers in Northeast Asia. Seoul once resisted this internationalization of security problems on the peninsula, but there is now greater confidence that these forums can reinforce South Koreans' vision of a more stable peninsula.

Another important motive for South Korea to push for regional multilateralism is economic. Although there is a continuing debate on whether East Asia constitutes a "natural" grouping, this region has witnessed rapid economic growth and increasing trade and investment flows over the past few decades. In 1960, the combined gross domestic product (GDP) of APT countries was only two-fifths of U.S. GDP. By 2003, the combined GDP of this group had become approximately 70 percent of U.S. GDP. By 2025, the combined GDP of APT countries is forecast to be slightly less than the U.S. GDP. Moreover, the transformation of East Asia from an export-production base for the rest of the world to an increasingly integrated market has significantly enhanced prospects for regional cooperation.[21] Against this background, South Korea is pushing for the construction of energy and transportation networks in the region, facilitating economic development not only in North Korea, but also in China's northeastern provinces and the Russian Far East. Such investment projects will also create business opportunities for firms from outside the region and allow them to share in the benefits of increased regional integration. Oil and gas pipelines from Siberia and Sakhalin are perhaps the best-known example of these proposed investment projects.[22]

In his speech to the European Union Chamber of Commerce in Korea in June 2003, Roh Moo-hyun presented this vision for an open and integrated Northeast Asia. Vowing to establish a virtuous cycle of peace and prosperity in Northeast Asia, he said: "The ultimate goal is to build a cooperative and integrated order in the Northeast Asian region. As Europe in the past was able to pursue economic integration by way of steel and coal, Northeast Asia will be able to create a new order of cooperation through railroad links and joint energy development." He added: "But regional cooperation designed for only Northeast Asian countries will have limits. Security can be improved and dynamism can be bolstered only when Northeast Asia provides an arena that will enable major international corporations to engage in energetic activities on the basis of improved relations among the countries in the region."[23]

As for identity politics, South Korea is inclined to take a historical and process-oriented view rather than just focus on the moment. Although South Koreans are quite proud of the nation's political and economic development over the past half century, they are wary of setting democracy and a market economy as preconditions for membership in regional multilateralism. To the extent that interaction with the outside world facilitates change, making engagement strictly conditional on the liberalization of the other side may actually impede such a transition. Although a system of governance based on accountability and transparency is likely to be conducive to regional cooperation, it is probably counterproductive for a nation to demand that another nation adopt such a system as a prerequisite for cooperation, especially when many nations in Asia have been making positive economic and political progress over the past few decades.[24] South Koreans appreciate the norm-building aspect of regionalism, as demonstrated by the Helsinki Accord of 1975, but they tend to differentiate between the building of mutually agreed-upon norms and the coercive imposition of norms.[25] In fact, some even regard the neoconservative variety of identity politics as a thinly veiled attempt to contain China.[26] The progressives tend to be particularly skeptical on this issue, given their own historical struggle against authoritarian regimes backed by Washington. In contrast, the conservative government of Lee Myong-bak that replaced Roh Moo-hyun in February 2008 has taken a more positive view of value-oriented diplomacy and the need for cooperation among democracies as South Koreans' view of the United States have improved and their view of China have begun to decline.[27] Nevertheless, even the conservatives can be expected to avoid any alliance of democracies that appears to confront or encircle China.

South Koreans also tend to believe that before the crafting of a shared regional identity that transcends national boundaries, nations that make up a potential community should first come to terms with history. Because nationalism was instrumental to the outbreak of historical hostilities in Asia as well as in other parts of the world, nationalism would have to inform the discussion on reconciliation and cooperation. Advocacy of a regional or supranational identity would ring rather hollow before national wounds are healed.[28]

In fact, historical issues have had a great deal of impact on both bilateral and multilateral relations in Northeast Asia. The best-known example is the relationship between South Korea and Japan over such issues as "comfort women" and the Yasukuni Shrine.[29] South Koreans feel that there is a fundamental contradiction in what Japanese conservatives are doing with regard to historical issues. Logically, Japanese conservatives should make their case to former imperialist powers in the West (not to Korea and China, which are victims of Japanese imperialist aggression) that it is unfair to lump Imperialist Japan with Nazi Germany and Tojo Hideki with Adolf Hitler. Geopolitically, however, Japanese conservatives seem to have made up their minds to build strong ties with the West (especially the United States) to guard against the rise of China. From a Korean perspective, an intellectually honest position would be to make a hard-nosed realist justification for Japan's imperialist aggression *and* apologize to the victims of this aggression, but Japanese conservatives have instead tried to beautify their past. Prime Minister Abe Shinzo's effort to justify Japan's wartime treatment of comfort women and the resulting criticism in South Korea and the United States demonstrate the trap Japanese conservatives have created for themselves. These retrogressions raise basic questions of trust and impede progress in bilateral and multilateral cooperation. Although the South Korea–Japan tensions over history that had peaked during the Roh-Koizumi years subsided considerably under Lee Myong-bak and Fukuda Yasuo, there is a cautionary tale in other apparent breakthroughs in their relations going back to the rapprochement led by Chun Doo-hwan and Nakasone Yasuhiro in the 1980s and Kim Dae-jung and Obuchi Keizo in the 1990s.

The controversy over the ancient kingdom of Koguryo in 2004 provides another example of how historical issues of identity can affect international relations and ultimately complicate regional community building.[30] With North Korea's becoming increasingly dependent on China, many South Koreans interpreted the Chinese action regarding Koguryo as an attempt to do the historical groundwork to expand its influence into the Korean Peninsula. Given China's efforts to present itself as a benign and nonhegemonic power under the slogan of "peaceful rise" or "peaceful development," the way it handled this delicate issue was something of a surprise, to say the least. The Koguryo controversy led many South Koreans to take a second look at China, despite continuing expansion in bilateral trade and investment ties.

BILATERAL ALLIANCE AND REGIONALISM: U.S.-CENTRIC, ASIA-CENTRIC, AND U.S.-IN-ASIA APPROACHES

Although there is a general consensus in South Korea that regional multilateralism can bring security and economic benefits, not everyone agrees that it should be given priority in South Korea's foreign policy, especially in relation to its bilateral alliance with the United States. Nor is there clear agreement on the membership and structure of multilateral cooperation. Of these two interrelated issues, there is far less disagreement regarding the membership and structure of multilateral cooperation. In fact, South Koreans tend to share similar views on existing multilateral arrangements; where they diverge is the future direction of these arrangements.

Most South Koreans believe that the Asia-Pacific Economic Cooperation (APEC) forum has lost much of its relevance in recent years and retains utility primarily as an opportunity for summit meetings. Of course, bringing national leaders together in one place and having a series of summits on pressing issues do have some value, but South Koreans think APEC has lost its focus on its primary missions of trade and investment liberalization and economic and technical cooperation in the Asia-Pacific region. Like many other countries in the region, South Korea has increasingly resorted to bilateral channels to address economic issues in recent years. Although some experts in South Korea have supported the expansion of APEC's agenda into security areas, most academics and practitioners prefer the narrower geographical scope of the "mini-CSCE" approach.[31] In fact, as previously mentioned, South Koreans believe that the Six-Party Talks have the potential to evolve into a multilateral security forum.

As for APT, most South Koreans regard it as a multilateral arrangement with substance that can serve as the basis of an East Asian community,[32] although the dream of creating such a community has suffered a setback in recent years due to deteriorating bilateral relations between major players in the region. How to expand this arrangement and address U.S. concerns about exclusion remains a challenge.[33] Many South Koreans also feel that China (with some help from Malaysia) might have overplayed its hand in creating the East Asian Summit (EAS). Although China, Japan, and South Korea found it somewhat awkward to participate as "guests" in a forum organized by ASEAN (i.e., APT), creating a separate forum was probably not the best way of securing an equal standing for Northeast Asian countries. China's proposal for the EAS aroused suspicions about its hegemonic ambitions, and Japan responded by insisting on broad membership that would include India, Australia, and New Zealand. Even after a contentious debate on its membership, however, no one seems to know how this body will evolve and differentiate itself from APT and how it will respond to U.S. concerns about its exclusion from multilateral arrangements in Asia.[34] In South Korea, there is no clear consensus on how to respond to these U.S. concerns. In fact, this issue is a critical element of the debate on South Korea's foreign-policy priorities.

With regard to South Korea's foreign-policy priorities, some analysts tend to attach overriding importance to the alliance with the United States. According to this "U.S.-centric" view, a multilateral security arrangement may easily degenerate into little more than "a talk shop" and thus cannot be a viable substitute for the bilateral alliance mechanism that has successfully deterred external security threats for more than half a century. By contrast, others tend to take an "Asia-centric" approach and give priority to building a regional community. Still others try to combine the benefits of bilateral alliance and regional multilateralism and thus support multilateral cooperation that includes the United States. The latter group essentially takes an "U.S.-in-Asia" approach.[35]

Those who attach overriding importance to South Korea's alliance with the United States argue that South Korea risks weakening the cornerstone of its security by giving priority to regional multilateralism. According to their alliance-centric view, the United States may interpret too much emphasis on regional multilateralism as a thinly veiled attempt to dismantle the alliance for the benefit of China or North Korea, especially when the membership of this multilateral arrangement excludes the United States. For this group, South Korea's best option is to curb its enthusiasm for regional multilateralism and strengthen its bilateral alliance with Washington, just as Japan did after its strained relationship with the United States in the first half of the 1990s.[36] This school of thought tends to project a quite ominous future for Asia, wherein South Korea essentially will be forced to choose sides between the United States and China. Rising tension between China on the one side and the United States and Japan on the other will make regional multilateralism little more than a pipedream, so South Korea should strengthen its alliance with the United States to guard against the rise of China as well as the threat from North Korea.

Some liberals in South Korea support a variant of this U.S.-centric approach under a somewhat different set of assumptions. They, too, project an ominous future for U.S.-China relations, but then argue that South Korea should strengthen its alliance with the United States not only to guard against Chinese hegemony, but also to prevent Japanese rearmament and to continue engagement with North Korea.[37] However, they do not explain why the United States would go along with this policy package under a strengthened alliance with South Korea.

By contrast, those who take an Asia-centric approach tend to emphasize that Asian nations' collective interests are best protected by building their own community. Some even argue that the partition of the world into three blocs would place Asian nations in a strong position to deal with Europe and the United States.[38] Although they do not necessarily want to terminate South Korea's alliance with the United States, they feel that strengthening the bilateral alliance runs counter to the objective of creating a regional community.

Those who support multilateral cooperation that includes the United States want to combine the benefits of the bilateral and multilateral approaches. According to their "U.S.-in-Asia" perspective, the exclusively U.S.-centric approach runs the risk of creating a self-fulfilling prophesy by exacerbating tension between the United States and China, and the Asia-centric approach is rather unrealistic because it basically assumes Japan will work with China to create a regional community that excludes the United States. In their view, a bilateral alliance by itself runs the risk of exacerbating the security dilemma. For example, with regard to the potential threat posed by China, the South Korea–U.S. alliance can serve as a mutually beneficial insurance; however, China might interpret a drastic strengthening of this alliance as an attempt to gang up on it. Although a bilateral alliance can provide a useful hedge against a third power, a multilateral arrangement can offer a more fundamental solution by addressing the security dilemma.

With the balance of power shifting in Asia due to end of the Cold War and the rise of China, those who support the U.S.-in-Asia approach regard regional multilateralism as a means of constraining the great powers and preventing continental-maritime confrontation in Asia. If the great powers agree to be bound by a multilateral cooperation arrangement, thanks in part to facilitation by middle powers in the region, such an arrangement would be an effective means of securing lasting peace. China's proactive multilateral diplomacy since the late 1990s has been putting pressure on the United States to reassess its multilateral policy in Asia, and this competitive dynamic may lead to the creation of multilateral arrangements that include the United States as well as China. In fact, the six-party security cooperation arrangement in Northeast Asia may become the precursor to this new trend in Asia. Those who support the U.S.-in-Asia approach believe that a combination of hedging alliances and inclusive multilateral arrangements will be a stabilizing force in the region.

In South Korea, the U.S.-centric, Asia-centric, and U.S.-in-Asia approaches appeal to different groups based on their beliefs and interests. In general,

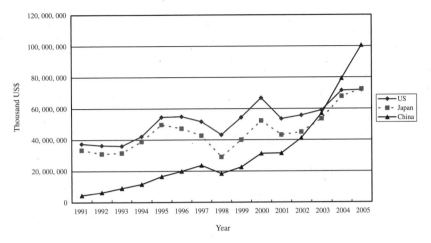

FIGURE 4.1 SOUTH KOREAN BILATERAL TRADE WITH
THE UNITED STATES, JAPAN, AND CHINA.

home-grown academics tend to have greater attraction to the vision of an East
Asian community, whereas U.S.-trained academics with a realist outlook are
unenthusiastic about the whole project, and those with a liberal outlook are favorably disposed to the idea of multilateral cooperation with a significant U.S.
role, especially in security areas.

Influenced more by commercial interests than by ideological beliefs, the
business community would like to take advantage of growing market opportunities in Asia while maintaining strong economic relations with the United States.
As shown in figures 4.1 and 4.2, although China overtook the United States and
Japan as South Korea's largest trading partner in 2004, South Korea still has
important trade and investment ties with the United States. Moreover, a significant share of South Korea's exports to China is processed in China to be
shipped to the United States and other advanced industrial nations. Consequently, the business community in South Korea tends to take a multipronged
approach by supporting the formation of an East Asian community as well as
free-trade agreements (FTAs) with China and the United States.[39] Seeking to
avoid a U.S.-China confrontation and to realize mutual gains through economic integration, this approach is similar in spirit to the U.S.-in-Asia approach.
Government officials also tend to take a similar position. As the Ministry of
Foreign Affairs and Trade handles South Korea's alliance relationship with the
United States and engages in middle-power diplomacy to promote regional multilateralism, it has to strike a fine balance between the two tasks. Other ministries are also well aware of this dual challenge.

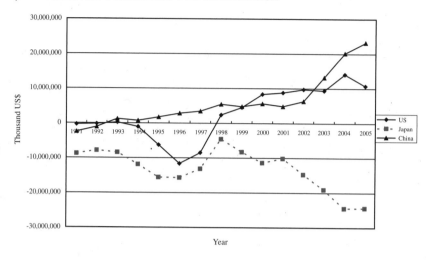

FIGURE 4.2 SOUTH KOREAN BILATERAL TRADE BALANCE.

In fact, South Korea's foreign policy under Roh Moo-hyun may be under-stood as an attempt to address this dual challenge—more through trial and error than design. Roh's anti-American rhetoric and Northeast Asian initiative seemed initially to suggest that he was taking an Asia-centric approach in his foreign policy. In fact, in the spring of 2005 his advocacy of a balancing role for South Korea in Northeast Asia raised questions about his commitment to South Korea's alliance with the United States. However, near the end of 2005 the Roh government abruptly shifted to a liberal variant of the U.S.-centric approach and formally launched negotiations for an FTA between South Korea and the United States in February 2006. This change of position came without any explanation and raised questions of trust, leaving to the next government the challenge of formulating and communicating South Korea's foreign-policy priorities. If anything, Roh's successor, Lee Myong-bak, has pursued this trend toward closer alignment with the United States and continued engagement and reconciliation with the North, but with greater demands for transparency and reciprocity.

Whether out of conviction or political calculation, Roh frequently projected the image of a maverick with an anti-American streak. In fact, during his presi-dential campaign in 2002, he went so far as to say, "What's wrong with being a little anti-American?" Even after taking office, he promoted himself as some-one who could stand up to the United States. His emotional remarks and fre-quent clashes with the George W. Bush administration over policy regarding North Korea created the impression that he was anti-American.[40] In addition, his vision for a peaceful and prosperous Northeast Asia was initially vague about the U.S. role in the region. By contrast, Roh was quite enthusiastic about strengthening South Korea's bilateral ties with China and Japan, at least early in his term. In fact, despite criticism at home, he made his first official visit to Japan on South Korea's Memorial Day and sought to secure support for his Northeast Asian initiative at the Japanese Diet in 2003. These actions suggested that the Roh government was adopting an essentially Asia-centric approach to building a regional community.

However, as noted, his Northeast Asian Cooperation Initiative suffered "historical" setbacks in 2004 with the controversy between China and South Korea over the ancient kingdom of Koguryo and the controversy between Japan and South Korea over Japanese prime minister Junichiro Koizumi's visits to the Yasukuni Shrine, which essentially turned back the clock on the Kim-Obuchi declaration of 1998. These developments among three major players in Northeast Asia raised questions about the feasibility of building a regional community. The Asia-centric approach to regional multilateralism suffered a further setback in early 2005 when Japan's Shimane Prefecture claimed ownership of the Tokdo Islands (called Takeshima in Japan) and the Japanese ambassador to South Korea reaffirmed this claim in Seoul. What was officially declared "a year of friendship" between Japan and South Korea quickly degenerated into a year of friction. To express his outrage at what he saw as a historical injustice, Roh Moo-hyun condemned Japanese actions in an open letter he posted on the Internet.

These developments formed the background of Roh's speeches on South Korea's new role as a balancer in Northeast Asia. Many Americans interpreted his remarks as expressing a desire to play the role of a balancer between the United States and China in the neorealist sense, despite South Korea's alliance with the United States. However, a close reading of the speech text suggests that *balancer* was a rather ill-defined term in Roh's mind. More than anything, he wanted to declare that South Korea would not be pushed around and that its choices would have a major impact on Northeast Asia.

In an address at the Korean Air Force Academy on March 8, 2005, Roh started out by making a reference to the nation's humiliation in the past. He said: "Korea sought peace one hundred years ago to no avail because it did not have the power to defend itself." After listing South Korea's accomplishments over the past century, he concluded by projecting a significant role for its armed forces: "We will safeguard peace in the region as an important balancing factor in Northeast Asia. For this purpose, we will take the lead in building a cooperative security structure in the region and [in] working together closely with other neighboring countries based on the Korea-U.S. alliance." In this context, being "an important balancing factor" does not seem to imply a neorealist balancer role for South Korea between China and the United States or between China and Japan. Instead, the speech text suggests that South Korea would resort to the combination of multilateral security cooperation and its alliance with the United States to safeguard peace.

Two weeks later Roh made a similar speech at the Korean Third Military Academy. He said: "The Korean armed forces have grown into a formidable military no one can take lightly. . . . We should play a balancing role for peace and prosperity not only on the Korea Peninsula but also for Northeast Asia. . . . The power equation in Northeast Asia will change depending on the choices we make."[41] Unlike in the previous speech, Roh made no explicit reference to the South Korea–U.S. alliance, but "a balancing role" in this context seems to imply a significant role, but not the neorealist notion of a balancer. In sum, what many interpreted as the height of Roh's anti-American remarks was largely a nationalistic response to Japanese actions on historical issues.[42] In fact, if anything, the Asia-centric position that Roh had displayed early in his term was changing in favor of the United States around this time. In late 2005, despite its earlier reservations, the Roh government officially accepted the U.S. principle of "strategic flexibility."

Roh's shift to a U.S.-centric position was most clearly demonstrated by dramatic changes in his FTA policy. The Roh government initially pursued FTAs in two directions.[43] First, it negotiated essentially "exploratory" FTAs with smaller countries that had a great deal of previous experience with FTAs and posed little threat to South Korea's vulnerable agricultural sector. As a result of these negotiations, South Korea signed FTAs with Chile, Singapore, and the European Free Trade Association. As a next step in this process, South Korea explored FTAs with middle powers such as Canada and Australia. Although these countries would likely demand agricultural liberalization, many experts believed that South Korea could negotiate on even terms with them and secure comparable concessions in return.[44] Second, the Roh government also pursued more "strategic" FTAs with a view toward promoting peace and prosperity in Northeast Asia. Building on the goodwill generated by the Kim-Obuchi declaration of a new partnership in October 1998, an FTA with Japan received top priority. By comparison, many felt that an FTA with China would be detrimental to South Korea's agricultural sector, even though it would give a significant boost to manufacturing exports. An FTA with the United States was widely regarded as a long-term project, driven more by high politics than by economics, for it would impose significant adjustment costs not only on South Korea's agriculture, but on its services as well, with less-tangible benefits for the manufacturing sector.

By early 2005, however, the Roh government began to seek new directions for various reasons. FTAs with Chile, Singapore, and the European Free Trade Association gave South Korean trade negotiators the confidence to pursue "simultaneous negotiations with multiple trading partners," including the United States. Then FTA negotiations with Japan broke down, and the controversy over historical issues further aggravated the prospects of these trade talks. And perhaps most important, faced with a deteriorating external security environment, the Roh government came to see the FTA with the United States as a way of compensating for the strains in the South Korea–U.S. alliance.[45] Although China expressed willingness to show flexibility with regard to rice and other "sensitive items" in its FTA negotiations with South Korea in August 2005,[46] the Roh government spurned this offer in part out of concern about the U.S. reaction. Furthermore, after concluding an FTA with the United States in April 2007, the Roh government started negotiations with the European Union rather than with its Asian neighbors. The idea of using "strategic" FTAs with Japan and China to build a regional community seemed a distant memory.

LOOKING AHEAD

Roh Moo-hyun's dramatic shift from an Asia-centric approach to a liberal variant of a U.S.-centric approach raised questions about South Korea's foreign-policy priorities. In less than a year, from the time of his speeches on South Korea's balancing role to the start of FTA negotiations with the United States, Roh managed to confuse the Americans and the Chinese about South Korea's geopolitical strategy. At the same time, his shift in position demonstrated how South Korea might respond to changes in its security environment—in this case, because of deterioration in its relationships with China and Japan. In the future, South Korea must formulate and communicate its position in a clear and consistent manner, striking a balance between its alliance with the United States and its pursuit of regional multilateralism. Roh's successor, Lee Myong-bak, sent early signals that he would continue pursuing regional community building while keeping a more secure and explicit mooring in the U.S.– South Korea alliance. For South Korea, the challenge will continue to be how to establish mechanisms for promoting regional cooperation in Asia, but in a way that is nonthreatening to the United States. Most important, a regional cooperation scheme should provide a "big picture" for the relations between China and Japan and the role of the United States in Asia. The resolution of the Korean question also has to be an integral part of such a scheme. These challenges can be best met by adopting a U.S.-in-Asia approach.

From South Korea's perspective, the United States plays a critical role in determining the future of the Korea Peninsula and of the region as a whole. This role can be negative or positive, however. In fact, there appear to be basically two options for the United States depending on what kind of relationship with China it envisions.[47] One is to place South Korea within a hub-and-spoke alliance against China, using the North Korean nuclear crisis as a catalyst. However, this policy is likely to find little support in South Korea and risks a nationalist backlash if the United States is increasingly viewed as an impediment to Korean unification and regional security. It would also increase the possibility of a shift in Korean preference from the United States to China, or it may perpetuate the division of the Korea Peninsula and exacerbate a continental-maritime confrontation in Asia. The United States would find itself increasingly tied to Japan, whose reluctance to come to terms with its past has limited the effectiveness of its diplomacy. Under this strategic vision, the United States essentially risks "losing" the Korean Peninsula in order to cement its relationship with Japan and to contain China.

The other alternative is for the United States to deal with South Korea on more equal terms and engage it as a partner in building a new order in the region, facilitating China's gradual transition, and resolving the North Korean nuclear crisis to usher in a new era in Asia. This alternative would require the United States to be more "equidistant" between China and Japan and consistently to signal China that the existing U.S. alliances with Japan and South Korea are not designed to threaten China. At the same time, the United States would also have to reassure Japan that this policy is not "Japan passing." The United States would assume the role of a stabilizer in Asia, much as it does in Europe. This approach would not only strengthen the U.S. position in the Korea Peninsula, but also enhance its policy options in dealing with China and Japan. It would also have the effect of encouraging Japan to improve relations with its neighbors. Under this vision, South Korea would play the role of an advocate for cooperation in the region, rather than a *balancer* in the neorealist sense of the term. South Korea is likely to support such a shift in U.S. policy because the last thing it wants is a continental-maritime division in Asia that would greatly complicate Korean unification and increase tension in the region. This strategic vision would not only serve the interest of the South Korea–U.S. alliance, but also enhance regional security.[48]

South Korea will continue to rely on the United States as the stabilizer in Northeast Asia, but new multilateral security arrangements that build confidence among the major powers in the region can supplement the U.S. role and help Korea to maintain a positive role as the land bridge of Northeast Asia without being caught between a continental-versus-maritime rivalry of great powers. The Six-Party Talks may serve as a predecessor to such a regime, though that process will by necessity be somewhat hostage to the pace of denuclearization by North Korea. A multilateral scheme to promote political reconciliation and economic integration more broadly in Asia will also serve Korean interests.

APT may provide the basis for further reconciliation and integration, but South Korea will have to be careful to ensure that a "Fortress Asia" does not exclude its critical ally and trading partner, the United States. Moreover, because South Korea is a major trading nation, its elected governments will want Asian regional integration to serve as a building block for global trade liberalization and economic integration. For Asia to secure peace and prosperity and to ensure that the Korean people never again have to endure what they did in the first half of the twentieth century, it is essential that the region contain the Sino-Japanese rivalry and maritime-continental confrontation and continue to expand economic interdependence with the rest of the world through trade and investment channels.

NOTES

1. Rhee was ambivalent about including Japan in this security pact. To strengthen South Korea's position in East Asia, he wanted to minimize Japan's influence in the multilateral arrangement. At the same time, he understood that the United States regarded Japan as the anchor of its East Asia strategy, especially after the defeat of the Nationalists in China. For a more detailed discussion of Rhee's position, see Park Jin-hee, "Syngman Rhee's Attitude Toward Japan and the Pacific Pact" [in Korean], *Critical Review of History* 76 (2006): 95–102.

2. Rhee wrote a letter to the *New York Times* warning the United States about the growing "red peril" on the Asian continent. See "Rhee Warns U.S. Red Peril Grows: Korean President Asks Arms for Asians to Keep Foe from Taking Continent," *New York Times*, May 9, 1954.

3. According to the Hallstein Doctrine, West Germany had the exclusive right to represent the entire German nation and would sever diplomatic relations with any state that recognized East Germany. However, Willy Brandt abandoned this principle of isolating East Germany and began to pursue *ostpolitik* in the late 1960s. A similar change in South Korea's unification policy came much later with the adoption of *nordpolitik* in the late 1980s.

4. Ironically, Henry Kissinger, the ultimate realist, supported the idea of cross-recognition.

5. For a more detailed discussion of Kim's position on Korean unification during the 1971 campaign, see Kim Dae-jung, *Union of Republics* [in Korean] (Seoul: Hak-minsa, 1991), 102–48.

6. Shin Wook-hee, "International Dynamics of the ROK-U.S. Alliance: A Search for an Analytical Framework" [in Korean], *National Strategy* 7, no. 2 (2001): 5–23. Looking at the South Korea–U.S. alliance from 1950 to 1972, Shin notes that the U.S. pursuit of détente tended to create strains in the alliance, especially in the years from

1968 to 1972. It is interesting to note that another "détente" brought about a reversal of roles in the 2000s, when the United States argued that South Korea was discounting North Korea's military threat, whereas South Korea urged the United States to engage North Korea to dismantle the Cold War structure on the Korea Peninsula. Over the previous three decades, the power balance between North Korea and South Korea had decisively shifted in favor of the South.

7. Roh Tae-woo, *Selected Speeches of President Roh Tae Woo* (Seoul: Presidential Secretariat, Republic of Korea, 1993).

8. On his visit to the Siberian city of Krasnoyarsk on September 16, 1988, Gorbachev called for a moratorium on nuclear weapons in the Asia-Pacific region, reduction of naval and air forces in Northeast Asia, and mutual abandonment of the U.S. bases in the Philippines and the Soviet bases in Cam Ranh Bay. He also made a proposal for a multilateral security conference in Asia.

9. "Agreement on Reconciliation, Nonaggression, and Exchanges and Cooperation Between South and North Korea," December 13, 1991 (effective February 19, 1992), http://www.isop.ucla.edu/eas/documents/korea-agreement.htm.

10. Lee Sang-kyun draws lessons from the European experience with regard to the U.S. role in regional multilateralism in "A Proposal for Multilateral Security Cooperation in Northeast Asia: European Experience and Korea's Choice" [in Korean], *National Strategy* 3 (1997): 200–201.

11. For more details on the mini-CSCE idea, see Han Sung-joo, "Fundamentals of Korea's New Diplomacy: New Korea's Diplomacy Toward the World and the Future," *Korea and World Affairs* 17, no. 2 (1993): 239. Han was the first foreign minister in the Kim Young-sam government.

12. Looking at South Korea's previous proposals for multilateral security cooperation in Northeast Asia, Cho Sung-ryol observes that the proposal for a Northeast Asia security dialogue can provide a useful benchmark for the forthcoming six-party negotiations on a multilateral security organization. See Cho Sung-ryol, "The Denuclearization of the Korea Peninsula and a Search for a New Order in Northeast Asia" [in Korean], paper presented at the Annual Unification Forum, Korean Council for Reconciliation and Cooperation, Seoul, April 12, 2007.

13. In this regard, the German case seems to offer a useful lesson: even if North Korea and its patrons simultaneously suffer a precipitous decline to make "unification by absorption" a realistic prospect for South Korea, it would still make sense for South Korea to have developed good relations with North Korea's patrons as well as with its own allies to facilitate unification. Adopting a hostile policy toward North Korea's patrons would be counterproductive.

14. See, for example, Kim Sung-hoon, Kim Tae-hoon, and Shim Eui-seop, *Northeast Asian Economic Region* [in Korean] (Seoul: Bibong Press, 1997); Kim Young-ho, "Economic Cooperation in Northeast Asia and Economic Integration of South and North Korea" [in Korean], *Review of Comparative Economics* 3 (1995): 205–25.

15. Kim Sun-hyuk and Lee Yong-wook, "New Asian Regionalism and the United States: Constructing Regional Identity and Interest in the Politics of Inclusion and Exclusion," *Pacific Focus* 19, no. 2 (2004): 185–231, http://www.korea.ac.kr/~sunhyukk/pfo4.pdf. Kim and Lee argue that the crucial feature of the "new" Asian regionalism in the postcrisis period has been its exclusionary nature. Using the constructivist theoretical framework, they point out that the West's initial "holier-than-thou" response to the Asian economic crisis helped the Asian nations to develop a new collective identity. However, as the acrimonious debate over historical issues in the region has since demonstrated, the stability of this new collective identity should be questioned.

16. In 1998, Kim Dae-jung and Obuchi Keizo came to terms with history and declared a new partnership for the twenty-first century between South Korea and Japan.

17. Kim Dae-jung, "The South-North Summit: A Year in Review," in *Building Common Peace and Prosperity in Northeast Asia*, ed. Woo Keun-min (Seoul: Yonsei University Press, 2002), 27–32. Looking back on the inter-Korean summit, Kim said: "Improvements in South-North relations will be realized when there is parallel progress in U.S.–North Korean ties. It goes without saying that U.S.–North Korean relations are inextricably linked with South-North relations. Successful South-North exchange and cooperation are unlikely to materialize when only progress in one area is visible. These two tracks must develop in unison with each other."

18. For details of this proposal, see Presidential Committee on Northeast Asian Cooperation Initiative, *Toward a Peaceful and Prosperous Northeast Asia* (Seoul: Presidential Committee on Northeast Asian Cooperation Initiative, 2004).

19. "Joint Statement in the Fourth Round of the Six-Party Talks on September 19, 2005," http://www.mofat.go.kr/me/me_a003/me_b041/me_c041/1226305_31377.html.

20. "Initial Actions for the Implementation of the Joint Statement on February 13, 2007," http://www.mofat.go.kr/me/me_a003/me_b041/me_c041/1226310_31377.html.

21. Lim Won-hyuk, "Economic Integration and Reconciliation in Northeast Asia: Possibilities and Limitations," in *Rethinking Historical Injustice in Northeast Asia*, ed. Gi-wook Shin, Soon-won Park, and Daqing Yang (New York: Routledge, 2007), 235–53. In this article, I look at the evolving pattern of economic relations in East Asia and analyze the possibilities and limitations of using economic integration to bring about historical reconciliation and regional cooperation.

22. For more details on energy, transportation, trade, and environmental cooperation projects, see Presidential Committee, *Toward a Peaceful and Prosperous Northeast Asia*.

23. Roh Moo-hyun, speech to the European Union Chamber of Commerce in Korea, June 2003, in *President Roh Moo-hyun's Speeches*, vol. 1 (Seoul: Blue House, 2004).

24. The economic and political development of Asian nations tends to weaken the old Japanese logic of *datsua* (escape from Asia) and to facilitate regional multilateralism in Asia.

25. The Helsinki Accord had three baskets. The first basket covered security issues such as confidence-building and arms-reduction measures. The second basket promoted cooperation in economic, science and technology, and environmental areas. The third basket covered cooperation in humanitarian and other areas through increased people-to-people interaction.

26. Cynics may view Japan's diplomatic initiative to create "an arc of freedom and prosperity" as the latest example of justifying China containment based on values.

27. Polling by the centrist *JoongAng Ilbo* found that the United States climbed from South Korea's third "most liked" country in 2006 to the top spot in 2007 (poll conducted by *JoongAng Ilbo* and *The Opinion* from September 1 to September 12, 2007, among twelve hundred adults; results published in *JoongAng Ilbo*, September 22, 2007). Meanwhile, the sense of threat about China increased in the same period, with 38 percent of South Koreans responding to a Korean Institute for Defense Analyses poll in 2006 that the greatest future threat was China, much greater than Japan or North Korea. See Korea Institute for Defense Analyses, March 20, 2006, cited in Scott Snyder, "China-Korea Relations: Kim Jong-il Pays Tribute to Beijing—in His Own Way," *Comparative Connections*, April 2006, http://www.csis.org/pacfor/ccejournal.html.

28. Choi Jang-jip, "Ideational Base for the East Asian Community" [in Korean], *Journal of Asiatic Studies* 47, no. 4 (2005): 119–20. Choi distinguishes "nationalism as an ideology" from "nationalism as a historical reality" shaped by the collective memory of struggle against foreign domination. He points out that attempts to deny and deconstruct nationalism as an ideology does not eliminate its existence as a historical reality.

29. The Yasukuni Shrine, a private Shinto temple in Tokyo, is a source of controversy owing to its tradition of honoring Japan's war dead, including those deemed war criminals in the post–World War II period, and the shrine's uncritical rendering of Japan's imperial history. The shrine becomes a particular source of controversy when visited by leading Japanese political figures, such as Prime Minister Koizumi Junichiro in the early 2000s.

30. With its territory extending from the northern half of the Korean Peninsula to Manchuria, the ancient kingdom of Koguryo has had the potential to develop into a contentious issue between South Korea and China for some time. A major controversy erupted in April 2004 when the Chinese Foreign Ministry deleted references to Koguryo from the Korean history (country profile) section on its Web site (http://www.fmprc.gov.cn). This official Chinese move followed the "academic" activities of the government-sponsored Northeast Project, which claimed that Koguryo was merely a Chinese vassal state or a Chinese regional province. When South Korea protested, China responded by deleting the entire pre–World War II history of Korea on the Foreign Ministry Web site.

31. Lee Dong-hui, for instance, supports APEC's new security agenda, pointing to the broader geographical scope of nontraditional threats in the post–September 11 world, whereas Han Yong-sup and colleagues advocate a tighter multilateral arrange-

ment focusing on traditional threats. The latter group would like to create a new multilateral security arrangement in Northeast Asia rather than expand the scope of APEC or ARF. See Lee Dong-hui, *The Development of the APEC and Its Future Agenda* [in Korean], Major International Issue Analysis no. 2004-30 (Seoul: Institute of Foreign Affairs and National Security, November 26, 2004); Han Yong-sup, Park Jong-chul, Yoon Hyun-keun, Hwang Byung-mu, Park Young-joon, Lee Sung-hee, Kim Young-ho, Lee Seo-hang, and Oh Seung-ryol, *Toward an East Asian Security Community* [in Korean] (Seoul: Nanam Press, 2005).

32. For details, see Park Beon-soon, *ASEAN Plus Three and East Asian Cooperation* [in Korean], Global Issues no. 9 (Seoul: Samsung Economic Research Institute, November 30, 2004).

33. With regard to this question, Bae-geung Chan argues that it is in South Korea's national interest to secure U.S. participation in regional cooperation initiatives, in *"Northeast Asian Cooperation Initiative" and Korea's Diplomatic Tasks: A Strategy for Regional Cooperation*, Policy Brief no. 2004-04 (Seoul: Institute of Foreign Affairs and National Security, November 2004).

34. See the roundtable discussion on this topic in the fall 2005 issue of *Changbi*.

35. For various perspectives on South Korea's foreign-policy priorities, see Bae Ki-chan, *Korea Standing Again at a Crossroads of Survival* [in Korean] (Seoul: Wisdom House, 2005); Jong-ryn Mo, "What Does South Korea Want?" *Policy Review* 142 (2007), http://www.hoover.org/publications/policyreview/6848122.html; Bae-geung, *"Northeast Asian Cooperation Initiative" and Korea's Diplomatic Tasks*; Han et al., *Toward an East Asian Security Community*.

36. For a comparative perspective on the U.S. alliances with Japan and South Korea, see Michael H. Armacost and Daniel I. Okimoto, eds., *The Future of America's Alliances in Northeast Asia* (Stanford, Calif.: Asia-Pacific Research Center, 2004).

37. For example, see Im Hyug-baeg, "East Asian Regionalism: Conditions and Constraints" [in Korean], *Journal of Asiatic Studies* 47, no. 4 (2004): 161–62.

38. Choi Won-sik, "East Asian Initiative as a Scheme to Partition the World into Three Blocs" [in Korean], in *Toward a Northeast Asian Community*, ed. Korean Solidarity for Northeast Asian Intellectuals (Seoul: Dong-A Ilbo, 2004), 9–24.

39. See, for instance, *Korean's FTA Roadmap and Additional Tasks* [in Korean], Federation of Korean Industries (FKI) Issue Paper no. 6 (Seoul: FKI, November 19, 2004); *Korea-U.S. FTA: A Corporate Survey* [in Korean], FKI Issue Paper no. 60 (Seoul: FKI, September 29, 2006); *Korea-China FTA: A Corporate Survey* [in Korean], FKI Issue Paper no. 62 (Seoul: FKI, December 6, 2006).

40. Roh did go out of his way to make pro-American statements on his first trip to the United States in May 2003, but when he came back home, he basically characterized his previous statements as theater for American consumption. His subsequent decisions to send combat troops to Iraq and accommodate the relocation of U.S. troops stationed in South Korea did little to win back Americans' trust.

41. "Roh Opposes Expansion of U.S. Troops' Role to Northeast Asia," *Yonhap News*, March 8, 2005, translated in World News Connection, KPP20050308000923; "Roh Envisions South Korea–U.S. Joint Defense Structure," *Yonhap News*, March 16, 2005, translated in World News Connection, KPP20070316971044.

42. The South Korean National Security Council later attempted to rationalize Roh's remarks by arguing that the term *balancer* really meant a "mediator, harmonizer, facilitator," and "initiator for peace" ("A Briefing on the Concept of a Balancer in Northeast Asia" [in Korean], April 27, 2005, http://www.president.go.kr/cwd/kr/archive/archive_view.php?meta_id = news_data&id = 3156e0ed75b5e6e6c5844a90).

43. For details on South Korea's FTA strategy as of early 2005, see Lim, "Economic Integration and Reconciliation in Northeast Asia."

44. In their view, it was imperative that South Korea set the pace and scope of agricultural and other trade liberalization depending on the concessions secured from the negotiating partner. For this reason, they felt that it made sense for South Korea to enter into negotiations first with middle powers such as Canada. In addition to achieving a more equitable outcome, such a sequencing strategy would allow South Korea's vulnerable sectors to adjust to liberalization before an FTA is negotiated with an economic superpower such as the United States.

45. Lee Joo-young, "Controversy over President Roh's Motive to Push for KORUS FTA Negotiations" [in Korean], *Kyunghyang Sinmun*, August 8, 2006, http://news.khan.co.kr/kh_news/khan_art_view.html?artid = 200608080747031&code = 910203.

46. "S. K. Nixed Trade Deal with China Under U.S. Pressure, Data Reveals," *Hankyoreh*, August 11, 2006, http://english.hani.co.kr/arti/english_edition/e_business/148185.html.

47. A similar argument is made in Kim Sun-hyuk and Lim Won-hyuk, "How to Deal with South Korea," *Washington Quarterly* 30, no. 2 (2007): 71–82.

48. In his remarks at the Korea Society Annual Dinner on September 15, 2005, in New York, Roh Moo-hyun spoke in favor of this latter alternative: "[I]t would be desirable to see the quest for a conciliatory and cooperative order for integration in the region assume primacy in U.S. policy toward Northeast Asia. . . . The hypothetical assumption of an adversarial constellation of forces in Northeast Asia will work to aggravate confrontation in the region, while the posting of reconciliation and cooperation will be similarly self-fulfilling." He added, "It would be far from the truth to claim that the uniting of Europe is fraying transatlantic ties. . . . It is high time for us to steadily pursue integration in Northeast Asia." These remarks were seemingly in line with a U.S.-in-Asia approach, but because of his previous inconsistencies it was unclear whether they represented his final say on the alliance and regional multilateralism.

5. Japan's Perspective on Asian Regionalism

Akiko Fukushima

From the Meiji Restoration to the present, Japan has used both bilateralism and multilateralism to pursue its foreign-policy goals. Although Japan was part of the ineffective system of Asian multilateral treaties in the years between the world wars and tried to construct its own "East Asian Coprosperity Sphere" during World War II, the primary instinct for Japanese strategists throughout modern history has been to focus on bilateral alliances with the perceived hegemonic power of the day: Great Britain from 1902 to 1922, Germany (and Italy) from 1940 to 1945, and the United States since 1952. However, since the end of the Cold War, the Japanese government has rediscovered multilateral diplomacy as a centerpiece of its foreign policy—not as a replacement for its strengthened bilateral alliance with the United States, but as a necessary complement. The new focus on multilateralism was initially prompted by the liberation of the United Nations from bipolar paralysis at the end of the Cold War. The 1990/1991 Gulf War had a particularly significant impact on Japanese thinking and led to the passage of the International Peace Cooperation Law in 1992, which enabled the dispatch of the Self-Defense Forces for peacekeeping operations abroad. Tokyo also began a sustained campaign for a permanent United Nations Security Council (UNSC) seat in 1994. Discouraged by the limited reform of the United Nations, including its own bid for a permanent UNSC seat, Japan increasingly turned its focus to regionalism in the Asia-Pacific region in the 1990s and then in East Asia beginning in the late 1990s.

Japan's record on regionalism has been mixed. At times, Japan has pursued an "independent foreign policy," focusing on Asian regionalism as a way to highlight differences between the United States and East Asian nations. Compared with the International Monetary Fund (IMF), it was more sympathetic and helpful in East Asia when the region was hit by the 1997 financial crisis,[1] and it has frequently lent its financial and diplomatic support to regional initiatives, though typically acting behind the scenes. At the same time, however, bilateralism, particularly with the United States, is still central to Japanese foreign policy. Playing in both of these arenas presents Japan with two challenges. The first is reconciling the two, particularly because East Asian regionalism does not include the United States. The second is whether and how Japan can lead regionalism in Asia, given the lingering and painful legacy of its history in the region.

Japan's role in community building in Asia will be shaped by how effectively Tokyo is able to manage these twin challenges. To examine these issues in more detail, this chapter first provides some historical background on Japan's approach to the regional architecture and community building. Next, it examines some of the ongoing debates in Japan concerning regional architecture. It then turns to the Japanese perspectives on the U.S. role in Asia and concludes with some thoughts about Japan and the future outlook for the Asian security architecture.

HISTORY OF JAPAN'S INVOLVEMENT IN ASIAN REGIONALISM

THE COLD WAR ERA: BILATERAL RELATIONS FAVORED OVER REGIONALISM

Although Japan applied for membership in the United Nations immediately after the conclusion of the San Francisco Peace Treaty at the end of World War II, the Soviet Union rejected Japanese accession for four years. Japan eventually joined the United Nations in December 1956, which it viewed as a critical step toward legitimization as a member of the international community. In February 1957, Prime Minister Kishi Nobusuke outlined the three pillars of Japan's postwar foreign policy: to center its foreign policy around the United Nations; to cooperate with the free, democratic nations of the Western alliance; and to identify closely with Asian nations.

Due to the UNSC's Cold War paralysis, the second pillar, bilateral alliance relations with the United States, loomed more prominently. Nevertheless,

United Nations–centered diplomacy remained at least rhetorically important in Japanese foreign policy, particularly as an antidote to concerns that Japan might become too dependent on the United States. Meanwhile, rhetoric regarding United Nations internationalism aside, Japan had an immediate interest in halting the expansion of communism in Asia. Unable and unwilling to become part of broader multilateral security arrangements in the region, such as the 1955 Southeast Asia Treaty Organization (SEATO), because of restrictive interpretations of Article Nine of the Constitution and a decision not to exercise the right of collective defense, Japan nevertheless expressed support for U.S. treaties aimed at containing communism in the region and took the initiative to convene the Ministerial Conference for the Economic Development of Southeast Asia in 1966 in which nine Southeast Asian countries participated.[2] In the case of both SEATO and the economic conference, the newly independent Southeast Asian countries, which had strong memories of Japanese and Western colonization, were unenthusiastic about a Japanese leadership role in the region, so for several decades Tokyo set aside its ambitions to help lead the regional campaign against communism.

In the meantime, Japan worked assiduously to resolve with its neighbors some outstanding issues from World War II. It normalized its diplomatic relations with South Korea in 1965 and with China in 1972. Next on the agenda was to negotiate significant aid agreements in lieu of reparations. Japan focused its aid on Indonesia, but also came to provide significant official development assistance throughout Southeast Asia and in China as well. However, despite generous Japanese economic assistance, many Asians eventually came to resent Japan's "economy first policy," a feeling that erupted in the form of anti-Japanese demonstrations in Thailand and Indonesia during Prime Minister Tanaka Kakuei's tour of Southeast Asia in 1974. In many respects, Japan was a victim of its own economic success, and the demonstrations against Tanaka reflected resentment in the region against the sudden surge of Japanese business activities in the still undeveloped economies of Southeast Asia.

In response a few year later, Prime Minister Fukuda Takeo announced in August 1977 what came to be known as "the Fukuda Doctrine": Japan would not become a military power; Japan would establish relationships built upon mutual trust; and Japan would partner with the Association of Southeast Asian Nations (ASEAN) and would support its efforts for peace and prosperity in Southeast Asia. This speech was warmly received by ASEAN countries and led to the Japan-ASEAN foreign ministers' meeting in 1978 and later to the ASEAN Post-Ministerial Conference with dialogue partners including Australia, Canada, the European Commission, Japan, and the United States. The U.S. withdrawal from Vietnam certainly helped change the region's view of Japan, whose economic aid and presence in the region suddenly took on a new importance.

For much of the Cold War period, Japan's cooperative regional policies in Asia were understood mainly as relations between Japan and Southeast Asia—more often as bilateral relations with individual Southeast Asian countries and sometimes with Southeast Asia as a region—but not as a collaboration between Japan and its Asian neighbors in a regional context. At the time, Asian nations lacked a strong sense of regional solidarity, and there was no infrastructure for regional cooperation in Asia like that in Europe. Ogoura Kazuo, a veteran of Japan's regional diplomacy, observed, "Before the war, Japan's international position was upheld by virtue of its military, political, and economic power and status *in Asia.*" After the war, however, its "position in Asia has been defined by its status in the international community as an industrially advanced *Western* nation." Thus, Japan did not have "a diplomatic strategy vis-à-vis Asia."[3]

At the private level, scholars and businesspeople tried to fill this gap by creating a series of regional forums since the 1970s. The Pacific Basin Economic Council, an annual meeting of businesspeople in pan-Pacific countries, was created in 1967 at the initiative of Goto Noboru, president of the Japan Chamber of Commerce. Prime Minister Ohira Masayoshi launched the Pacific Economic Cooperation Council (PECC),[4] a tripartite meeting of academics, businesspeople, and government officials with Australian prime minister Malcolm Fraser in 1980. PECC holds a major conference every two years and has hosted forums and working groups on energy and trade policy, but it has not developed into an intergovernmental organ. Despite these acts, the Japanese government's direct role in Asian regionalism remained limited.

THE POST–COLD WAR ERA: FROM ASIA PACIFIC TO EAST ASIA

With the end of the Cold War, as the tide of democratization came ashore in Asian countries, Asian regionalism began to bud, stimulated by European regional integration and the North America Free Trade Agreement (NAFTA). Japan took an active part. In 1988, the *Sakamoto Report*[5] from the Japanese Ministry of International Trade and Industry (MITI) laid down an important marker by recommending not a closed economic bloc, but rather multilateral cooperation open to economic partners outside the region. In particular, the report focused on trade and investment facilitation and human resources development rather than on the more politically sensitive goal of trade liberalization. MITI officials disseminated these ideas throughout the region and found particular support in Australia, leading to a well-coordinated Australian proposal in January 1989 to establish the Asia-Pacific Economic Cooperation (APEC) forum. Tokyo supported Australia in convening the first APEC foreign and trade ministers meeting in November 1989 and insisted on the inclusion of the United States in APEC to assure the trans-Pacific nature of the grouping.[6] This was a good case of Japan's catalyzing ideas for regional cooperation, but avoiding the conspicuous appearance of regional leadership. It was also a successful case of Tokyo's managing its twin challenges of leading on Asia regional integration without weakening Japan's critical alliance with the United States.

Over the course of the 1990s, however, Japan also began increasingly to accept the notion of East Asian (as opposed to trans-Pacific) regionalism as well. Malaysian prime minister Mahathir bin Mohamad strongly hoped for Japanese participation and a leadership role in the East Asia Economic Group, which he had proposed in 1990 and which was later renamed the East Asia Economic Caucus (EAEC). With strong U.S. opposition to any group that would exclude the United States (U.S. secretary of state James Baker famously said during his visit to Japan in November 1991 that the EAEC would "draw a line down the Pacific"),[7] Tokyo did not back the proposal. Sakamoto Yoshihiro, then deputy minister of international trade, recalls that it was not U.S. pressure, but Japan's own concern about the EAEC that led to its change in position on the EAEC. Sakamoto explains that some Japanese were concerned that the EAEC might provoke tension, if not another Pacific war, between Japan and United States based on the latter's fear that Japan would control Asian economic interests by leading the EAEC.[8] Japan was torn between its allegiances with Washington and its interest in an Asian version of NAFTA. With the industrialization and democratization of many of Southeast Asian countries, the advent of globalization, and the stagnation of the Japanese economy, Japan edged further in the direction of Asian regionalism, especially in the economic sphere. With the advent of the Asian financial crisis in 1997 and the perceived failure of the U.S.-led APEC to respond, a greater awareness emerged in Japan and the region regarding the importance of constructing measures to help address and alleviate financial threats. Hence, the Japanese Ministry of Finance proposed the creation of a new Asian monetary fund in the summer 1997 to supplement the IMF with a U.S.$100 billion reserve in emergency funds. Washington was surprised by the proposal and concerned that it was being portrayed as a regional alternative to the IMF. Beijing also objected because of worries that the fund would force a convergence of regional currencies. Hit from both Washington and Beijing, the proposal died early on. However, as one observer noted, "the desire to stabilize regional finance under Japanese leadership even in competition with the United States died hard among Japanese policymakers, and expectation of an active Japanese role lingered among some Asian leaders from 1997 to 2000."[9] Although the Asian monetary fund proposal died, the Japanese government introduced a scheme called "the new Miyazawa Initiative," worth

U.S.$30 billion, to help the region meet emergency financial needs. This proposal was given a warmer reception in Washington because it was framed as a supplement rather than an alternative to the IMF.

In another Japanese move, Prime Minister Hashimoto Ryutaro visited Brunei, Malaysia, Indonesia, Vietnam, and Singapore in January 1997 and proposed an annual Japan-ASEAN summit.[10] Prime Minister Mahathir of Malaysia thought that an annual meeting between ASEAN and Japan might make China uneasy and therefore suggested a summit meeting bringing together the ASEAN states with Japan, China, and the South Korea, rather than with Japan alone.[11] The 1997 subsequent Asian monetary crisis gave a push to this process and the ASEAN Plus Three (APT) Summit became an annual event, with other related ministerial meetings subsequently established among the members as well. A major achievement of APT has been the Chiang Mai Initiative (CMI) launched in 2000, which creates a web of bilateral currency-swap mechanisms at a time of crisis (detailed in chapter 9 in this volume).[12]

In order to stimulate debates for the APT meetings and provide concrete ideas for the building of an East Asian community, the Japanese government prepared three issue papers in 2004: on an East Asian community, on functional cooperation, and on the East Asia Summit (EAS).[13] The issue papers pointed out that regionwide institutional arrangements and the creation of a sense of community are future objectives. They cautioned that many points about the EAS had to be given further consideration, including the differences between it and the APT Summit. The papers highlighted a functional approach—focusing on such issues as trade, investment, information technology, finance, development assistance, energy security, environmental protection, food safety, public health, and intellectual property—as the key concept around which to enhance regional cooperation.

In commenting on the EAS, the Japanese foreign minister noted in March 2005 that "[the East Asian community] has to be an open community; India and Australia are welcome; the United States is welcome as an observer; it is important that Russia participates in some form as well."[14] Although Foreign Minister Machimura Nobutaka suggested the participation of the United States as an observer, the proposal did not receive sympathetic reaction from other APT members. Moreover, the United States itself was not thrilled with only observer status in the organization.[15]

In the wake of these developments, Japan has negotiated bilateral free-trade agreements (FTAs) or economic partnership agreements (EPAs, which include FTAs as well as agreements on the free movement of people, goods, and capital), first with Singapore (concluded in November 2002), subsequently with Malaysia (December 2005), and with many other countries as shown in figure 5.1.[16]

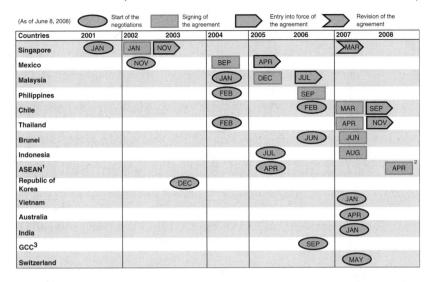

FIGURE 5.1 CURRENT STATUS OF EPA AND FTA NEGOTIATIONS
BY JAPAN.
[1]*Association of Southeast Asian Nations.*
[2]*Japan and ASEAN reached an agreement in November 2007.*
[3]*Gulf Cooperation Council.*
Source: Created by the author based on the Web sites of the Ministry of Economy, Trade, and Industry and the Ministry of Foreign Affairs, Japan.

In addition, in 2006 the Ministry of Economy, Trade, and Industry (METI) announced the Nikai Initiative, which included two elements: the Comprehensive Economic Partnership in East Asia (CEPEA) and the Economic Research Institute for ASEAN and East Asia (ERIA, which is conceived as an East Asian version of the Organization for Economic Cooperation and Development). CEPEA aims to form an EPA among ASEAN Plus Six, capitalizing on bilateral EPAs that have been forged or are in the process of negotiation. It will deal with such issues as trade in goods, countries of origin, services, investments, and intellectual property. ASEAN welcomed the initiative, but Beijing and Seoul were less responsive because both prefer to develop the APT framework. In contrast, India welcomed the Nikai Initiative because it is explicitly included in CEPEA. At the second EAS held in Cebu, Philippines, in January 2007, members agreed to commission an expert study on CEPEA.[17] In June 2007, the first track-two study group met in Tokyo to explore further a path toward CEPEA. The group submitted a progress report to the EAS in November 2007 and is to submit a final set of recommendations to the fourth EAS in late 2008.

The Nikai Initiative's ERIA, a regional think tank, would provide policy recommendations and coordination on statistics, trade, investment, industrial policy, energy, environment, standards and certification, and intellectual property. It also is meant to supplement the work of the ASEAN Secretariat. It would be composed of a web of research institutions from ASEAN Plus Six, and it would eventually be established in ASEAN, with researchers to be seconded from member institutions as a first step.[18] ERIA was proposed at the second EAS, which "welcomed" it, and it will soon be established in collaboration with think tanks in the ASEAN Plus Six countries.[19] It is working on test-run projects on issues not covered by CEPEA, such as regional cooperation to correct inequality as well as energy and environmental issues, and will submit its policy recommendations to ASEAN, ASEAN Plus One meetings (where ASEAN meets separately with China, Japan, and South Korea, respectively), APT, and ASEAN Plus Six. According to METI, "ERIA will make intellectual contributions to the regional efforts driven by ASEAN through policy studies and recommendations,"[20] as figure 5.2 shows.

Japan also took on an active role in the multilateral processes concerned with security in Asia, beginning with the ASEAN Regional Forum (ARF), but with a particular focus on Northeast Asia through the Korean Energy Development Organization and the subsequent Six-Party Talks on Korean Peninsula security. Regarding the Six-Party Talks, Japan had suggested a multilateral framework for resolving regional differences long before the six-party process was initiated. In February 1998, Foreign Minister Obuchi Keizo stated that "[i]n the Asia-Pacific region . . . it is essential to ensure the cooperation among Japan, the United States, China, and Russia toward the establishment of a framework for peace and stability in the region. . . . I believe that as these quadripartite relations evolve, we should be aware of the possibility of the four nations meeting together in the future to have discussions on various matters of mutual concern."[21] Obuchi visited the United States as prime minister in September 1998 and suggested to President Bill Clinton the need to hold six-party rather than four-party talks on North Korea.[22] When the George W. Bush administration proposed a multilateral approach to resolving the impasse with North Korea in early 2003, Japan warmly welcomed the initiative. As the participants list appeared to grow beyond Northeast Asia to include the United Nations, the European Union, and Australia, however, Japanese foreign minister Kawaguchi Yoriko convinced visiting U.S. secretary of state Colin Powell in February 2003 to limit the numbers to the six parties of Northeast Asia (China, Japan, North Korea, Russia, South Korea, and the United States). In Tokyo, there has been enthusiasm about the Six-Party Talks process, which empowers Japan in the diplomacy regarding the Korean Peninsula in the most significant way since World War II, but there is also apprehension that the process may lead to collective pressure on Japan to make concessions to North Korea on sensitive issues such as North Korea's abduction

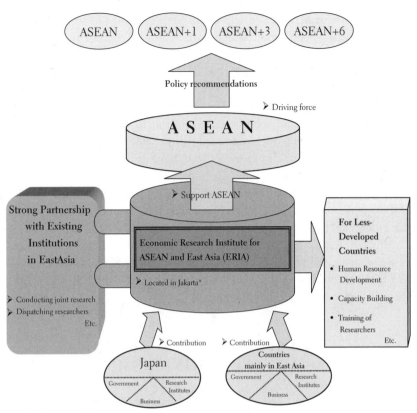

*Established on June 3, 2008

FIGURE 5.2 ERIA CONCEPT.
Source: Modified from a figure in Ministry of Economy, Trade, and Industry (METI), Japan, White Paper, chap. 4, sec. 3, p. 374, http://www.meti.go.jp/english/report/data/gWT2007fe. html, or http://www.meti.go.jp/english/report/downloadfiles/2007WhitePaper/Section4-3.pdf.

of Japanese citizens in the late 1970s and early 1980s.[23] Overall, the Six-Party Talks establishment in February 2007 of working groups related to denucleariza-tion, peace mechanisms on the peninsula, and regional confidence building will ensure that Japan remains an active participant.

The objectives and conditions for Japan's role in reconciliation on the penin-sula were outlined by Prime Minister Koizumi Junichiro during his September 2002 visit to Pyongyang: Japan will be prepared to normalize relations with Pyongyang and provide economic aid as it did when normalizing with South Korea in 1965, but only when North Korea resolves the abductee issue and the nuclear threat (including missiles) to Tokyo's satisfaction. Although future prime ministers may vary tactically on defining resolution, the conditions put forward by Koizumi are unlikely to change significantly.

In parallel with an increased activism in Northeast Asian security multilateralism, Japanese scholars and researchers have also been active in multilateral confidence-building exercises. Examples range from the Conference for Security and Cooperation in the Asia Pacific, which tracks with the ARF membership, to trilateral U.S.-Japan-China forums run by the Asia Foundation, the Brookings Institution, and the Center for Strategic and International Studies with Chinese think tanks and institutions in Tokyo such as the Japan Institute for International Affairs and the business federation Keidanren.

Japanese experts have also been active in the Network of East Asian Think Tanks, which was established in 2003 to debate the concept of an East Asian community. Parallel discussions are also occurring in Japan among a number of think tanks joined together in the Council on East Asian Community, which was established in May 2004.[24]

Although it is difficult to quantify the impact of this "paradiplomacy," Japanese diplomats and officials' frequent participation in these dialogues ensures that themes addressed in first-track forums such as the ARF or Six-Party Talks receive a fuller vetting around the margins.

JAPANESE DEBATES ABOUT ASIAN REGIONALISM

As the previous section demonstrates, Japan has overall been quite active in promoting regional cooperation in Asia, even as it maintains and strengthens its bilateral relationships, particularly with the United States. But what are the domestic debates about Japan's approach to Asian regionalism? This section examines several key debates and drivers behind that approach.

From an official Japanese standpoint, the driving force for regionalism in East Asia is economic interest due to the significant increase of Asia's involvement in trade and investment. Without a deepening of economic interdependence within Asia, regionalism could not have gathered much steam in Japan. The consensus among strategic thinkers in Japan is that the building of an East Asian community should be a long-term goal, but also an important ongoing process. In promoting the building of an East Asian community, Japan has emphasized functional cooperation. A majority view in Japan also holds that East Asia should start by building an economic community, move on to establishing a regionwide FTA/EPA, and then perhaps establish some sort of financial and monetary cooperation.

Beyond the broad consensus on economic integration, however, opinions diverge. As described later in this section in detail, some argue that regionalism should stop at the level of economic cooperation.[25] Others argue that functional cooperation should go beyond the economic area to nontraditional security issues to lay the foundations for an eventual security community.[26]

There is a consensus in the Japanese government on the merit of building an Asian community when it is cast as a future goal. References to community building can be found in numerous government documents. Prime Minister Koizumi alluded to it in his Diet Policy Speech in January 2005 and stated that "the Government will play an active role in the creation of an East Asian community, an open community that shares economic prosperity, while embracing diversity."[27] However, Japan's various ministries differ in their approaches.

For example, the Ministry of Finance promotes APT rather than the EAS because of the former's experience with the Miyazawa Initiative and the CMI. At the time of the 1997 Asian monetary crisis, it had a bitter experience with its Asian monetary fund initiative. Therefore, in its view, APT is more manageable.[28] In contrast, the Ministry of Foreign Affairs takes the official position of promoting both the EAS and APT. However, it believes that the EAS, which includes Australia, India, and New Zealand, is a more balanced venue for regionalism. The Foreign Ministry considers functional cooperation as the basis of community building and believes in open regionalism and the universal values to be shared.[29] In METI, some are for the EAS and others are for APT. However, extrapolating from the ERIA and CEPEA initiatives mentioned earlier, the ministry as a whole seems to favor the EAS.[30] For Japanese policy, the EAS and APT will likely continue to coexist in a sort of tug-of-war relationship. These two frameworks coexist because countries have different views on how large the footprint of Asian community building should be. Until this question of the community's scope is resolved, the EAS and APT will have to coexist—and Tokyo will need to work to balance the benefits and drawbacks of both.

Among academics, there are wide and varied viewpoints toward Asian regionalism and community building. Kokubun Ryosei, a respected China scholar at Keio University, has observed that the debate in Japan peaked at the time of the first EAS in December 2005. Debate over community building declined after that point because of the seemingly intractable tensions between Japan and China—there were bilateral collisions over the controversial Yasukuni Shrine visits[31] and China's aggressive efforts to block Japan's bid for a permanent UNSC seat. These tensions culminated in anti-Japan demonstrations in China in the spring of 2005. Since then, the debate on Asian community building has shifted away from lofty notions of community and on to the harder work of Sino-Japanese reconciliation. Kokubun argues that it is wrong to expect that China and Japan alone can determine the fate of Asian community building, but if the two continue to antagonize each other, Asia cannot come together.[32]

The Japanese skeptics regarding community building argue that despite growing economic regional interdependence, East Asia remains too dependent on trans-Pacific trade and financial ties to establish a separate economic community. They see visions of multilateral security cooperation as a potential trap for Japan in light of China's growing military modernization and diplomatic clout. They see a longer-term trend of Sino-Japanese rivalry that has to be addressed by reaching out to like-minded democracies rather than by embracing a pan-Asian identity that narrows the number of like-minded states that will help Japan balance China's influence. These observers tend to be conservative realists in their ideological outlook and to dismiss the advocates of community building as misguided liberal idealists.[33]

Those who remain enthusiastic about community building generally acknowledge that the pace will be slow and the focus will remain on finance and trade issues for the foreseeable future. They argue that the process should not be abandoned because of the different value systems to be found in Asia, but rather used to narrow the differences and to encourage China and other more authoritarian states to move steadily closer to the open liberalism that characterizes Japan. Former deputy foreign minister Tanaka Hitoshi is best known for this view. Tanaka underscores the importance of enhanced regional cooperation that includes China and encourages it to abide by the rules instead of seeking hegemony.[34] He argues that "over the long term, it is even plausible to think that nationalism in the region can eventually be complemented and perhaps absorbed by a sense of regionalism and common identity."[35] Enthusiasts for community building also see the potential for developing a sense of common security interests as several countries together tackle common transnational threats such as avian influenza.[36] Some scholars also see significance in the "epistemic" security communities that are developing in second-track and civil-society engagement across the region.[37]

The increasing emphasis on strengthening common values in regionalism and community building has broad support among scholars and officials in Japan, but there is still an active debate about how much to emphasize democracy and human rights rather than more functional cooperation on rule of law, protection of intellectual property rights, economic transparency, and good governance. The Japanese government argued for regionwide norms to be built at the first EAS, which is reflected in the summit declaration: "the East Asia Summit will be an open, inclusive, transparent, and outward-looking forum in which we strive to strengthen global norms and universally recognized values with ASEAN as the driving force working in partnership with other participants of the East Asia Summit."[38] During a visit to Southeast Asia in 2002, Prime Minister Koizumi launched the aforementioned Initiative for the Development of the Economies of Asia, which included good governance, the rule of law, and economic transparency, although the initiative did not bloom in full.[39] Prime Minister Abe Shinzo stated in his Policy Speech to the Diet on January 26, 2007, "With the ASEAN countries and also with countries with which we share fundamental values, such as India and Australia, we will promote exchange at the top level, as well as strengthen economic partnerships."[40] Foreign Minister Aso Taro launched "value-oriented diplomacy," more specifically the values of freedom and prosperity, as the new base for Japanese foreign policy in his speech at a Japan Institute of International Affairs seminar on November 30, 2006.[41] In his speech, he stated that Japan places emphasis on "universal values such as democracy, freedom, human rights, the rule of law, and the market economy as we advance our diplomatic endeavors." This emphasis goes beyond Asia and reaches to the Eurasian continent building the Arc of Freedom and Prosperity. Such values are also underscored in the Japan-Australia Joint Declaration on Security Cooperation announced on March 13, 2007, during the visit of Prime Minister John Howard to Japan. The Joint Declaration affirmed that "the strategic partnership between Japan and Australia is based on democratic values, a commitment to human rights, freedom, and the rule of law."[42] Although the relative emphasis on democracy and human rights versus more functional rule making will likely ebb and flow in Japanese approaches to regionalism over the coming years, there is no doubt that Tokyo seeks a community-building process that narrows the differences among states and links them more closely to global norms.

PERSPECTIVES ON THE U.S. ROLE

Japan has tried to give expression to its Asian identity and the desire for Asian-only forums, while reinforcing global norms shared with the United States and maintaining a concept of open regionalism and trans-Pacific ties. There is a strong view in Tokyo that the United States will ultimately benefit from an Asian economic community that reinforces stable economic growth and retains open ties to the United States through APEC, new initiatives such as the U.S.–South Korea FTA, and eventually—as increasing numbers of Japanese business leaders are urging—a U.S.-Japan EPA or FTA. Moreover, just as North America has NAFTA and Europe the European Union, there is no reason for Asia not to have its own economic community. In Asia, economic cooperation may take the form of a regional FTA, but given some members' level of economic development, it will more likely take the form of economic assistance,.[43] which can also benefit the United States.

On traditional security, the majority view in Japan is that Japan, given its security environment, must rely on the bilateral alliance with the United

States and on increased cooperation with other U.S. allies in the region, such as the South Korea and Australia. There is also increased interest in engaging India as a strategic partner in a broader Asian context, as reflected in increased diplomatic and security exchanges and Japan's active support for Indian membership in the EAS. But at the end of the day, most Japanese experts would argue that there is no point in taking up hard-security issues in a regional architecture without including the United States. There is a bipartisan consensus behind strengthening security cooperation on areas ranging from missile defense to coalition operations; North Korea's nuclear and missile programs and the People's Liberation Army military buildup are likely to keep that consensus more or less intact for the foreseeable future.

Japanese officials and experts also believe that the United States should take comfort in Tokyo's effort to advocate regional integration based on a philosophy of universal values rather than Asian exceptionalism (which was more characteristic of Japanese thinking a decade ago). Many Asian countries are adhering to universal norms, but do not want a single power, such as the United States, to be the champion of these values. Certainly, Japan wants to see the United States continue to offer constructive proposals and to engage in regional leadership, and it is not alone in that view. U.S. efforts to revitalize APEC and other trans-Pacific mechanisms would be particularly welcome and would enjoy strong Japanese support. Japan does not want to be seen in Washington as building an architecture that excludes the United States and wants to ensure its ally that community building in Asia is based on regional interdependence and not driven by anti-Americanism. From Japan's perspective, community building and regionalism should embrace globalization, not reject it. The United States encouraged its allies in Europe to build the European Community, and the prevailing hope in Japan is that the United States will take a similarly supportive view of Japan's efforts in Asia. If Japan cannot find a way to win U.S. confidence in its strategic approach on regionalism, a national consensus and an active role in community building will prove far more difficult for future Japanese governments.

CONCLUSIONS: ENDURING PRINCIPLES, EMERGING PROSPECTS

With regard to the future, Japan wants to take a leadership role and participate as a relevant player in regional architecture in Asia. Given the great changes taking place in Asia, Japan wants to adapt to the changes and redefine its role in the region in a way that increases its own visibility. Regionalism is certainly one of the paths for it to choose. It wants to build a stable neighborhood for its own sake and for the sake of regional peace and prosperity, and it would certainly benefit from such stability. To take an active part in this process and realize its own interests and those of the region, it should aim for a regional architecture undergirded by five main principles.

First, as has been noted, the regional architecture must allow both bilateralism and multilateralism to flourish and complement one another. However, from the Japanese perspective, regionalism in East Asia has not been and should not be led by a top-down, institutionalized integration. Rather, it has been and should continue to be driven by de facto regionalization backed by deepening interdependence. Growing intraregional trade is one such example. During the past ten years, the trade volumes between Japan and China, China and South Korea, and China and the ASEAN nations have increased four-, eight-, and sixfold, respectively. In the figures for 2003, the East Asian intraregional trade share amounted to 53.3 percent (including Taiwan and Hong Kong), whereas it had been only 33.6 percent in 1980. The figure exceeded the NAFTA rate (44.5 percent) and was getting closer to the European Union rate (60.3 percent). Its share of the global gross domestic product is one-fifth, and the countries in the region now hold about one-half of the world's foreign reserves. Moreover, with the increased trends of horizontal production networks in the manufacturing sectors, East Asia has provided a cross-border "integrated economic space" to forge dynamic competitiveness.

Second, the future regional architecture should promote both healthy cooperation and competition. Regional institutions are arenas for national power competition as well as for cooperation, and both competition and cooperation spur Japan's policies toward Asian regionalism and help create an atmosphere for more effective community building. For example, the initiation of FTA/ EPA discussions by Japan and China derives in part from a competition between the two. Japan started its FTA/EPA negotiations with Singapore earlier than the offer made by China to ASEAN as a region. The Japan-Singapore EPA was signed in January 2002. Meanwhile, China proposed its FTA with ASEAN as a group and concluded its framework agreement in November 2002, with the intention of concluding an FTA by 2010 (the parties have introduced some tariff reductions since 2004). Meanwhile, Prime Minister Koizumi proposed a Japan-ASEAN EPA in January 2002 during his visit to Singapore, the framework of which was signed in October 2003.[44]

In another example, the framework for the EAS came about in part from competing visions between Japan and China. Press reports on the APT Summit and the first EAS in December 2005 portrayed the tense relations between Japan and China as undermining the process of achieving regional cooperation in East Asia. It was reported that there were intense debates as to whether APT or the EAS should be the venue for discussing the East Asian community. China apparently insisted that APT, where China could exert more influence, should be that venue. In contrast, Nishiguchi Kiyokatsu, a professor at Takushoku University, asserted that Japan wanted to use the EAS to discuss the East Asian community in order to reduce Chinese influence.[45] In the end, a compromise was struck between the Chinese and the Japanese positions. The Kuala Lumpur Declaration of the APT Summit in December 2005 stated that "the ASEAN+3 process will continue to be *the main vehicle* in achieving [an East Asian community]."[46] Meanwhile, the EAS Declaration in the same month stated that "the East Asia Summit could play *a significant role* in community building in this region."[47]

Ideas matter in promoting regionalism. Since the creation of APEC, the ARF, and the EAS, Japan has tried to offer ideas for regional cooperation. As Michael Green describes, we may in the future see more of a balance of ideas rather than a balance of power in the context of regionalism.[48] There are certainly areas in which Japan can better take the leadership and areas in which China can better take the leadership. In creating a rule-based market, for example, Japan should be the leader. In nontraditional security cooperation, we have a variety of issues from drug trafficking and environmental preservation to curbing the spread of infectious diseases. Each area has potential leaders and members, and a healthy spirit of cooperation and competition will help spur effective ideas.

Third, the future regional architecture should offer "open regionalism." However, for the foreseeable future, Japan will likely support forms of regionalism in which ASEAN will still play a central role, while also promoting greater inclusivity and participation by non-ASEAN players. Since the first EAS, Japan has perceived that those who promote APT regard it as a core for concrete regional cooperation and see the EAS as a leaders' forum that is not meant to be a venue for discussing specific cooperation, but rather for generally discussing regional cooperation overall. Those who promote the EAS, however, want the EAS to conduct concrete measures of cooperation for the East Asian community and to create senior officials' and ministerial meetings. Japan, after being perceived as more in favor of the EAS and less in favor of APT, has tried not to debate which is to be used for regional community building, but instead has promoted the use of both for regional cooperation. Some have even wondered whether Japan was trying to kill APT and have tried to remove such doubts.[49] In fact, Japan is trying to excise the belief that it wants to promote the EAS at the expense of APT and attempting to replace that belief with the assurance that it wants to use both for regional cooperation.[50] The chair's statement at the APT Summit in January 2007 claimed that "ASEAN+3 is an essential part of the evolving regional architecture, complementary to the East Asia Summit and other regional fora."[51] The EAS chair's summary in December 2005 stated that "the East Asia Summit complements other existing regional mechanisms, including the ASEAN dialogue process, the ASEAN+3 process, the ARF and APEC in community building."[52]

Some Japanese government officials have explained that Japan has intentionally let ASEAN take the drivers' seat in East Asian regionalism in order to avoid rivalry with China. They have also explained that ASEAN's leadership in regionalism is more acceptable to members of the region because it is nonthreatening. Japan has been consciously trying to develop ASEAN's governorship of regionalism at the EAS. There is a prevailing view that if ASEAN sits in the driver's seat, then regional institutions are easier to control. It is considered wise for Japan to let ASEAN take the lead.[53] In contrast, in Japan it is perceived that ASEAN does not have the same sense of ownership of APEC.

In addition, given its alliance with the United States, Japan wants to play a bridging role in the Pacific region and for other key non-ASEAN regional players. In a speech in Singapore on January 14, 2002, Prime Minister Koizumi proposed the creation of a "community that acts together and advances together." In his proposal of such a community, for which he used the term *chiiki shakai* (regional society) rather than *kyodotai* (community), Koizumi included as members Australia and New Zealand in addition to the APT nations.[54] In his speech in Sydney on May 2003, he again named Australia and New Zealand as core members of the East Asia community. At the time, APT was making progress, so Koizumi's sudden inclusion of Australia and New Zealand perplexed ASEAN and even Australia and New Zealand themselves. This speech, however, succeeded in creating an impression of inclusiveness, contrasting somewhat with China's focus on the thirteen APT countries.[55] Japan insisted that these two countries should be included not only because they are advanced democracies, but also because they would help the community achieve a more balanced blend of ethnic backgrounds.[56] Meanwhile, although Japan did not originally include India in its blueprint of East Asia regional cooperation, it started to do so more actively with ASEAN Plus Six in mid-2005 as Singapore advised in running up to the first EAS. Furthermore, Prime Minister Abe Shinzo and his government has been more forthcoming than ever in including India in its Asian cooperation efforts. In his first Policy Speech to the Diet in September 2006, he proposed a security dialogue among Japan, the United States, Australia, and India.[57] When Foreign Minister Aso attended the South Asian Association for Regional Cooperation (SAARC) Summit meeting in April 2007, he stated in his speech that South Asia "makes a central pillar of 'the Arc of Freedom and Prosperity,'" the initiative that he was advancing.[58] Japan hopes to achieve an outward-looking, not anti-American or anti-West, regional architecture in Asia.

Fourth, the future regional architecture should reflect a respect and realization of democracy, human rights, and other universal values. Japan is not alone in advancing these ideals in Asia, but the Japanese government has been particularly active in advancing this concept through Foreign Minister Aso's Arc of Freedom and Prosperity and other efforts at the governmental and second-track levels. The Japanese interest in narrowing the differences among Asian nations with respect to rule making dates back to the 1990s and naturally reflects Japanese interests in stabilizing the environment for trade and investment. The focus on universal human rights and political freedoms has been a part of Japan's domestic identity since the end of World War II, but has been less pronounced as a matter of foreign-policy identity until more recently. The Japanese government will continue to debate how to operationalize these universal values in the areas of foreign aid and diplomacy toward outlying regimes such as Myanmar (Burma). There will likely be tension from the growing competition with China for access and influence and over defining regional values. However, the goal of narrowing the normative differences among members of the community will continue for some time to involve a contrast between Japan's approach and China's (which seeks to preserve diversity).

Fifth, the future regional architecture should be driven by a functional approach that helps address the many political, economic, and security challenges the region faces. Thus, it should be structured in a way that goes beyond conferences and undertakes effective action ranging from EPAs to nontraditional security measures. How Japan and the region can realize functional cooperation in a substantive manner will be a first hurdle to clear. If the architecture does not produce concrete results, it will lose momentum. In ten to fifteen years, those existing regional institutions that prove to be effective will survive and will compose the future regional architecture in East Asia. In economics and trade, APT and India will most probably strengthen their linkages, whereas in the area of traditional security Japan, the United States, and possibly South Korea, Australia, and India may have stronger ties. On traditional security, the majority view in Japan is that there is no room for multilateral hard-security cooperation in East Asia. Hard security should best be left to the web of bilateral alliances such as those between the United States, on the one hand, and Australia, Japan, and South Korea, on the other.

Thus, after the first EAS and running up to the second, Japan tried to argue that the EAS ought not to replace APT and pointed out that there are areas in which the EAS can effectively promote cooperation, such as energy, terrorism, disaster prevention, and trade and investment. Japan and Malaysia organized ministerial meetings on gender equality, science and technology, and economics in order to reduce some countries' allergic reaction to ministerial meetings held under EAS auspices. Around the summer of 2006 at an EAS informal foreign ministers' meeting, ASEAN suggested energy, disaster prevention, education, avian flu, and finance as agenda items for cooperation at the EAS. This proposal was reflected in the outcome of the second summit.[59] At this second summit in Cebu, Philippines, Japan took the position of emphasizing the adoption of the Second Joint Declaration in 2008 as the focal point of both APT and the EAS in order to achieve concrete regional cooperation on such issues as energy security.

The terrorist attacks of September 11, 2001, sent a message to the region that it can respond better collectively to nontraditional security issues such as terrorism, illicit drug trafficking, sea piracy, human trafficking, and the spread of infectious disease. A cooperative security framework involving Australia, China, India, Japan, Russia, South Korea, and the United States—an Asian version of the Organization for Security and Cooperation in Europe—or something like Tanaka Hitoshi's proposal for an East Asian security forum is conceivable. In the meantime, Japan will support a plethora of Asian institutions with ASEAN as a hub, from APEC, the ARF, and the Asia Europe Meeting to APT and the EAS—all of which offer ideas for regional cooperation. As the future regional architecture is constructed, numerous old and new frameworks will form a multilayered structure, waiting for upcoming generations to give it its final shape.

Thus, in Japan, there is a converging view that the building of an Asian community should be a goal, however far-fetched it may seem. The focus should not be on institution building for its own sake, though, but rather on the process of moving toward regionalism. In building a community, Asia should promote functional cooperation first on an economic front, through FTAs and EPAs, for example; second on nontraditional security challenges such as export control and counterpiracy; and third on cultural exchange, perhaps through youth exchange programs. Concerning culture, middle-class urban people throughout Asia are now sharing music, movies, and other cultural activities. Korean TV dramas have been watched in Japan and China. A deepening of cultural relations may help in regional identity building. In approaching regionalism in Asia, the prevailing consensus in Japan is that de facto regionalization should take precedence over institutionalization. An Asian community will not necessarily be the same as the Europe community.

Japan also hopes that a functional regional architecture will help deal with nationalism and anti-Japanese sentiments in Asia arising from unresolved historical differences. It sees regionalism as a way to capitalize on the relationships with Southeast Asian countries that it has cultivated bilaterally since the end of World War II through official development assistance and people-to-people exchange. Another key functional activity for future regional cooperation should be an increase in military transparency and confidence building.

For Japan, bilateralism, regionalism, and multilateralism are not choices from which it must select only one. Rather, it must use all three approaches to remain a relevant player, realize its interests, and promote prosperity and peace regionally and globally. Given the changes in its relative power, it will strive more diligently to be a player, to try to reconcile its past, and to make a positive contribution to Asia's future.

NOTES

1. Michael Jonathan Green, *Japan's Reluctant Realism* (New York: Palgrave, 2001), 7.

2. Tadokoro Masayuki, "Keizai taikoku no gaikōno genkei" [The prototype for diplomacy by an economic superpower], in *Sengo Nihon gaikōshi* [*The diplomatic history of postwar Japan*], ed. Iokibe Makoto (Tokyo: Yuhikaku, 2001), 132–34.

3. Kazuo Ogoura, "Japan's Asia Policy: Past and Future," *Japan Review of International Affairs* 10, no. 1 (1996): 7, emphasis added.

4. The PECC participants were Australia, the United States, New Zealand, Japan, the ten ASEAN nations, the Republic of Korea, Papua New Guinea, Fiji, and Tonga.

5. The study group headed by Sakamoto Yoshihiro compiled this report. Toyoda Masakazu was its chief drafter.

6. Sakamoto Yoshihiro, Ministry of Economy, Trade, and Industry (METI) official, interview by author, April 25, 2007, Tokyo.

7. Yoichi Funabashi, "Japan and the New World Order," *Foreign Affairs* 70, no. 5 (1991–1992): 58–74.

8. Sakamoto Yoshihiro, interview.

9. Saori N. Katada, "Japan's Counterweight Strategy: U.S.-Japan Cooperation and Competition in International Finance," in *Beyond Bilateralism: U.S.-Japan Relations in the New Asia-Pacific*, ed. Ellis S. Krauss and T. J. Pempel (Stanford, Calif.: Stanford University Press, 2004), 186.

10. Hashimoto Ryutaro, "Nihon-ASEAN shinjidai he no kaikaku: Yori hiroku yori fukai pa-tona-shippu" [Japan-ASEAN and a new era for transformation: Broader and deeper partnership], speech at the ASEAN Summit, Singapore, January 14, 1997, http://www.mofa.go.jp/mofaj/press/enzetsu/09/eha_0114.html.

11. Tanaka Akihiko and Jimbo Ken, "Higashi ajia kyodotairon no haikei to hokosei" [The background and orientation of discussion on East Asia community building], in *Higashi ajia kyodotai to Nihon no shinro* [*An East Asian community and Japan's thrust*], ed. Itoh Kenichi and Tanaka Akihiko (Tokyo: Nihon Hoso Shuppan Kyoukai, 2005), 46–47.

12. Phillip Y. Lipscy, "Japan's Asian Monetary Fund Proposal," *Stanford Journal of East Asia Affairs* (Singapore) 3, no. 1 (2003): 93–104.

13. Issue papers prepared by the government of Japan, June 25, 2004, following the discussion at the APT Summit held in Yogyakarta, Indonesia, on May 11, 2004, to suggest issues for an East Asia community, the functional cooperation in Asia, and an East Asia summit.

14. "Sankakoku kakudaihe seifu ugoku: Chugoku nanshoku, shudoken arasoi" [The government moves toward expanding member states: China is reluctant. Who will take the lead?], *Asahi Shimbun*, March 31, 2005.

15. Robert Zoellick stated in Singapore on May 10, 2005, that the United States would not participate as an observer, which was reported by *Asahi Shimbun* on May 15, 2005.

16. Details are available at http://www.meti.go.jp/policy/trade_policy/epa/index.html.

17. ASEAN Secretariat, "Chairman's Statement of the Second East Asia Summit," Cebu, Philippines, January 15, 2007, paragraph 12.

18. METI official, interview by author, November 2, 2006, Tokyo.

19. ASEAN Secretariat, "Chairman's Statement of the Second East Asia Summit," paragraph 12.

20. METI official in charge, e-mail message to author, July 20, 2007.

21. Obuchi Keizo, Foreign-Policy Speech to the Diet, 142d sess., February 16, 1998, http://www.mofa.go.jp/mofaj/press/enzetsu/10/eo_0216.html.

22. Nakanishi Hiroshi, "Reisen shuryogo no Nihon no henyou" [Japan's transformation after the end of the Cold War], in *Nihon no Higashi-Ajia Kousou [Japan's East Asian initiatives]*, ed. Soeya Yoshihide and Tadokoro Masaaki (Tokyo: Keio University, 2004), 290.

23. Agents of the North Korean government abducted Japanese citizens in the late 1970s and early 1980s to serve as teachers to train North Korean spies in Japanese language and culture. When Japanese prime minister Koizumi Junichiro visited North Korea in September 2002, Pyongyang for the first time acknowledged the abductions. Negotiations continue for the release of all abductees officially recognized by the Japanese government who are believed to be in North Korea still.

24. Council on East Asian Community, *Policy Report: The State of the Concept of an East Asian Community and Japan's Strategic Response Thereto* (Tokyo: Council on East Asian Community, August 2005), 7, http://www.ceac.jp/e/pdf/policy_report_e.pdf.

25. Hatakeyama Noboru, "Higashi Ajia Kyōdōtai no gensō o suteyo" [Give up the fantasy of an East Asia community], *Chūūō Kōron*, September 2005, 154–61.

26. In fact, the EAS has already taken on transnational issues such as tsunami-detection systems and avian flu. For more on views of community building, see Tanaka Hitoshi, "21-seiki Nihon gaikō no senryaku-teki kadai" [Strategic agenda for Japanese diplomacy in the twenty-first century], *Gaikō Forum*, no. 207 (2005): 8–13; Taniguchi Makoto, "Kikiteki Ajia gaikō wo ikani tate-naosu ka?" [How will we remake Asian diplomacy?], *Chūō Kōron*, April 2006, 314; Soeya Yoshihide, "Higashi Ajia Kyōdōtai

tenbō to kadai: Kyūkyo wa anzen hoshō kyōdōtai" [East Asia community: Problems and prospects: A security community is the ultimate goal], *Nihon Keizai Shimbun*, November 28, 2005.

27. Koizumi Junichiro, General Policy Speech to the Diet, 162d sess., January 21, 2005, http://www.kantei.go.jp/foreign/koizumispeech/2005/01/21sisei_e.html.

28. Based on Ministry of Foreign Affairs (MOFA) official, interview by author, October 25, 2006, Tokyo.

29. MOFA official, interview by author, November 2, 2006, Tokyo.

30. Japanese government official, interview by author, January 30, 2007, Tokyo.

31. For an explanation of the Yasukuni Shrine controversy, see chapter 4, note 29.

32. Kokubun Ryosei, "Ima wo yomitoku: Higashi Ajia kyodotai no mirai" [Interpreting current issues: The future of the East Asian community], *Nihon Keizai Shimbun*, March 18, 2007.

33. In his influential report to Japan's House of Councilors in 2005, Tanaka Naoki, president of the 21st Century Public Policy Institute, argued that despite growing economic regional interdependence, East Asia cannot form a regional economic network by itself, given the continued importance of transpacific trade and financial ties. He concluded that in economic terms, any concept of an East Asian community that excluded the United States would not make sense. He also noted the growth of transpacific trade deals, such as the South Korea–U.S. FTA, which would ultimately complicate the building of a narrower community in East Asia. See Tanaka Naoki, *Higashi Asia kyoudoutai kousou jitsugen heno kadai* [*Steps for realizing the East Asia community plan*] (Tokyo: 21st Century Public Policy Institute, April 22, 2005), http://www.21ppi.org/japanese/hitokoto/tanaka215.html. Nakajima Mineo, president of Kokusai Kyoyo University, asserts that East Asia's political and cultural diversity is too overwhelming to make economic or functional cooperation feasible. He points in particular to China's continental nature, Korea's peninsular nature, and Japan's insular nature, which together create cultural and civilizational differences too large to bridge. See Nakajima Mineo, "Higashi Ajia Kyōdōtai wa genjitsuron na no ka?" [Can the building of an East Asian community become a reality?], *Sankei Shimbun*, August 1, 2005. Yoshino Fumio, a professor with Takushoku University, argues that East Asia has achieved regional interdependence without institutional integration and the ceding of sovereignty. For Yoshino, an Asia community based on institutionalization will only lead to a clash of national interests. Moreover, he argues that the future of Chinese economic growth, which is the incentive for community building, is uncertain. Like other realists in Japan, he calls the advocates of an East Asian community misguided romantics rather than liberalists and says they are not qualified to discuss real policies. See Yoshino Fumio, *Higashi Ajia Kyodotai ha honto ni hitsuyo nano ka?* [*Is an East Asia community really necessary?*] (Tokyo: Hokuseido, 2006), 219–30.

34. Tanaka Hitoshi, e-mail message to author, May 13, 2007.

35. Hitoshi Tanaka, "Nationalistic Sentiments in Japan and Their Foreign Policy Implications," *East Asia Insights* 2, no. 71 (2007): 1–5. Tanaka, a former deputy minister of foreign affairs and key architect of the Koizumi government's approach to regionalism, ardently promotes the Asian community concept as a way to build a "better Asia." He acknowledges, however, that the process will also require governments across the region to improve their governance. See Tanaka Hitoshi, "Higashiajia, Nihon, setumei sekininn" [East Asia, Japan, and accountability], *Asahi Shimbun*, February 5, 2007. In other words, rather than be stymied by the lack of common values in the region, Japan can use the community-building concept to help narrow the normative gap among nations. For Tanaka, this option is a matter of realism rather than idealism. Japanese foreign policy is at a crossroad sixty years after the end of the World War II as the relative population declines and other powers such as India and China are set to increase their influence over the next fifteen years. Shaping the regional strategic environment will be critical for Japan, and community building based on functional cooperation can help to narrow mistrust and gradually create common values that will help to underpin Japanese security during a period of shifting power dynamics. See Tanaka Hitoshi, "21 seiki Nihongaikō no senryaku-teki kadai" [Strategic agenda for Japanese diplomacy in the twenty-first century], *Gaikō Forum*, no. 207 (2005): 8–13. Tanaka sees multilayered regionalism such as CEPEA and the Six-Party Talks as necessary, and he specifically proposed an East Asia security forum—with the core members of ASEAN Plus Six and the United States—as a cooperative security framework on nontraditional security issues such as nonproliferation of weapons of mass destruction, counterterrorism, counterpiracy, and human security. See Hitoshi Tanaka, "East Asia Community Building: Toward an 'East Asia Security Forum,'" *East Asia Insights Toward Community Building* 2, no. 2 (2007), http://www.jcie.or.jp/insights/2-2.html. Other influential scholars who remain confident about the potential for community building include Watanabe Toshio, president of Takushoku University, who admits that an Asian community will not be possible as long as China and the two Koreas continue institutionalizing anti-Japanese sentiment in order to retain a cohesive national identity. However, he sees the merit of a regional East Asian FTA because governments in the region also have an indispensable national interest in trade and investment. See Watanabe Toshio, "Higashi Ajia Kyōdōtai wa seiritsu suru ka?" [Can an East Asian community be built?], in *Nihon no Higashi Ajia senryaku* [*Japan's strategy toward East Asian economic integration*] (Tokyo: Toyo Keizai Shinpo Sha, 2005), 207, 218. Hatakeyama Noboru, former METI vice minister, argues that community building requires that members share values and are willing to share burdens with other members, conditions that do not characterize current relations among Japan, South Korea, and China. However, work on an East Asian FTA would not necessarily require a loss of sovereignty in areas related to values or security. See Hatakeyama Noboru, "Higashi Ajia Kyōdōtai no gensō o suteyo" [Give up the fantasy of an East Asia community], *Chūō Kōron*, September 2005, 154–61.

36. Senior MOFA official Kohara Masahiro captures this view when he argues that transnational cooperation in the region will provide economic benefits and will institutionalize "win-win relations" in an era of globalization and interdependence. See Kohara Masahiro, *Higashi Ajia kyodotai: Kyodaika suru Chugoku to Nihon no senryaku* [*The East Asian community: Growing Chinese power and Japanese strategy*] (Tokyo: Nihon Keizai Shimbun Sha, 2005), 248–50). Shindō Eiichi, professor emeritus of Tsukuba University, echoes this view, noting that the information revolution will increasingly reinforce a sense of common challenges and common purpose. See Shindō Eiichi, *Higashi Ajia kyodotai wo dou tsukuruka* [*How to build an East Asian community*] (Tokyo: Chikuma Shobo, 2007). Others, such as Iwate University president Taniguchi Makoto, see in Asia's current cooperation the seeds of what eventually led to full integration in Europe. See Taniguchi Makoto, "Kikiteki Ajia gaikō wo ikani tate-naosu ka?" [How will we remake Asian diplomacy?], *Chūō Kōron*, April 2006, 314. Shiraishi Takashi, vice president of the National Graduate Institute for Policy Studies, highlights functional cooperation in the area of nontraditional security in East Asia and notes that although European-style community building may be difficult for Asia, there is a prospect for linking the strands of strong bilateral relationships in Asia into a network that reinforces broader regional peace and stability. See Shiraishi Takashi, "ASEAN jiku ni tenkai" [The development of an East Asian community around ASEAN], *Yomiuri Shimbun*, September 4, 2005.

37. Soeya Yoshihide, "Higashi Ajia Kyōdotai tenbō to kadai: Kyūkyoku wa anzen hoshō kyōdōtai" [East Asian community, problems and prospects: Security community is the ultimate goal], *Nihon Keizai Shimbun*, November 28, 2005.

38. ASEAN Secretariat, "Kuala Lumpur Declaration on the East Asia Summit," Kuala Lumpur, Malaysia, December 14, 2005, http://www.mofa.go.jp/region/asia-paci/eas/joint0512.html.

39. Koizumi Junichiro, "Japan and ASEAN in East Asia: A Sincere and Open Partnership," remarks, Singapore, January 14, 2002, http://210.163.22.165/region/asia-paci/pmv0201/speech.html.

40. Abe Shinzo, Policy Speech to the Diet, 166th sess., January 26, 2007, http://www.kantei.go.jp/foreign/abespeech/2007/01/26speech_e.html.

41. Aso Taro, "Arch of Freedom and Prosperity: Japan's Expanding Diplomatic Horizons," remarks, Japan Institute of International Affairs, Tokyo, November 30, 2006, http://www.mofa.go.jp/announce/fm/aso/speech0611.html.

42. "Japan-Australia Joint Declaration on Security Cooperation," March 13, 2007, http://www.mofa.go.jp/region/asia-paci/asutralia/joint0703.html.

43. METI official, interview by author, October 25, 2006, Tokyo.

44. Koizumi, "Japan and ASEAN in East Asia."

45. "Higashi Ajia shunōo kaigi 14 nichi Mareshia de kaisai" [East Asia Summit to start in Malaysia on the 14th]," *Sankei Shimbun*, December 8, 2005; "Kinrin gaikō, heisoku tsuyomaru" [Relations with neighbors becoming tense], *Tokyo Shimbun*, De-

cember 5, 2005. See also Nishiguchi Kiyokatsu, "Higashi Ajia no kyodotai kochiku to Nihon no senryaku" [East Asia community building and Japanese strategy], in *Higashi Ajia kyodotai no kochiku* [*East Asia community building*], ed. Nishiguchi Kiyokatu and Go Ka (Tokyo: Mineruva Shobo, 2006), 3.

46. ASEAN Secretariat, "Kuala Lumpur Declaration on the ASEAN + 3 Summit," Kuala Lumpur, Malaysia, December 12, 2005, http://www.mofa.go.jp/region/asia-paci/asean/conference/asean3/jointo512.html, emphasis added.

47. ASEAN Secretariat, "Kuala Lumpur Declaration on the East Asia Summit," emphasis added.

48. Michael J. Green, "Democracy and the Balance of Power in Asia," *American Interest* 2, no. 1 (2006): 96.

49. MOFA official, interview by author, January 30, 2007, Tokyo.

50. Ibid.

51. ASEAN Secretariat, "Kuala Lumpur Declaration of the ASEAN + 3 Summit."

52. ASEAN Secretariat, "Kuala Lumpur Declaration on the East Asia Summit."

53. MOFA official, interview by author, November 2, 2006, Tokyo; METI official, interview by author, October 25, 2006, Tokyo.

54. Koizumi, "Japan and ASEAN in East Asia."

55. Koizumi Junichiro, "Japan and Australia: Toward a Creative Partnership," speech, Sydney, Australia, May 1, 2003, http://www.mofa.go.jp/region/asia-paci/pmv0204/speech.html.

56. MOFA official, interview by author, November 2, 2007, Tokyo.

57. Abe Shinzo, Policy Speech to the Diet, 165th sess., September 29, 2006, http://www.kantei.go.jp/jp/abespeech/2006/09/29syoshin.html.

58. Aso Taro, "Statement at the Fourteenth SAARC Summit," New Delhi, April 3, 2007, http://210.163.22.165/region/asia-paci/saarc/state0704.html.

59. MOFA official, briefing given to author, January 30, 2007.

6. India and the Asian Security Architecture

C. Raja Mohan

MULTILATERALISM: REGIONAL AND GLOBAL

Multilateralism, whether regional or global, has always had a powerful appeal in the Indian foreign-policy discourse. The near century-long Indian national movement, built as it was on liberal ideas, was strongly devoted to the notion of internationalism. As India approached its independence after the end of World War II, it was commonplace for the Indian elite to argue that power politics was passé and to emphasize the importance of building collective security. Linked to this approach was the Indian enthusiasm for global and regional multilateral institutions as effective instruments for dealing with the postwar challenges of security and development. At the regional level, the idea of "Asian unity" and "solidarity of the newly decolonized states" lent a powerful impetus to the notion of multilateralism. Jawaharlal Nehru, India's first prime minister, often talked about an "Eastern federation" encompassing India, China, and a number of Asian nations to the east and west of India. Months before its independence, India took the lead in organizing the Asian Relations Conference in 1947 to focus on regional political cooperation.[1]

However, for a variety of reasons, this initial interest in multilateralism soon gave way to a more narrowly defined wariness that in many ways left India marginalized from the political and economic dynamics of Asia. Beginning in the 2000s, though, multilateralism and Asian regionalism again emerged as a top foreign-policy priority for New Delhi and the Indian foreign-policy elite. Today India has reached the determination to be a part of the regionalism forming in Asia and even to take a leading role where it can, with all of the challenges and opportunities that will entail. To review and assess these developments, this chapter first provides a historical overview of India's approach to regional security architectures and looks at the sources and debates around these issues in Indian circles. It then spells out Indian perceptions of the U.S. role in the region and concludes with a look at some of the enduring Indian principles regarding the security architecture in Asia.

HISTORICAL OVERVIEW

Despite their enduring rhetoric in favor of liberal internationalism, Indian governments repeatedly had to confront the tension between supporting multilateralism and liberal internationalism, on the one hand, and pursuing India's national interests, on the other. India's decision to take its dispute with Pakistan regarding Jammu and Kashmir to the United Nations Security Council (UNSC) in 1948 on a voluntary basis was premised on the hope that the United Nations would be fair in its approach to the conflict with Pakistan.[2] But the responses of the Western powers in the UNSC and their tilt toward Pakistan made India determined thereafter to prevent the multilateral system's intrusion into areas that related to its own national security and territorial integrity. The induction of Pakistan into U.S. regional security alliances such as the Southeast Asia Treaty Organization and the Central Treaty Organization made India deeply critical of the U.S. alliance systems in the region, pushed it closer to the Soviet Union, and reinforced the domestic consensus in favor of nonalignment.[3] The Cold War's impact on the subcontinent and Asia, the growing tensions with China on Tibet and the border, and the deepening divisions within Asia put paid to the prospects of Asian unity that Nehru had sought to promote. The inward-looking economic orientation mandated by state socialism not only turned India against economic multilateralism, but also undermined the historic trade and commercial linkages between India and its neighboring regions in Asia. As a consequence, India became increasingly marginal to the dynamics of Asia.[4]

The Indian focus tended to be global, thanks to its presumed leadership of the Nonaligned Movement. India vigorously pursued a whole range of issues regarding a new international economic order that sought to redefine the unequal relationship between the developed North and the underdeveloped South within the framework of the G-77 at the United Nations General Assembly. The only regional exception to this preoccupation with multilateralism and Third

Worldism at the global level during the Cold War was the South Asian Association for Regional Cooperation (SAARC), which was established in 1985. In many ways, SAARC was the exception that proved India's entrenched disinterest in regional multilateralism.[5] When Bangladesh first floated the idea for SAARC, India was deeply suspicious of it. India feared that its smaller neighbors, with which it had increasingly frayed relations, would use the forum to gang up on India. New Delhi was also apprehensive that Pakistan might use SAARC to rake up the dispute over Jammu and Kashmir in a multilateral context. Unable to say "no," India made sure that the SAARC Charter would exclude the discussion of all bilateral disputes and underline the necessity of unanimity in all of the forum's key decisions. All South Asian countries were stuck with the notion of building "socialism in one country," so there was no real prospect that South Asian regionalism would take off when SAARC was constructed.[6]

It was only with the end of Cold War and the launch of sweeping economic reforms in 1991 that India rediscovered the importance of economic multilateralism. Recognizing the importance of accessing external finance and technology markets, finding itself completely isolated from the Asian economic dynamism, and becoming apprehensive about Chinese economic successes, India launched its "Look East" policy in the early 1990s by befriending the Southeast Asian nations.[7] India thereafter steadily became an active part of the Association of Southeast Asian Nations (ASEAN), including its security adjunct the ASEAN Regional Forum. The postreform years also saw India engage in a variety of other regional multilateral forums. One was the Indian Ocean Rim Association for Regional Cooperation established by thirteen countries, including Australia, India, Indonesia, Singapore, and South Africa. Although this association presented India with an opportunity to assume economic leadership in an area that was its natural strategic *spielraum*, India was as yet unprepared for substantive regional integration. In addition, on the political front it had differences with other participants on the question of taking up security-related issues in the forum.[8]

India was wary of a proposal from Beijing in the late 1990s, called the Kunming Initiative, to promote regional cooperation between China's southwestern provinces, on the one hand, and Burma (Myanmar), Bangladesh, and India's northeastern regions, on the other. Unwilling to forget Chinese support of insurgencies in India's northeastern provinces in the past and apprehensive about throwing open the restive provinces to transborder cooperation, India held back from official participation in the initiative.[9] More significant, concerned about China's rising profile in India's eastern neighborhood, and underlining the need to counter it in some form, India unveiled the so-called Mekong Ganga Initiative for regional cooperation with Burma, Cambodia, Laos, Thailand, and Vietnam. The Indian proposals were clearly driven by a desire to create regional forums that excluded China.[10] India was also enthusiastic about a Thai initiative called the Bay of Bengal Initiative for Multi-Sectoral Technical and Economic Cooperation (BIMSTEC), which was to bring together parts of South Asia with Southeast Asia.[11]

Toward the end of the 1990s, India saw the importance of injecting some life into SAARC and began to press for greater economic cooperation within the subcontinent. It also began to redefine its trade relations with some of its smaller neighbors on a bilateral basis. It had always had a fairly open trading regime on a bilateral basis with Nepal and Bhutan, and in 2000 it unveiled a similar arrangement with Sri Lanka.[12] It has actively supported the negotiation of a free-trade agreement (FTA) for the region, but enduring conflict between India and Pakistan and the wariness between India and its smaller neighbors has prevented an accelerated movement toward regional integration.[13] Until its partition along religious lines in 1947, the subcontinent was a single integrated economic space. Yet by 2007 South Asia had become one of the least-integrated regions of the world.[14] Recognizing the political and economic dangers of the status quo, India has increasingly sought to accelerate South Asian economic integration, through unilateral means if necessary.[15]

But it was ASEAN that became the principal vehicle for India's Asian regionalism. By the turn of the millennium, India was being increasingly socialized into the ASEAN structures, and as its own economic reforms gathered momentum, it began to take up the prospect of both bilateral and multilateral FTAs with the ASEAN states. India signed an FTA with Thailand in 2003 and the Comprehensive Economic Cooperation Agreement with Singapore in 2005, which also involved liberalization of services. The early years of the new century saw India embark on negotiations with a large number of countries and regional organizations on preferential and free-trade arrangements.[16]

At the political level, India steadily expanded the ambit of its Look East policy. In geographic terms, it was now including Australia, China, Japan, the Korean Peninsula, and the South Pacific in its single most important post–Cold War diplomatic initiative. Once it became part of the ASEAN structures in the late 1990s, it began to emphasize the restoration of physical connectivities with the neighboring regions of Asia. Security cooperation, initially latent in the Look East policy, acquired a new prominence as the Indian navy began to acquire a more solid outward orientation. The negotiation of a bilateral defense cooperation agreement with Singapore in 2003 marked India's first substantive and explicit security arrangement in the region. India's wide-ranging military exercises with a number of major powers and regional actors in the Asia-Pacific and Indian Ocean regions since the early 1990s began to acquire a more institutional traction.[17]

As Asian multilateralism and regional security cooperation reemerged at the top of the Indian foreign-policy agenda, New Delhi had to stay abreast of the rapid diplomatic developments on the new plans in Northeast and Southeast

Asia to forge an East Asian community. As the initial debates in ASEAN began, India put forward its own interest in Asian economic integration by suggesting an FTA among ASEAN, China, India, Japan, and South Korea. In an address to the India-ASEAN business summit in New Delhi in October 2004, Prime Minister Manmohan Singh said:

> It is only inevitable that we seek to take the existing India-ASEAN relationship to a higher level, where we envision an Asian Economic Community, which encompasses ASEAN, China, Japan, Korea and India. Such a community would release enormous creative energies of our people. One cannot but be captivated by the vision of an integrated market, spanning the distance from the Himalayas to the Pacific Ocean, linked by efficient road, rail, air and shipping services. This community of nations would constitute an "arc of advantage," across which there would be large-scale movement of people, capital, ideas, and creativity. Such a community would be roughly the size of the European Union in terms of income, and bigger than NAFTA [North American Free Trade Agreement] in terms of trade. It would account for half the world's population and it would hold foreign exchange reserves exceeding those of the EU and NAFTA put together. This is an idea whose time is fast approaching, and we must be prepared for it collectively.[18]

Implicit in this statement was the political determination that India should not be left out of the potential new regional arrangements taking shape in East and Southeast Asia. Having found itself outside the earlier transregional institutions such as the Asia-Pacific Economic Cooperation (APEC) forum and the Asia Europe Meeting, India was focused this time on ensuring a place at the proposed first East Asia Summit (EAS). Amid a furious ASEAN debate on which countries should be invited to the EAS, India embarked on a purposeful diplomatic campaign within ASEAN to secure an invitation. With strong support from Indonesia, Vietnam, and Singapore, ASEAN finally decided to invite India to the first EAS. Sino-Indian competition was also reflected in issues of EAS membership. Whereas China sought to keep India out of the membership and to subordinate the role of the EAS to that of ASEAN Plus Three, India devoted considerable diplomatic energy to gaining membership in the EAS and steering it toward a potential leadership role in the creation of an Asian order, even in the face of strong opposition from Beijing.[19] In any event, India's membership in the EAS marked its return to the center stage of East Asia, a region that for decades had argued that India had no place in it. Yet membership also opened up new political challenges in influencing the new regional multilateralism and the future security architecture of Asia.

INDIA'S ASIAN REGIONALISM: SOURCES AND DEBATES

Asian solidarity against colonialism, a shared sense of an Asian cultural identity superior to Western civilization, and the idea that India should shoulder the responsibility to lead Asia were three powerful notions that shaped India's attitudes to regionalism in the early years of the twentieth century. As the Indian national movement gained momentum in the period between the world wars and the new elite began to rediscover India's own history and its rich interaction with the rest of the continent, romanticism about Asia overpowered most Indian leaders, including Rabindranath Tagore, Mohandas Karamchand Gandhi, and Jawaharlal Nehru. Although these ideas crashed against unpleasant realities after the decolonization of Asia, they continued to provide stimuli for India's Look East policy in the final years of the twentieth century.[20]

However, the fact that India's new pan-Asian consciousness was built on a foundation of Indian nationalism complicated India's conduct of its foreign policy toward Asia. As one analyst put it, "While Pan-Asianism was based initially on the premises of Asian cultural and spiritual unity, the unique moral mission of the Orient, and the desirability of reviving Greater India, nationalist Indians injected a political character into the concept by advancing the notion of creating some form of Asian political federation under Indian leadership".[21] This notion, however, was premature and ultimately disillusioned. According to the same analyst,

Emerging imperialism in Japan, Indian ambivalence toward the Nationalist Government in China, growing anti-Indian feelings in South and Southeast Asia, and the paucity of contacts between Indian nationalists and their counterparts in many Asian countries, all boded ill for Asian political unity—and the actual attempts to promote solidarity reflected these problems. . . . Once promulgated, however, the Pan-Asian idea was difficult to dispel, and it persisted into the independence period, thereby heightening India's sense of disillusionment when the concept's inevitable demise occurred. One unfortunate result was the subsequent Indian neglect of the potential for more limited—but more practical—forms of regional cooperation.[22]

India's difficulties in bringing Asia together were evident pretty quickly at the Asian Relations Conference in 1947. A contemporaneous review summed up the problems: "The aim of India was also to acquire implicitly some form of leadership in Asia. It was therefore significant that the meeting was boycotted as a maneuver of 'Hindu Imperialism' by Jinnah's Muslim League, which a few months later became the government of Pakistan. The small countries of South East Asia and Ceylon favored in principle the creation of an Asian bloc. At the same time they emphasized their fear that European imperialism might be replaced by Indian or Chinese imperialism." Even on the question of shared objectives of decolonization, "there was considerable divergence of opinion between the Indonesians and Vietnamese who wanted armed help and Nehru who favored moral support."[23]

The notion of Indian leadership of Asia had a source other than a nationalist romantic view of Asian unity. It was inspired by Lord Curzon, easily the most remembered British viceroy to India at the turn of the twentieth century, who laid out a vision of Indian primacy in the Indian Ocean and southern Asian regions.[24] Conceived at the peak of British imperial power, rooted in India's geographic location, and based on the real contributions of the Indian army in the maintenance of regional peace and security during the period from the mid–nineteenth century to the beginning of the twentieth century, Curzon's conceptions of India's primacy seeped into the strategic thinking of the Indian establishment. Central to this legacy is the notion of Indian primacy or veto in a region stretching from the Aden to the Malaccas. A section of the British establishment articulated this notion right until the final days of the empire in the subcontinent and insisted that independent India must remain at the center of any Western strategy of securing Asia.[25] An Indian realist tradition too emerged that rejected Gandhi's commitment to "nonviolence" and the pervasive growth of Indian pacifism. A leading proponent of this realist school argued that "once we are free from the effects of this idea [pacifism], and are thus enabled to look at facts in the face, it will be clear that Indian freedom can be achieved and upheld only by firmly deciding to shoulder our share at all costs in the active defense of the areas necessary for our security".[26] K. M. Panikkar called for strong defense capabilities, consolidation of security relationships with key nations in Southeast Asia and the Persian Gulf, and the development of a robust maritime strategy. Even as he underlined the centrality of India in the defense of Indian Ocean littoral, Panikkar called for a multilateral approach in the form of a "regional council" to underwrite security. "Clearly no country in the region is able on its own to undertake the responsibility of ensuring peace and security in the area," he wrote. "Owing to the weakness of the units comprising this area and their great importance as the reservoir of raw materials, the organization of the region for security is of vital importance to future world peace." Panikkar went on to point out that "[i]n population, resources and the general potential for ensuring security, India alone in [South Asia] is in a position to make an effective contribution."[27]

The idea of India's leading the future political and security arrangements in Asia and the Indian Ocean was not limited to just a section of the Indian establishment. It was at the core of Jawaharlal Nehru's conception as he led India for the first seventeen years after its independence in 1947. Speaking to the Indian Constituent Assembly in January 1947, Nehru declared that India's independence "will lead also to the freedom of the countries of Asia, because in a sense, however unworthy, we have become—let us recognize it—the leaders of the freedom movement of Asia, and whatever we do, we should think of ourselves in these larger terms. . . . [W]e shoulder . . . the responsibility of the leadership of a large part of Asia, the responsibility of being some kind of guide to vast numbers of people all over the world."[28]

New Delhi's enthusiasm for leading postcolonial Asia, however, was continually undermined by India's complex and volatile relationship with China. For much of the world, the rise of China is a recent phenomenon. For Indian nationalists, however, the putative emergence of China as a powerful force in world politics was an acknowledged reality from the early decades of the twentieth century. From the interwar period, the belief that the two Asian giants were destined to be partners was in many ways emblematic of India's romanticization of Asia, but in confronting different imperial powers in their own liberation struggles, the Indian and Chinese nationalists found it impossible to agree on common positions on world issues or to construct a stable relationship with each other.[29] Beijing's assertion of control over Tibet in 1950 made China a neighbor of India and produced new challenges in defining an agreed border. Nehru sought to cope with the new situation by a policy of simultaneous engagement and containment. The mutual distrust over Tibet resulted in India's concluding bilateral security treaties with the vulnerable kingdoms of Nepal, Bhutan, and Sikkim during 1949 and 1950. At the same time, Nehru hoped that engaging with Communist China and bringing it into the mainstream of Asian politics would be better than seeking to isolate it. With this perspective, much to the dismay of the West and some Asian countries, he invited China to the Bandung Conference in 1955 and hoped to "introduce" his friend Zhou Enlai to other Asian leaders. Instead, the charming and conciliatory Zhou took advantage of the opportunity to upstage Nehru.[30] The Bandung Conference, which essentially was about celebrating newly won freedom and exploring prospects for cooperation, produced a shift in the regional balance that was not to India's benefit. The group that founded the Bandung Conference—Burma, India, Indonesia, Pakistan, and Sri Lanka—faded as a cohesive force, China and Pakistan drew closer, and India became marginalized from Asia.[31] China's coup de grace against India's ambitions to lead Asia came in 1962, when Beijing inflicted a humiliating military defeat on New Delhi on the Indo-Tibetan borders. China, in pursuit of international recognition of its standing as a great power, had first to befriend India—at the time preeminent in Asia—then to humble it.

After 1962, India's emphasis was on containing China. Whether in its active support for the Tibetan cause, its enduring alignment with Moscow, or its support of Hanoi's intervention in Cambodia, India's foreign policy in the 1960s and 1970s revolved around its hostility toward China. Beginning in the late 1980s, India sought a rapprochement with Deng Xiaoping's China. Despite some bumps on the road, the depth and range of the relationship have steadily expanded since then. That expansion in no way, however, erases the determination in New Delhi to compete and catch up with Beijing, which has marched ahead of India since the late 1970s.[32] China serves a number of functions in the Indian political discourse on Asian security. It is a constant spur for India to overcome its own inhibitions in thinking big about Asian regionalism. Whether regarding domestic economic reform or the need for India to play a greater role in Asia, the Chinese example tends to be the clincher in the domestic debates on Asia. Underlying this attitude is the simple reality that India will not accept any political ranking behind China. Despite the current positive phase in Sino-Indian relations, balancing China remains an overriding strategic objective for India.

The reestablishment of India's centrality in Asian economic and security politics has undoubtedly become an important national strategic objective in New Delhi. The political leadership at the highest level recognizes that India has fallen behind China and has marginalized itself from the Asian dynamism since the 1970s. Indian leaders also recognize that the challenge since the early 1990s has not been how to "lead" Asia, but how to find ways to emulate it in the economic arena. New Delhi's attempt to regain India's standing, however, is complicated by the domestic politics of economic reform. Two very different governments—one led by the right-of-center Atal Bihari Vajpayee that ruled India between 1999 and 2004 and the other led by the left-of-center Manmohan Singh beginning in 2004—fully understood the historic nature of the structural shift in the global balance of power toward Asia and the importance of India's ensuring its rightful place in the future security architecture of Asia. Reflecting this understanding, the Foreign Office has been actively focused on ensuring India's participation in a range of Asian institutional initiatives. Whether in the initial drive toward becoming a part of ASEAN structures or in the more recent campaign to ensure an invitation to the first EAS, the Foreign Office has been at the forefront of India's engagement with Asia. Both Vajpayee and Singh were strong supporters of expanded engagement with Asia and often sided with the Foreign Office to overrule opposition from other sections of the government.[33]

Yet the resistance from domestic economic interests and the inherited negotiating strategies in world economic forums have undermined India's ability to respond effectively to the new challenges it has confronted in a globalizing

Asia. Although India did alter its grand economic strategy from inward socialist development to liberalization and globalization in 1991, it has continuously struggled to overcome resistance from different sections of the national establishment. The most important of these sections is the Indian capitalist class itself. Battened for years under protectionist policies, large sections of the private sector are not ready to yield their domestic markets to foreign competition. Although the dynamic sectors of the Indian capital are making waves around the world, the resistance from those demanding protection is substantive. Put another way, the Indian capitalist class is at a crossroads. Until there is new consensus that gaining access to external markets is more important than defending one's own turf, there will be pressure on India not to yield on trade liberalization. Even the industry associations, which have emerged as general champions of liberalization at home, often campaign against FTAs.[34] Agriculture is in a unique category of its own, and no political leader in India is prepared to open up that sector for cheap imports and present himself as an opponent of the Indian peasant and farmer. Unlike in the West, where the farming community is miniscule in comparison to the total population, in India it remains a large segment of the population.

Beginning in the late 1980s, even as the protected capitalist class insisted on continued protection—or at least a sequence in which the domestic industry would be better placed to compete with cheaper exports from outside—the left, the liberals, and the populist right together whipped up fears about the General Agreement on Tariffs and Trade (GATT) and the World Trade Organization (WTO) and their supposed aim to undermine India's sovereignty. The agrarian interests were afraid that cheaper imports would undercut their high-cost production; the Indian trade unions opposed trade liberalization; and newly mushrooming nongovernmental organizations and free-standing radicals joined forces with the movement against globalization around the world. Although India was in many ways a significant beneficiary of the new wave of globalization, few constituencies in India were willing to call for unabashed trade liberalization and opening of the Indian market. This resistance in turn made it more attractive for Indian political leaders to grandstand against the WTO rather than to engage in effective bargaining and mutual give and take.[35] From the perspective of the Indian establishment as a whole, a pragmatic approach to trade liberalization should have come from the professional bureaucracies manning the Commerce Ministry, the lead agency in external trade negotiations. A deeply ingrained tradition of defending the protectionist impulses and an emphasis on standing firm rather than winning beneficial outcomes through compromises became India's negotiating style at GATT and WTO meetings. Although this approach might have made sense before the era of economic reforms, India's persistent negativism has since then tended to produce suboptimal outcomes for the nation's collective interests. Much of this strategy has often been justified as defending the interests of the developing world, but in reality it only underlines the problems of transition from a "developing country identity" to an "aspiring great power identity."[36] India's hard line at the WTO can be presented as a North-South confrontation, but its failure to move toward FTAs with its developing country neighbors either in Southeast Asia or the subcontinent reflects the power of the Indian capitalist class, which is unwilling to cede its market space to outsiders. This unwillingness, in turn, is reinforced by a strategic culture that has often reveled in saying "no."[37]

The Indian political leadership recognizes the long-term dangers of going slow on economic integration with East Asia. Despite strong political commitments made by Indian leaders in the engagement with the ASEAN leaders, its industry and bureaucracy have tended to slow down the process, which at one point led to political embarrassment from a public spat between India and ASEAN on the eve of the first EAS.[38] India's credibility as a regional player will hinge in a large measure on the political leadership's strength to pull together the diverse elements in India in order to accelerate integration with East Asia and South Asia.

INDIA'S CHANGING RELATIONSHIP WITH THE UNITED STATES

India, with nonalignment as the presumed leitmotif of its foreign policy, was always perceived to be in opposition to alliances in general and especially to those formed by the United States in Asia. That India was opposed in principle to the notion of alliances is a carefully nurtured national myth.[39] A simpler explanation is that India employed nonalignment as a balance-of-power strategy to protect its autonomy: "Such a policy is aimed at maintaining the security of a relatively weak state intact against the possible pressures, stemming from international conflicts, of overwhelmingly powerful states. . . . [Nehru] has created an extremely potent myth in the Asian and African world, that of [India's] dissociation from the power politics of the great powers. Under its cover, a nonaligned policy can manipulate in a variety of directions"[40]

It is possible to view India's relationship with the Soviet Union, in particular during the 1970s and 1980s, as a de facto alliance that was aimed at balancing the U.S. partnership with Pakistan and China. India was opposed to the U.S. alliance system in the region not because of the principle of nonalignment, but because the system included India's principal adversaries. Although it was in fact prepared to embark on alliances, as it did with the Soviet Union, it was not prepared to become a junior partner to Moscow. The need to protect its freedom of action tended to prevail over the demands of discipline and the subordination of interests that a formal alliance would entail. In that sense, *nonalignment* was a code word for "independent foreign policy."

Amid the unfolding structural changes in the Asian balance of power, India's future orientation toward U.S. alliances in the region and the prospect of New Delhi's alliance with the United States have become consequential questions. India's defense cooperation with the United States significantly expanded under the George W. Bush administration in the 2000s. India carefully considered the deployment of a division of troops to Iraq in 2003, but held back in the end because of domestic political considerations.[41] At the end of 2004, it participated in coalition operations for tsunami relief and signed a broader framework for military cooperation with the United States in June 2005.[42] For the first time, India was outlining broad missions for its armed forces in cooperation with other major powers. It had long been a major participant in the United Nations peacekeeping operations and has often used force beyond its own borders within the subcontinent. Yet it traditionally has been reluctant to send troops beyond its presumed sphere of influence without United Nations authorization. The duality in the Indian policy can be interpreted as a prudent management of political risk in foreign interventions rather than as a high principle. India's serious consideration of sending troops to Iraq, its probable interest in contributing to the international stabilization force in Afghanistan, and its willingness to join the tsunami relief operations suggest that it might increasingly be ready to join U.S.-led military coalition operations in Asia.[43]

During the Bush years, the intensified exchanges between the two armed forces have begun to clear the ground for a significant arms-transfer relationship. India's decision to acquire the USS *Trenton* in 2006 and six C-130 military transport aircraft in the same year marks the first transfers of major weapons platforms by Washington to New Delhi. The Bush administration's decision to assist India's rise to power, especially its military capabilities, has opened the door for unprecedented defense industrial collaboration between the two nations. As the U.S. defense industry comes to terms with globalization, and as India begins to encourage private-sector participation in a defense production long dominated by inefficient public-sector enterprises and to leverage the massive size of its armament procurement, a new synergy has begun to emerge between the two nations.[44] Expanding Indo-U.S. defense cooperation has often been perceived in terms of the rise of China. It is important, however, not to miss the nuances here. Neither the United States nor India has made a decision in favor of containing China. Both nations nevertheless find deeper bilateral security cooperation a prudent hedge against the rise of China.

Two broad propositions might be stated here. India's main objective is to emerge as an indispensable element in the Asian balance of power. Given its history and location, India is likely to pursue this objective irrespective of an alliance with the United States. But strategic cooperation with the United States might immensely strengthen India's future options. Given India's reluctance to enter into unequal alliances, strategic coordination with the United States, something less than an alliance, would be a more likely option for Indian planners.[45] Amid the rise of China and its geopolitical consequences for the regional balance of power, India has been more willing than ever before to expand security and political cooperation with the United States not merely in a bilateral framework, but also in multilateral forums.

At a time when the Bush administration was widely criticized in Asia for its unilateralism and its opposition to multilateralism, India was surprisingly silent. Traditionally the biggest champion of multilateralism, it now found the new opportunities for bilateral cooperation with the United States too valuable to indulge in its traditional rhetoric. India's reluctance to join the rest of the world in the chorus against U.S. unilateralism was a reflection not merely of diplomatic opportunism, but of the somewhat poorly understood complexity of the Indian attitudes to both multilateralism and national sovereignty. India's enthusiasm for Third Worldism and collective bargaining by the undeveloped countries against the developed never completely obscured its own ambitions to become a major power in its own right or its unwillingness to limit its sovereignty under the presumed advantages of multilateralism. An appreciation of India's "great-power attitude" perhaps also explains the interesting convergence with U.S. policies in the 2000s on a range of controversial issues, such as missile defense, the International Criminal Court (ICC), and global warming. On missile defense, India's security interests in breaking out of the nuclear box in which it had been locked with Pakistan and China has now become aligned with Bush administration views.[46] Reflecting India's strong belief in the notion of sovereignty, New Delhi has taken positions on the ICC similar to Washington's. On global warming, India's emphasis on growth without constraint has converged with the Bush administration's.

On the trade and economic front, India has had no choice but to partake actively in the various regional proposals for integration. The pace and intensity of Indian participation in these areas will depend on domestic pressures and external stimuli. On other issues, especially political and security questions, India's response to the few multilateral initiatives taken by the Bush administration has been varied, suggesting that Indian attitudes to Asian multilateralism will depend on specifics of the issue at hand rather than consist of an omnibus support or rejection. India was pleased to join in the U.S. initiative for cooperation among key Asian countries for clean development, which recognized the Indian weight in the debate and framed the issue outside the Kyoto Protocol.[47] On the U.S.-proposed Proliferation Security Initiative (PSI), the Indian government was quite keen to join in and promised the Bush administration to do so as part of its nuclear agreement with the United States in July 2005. What held India back was not a principle, but the management of domestic politics, where opposition to the PSI crystallized around traditional arguments of legality and conformity with classical multilateralism.[48] The United States has not yet included India in its attempts to develop multilateral responses to proliferation threats in Asia—such as in North Korea and Iran. On a range of maritime security issues in the Asia Pacific, India has been eager to join in multilateral efforts, but is often confronted with the paradox of being an "outsider." Just as India urged the great powers to leave the Indian Ocean during the 1970s and 1980s, some of the littoral countries of the Malacca Straits oppose an Indian role in securing the passage. India argues that it is part of the straits because it is present at their entry and thus should not be treated as an outside power. With this approach, it has succeeded in working out a range of bilateral arrangements with the littoral states for coordinated patrolling of the straits.[49]

On the sensitive question of joining U.S.-led initiatives on the promotion of democracy in Asia, India became one of the cosponsors of the United Nations Democracy Fund (along with the United States and others) in 2005. It also supported the broad idea that Asian democracies work together, proposed by Prime Minister Abe Shinzo of Japan in 2006. In a joint statement with Abe in December 2006 in Tokyo, Manmohan Singh agreed on "the usefulness of having dialogue among India, Japan and other like-minded countries in the Asia-Pacific region on themes of mutual interest."[50] The cautiousness of this formulation was due less to Indian reluctance and more to the U.S. hesitation in offending China at a time when Beijing's role in the Six-Party Talks in North Korea had assumed substantive diplomatic significance.

India participated for the first time in a trilateral naval exercise with the United States and Japan off Guam in 2007. This participation underlines a new political will in New Delhi, suggesting its readiness to play the balancing game within Asia. On democracy promotion, however, India's attitudes are likely to be more prudent than crusading. India's emphasis will likely remain on the demonstration value of its democracy rather than on forcing it upon others. India is thus unlikely to join the United States or even the United Nations in expanding sanctions against the military regime in Burma. India's interests in Burma cut too close to the bone in New Delhi.[51]

Unlike many others in Asia, the Indian establishment is unlikely to complain about the absence of American leadership or initiatives toward collective security structures in Asia. India recognizes that the alliance system at the center of U.S. political engagement in Asia, and the prospect of any substantive new initiatives in favor of Asian multilateralism are unlikely.

Nor would India reject as a matter of principle American proposals for functional multilateral cooperation in specifically defined areas. It has signaled its interest in working with the United States, other major powers, and regional actors in a multilateral framework to combat terrorism, protect sea-lanes, and prevent the spread of weapons of mass destruction. It is prepared to join U.S.-led coalition operations in the region, but will evaluate them on a case by case basis. It has also shown an unprecedented willingness to work in the security realm either singly with the United States or jointly with the United States and its allies.

Nothing captures the transformed relationship between India and the United States better than the controversial civil nuclear initiative announced by President Bush and Prime Minister Singh at the White House on July 18, 2005.[52] The difficulties that India has faced in implementing a deal so patently in its favor also underlines the challenges in consolidating the historic breakthrough in bilateral relations. In essence, the civil nuclear initiative offered India a way out of the nuclear isolation that it found itself in after its first nuclear test in May 1974 and that was deepened by its second round of tests in May 1998. Under the rules of the international nonproliferation regime, India can either keep its nuclear weapons or have access to civilian nuclear cooperation. It cannot have both. In a bold move, Bush opened a way out by promising to change U.S. domestic nonproliferation law and to persuade the international community to change its rules to facilitate renewed global cooperation with India on its civilian nuclear program. On its part, India promised to separate its civilian and military nuclear facilities and to place the former under international safeguards. It also agreed to strengthen the global nonproliferation regime by undertaking a number of commitments. There was no shortage of critics of this deal, especially from the arms control community, who attacked it as a reckless act by the Bush administration to curry favor with India at the cost of the global nuclear order.[53] Despite widespread criticism, the U.S. Congress extended strong bipartisan support for the deal by altering U.S. nonproliferation legislation in December 2006.

If the Bush decision to invest in a long-term strategic relationship with India found a resonance within the U.S. establishment, it encountered intense and unexpected criticism in India. It was India's atomic energy establishment that first raised a series of technical objections to the deal. A victim of prolonged U.S. high-technology sanctions, the Indian Department of Atomic Energy was not prepared to accept at face value the fundamental change in U.S. nuclear policy toward India. Once these technical objections to the civil nuclear initiative were overcome, it was the turn of the Communist partners of India's ruling coalition to oppose the deal on political grounds. They saw, not incorrectly, the deal as a transformative event in India's foreign policy and an irretrievable shift toward a security partnership with Washington. The intensity of the resistance to the nuclear deal and the Communists' threat to pull down the government on the issue surprised American observers. One of them called it "the classic case of putting a bullet in a gift horse's forehead."[54] The depth of the domestic political crisis over the nuclear deal underlined its ambitious scope and significance as well as the entrenched fears within the Indian political classes about the danger of becoming a strategic subaltern to the United States. For the very same reason, the eventual implementation of the civil nuclear initiative might also mark the marginalization of long-accumulated anti-Americanism in India.

LOOKING AHEAD: ENDURING PRINCIPLES

Four enduring elements in New Delhi's strategic thinking will likely shape future Indian policy toward the evolving security architecture of Asia. First, political realism has long characterized its security policies, despite the strong rhetoric of idealism that dominated India's foreign-policy articulation for decades. Although Indian leaders have tended to downplay the significance of the notion of balance of power, this notion has always played a part in its policy toward its Asian neighbors. After its experimentation with the United Nations on the Kashmir question, India has had no stomach for placing faith in collective security arrangements. The conflicts with Pakistan on Kashmir and the confrontation with China convinced India that it must rely on itself to secure its interests. This conviction also implied the recognition of the dangers that collective security or multilateral arrangements might pose to India's own freedom of action. India repeatedly rejected proposals from the Soviet Union for collective security in Asia, despite the fact that New Delhi was in a de facto alliance with Moscow through much of the Cold War. When Soviet leader Leonid Brezhnev proposed collective security arrangements in Asia in the late 1960s and early 1970s, India remained lukewarm in public and firm in its rejection in private.[55] Similarly, when Soviet president Mikhail Gorbachev unveiled his proposal for Asian security for the first time in his meeting with Indian prime minister Rajiv Gandhi in 1985 and repeated it in his address to the Indian Parliament in 1986, India remained steadfast in its silence and was focused more on the potential implications of the unfolding Sino-Soviet rapprochement under Gorbachev.[56]

From that quiet opposition to collective security notions, India's decision makers have become increasingly bold enough to define their policy in terms of a balance of power. India's defense minister outlined two fundamental principles in 2005: "First, the maintenance of an equitable strategic balance and prevention of regional rivalries from destabilizing the region. . . . Second and more importantly, India would like to engage all players both bilaterally and collectively through institutions like the ASEAN Regional Forum. Toward this end, India has initiated a security dialogue to constructively engage all the major players in the region."[57] This probably was the first time in decades that the notion of balance found explicit articulation among Indian political leaders. Addressing an international gathering in New Delhi at the end of 2005, the Indian foreign secretary Shyam Saran further developed the case for a balance of power in Asia:

> If we are looking at Asia in the coming years, there is no doubt that there is a major realignment of forces taking place in Asia. There is the emergence of China as a global economic powerhouse. There will be increased capabilities that China will be able to bring to bear in this region and even beyond. . . . I think India and the United States can contribute to a much better balance in the Asian region. . . . We believe that in terms of managing the emerging security scenario in Asia we need to bring more and more countries within the discipline of a mutually agreed security paradigm for this region. I think both the United States and India can contribute to that.[58]

That the new security paradigm on Saran's mind was balance of power did not escape the liberal section of the Indian political class. One analyst inferred: "China, presumably, is the main country needing the 'discipline' of a 'security paradigm' to which India and the U.S. can 'contribute.' It doesn't take a lot of analysis to recognize that these ideas run counter to the new spirit so evident in Asia."[59] Given such debates and constraints, India might well consider arrangements for a system of Asian security based on a concert of great powers, but it is unlikely to endorse a collective security system for the region.

Second, India's commitment to national sovereignty in the security realm is near absolute and is unlikely to accept any proposal seeking to build supranational structures. Two factors are at work. One stems from big-power sensibility. Much like China, or for that matter the United States, India is not willing to cede power over its national-security decisions to a multilateral organization. Indian decision makers are perfectly at home with the dictum of great powers articulated by the Clinton administration: "multilateralism where convenient, and unilateralism where necessary." The other factor is memory. For decades after India took the Kashmir question to the United Nations, Indian diplomacy has sought to fend off great-power intervention in its own internal affairs. India's insistence that the Kashmir question must be resolved entirely within the bilateral framework with Pakistan and its relentless opposition to third-party intervention are largely similar to China's and Russia's reluctance to accept international intervention in Tibet and Chechnya, respectively. India, like China, might be a rising power on the Asian stage, but it is also acutely aware of its internal vulnerabilities and has a long memory of past international attempts to manipulate its domestic conflicts. Both states have also yet to complete their territorial consolidation, which in turn has led to an obsessive defense of the concept of national sovereignty. India, for example, was among the few countries that abstained in the voting to establish the ICC in 1998. Its attitude was shaped largely by the fear that the ICC may act as a judicial bully and that other powers might leverage the ICC to exploit individual nation's (i.e., India's) domestic political problems. A certain "cynicism" informs the Indian perspective that "the ICC could be a mere tool in the political game-playing of nations."[60]

This is part of a larger picture in which India finds itself in the company of many Asian and other developing states that oppose the West's robust interventionist approach to deal with bad actors' violation of human rights. India is deeply wary of letting the international system get a handle on the million mutinies that are playing out in India. That India is a vibrant democracy does not alter the strong perception in New Delhi that international interventions cannot be separated from international politics and that insulating its own internal transformation is a more prudent course.

The third set of enduring principles relates to significant ambiguities in India's approach to sovereignty and intervention. That India is determined to defend its own sovereign space against meddling by other great powers does not mean that it treats nonintervention in international affairs as a supreme and inalienable principle. Its own record, especially in its neighborhood, has been one of frequent military interventions: for example, Goa in 1961, East Pakistan in 1971, and Sri Lanka from 1987 to 1990. All these interventions did have seemingly high moral justification: the liberation of Goa from Portuguese colonial rule, the need for a humanitarian intervention to end the army's genocide in East Pakistan, and the preservation of Sri Lanka's territorial integrity and the promotion of federalism to satisfy the aspirations of the Tamil minority. Yet many critics have found the basis for Indian interventions ethically inadequate.[61] Others have seen these interventions in more structural terms as attempts to exercise political hegemony in India's immediate neighborhood.[62] What stood out in India's policy was a twofold objective: to prevent other great powers from intervening in the internal affairs of South Asia and to retain the right of intervention for itself—a form of the Monroe Doctrine practiced by the United States in the Western Hemisphere.[63]

However, this Indian Monroe Doctrine has evolved since the end of the Cold War. With the failed intervention in Sri Lanka in the late 1980s, the Indian establishment became more reluctant to undertake direct military interventions in its neighborhood. The current reluctance may be attributable in part to overextension of security commitments in the final years of the twentieth century.[64]

A range of other factors—including a structural crisis in the relations with neighboring countries, the preoccupation with setting its own house in order, and the pressures to cope with the new globalization of South Asian security—has encouraged India to modify its intervention policies.[65] These changes have included an acceptance of third-party mediation in South Asian conflicts. For example, New Delhi accepted the work of Norway in Sri Lanka and a limited United Nations role in ensuring a peaceful democratic transition in Nepal after the popular rebellion in the spring of 2006. New Delhi also took part in active diplomatic cooperation with the United States, the European Union, and the United Kingdom in managing the political crisis in Nepal during 2005 and 2006. In addition, India accepts a continuing dialogue with the United States on regional security issues and supports the participation of China, the European Union, Japan, and the United States as observers in SAARC. Underlying these changes is the political recognition in New Delhi that India's primacy in South Asia can no longer be sustained on the basis of denial alone and that cooperation with other major powers may in fact facilitate the achievement of India's own regional objectives. The declining distrust of the U.S. role in South Asia, encouraged in part by Washington's willingness to defer to India's leadership on some of the regional issues and the political prudence in minimizing New Delhi's risks in acting as the sole security manager of the subcontinent, has created a basis for considering security multilateralism as a potential instrument of foreign policy. Increasing Indian self-confidence that its own territorial sovereignty remains invulnerable to external pressures and a growing self-assurance that multilateralism need not necessarily hurt the pursuit of national interests is likely to make India less opposed to future cooperative endeavors on building an Asian security order. These attempts, however, will remain subject to the test of India's own national-security interests.

Finally, India prefers an "inclusive" rather than an "exclusive" structure for a future Asian security order. This preference perhaps stems as much from the imperatives of realpolitik as it does from normative considerations. Addressing the issue normatively, Indian spokesmen have argued that "we have an interest in seeing a more multi-polar world emerge. That is, if there are more centers of economic activity, if there are more centers of political influence, if the world order or the regional order becomes more diversified, we believe, the greater the chances of maintaining peace and stability."[66] India's emphasis on the importance of creating "multipolarity" has often been seen in terms of finding space for itself in a unipolar world. The same logic also applies equally to its concerns about a potential "unipolar Asia" dominated by China. India has little time for conceptions of a Sino-centric Asian order. Its traditional rivalry with China for influence in Asia has not been mitigated by the current state of expansive cooperation between New Delhi and Beijing. As a rising power, India argues for a regional balance between India and China within a multipolar framework and rules out the prospect of joining a containment ring against Beijing. India's foreign minister Shyam Saran put it well when he argued that New Delhi and Beijing must be "sensitive to each other's interests and aspirations," that "there is enough space and opportunity in Asia and beyond for the two countries to grow," and that "India and China, as two continental-size economies and political entities, are too big to contain each other or be contained by any other country."[67]

Based on India's traditional foreign-policy rhetoric, it would have been easier to assume that India would have joined the Chinese bandwagon on "Asia for Asians" and supported the exclusion of the United States and other "non-Asian" participants in the EAS. Although China's successful exclusion of the United States from the EAS is for the moment a secondary diplomatic issue for India, it is of concern in the longer term. India might not articulate this attitude explicitly, but it clearly values the continued role of the United States in constraining Chinese behavior in Asia—hence, the emphasis on promoting "equilibrium" in Asia that increasingly guides India's relations with the United States and Japan. Whether it is the EAS or the Shanghai Cooperation Organization (SCO), India has been reluctant to endorse the Chinese agenda on excluding "external powers." Despite India's own past rhetoric against the involvement of external powers in Asia and the Indian Ocean, India has not backed the SCO's call for withdrawal of U.S. and other foreign troops from Central Asia. Such a withdrawal, India is aware, would only benefit the extremist forces in the region, including the Taliban.[68] India's interests regarding a balance of power in Asia, then, fit in with the normative considerations of "inclusiveness" in any future regional security order.

Contrary to the widespread internal and external perceptions that India's Asian policy is driven by normative impulses, however, there is concrete evidence that it is driven by solid considerations of realpolitik. If the memory of its own past experience in promoting Asian unity on the basis of idealism makes India somewhat cold to the notion of collective security mechanisms in Asia, its new awareness as a rising power increasingly encourages it to take on the responsibility for creating and sustaining a new regional order beyond its neighborhood. Since the end of the Cold War, India's emphasis has been on catching up and being present in the new institutions. As the rise of China generates a fundamental redistribution of power in Asia and the world, India is bound to come under greater pressure to move beyond mere establishment of a presence to system-shaping actions in the future.

Given the complex internal struggles regarding the pace of globalization, India's integration with the East Asian economies is most likely to be gradual and grudging. Yet an India that grows at 8 percent per annum will inevitably influence future outcomes on regional integration. Although Asian institution building has been quite dynamic in the economic arena, it is quite thin on the security front. India is certainly not betting on the emergence of a single over-arching structure of Asian security in the near future. Asia is quite far away from forming a European-style security community. Collective Asian efforts aimed at resolving intrastate, interstate, and regional conflicts have not been impressive. Even weak states' capacity to defy presumed norms by playing great powers against each other has been demonstrated by both Burma and North Korea. Even when great powers seem united—as in the strong consensus in op-position to North Korea's nuclear ambitions—their capacity to deter, dissuade, and compel seems limited.

The current hopes of building Asian security institutions are premised rightly on the value of limiting conflict in the region amidst a fundamental change in the distribution of power. But the very process is not immune from the new dynamic of mutual suspicion and rivalry among the great powers. Most powers in the region do believe that although multilateral arrangements are useful, they are no substitute for building credible alliances, both formal and informal. India is no exception. Amid all the debate about a multilateral secu-rity architecture in Asia, the real challenge might be about engineering a cred-ible balance of power. The stronger India becomes, the more eager it will be to construct a new balance-of-power system for Asia. India's preparedness for greater strategic coordination with the United States and Japan as well as for expanded engagement with China and deepening security ties with other coun-tries of the region positions it well to become a critical element of any security system that may emerge in Asia.

NOTES

1. For the official documentation from the conference, see Asian Relations Orga-nization, *Asian Relations: Being the Proceedings and Documentation of the First Asian Relations Conference, March–April 1947* (New Delhi: Asian Relations Organization, 1947). A reprint is available as *Asian Relations: Report of the Proceedings and Docu-mentation of the First Asian Relations Conference New Delhi, March–April, 1947* (Delhi: Authors Press, 2003).

2. For India's motivations and logic in taking the Kashmir question to the UNSC, see Chandrashekhar Dasgupta, *War and Diplomacy in Kashmir, 1947–48* (New Delhi: Sage, 2002).

3. For an account of the impact of U.S. Cold War policies on the subcontinent, see Robert McMahon, *The Cold War on the Periphery: The United States, India, and Paki-stan* (New York: Columbia University Press, 1994).

4. Man Mohini Kaul, "ASEAN–India Relations During the Cold War," in *India and ASEAN: The Politics of Look East Policy*, ed. Frederic Grare and Amitabh Mattoo (New Delhi: Manohar, 2001), 43–88.

5. For an assessment of the early Indian debates on SAARC, see S. D. Muni and Anuradha Muni, *Regional Cooperation in South Asia* (New Delhi: National Publishing House, 1984), 29–31.

6. For an analysis of SAARC's failure to build regional cooperation, see Kishore C. Dash, "The Political Economy of Regional Cooperation in South Asia," *Pacific Affairs* 69, no. 2 (1996): 185–209. See also Devesh Kapur and Kavita Iyengar, "Limits of Integration in Improving South Asian Security," in *Strategic Asia, 2006–07: Trade, Interdependence, and Security*, ed. Ashley Tellis and Michael Wills (Seattle: National Bureau of Asian Research, 2006), 241–70.

7. Kripa Sridharan, *The ASEAN Region in India's Foreign Policy* (Aldershot, Eng.: Dartmouth, 1996). See also Sandy Gordon and Stephen Henniggham, eds., *India Looks East: An Emerging Power and Its Asia-Pacific Neighbors* (Canberra: Strategic and Defense Studies Centre, Australian National University, 1995).

8. P. V. Rao, ed., *Regional Cooperation in the Indian Ocean: Trends and Perspectives* (New Delhi: South Asian, 2001).

9. P. V. Indiresan, "The Kunming Initiative," *Frontline*, April 1–14, 2000, http://www.flonnet.com/fl1707/17070980.htm.

10. Amit Baruah, "Looking East," *Frontline*, November 25–December 8, 2000, http://www.hinduonnet.com/fline/fl1724/17240490.htm. See also Faizal Yahya, "India and Southeast Asia: Revisited," *Contemporary Southeast Asia* 25, no. 1 (2003): 79–103. An Indian official fact sheet on BIMSTEC published in August 2005 is available at http://meaindia.nic.in/onmouse/BIMSTEC.pdf.

11. T. Nirmala Devi, ed., *India and the Bay of Bengal Community: The BIMSTEC Experiment* (New Delhi: Gyan, 2007).

12. Saman Kelegama and Indra Nath Mukherjee, *India–Sri Lanka Bilateral Free Trade Agreement: Six Years Performance and Beyond*, Research and Information System Discussion Papers no. 119 (New Delhi: Research and Information System for Developing Countries, 2007).

13. Aparna Shivpuri Singh, *The South Asian Trade Labyrinth and India's Regional Trade Policies*, Institute for South Asian Studies (ISAS) Background Brief no. 2 (Singapore: ISAS, May 2005). See also Shaheen Rafi Khan, Faisal Haq Shaheen, Moeed Yusuf, and Aska Tanveer, *Regional Integration, Trade, and Conflict in South Asia* (Islamabad: Sustainable Development Policy Institute, January 2007), http://www.iisd.org/pdf/2007/tas_rta_south_asia.pdf.

14. World Bank, *South Asia: Growth and Regional Integration* (Washington, D.C.: World Bank, December 2006), http://www.wds.worldbank.org/external/default/WDS-ContentServer/WDSP/IB/2007/02/07/000020439_20070207135607/Rendered/PDF/378580SAS.pdf.

15. Prime Minister Manmohan Singh highlighted India's commitment to a new unilateralism on the economic front when at the fourteenth summit in New Delhi in April 2007 he offered to open the Indian market to the least-developed countries of SAARC without insisting on reciprocity. See Manmohan Singh, "Address to the 14th SAARC Summit," New Delhi, April 3, 2007, http://www.mea.gov.in/.

16. For an official summary of India's FTAs by the Ministry of Commerce, India, see http://commerce.nic.in/india_rta.htm.

17. For a comprehensive narrative on the evolution of the security dimension in India's engagement with Southeast Asia, see Sudhir Devare, *India and Southeast Asia: Towards a Security Convergence* (Singapore: Institute for Southeast Asian Studies, 2006).

18. Manmohan Singh, "Address at the Third India-ASEAN Business Summit," New Delhi, October 19, 2004, http://pmindia.nic.in/speech/content.asp?id = 35.

19. Bruce Vaughn, "East Asia Summit: Issues for the Congress," *CRS Report to the Congress*, December 9, 2005, http://fpc.state.gov/documents/organization/58236.pdf. See also Mohan J. Malik, "The East Asia Summit," *Australian Journal of International Affairs* 60, no. 2 (2006): 201–6.

20. Christophe Jaffrelot, "India's Look East Policy: An Asianist Strategy in Perspective," *India Review* 2, no. 2 (2003): 35–68.

21. T. A. Keenlyside, "Nationalist Indian Attitudes Towards Asia: A Troublesome Legacy for Post-independence Indian Foreign Policy," *Pacific Affairs* 55, no. 2 (1982): 229.

22. Ibid., 230.

23. Lennox A. Mills, review of *Asian Relations: Being the Proceedings and Documentation of the First Asian Relations Conference, New Delhi, March–April 1947*, by Asian Relations Organization, *Annals of the American Academy of Political and Social Science* 264 (1949): 138–39.

24. Lord Curzon of Kedleston, *The Place of India in the Empire* (London: John Murray, 1909).

25. Peter John Brobst, *The Future of the Great Game: Sir Olaf Caroe, India's Independence, and the Defense of Asia* (Akron, Ohio: University of Akron Press, 2005).

26. K. M. Panikkar, *India and the Indian Ocean: An Essay on the Influence of Sea Power on Indian History* (London: Macmillan, 1945), 16–17.

27. K. M. Panikkar, "Regional Organization for the Indian Ocean Area," *Pacific Affairs* 18, no. 3 (1945): 248–49.

28. Quoted in Jaffrelot, "India's Look East Policy," 42.

29. Guido Samarani, *Shaping the Future of Asia: Chang Kai-shek, Nehru, and China-India Relations During the Second World War Period*, Working Papers in Contemporary Asian Studies no. 11 (Lund, Sweden: Centre for East and South-East Asian Studies, Lund University, 2005), http://www.ace.lu.se/images/Syd_och_sydostasien-studier/working_papers/Samarani.pdf.

30. Guy Wint, "China and Asia," *China Quarterly*, no. 1 (1960): 65.

31. A. W. Stargardt, "The Emergence of the Asian System of Powers," *Modern Asian Studies* 23, no. 3 (1989): 593. The Colombo powers, which were actively leading the Asian diplomatic efforts, were India, Pakistan, Sri Lanka, Burma, and Indonesia.

32. John Garver, *Protracted Contest: Sino-Indian Rivalry in the Twentieth Century* (Seattle: University of Washington Press, 2001).

33. For the specific instance of the trade negotiations with Singapore, see See Chak Mun, "C.E.C.A: Strategic Imperatives," *Singapore Yearbook of International Law* (2006): 233–42.

34. V. Sridhar, "Free Trade Fears," *Frontline*, May 7–20, 2005, http://www.hinduonnet.com/fline/fl2210/stories/20050520002709800.htm. See also "FICCI Urges Caution on Free Trade Pacts," *Hindu Business Line*, July 15, 2005, http://www.thehindubusinessline.com/2005/07/15/stories/2005071501241700.htm.

35. Amrita Narlikar, "Peculiar Chauvinism or Strategic Calculation? Explaining the Negotiating Strategy of a Rising India," *International Affairs* 82, no. 1 (2006): 59–76.

36. Andrew Hurrell, "Hegemony, Liberalism, and Global Order: What Space for Would-be Great Powers?" *International Affairs* 82, no. 1 (2006): 1–19.

37. Stephen Cohen, *India: Emerging Power* (Washington, D.C.: Brookings Institution Press, 2001). See also Rodney W. Jones, *India's Strategic Culture* (Washington, D.C.: Science Applications International Center, 2006).

38. R. Ravichandran, "ASEAN Concerned About India's Position on FTA," *Bernama*, December 13, 2005, http://www.bilaterals.org/article/php3?id_article = 3261; "FTA Consensus Unlikely During ASEAN Summit," *Business Standard*, January 6, 2007, http://www.bilaterals.org/article.php3?id_article = 6844; Amiti Sen, "Hurdles Galore on Road to FTA with ASEAN," *Economic Times*, January 29, 2007, http://www.bilaterals.org/article.php3?id_article = 7032.

39. For a critical reflection of the origins and evolution of India's conception of nonalignment, see T. A. Keenlyside, "Prelude to Power: The Meaning of Nonalignment Before Indian Independence," *Pacific Affairs* 53, no. 3 (1980): 461–83.

40. A. P. Rana, "The Intellectual Dimensions of India's Nonalignment," *Journal of Asian Studies* 28, no. 2 (1969): 309.

41. India offered the excuse of the lack of a United Nations mandate to back off from the initial enthusiasm for sending troops to Iraq: "The Government of India has given careful thought to the question of sending Indian troops to Iraq. Our longer term national interest, our concern for the people of Iraq, our long-standing ties with the Gulf region as a whole, as well as our growing dialogue and strengthened ties with the U.S. have been key elements in this consideration. India remains ready to respond to the urgent needs of the Iraqi people for stability, security, political progress and economic reconstruction. Were there to be an explicit UN mandate for the purpose, the Government of India could consider the deployment of our troops in Iraq" (Ministry of External Relations, India, Press Release, "Statement on the Question of Sending Troops to Iraq," New Delhi, July 14, 2003, at http://www.mea.gov.in).

42. "New Framework for the U.S.-India Defense Relationship," Washington, D.C., June 28, 2005. The text of the agreement signed by U.S. defense secretary Donald Rumsfeld and Indian defense minister Pranab Mukherjee is available at http://www .indianembassy.org/press_release/2005/June/31.htm.

43. For a discussion of the new approach and the controversy it generated at home in India, see C. Raja Mohan, *Impossible Allies: Nuclear India, United States, and the Global Order* (New Delhi: India Research Press, 2006), 99–130.

44. For an assessment of the prospects, see Pramit Mitra and John Ryan, *Gathering Steam: India and the United States Extend Military Ties*, South Asian Monitor no. 99 (Washington, D.C.: Center for Strategic and International Studies, 2006).

45. Ashley Tellis was the first to use the term *strategic coordination*. See House Committee on International Relations, *The United States and South Asia: Hearing Before the Subcommittee on Asia and the Pacific*, 109th Cong., 1st sess., June 14, 2005, 35, http://www.foreignaffairs.house.gov/archives/109/21800.pdf.

46. Ashley Tellis, "The Evolution of U.S.-Indian Ties: Missile Defense in Emerging Strategic Relationship," *International Security* 30, no. 4 (2006): 113–51.

47. Office of the Press Secretary, White House, "President's Statement on U.S. Joining New Asia-Pacific Partnership," Washington, D.C., July 27, 2005, http://www .whitehouse.gov/news/releases/2005/07/20050727-9.html.

48. For a flavor of the initial Indian reaction to the PSI, see G. S. Khurana, "Maritime Non-proliferation Initiatives: India's Bulwarks Against Nuclear Terrorism?" in *Emerging Nuclear Proliferation Challenges*, ed. C. Uday Bhaskar and C. Raja Mohan (New Delhi: Institute for Defense Studies and Analyses, 2005), 111–13.

49. G. S. Khurana, "Safeguarding the Malacca Straits," *Strategic Comments*, Institute for Defense Studies and Analyses, January 5, 2005, http://www.idsa.in/ publications/stratcomments/gurpreetkhurana50105.htm.

50. Manmohan Singh and Abe Shinzo, "Towards India-Japan Strategic and Global Partnership," joint statement, December 15, 2006, http://www.mofa.go.jp/region/asia -paci/india/pdfs/joint0612.pdf.

51. For an assessment of India's ambiguities on the promotion of democracy, see C. Raja Mohan, "Balancing Interests and Values: India's Struggle with Democracy Promotion," *Washington Quarterly* 30, no. 3 (2007): 99–115.

52. For a comprehensive review of the origins of the civil nuclear initiative, see Mohan, *Impossible Allies*.

53. Strobe Talbott, the deputy secretary of state in the Clinton administration who negotiated the nuclear question with India from 1998 to 2000, put out the simplest yet most succinct critique of the deal within days of its announcement. See Strobe Talbott, "Good Day for India, Bad Day for Non-proliferation," *Yale Global Online*, July 21, 2005, http://yaleglobal.yale.edu/display.article?id = 6042.

54. "Strobe Talbott Surprised at Opposition to the Nuclear Deal," *Economic Times*, February 27, 2008.

55. Alexander O. Ghebhardt, "The Soviet System of Collective Security in Asia," *Asian Survey* 13, no. 12 (1973): 1075–91; Arnold Horelick, "The Soviet Union's Asian Collective Security Proposal: A Club in Search of Members," *Pacific Affairs* 47, no. 3 (1974): 269–85.

56. Gail W. Lapidus, "The USSR and Asia in 1986: Gorbachev's New Initiatives," *Asian Survey* 27, no. 1 (1987): 1–9; Stephen M. Young, "Gorbachev's Asian Policy: Balancing the Old and the New," *Asian Survey* 28, no. 3 (1988): 317–39.

57. Pranab Mukherjee, concluding address to the seventh Asian Security Conference, Institute of Defense and Analyses, New Delhi, January 29, 2005, http://www.idsa.in/speeches_at_idsa/7ASCConcluding.htm.

58. Shyam Saran, address to the India Economic Summit, New Delhi, November 28, 2005, http://www.mea.gov.in//speech/2005/11/28ss01.htm.

59. Siddharth Varadarajan, "Asian Interests and the Myth of 'Balance,'" *The Hindu*, December 13, 2005.

60. Usha Ramanathan, "India and the ICC," *Journal of International Criminal Justice* 3, no. 3 (2005): 634.

61. For a critical assessment of India's intervention, see Ralph Buultjens, "The Ethics of Excess and Indian Intervention in South Asia," *Ethics and International Affairs* 3, no. 1 (1989): 73–100.

62. For a perceptive analysis, see Mohammed Ayoob, "India in South Asia: The Quest for Regional Predominance," *World Policy Journal* 7, no. 1 (1989–1990): 107–33. See also Mohammed Ayoob, "India as a Regional Hegemon: External Opportunities and Internal Constraints," *International Journal* 46 (1991): 420–48.

63. See, for example, Devin Hagerty, "India's Regional Security Doctrine," *Asian Survey* 31, no. 4 (1991): 363.

64. Neil Devotta, "Is India Over-extended? When Domestic Disorder Precludes Regional Intervention," *Contemporary South Asia* 17, no. 3 (2003): 365–80.

65. C. Raja Mohan, "Beyond India's Monroe Doctrine," *The Hindu*, January 2, 2003.

66. Shyam Saran, "Present Dimensions of the Indian Foreign Policy," address at the Shanghai Institute of International Studies, January 11, 2006, http://www.mea.gov.in//speech/2006/01/11ss01.htm.

67. Ibid.

68. For the Indian ambiguities on the SCO, where New Delhi has an observer status, see B. Raman, "Shanghai Summit: Indian Misgivings," July 5, 2006, http://www.saag.org/papers19/paper1847.html.

7. Australia's Pragmatic Approach to Asian Regionalism

Greg Sheridan

Australia is a unique nation in that its culture, history, geography, security environment, economic partnerships, and key security alliances all tend to push it in different directions rather than reinforcing each other. In international and security matters, many nations, in particular European nations, are concerned primarily with their nearest neighbors, even if the relationship is not always amicable. By contrast, Australia is a more truly globalized nation. Its history, since European settlement in 1788, is predominantly European. Its institutions are British, with a conscious admixture of American influences. Its closest neighbors are small South Pacific Melanesian and Polynesian states. Its closest big neighbor is the world's largest Muslim nation, Indonesia. Its primary security environment is Southeast Asia. Its biggest trade partners are in Northeast Asia (Japan, China, South Korea). Its central security relationship is its military alliance with the United States.

Although its population remains predominantly European in origin, for most of the past twenty years approximately one-third of its immigrants have come from Asia. Thus, 5 percent of its population is Asian, 2 percent is Aboriginal, and nearly 2 percent is Muslim.

These diverse influences have been reflected both in Australian regionalism and in its basic security policy. Australia has always sought to provide for its security through a combination of great-power alliance, proactive regional engagement, and a degree of self-reliance in defense.

Nonetheless, contradictions and tensions have existed in each of these three central dynamics. Australia has had two great-power alliances, the first with the United Kingdom, the second with the United States. Each has always occasioned contentious domestic debate.

Australia's public culture is deeply pragmatic. Beyond a broad commitment to democracy, Australia is a nonideological society. British empiricism is the prevailing intellectual mood in public policy. The most powerful word of Australian political rhetoric is not *liberty* or *justice*, but *practical*. To describe a policy as practical and effective is the highest claim that can be made for it.

With this characterization in mind, this chapter delves into Australian approaches to regional security structures in Asia. After a historical overview of Australian approaches, the chapter then turns to the current debate in Australia about the emergent Asian regionalism. It offers perspectives on the role of the United States as part of the future regional architecture and concludes with a look ahead to how the region can best organize itself to meet the future challenges it faces.

HISTORICAL BACKGROUND TO AUSTRALIA'S REGIONAL SECURITY POLICIES

As suggested earlier, Australia's great-power alliances have always been subject to practical tests. How far can the British provide for Australian security? Would it be wise to balance British influence with American influence? Former defense minister Kim Beazley has argued that Australia's commitment to World War I was rooted in a deep appreciation of national self-interest. Earlier, Prime Minister Alfred Deakin in 1908 had invited U.S. president Teddy Roosevelt to send "the great white fleet" to Australia, partly as a way of building an alternative to British protection, which intensely annoyed the British Foreign and Colonial Office. Finally, in 1941, wartime prime minister John Curtin declared in a newspaper article that Australia looked to the United States free of any pangs of traditional loyalty to the United Kingdom—for the simple and entirely practical reason that the United States could provide assistance to Australia in the war against Japan, which the United Kingdom could not.[1]

Similarly, proactive regional engagement has meant many different things over the course of Australian history. Australia's first military act in World War I was against the Germans in New Guinea. As soon as the British colonies of Australia federated and became a nation, the Australian Parliament passed laws to give effect to the White Australia policy, which was designed to exclude Asians from Australia. However, this policy coexisted with an understanding of the deep need to engage with Asia and with Australia's neighbors more broadly. A provision was included to allow New Zealand to join the Australian federation if it so desired. Deakin, the dominant politician of the era, was a student of Asian civilization, especially of India, and desired that the racial exclusion not preclude productive engagement.

And finally, defense self-reliance was itself intensely contested. There have always been two great traditions in Australian military policy—expeditionary and continental. The former was an early form of multilateral security—in other words, seeking security in part through alliances. It rested on two insights. The first was that Australia's security was best provided for in a global security order that was guaranteed by its allies, that embodied its values, and that specifically provided for Australian interests. Thus, Australian leaders believed the dominance of the British Empire provided for all these interests. By providing forces, Australia made more sustainable the international security order from which it benefited and that it believed was a global good. At the same time, by providing troops for empire needs, such as in the Boer War, Australia imposed a reciprocal obligation on its great-power ally. The second insight was that Australia's own armed forces acquired a high degree of competence and professionalism by its participation in great-power military activities.

The point of this brief historical survey is the high degree of continuity of all these factors after World War II. That war was certainly a fundamental discontinuity for Australia, but after it Australia emerged with a new great-power orientation, looking toward the United States, although this relationship took some years to formalize. In addition, Australian policy included a deep involvement in the new global multilateral institution, the United Nations, in which Australia's foreign minister, H. V. Evatt, was the first president of the General Assembly; a new relationship with its near neighbors that was evident in its representation of Indonesia in United Nations negotiations; and a realization that it needed a larger population, which would require a more diverse population. At the same time, with the emergence of communism in China and of Communist parties throughout Southeast Asia, there was a fundamental, new security challenge.

There has always been a certain promiscuity in Australian institutional engagement, in part because of the characteristic Australian empiricism and the complex and unusually diverse nature of the influences on its national policy. Thus, in 1950 Australia sponsored the Colombo Plan, which was a miniature Marshall Plan for Asia.[2] This sponsorship was made out of genuinely humanitarian motives, but also from an explicit recognition that economic development and stability in Asia would directly contribute to Australian security. It had another vitally important effect. Because it involved large numbers of scholarships for Asian students to study in Australia, it was one of the first occasions in which large numbers of Asians were officially welcomed into Australia. In retrospect, this episode is typical of Australian gradualism, introducing by a cautious, incremental step what would eventually become a radical change.

The most important institutional ambition for Australia after World War II was the establishment of a formal military alliance with the United States. The ambition of the first postwar Labor government of Prime Minister Ben Chifley, it went unfulfilled. Washington was at that time reluctant to enter into new security commitments. However, the Australian government changed hands in 1949, and with adroit diplomacy from the conservative foreign minister Percy Spender, a formal security treaty was negotiated between Australia, the United States, and New Zealand, which came into force in 1951. This particular episode illustrated Canberra's ability to exploit the mixing dynamics of two separate historical periods—the end of the immediate postwar period and the beginning of the Cold War. Australia essentially accepted a soft peace with Japan in exchange for the security guarantee. The United States was motivated by the desire to shore up Japan as a Cold War ally and to solidify its position in Asia to resist communism. Nonetheless, in the personal diplomacy between U.S. president Harry Truman and Foreign Minister Spender, Truman alluded to the high quality of the Australian military, which he had experienced directly in World War I.[3] Again, this episode was typical of Australian diplomatic history in the region. A military connection was used to leverage a desired result from the United States, which in turn was leveraged as influence in Asia.

At least since 1941 (in reality from much earlier, although it was less explicit in earlier decades), it has been a fixed object of Australian foreign policy to involve the United States closely in the security affairs of Southeast Asia and the Asia Pacific more generally. Thus, Australia was an enthusiastic participant in the effort to multilateralize U.S. involvement when in 1954 it joined with the United States, the United Kingdom, France, New Zealand, Pakistan, Thailand, and the Philippines to form the Southeast Asia Treaty Organization (SEATO). This body was ill fated, justly derided as "the Southeast Asian Treaty Organization minus Southeast Asia." However, SEATO gave expression to Australia's chief security concern in this period—the rise of Asian communism. Canberra was a strong advocate of U.S. involvement in the Vietnam War. When the Communists triumphed in Indochina, Australia supported the establishment of the Association of Southeast Asian Nations (ASEAN) in 1967 and became ASEAN's first dialogue partner.

Throughout the 1950s, Australia had simultaneously pursued a growing trade relationship with Asia, signing a ground-breaking trade treaty with Japan in 1957. Coming so soon after the brutalities of World War II, this treaty was a matter of some controversy within Australia. Some Australian war veterans offered distinguished moral leadership in promoting reconciliation with Japan, but it is fair to see this treaty as essentially another episode of Australian pragmatism and a straightforward desire to make things work.

AUSTRALIAN DEBATES ABOUT ASIAN REGIONALISM AND COMMUNITY BUILDING

Within the Australian political system, a mild doctrinal disagreement over the tools of foreign policy developed after World War II. The conservative parties—the Liberal Party and its coalition allies, first the Country Party and later the National Party—emphasized bilateral relationships and traditional alliances and friendships. These relationships did not have to be exclusively European and North American. Japan became a strong card in the conservative foreign-policy repertoire. Moreover, those Asian nations that had been part of the British Commonwealth, in particular Malaysia and Singapore, were also easily absorbed into the conservative narrative of Australian foreign policy. Indeed, a conservative government entered into the Five Power Defense Arrangements with Malaysia, New Zealand, Singapore, and the United Kingdom for the defense of peninsular Malaysia and Singapore in 1971. This agreement was designed originally to reassure Malaysia after the era of confrontation between Indonesia and Malaysia, but it developed into a general security relationship that, perversely perhaps, tended to have greater military than political intimacy. The Labor Party, in contrast, placed more emphasis on multilateralism, especially the United Nations. It had opposed Australian participation in the Vietnam War, which meant that at least some in the Labor Party were more ambivalent than their conservative counterparts about the U.S. alliance.

These doctrinal differences persist today.[4] However, it is easy to exaggerate their significance. Australia has a strong diplomatic corps and professional military, both of which provide independent policy advice to governments. Australian policy has a high degree of continuity. Both sides of politics emphasize their pragmatism, centrism, and even conservatism. The differences are much more points of emphasis than questions of fundamentals. Conservative Australian governments participate energetically in the works of the United Nations; Labor governments are steadfast in their fidelity to the U.S. alliance.

The latter was evident in the foreign-policy approach of the Labor government of Prime Minister Bob Hawke, who took office in 1983. As Hawke's long-term foreign minister Gareth Evans has written, "With Bob Hawke's strong personal commitment to external policy matters a prevailing feature of his

Prime Ministership, priorities were quickly established: firm and clear support for the alliance with the United States, coupled with initiatives on disarmament; an economic focus on the Asia Pacific region; diplomatic effort to resolve the deadlock on a peace settlement in Indo-China; the intensification of pressure against apartheid in South Africa; and strong support for the role of the United Nations."[5] Evans wrote this assessment in 1995, not long before the Labor government was defeated by John Howard the next year. It is worth quoting in part because of its representative sampling of Labor foreign-policy issues. The top priority is security, and the expression of that security is the U.S. alliance. The next priority is economic relations in the Asia Pacific, followed by a mixed menu of regional and global issues, including a commitment to the United Nations.

DEBATES ABOUT THE ASIA-PACIFIC ECONOMIC COOPERATION FORUM

The Labor governments of Bob Hawke (1983–1991) and Paul Keating (1991–1996) were responsible for several pieces of regional architecture of lasting importance, but the establishment of these pieces was not without controversy and debate. The most significant was the Asia-Pacific Economic Cooperation (APEC) forum. Ideas for a regional body for economic cooperation had been kicking around for years and had been promoted particularly by Japan and Australia, but it was Hawke, in a speech in Seoul in January 1989, who formally proposed APEC. The first APEC ministerial meeting of foreign, trade, and industry ministers was held in Canberra in November 1989. In Hawke's original speech in Seoul, he did not mention the United States by name, which led to some tense exchanges between U.S. and Australian officials.[6] However, the Australian concept was soon refined into one in which an integral selling point was its trans-Pacific nature.

APEC remains a unique episode in the history of Australian diplomacy. It is the only such organization that Australia has founded, and it was to serve specifically Australian, but also more broadly regional purposes. The regional purpose were clear enough: essentially to enhance regional economic cooperation and consultation. Asia was economically strong but institutionally weak. By 1989, a number of Asian nations had only relatively recently established formal diplomatic relations with China. Before APEC came into existence, China's and Japan's leaders did not regularly meet. The widespread view was that Asian institutions were anemic or absent.

The original vision for APEC was that it would embody open regionalism, which meant that it would not become a customs union or erect trade barriers for countries outside the group. However, from Canberra's point of view, the specifically Australian purposes that APEC served were more important. First, it was a highway down which Canberra could drive to the Asia-Pacific region. Before APEC, Australia was a member of no natural regional or trade grouping. Apart from the U.S. alliance, traditional linkages with the United Kingdom, and membership in the United Nations, Australia had full and active membership in only two significant international organizations—the British Commonwealth and the South Pacific Forum. The Commonwealth had no operational coherence or obvious commonality of interest. The South Pacific Forum was designed to assist the small states of the South Pacific, its only other substantial member being New Zealand. By contrast, APEC moved Australia to a much greater focus on Asia.

Further, by 1989 Asian economic dynamism was well established. Australian policy and business leaders wanted more and better methods of regional interaction. APEC also further established the legitimacy of Australian leadership within the region. This legitimacy was not a claim to permanent leadership status, but simply the acceptance that an Australian initiative could find support and come to life in the Asia Pacific.

Because APEC involved the United States, it also served the long-standing Australian goal of helping to anchor the United States in East Asia (meaning both Northeast Asia and Southeast Asia). APEC quickly became an important national icon within Australia. Its success was seen as a national project, a source of pride. Australians felt protective and affectionate toward APEC. Both sides of the political spectrum competed over who could manage APEC best. No serious figure in Australian politics has ever opposed APEC as such. Some occasionally argue that it has become less relevant or has lost steam, but no serious figure has ever argued that APEC's existence is not in Australia's interests. When Keating succeeded Hawke as prime minister in 1991, he quickly became an APEC enthusiast. He suggested publicly that APEC should become a leaders' meeting and devoted a great deal of effort into convincing U.S. president Bill Clinton to convene such a meeting in Seattle in 1993. He also engaged in vigorous, personal diplomacy with Indonesia's then president Suharto to make sure that Suharto supported the concept of the leaders' meeting.[7]

Keating used APEC's dynamic to try to improve U.S.-Indonesia relations in part because the improvement would greatly benefit Australia. He told Clinton that he could not build a successful leaders' meeting without the support of Suharto because of Indonesia's dominance within Southeast Asia. To secure Suharto's support, Keating told Clinton, it was necessary for Washington to moderate pressure on Indonesia regarding human rights, the environment, and labor standards. Keating urged Clinton to moderate such pressure in the interests of getting Suharto on board in APEC, which, in turn, would make it more likely that Indonesia would listen to U.S. arguments on these issues. Keating similarly told Suharto that some pressure from the United States on human rights, the environment, and labor standards was absolutely inevitable. If this pressure came in a multilateral context, it would be less disagreeable to Indonesia, and over time the United States would be socialized into behaving in a somewhat more "Asian way."[8]

This episode is important in an illustrative sense. It demonstrates how the achievement of an institutional end—the creation of the APEC Leaders' Meetings—required intense bilateral negotiations among key players. But it also demonstrates how the institution itself can facilitate the achievement of national goals and how the process of building a regional institution can itself become an element in regional power politics.

In 1994, Keating associated himself intensely with the free-trade goals to which APEC leaders committed themselves in Bogor, Indonesia. APEC's defenders would later argue that although these goals were never fully achieved, they did help maintain momentum toward trade liberalization.

Both Keating and Evans expressed a degree of hostility to European Union membership (or the European Community as it was then known as an institution) in APEC, for two reasons. First, their vision for Asia-Pacific regionalism was always meant to be clearly distinguished in style and purpose from European regionalism. There was to be for APEC no Brussels-style bureaucracy, no pooling of national sovereignty, and no making of broad transnational rules other than those governing trade. Second, in relation to pure power politics, both Keating and Evans believed that the mere existence of an Asia-Pacific alternative could pressure the Europeans on trade. Indeed, numerous commentators have attributed to APEC some role in pressuring the Europeans into making compromises that finally led to the conclusion of the Uruguay Round of the General Agreement on Tariffs and Trade (which subsequently became the World Trade Organization).

The other issue of contention over Asian regionalism during Keating's time as prime minister was his debate throughout the 1990s with Malaysia's prime minister Dr. Mahathir bin Mohamad.[9] Although this debate had its domestic political, personal, and at times petty aspects, it was really a clash of visions for regional organizations. Dr. Mahathir initially proposed an East Asian economic group as an East Asians–only alternative to APEC. It was meant to be centered on ASEAN, but would include the big Northeast Asian powers—China, Japan, and the Republic of Korea. It would overtly and self-consciously exclude the United States and Australia. Dr. Mahathir famously declined to attend the 1993 Seattle APEC Leaders' Meeting in order to demonstrate his displeasure with the elevation of APEC and his continuing commitment to an East Asia–only vision.

Canberra opposed Dr. Mahathir on two grounds. First, his vision of Asian regionalism excluded Australia and therefore at the most basic level contradicted Australia's national interests. Second, Australian policymakers believed that trans-Pacific regionalism, involving the United States specifically, was the best version of regionalism for Asia itself. The United States was central to Asian security and central to the Asian economy.

It is fair to say that in the end neither Keating nor Mahathir decisively prevailed. In terms of the direction of APEC's development, Mahathir was defeated. APEC became more and more established and more and more significant. However, Mahathir's vision also flourished. It formed the basis of what became ASEAN Plus Three (APT): the ten ASEAN countries (Brunei, Burma, Cambodia, Indonesia, Laos, Malaysia, the Philippines, Singapore, Thailand, and Vietnam) plus China, Japan, and South Korea. APT's emergence owed much to the failure of regional institutions in the 1997 Asian economic crisis, but it also owed a great deal to Mahathir's consistent advocacy over many years. The Keating-Mahathir contest and the fact that both visions ultimately found an institutional life demonstrate that regional institutions can be sites for power rivalry between nations and between individual leaders. It also shows that regional institutions are inherently flexible and that the region can accommodate numerous different institutions. For a long time, Canberra overtly opposed APT, but nonetheless made fitful efforts to join it. After John Howard became prime minister in 1996, one of his early decisions was that Australia would no longer apply to join organizations it had be refused admittance to. Canberra eventually came to an uneasy acceptance of APT.

DEBATES ABOUT THE ASEAN REGIONAL FORUM

The other important regional institution that Canberra played a role in creating was the ASEAN Regional Forum (ARF). Foreign Minister Evans's belief was that existing regional institutions were not sufficient to manage emerging security problems in the region. This view was driven in particular by disputes over sovereignty within the South China Sea. When Australia, in cooperation with Japan, proposed the multilateral forum that eventually became the ARF, U.S. officials were at first unhappy. At that stage, they were opposed to the multilateral approach to security within the Asia Pacific because they believed such an approach could detract from the system of U.S. bilateral security alliances, which were the effective security system in Asia. U.S. secretary of state James Baker protested strongly to Evans that Australia should not have proceeded with such an initiative without consulting its American ally first.[10].

Evans has written that it took nearly two years to convince Baker and other U.S. officials that the ARF would not seek in any way to limit U.S. freedom of maneuver in the Pacific, especially in relation to the U.S. Navy. However, Evans stressed that the ARF was to be a dialogue and perhaps a confidence-building body, but not a deliberative body. In Evans's telling of the story, he was successful in convincing Baker that the ARF would have no restrictive consequence for the United States in Asia. Before Baker left office, he gave in-principle support to a multilateral security dialogue, but also stressed the overriding importance of the traditional bilateral alliances. The Clinton administration, as Evans tells it, was an enthusiastic supporter of the ARF from the start.[11]

In spite of Australia's commitment to this institution, virtually all of its ministers, government officials, and commentators agree that the ARF has not lived up to its potential—that its consultative processes add some value, but that it has not been of great importance in confidence building or norm setting or dispute resolution. Australia continues to play an active role in the ARF. It is a fair conclusion that because the ARF has produced very little in terms of outcomes, it has been the focus of relatively less-senior Australian attention. But Australian foreign ministers have been conscientious in attending every ARF meeting and using the presence of so many other foreign ministers to pursue bilateral meetings and issues. Similarly, although Australia supports the ARF's move to confidence-building measures and the like, no very great Australian effort has been directed at ARF reform.

SHIFTING DEBATES UNDER THE HOWARD GOVERNMENT

John Howard was elected prime minister in a landslide victory over Paul Keating in 1996. However, Howard promised to continue the main lines of Keating's foreign policy, including making engagement with Asia the top foreign-policy priority. Nonetheless, although a conscientious regionalist and multilateralist, he as a matter of doctrine put more emphasis on bilateral relations. In any event, four external events completely transformed Australia's foreign policy and with it substantially transformed the Howard government's approach to regional architecture: the East Asian economic crisis of 1997; the fall of Suharto and the rise of Indonesian democracy in 1998; East Timor's independence in 1999; and the terror attacks of September 11, 2001, in the United States.

The East Asian economic crisis showed the inadequacy of existing Asian institutions for dealing with such shocks, but it also discredited the International Monetary Fund (IMF) and the Washington Consensus on economic policy. It also greatly reduced the political self-confidence of Southeast Asian governments and of ASEAN as an institution. The fall of Suharto and the rise of Indonesian democracy was a good development for Australia, but in the chaotic early years after Suharto, Jakarta lost its natural dominance in Southeast Asian diplomacy and regionalism. This change ironically did not make Southeast Asian regionalism more democratic, but instead robbed it of much of its effectiveness. Although the vote for independence in East Timor eliminated the one great long-term problem in the critically important relationship between Australia and Indonesia, it also generated a great deal of short-term mutual antagonism between the two societies. It also brought the army back to the center of Australian national affection. And finally, the war on terror, unleashed by the September 11, 2001, attacks, led to an unprecedented closeness between Howard and U.S. president George W. Bush. Howard backed Bush in Afghanistan and, much more controversially, in Iraq. Australia contributed two thousand troops to the military campaign in Iraq, a small but nonetheless significant number that included special forces who did militarily difficult and effective work.

Taken together, these factors increased Canberra's closeness to Washington and somewhat diminished its investment in regionalism. It became particularly attracted to purpose-built "coalitions of the willing" designed to address particular regional problems. Such groups could be temporary—as was the Regional Core Group formed by the United States, Japan, India, and Australia to render rapid assistance to the Asian nations devastated by the December 2004 tsunami—or more permanent, such as the Asia-Pacific Partnership on Clean Development and Climate, designed to promote a technology-centered approach to reducing greenhouse gas emissions.

Similarly, all these factors changed the power dynamic between Southeast Asia and Australia. This change led to clumsiness on Canberra's part and to some Southeast Asians' perception of its arrogance, as when in an interview Howard allowed Australia to be described as the "deputy sheriff" to the United States.[12] Nonetheless, these factors also contributed to underlining Australia's utility to the region. Australia was, with Japan, one of only two nations to contribute to all three IMF financial bailouts for nations worst hit by the 1997 economic crisis (Indonesia, South Korea, and Thailand). Similarly, after the Bali terrorist bombings in Indonesia in 2002, Canberra and Jakarta drew together in counterterrorist cooperation. Australia contributed a great deal of financial and technical assistance to Indonesia, and the two governments together hosted a series of regional ministerial meetings to enhance regional cooperation in counterterrorism. This model seems to be effective. Despite the panoply of existing regional organizations, or perhaps because of the habits of consultation they have encouraged, when something urgent is required, the region can easily group together in a task-oriented fashion. This approach is inherently untidy and perhaps unappealing to classical diplomats or international-relations theorists, but it passes the most basic test—it works. At the same time, Canberra's closeness to Washington became a positive asset with Indonesia, particularly so in the long-running campaign to get the Americans to resume military-to-military cooperation with Indonesia.[13]

Howard believed that all of these developments were a clear vindication of his preference for bilateralism over multilateralism or overt regionalism. Nonetheless, the Howard government did not want Australia to be left out of any important regional organization it might join. It had a substantial internal debate over whether it should seek to join the East Asia Summit (EAS) mechanism.[14] The prime minister's department and indeed his own office believed strongly that signing the ASEAN Treaty of Amity and Cooperation, which became a condition for joining the EAS, was a bridge too far. In the end, Canberra signed the treaty but made a declaration that in effect it had no meaning or, specifically, would not affect Australia's military alliances, in particular the alliance with the United States. Indonesia, Japan, and Singapore, supported EAS membership for Australia and India, which reflected not only their consideration of their bilateral relations with Australia and India, but also their desire to balance China's influence within the EAS. The strategy here is not one of containing China, but of prudently balancing China, which can go hand in hand with jumping on its bandwagon.

The influence of the East Asian economic crisis, the changes in Indonesia, and the war on terror also affected the development of APEC and Australia's involvement in it. The Leaders' Meetings have become the most significant part of APEC. Although APEC is not supposed to address security issues and is technically a gathering of economies rather than nations, the leaders proverbially address whatever they like. In response to the war on terror, APEC has embarked on a substantial program of trade-related security-enhancement cooperation. However, from Australia's point of view, perhaps the most decisive APEC Leaders' Meeting was the one held in New Zealand in 1999. Canberra, perhaps unwisely, had become deeply involved in the politics of East Timor's move to independence, although it had never been Australian policy to seek East Timorese independence. After the vote for independence by the East Timorese in a plebiscite, pro-Indonesia militias went on a spree of destruction through East Timor, causing much terror, loss of life, and destruction of East Timor's fairly primitive infrastructure. The Howard government was under intense domestic pressure to send a peacekeeping force to East Timor, but it could not do so without Indonesian acquiescence. It was necessary for the United States to put a great deal of diplomatic pressure on Jakarta to achieve this goal. The APEC meeting in New Zealand allowed Howard to negotiate directly with Clinton and other national leaders in relation to East Timor, which led to a renewed burst of prestige for APEC within Australia and demonstrated once more the flexibility of the APEC Leaders' Meetings.

Contemporary Australian attitudes emerge directly out of this experience. The formation of the EAS provoked some Australian commentators to believe that the formation of a full East Asian community was just around the corner. Foreign Minister Alexander Downer was more skeptical, but believed that an East Asian community might develop over time as a result of both the EAS and the interaction among all the various regional and subregional groupings. Others were even more skeptical because it seemed unlikely that an East Asian community could be built when the China-Japan relationship had recently gone through one of its stormiest passages in several decades.

VIEWS ON THE U.S. ROLE IN REGIONAL COMMUNITY BUILDING

Certainly, the fears that an East Asian community would be designed to exclude the United States appear exaggerated. There seems to be no reason why U.S. allies such as Japan would see such a development as in their interests. Within most of East Asia, a strong consensus still exists that the U.S. security presence is a substantial stabilizing factor for the region. Very few want to chase the United States out of the region. Similarly, although intra-Asian trade has grown, the United States remains the biggest economy in the world, and most Asia-Pacific nations want the U.S. attention in the region that trans-Pacific regionalism—such as APEC—brings. They also want the access to U.S. officials and political leaders that trans-Pacific regionalism provides.

At times, there is some skepticism about whether the United States has the patience for all aspects of Asian diplomacy. It is hard to imagine any Australian opposition to U.S. membership in the EAS, but membership would be valuable only if the United States fully committed to all of the summit's works and disciplines, mainly the need for the president to attend the summit each year. Most Australians would strongly not want growth in the EAS to be at the expense of the APEC Leaders' Meetings, but in addition to them. Because of the primacy Australians accord to APEC, there is no great demand for the United States to energize the EAS. And although Canberra has been unusually close to Washington in the past decade, Australian foreign policy, especially toward Asia, is less normative than U.S. foreign policy. It is a matter of degree rather than fundamental direction.

Throughout Australia's history, it has virtually always been an object of policy to seek the maximum U.S. involvement in Asia and Asian institutions. This is not to say that Canberra always agrees with Washington on Asian policy. Throughout the 1980s and 1990s, there were sharp disagreements over China and Japan. Canberra opposed the punitive U.S. Super 301 trade legislation against Japan, and it equally opposed the Clinton administration's early linking of China's most-favored nation trade status to human rights. Nonetheless, the United States and Australia share so many civic values (democracy, capitalism, civic freedoms), have such similar cultures, and are so closely linked in security alliance that excluding the United States from any part of regional architecture can never be in Australia's interests. Australian policymakers do not feel over-awed by U.S. power, but rather that they have a good chance of influencing U.S. policy and that this chance is enhanced the more deeply the United States is involved in Asia. Nonetheless, Australia is happy to join, in its own interests, organizations the United States may not join. Australian policymakers under-stand that their national interests are affected by the way the United States conducts its Asian diplomacy.

Australian policymakers are keen, for example, for Sino-U.S. relations to be stable. During the simultaneous life of the Bush administration in Washington and the Howard government in Canberra, there were at times some disagree-ments between Australia and the United States over China policy. Canberra, which enjoyed a vast trade surplus with China, tended not to see Chinese mer-cantilism as an obvious economic threat. As previously noted, Australia's diplo-matic style is less normative than the U.S. style, and its diplomacy toward China over human rights, although sharing the same goals as Washington, is much quieter. Similarly, Canberra is always willing to reiterate its opposition to the use of force by China over Taiwan, but does not share the same security guarantee that binds the United States to Taiwan. Nonetheless, it is easy to over-state these differences. They are matters of nuance more than substance, and they have a long lineage. Throughout the Clinton administration, Australia objected to the early Clinton policy linking China's trade status to its human rights policy. Earlier than that, Richard Nixon's opening to China occurred at a time when Australia was more hostile to China. Some overexcited commenta-tors foretold a fundamental clash between the United States and Australia over China policy, especially given Australia's booming trade relationship with China. Some said this clash was likely to occur in the event of hostilities be-tween the United States and China over Taiwan. This fear was wildly over-blown. Both John Howard and his successor, the Labor Party's Kevin Rudd, have consistently stressed the absolute centrality of the U.S. alliance to Austra-lian foreign policy and more broadly to Australia's sense of itself. They both have also made it clear that they will not abridge, limit, or much less abandon the alliance in the interests of better relations with China. Therefore, although disagreements between Canberra and Washington may from time to time occur over China policy, a fundamental breach between the two countries is extremely unlikely.[15]

Stability, as is generally thought in Australia, is enhanced by the maximum exposure of the United States to Asian institutions and the maximum exposure of Asian leaderships to the United States through a trans-Pacific architecture. However, provided these linkages are in good order, Australian policymakers are not paranoid about the development of an Asian architecture in which the United States is not a part, provided that this architecture does not indicate hostile exclusion of the United States or U.S. neglect of Asia.

CONCLUSIONS AND A LOOK AHEAD

Debate over the future of regional architecture is robust within Australia but occurs among a small minority of specialists and does not engage significant political interest when it occurs in the abstract. The political system is motivated only when a specific proposal to exclude or include Australia is at hand or a specific problem, such as terrorism, is to be addressed.[16] Nevertheless, there remains a wide range of views within Australia's policy community about what shape the future regional architecture should take. In general, however, four propositions represent a broad Australian consensus.

First, the basis of Asian security is the U.S. alliance system, and Australia's participation in its bilateral military alliance with the United States is nonnegotiable and more important than any regional consideration. At the same time, the U.S. alliance is not seen as being seriously in conflict with Australia's distinctive interests in the region. It is in the region's interests and overwhelmingly in Australia's interests for the United States to have the maximum constructive involvement possible in the Asia-Pacific region.

Second, APEC is the organization most important to regional architecture and most friendly to Australian interests. Australians regard APEC as flawed by an excessively large membership, and there is much criticism of the United States for championing Latin American and Russian membership in the organization. Nonetheless, although APEC's flaws are recognized, it is regarded as providing real benefits to the region and specifically to Australia.

Third, Australia desires to make a constructive contribution to community building—such as in the formation and retention of the EAS—but most Australian officials have an open mind about where such regionalism can go and what it can do. There is a great deal of skepticism about what the EAS will deliver, but no desire to prevent it from delivering anything worthwhile. At the same time, there is no burning Australian desire to make the EAS work wonders. Australians are growing more comfortable with an Asian pace of institutional development. Australian empiricism is relaxed about task-oriented groups or coalitions of the willing being formed as and when necessary. For example, the region's greatest security problem, North Korea, has been well managed by the Six-Party Talks and would be unlikely to benefit noticeably from any institutional development in prospect. The same is probably true for the Taiwan issue. Australians have no great interest in the formation of an Asian community unless this community includes Australia, and it can include Australia only if it does not abridge Australia's national identity. There is little feeling in Australia that regional organizations should promote political norms such as democracy, which is not to say that outrageous human rights abuses should not be condemned. There tends to be more faith that norms can be established in areas such as trade and economic governance and that economic development over time is likely to produce sustainable political and human rights development.

Fourth, although the Labor Party under Kevin Rudd won a sweeping election victory in November 2007, his government will not likely dramatically alter Australia's approach to Asian regionalism. Over many years, Rudd repeatedly stressed the "three pillars" of his foreign policy: the U.S. alliance, the deepest possible engagement with Asia, and the strongest possible participation in the United Nations. A serious breach with underlying Howard policy is not likely, although Rudd did immediately ratify the Kyoto Protocol on Climate Change, which Howard, like George W. Bush, had refused to do. However, this act indicated something less than what met the eye because, even under Howard, Australia was already on track to meet its admittedly generous Kyoto targets. The emphasis on the U.S. alliance and engagement with Asia mean there will be little change in these main aspects of Australian foreign policy.

Similarly, although Labor is more instinctively multilateral than its conservative opponents, the Howard government had already engaged in a great deal of task-oriented and ad hoc regional multilateralism on issues such as combating terrorism and controlling refugee flows and people smuggling. The Rudd government will continue these initiatives and seek to intensify Australian involvement in the United Nations. A substantial feature of Australian foreign policy in recent years has been interventions in Melanesia to provide short-term security, relief from disasters, and long-term aid. The security element has been evident in Australian troop deployments to East Timor and the Solomon Islands, and Australia pursues extensive aid relations with other Melanesian nations, most notably Papua New Guinea and Vanuatu, but less intensely with Polynesian nations. However, with the exception of the original East Timor intervention, which coincided with an APEC Leaders' Meeting, Asian regional institutions have not been important in these Australian initiatives. These initiatives have substantially been unilateral Australian operations, although other nations sometimes supported them. Insofar as there has been an overarching multilateral authority to the missions, it has been provided by the United Nations in East Timor and by the South Pacific Forum in the case of the Solomon Islands.

Finally, there is a realization that the region has to manage the rise of China and in due course the rise of India. This management does not mean agreeing with every Chinese position—far from it—but it will be useful to embrace China as a "responsible stakeholder," in the words of former U.S. deputy secretary of state Robert Zoellick. This task is one of the many that need to be done by Asia-Pacific regionalism in coming years.

There is great pragmatic wisdom in the Chinese proverb about crossing the river by feeling the stones. It does not imply that you do not make progress, but that you should make progress slowly and gradually and on the basis of performance. For Australia, this kind of pragmatism and careful weighing of interests will define its approach to the future Asian regional architecture.

NOTES

1. John Edwards, *Curtin's Gift: Reinterpreting Australia's Greatest Prime Minister* (Sydney: Allen and Unwin, 2005), 3.

2. Gareth Evans and Bruce Grant, *Australia's Foreign Relations* (Melbourne: Melbourne University Press, 1995), 23.

3. Paul Kelly, *100 Years: Australian Story* (Sydney: Allen and Unwin, 2001), 230–33.

4. Michael Wesley, *The Howard Paradox: Australian Diplomacy in Asia, 1996–2006* (Sydney: ABC Books for the Australian Broadcasting Corporation, 2007).

5. Evans and Grant, *Australia's Foreign Relations*, 29.

6. Ibid., 128–29.

7. Greg Sheridan, *Tigers: Leaders of the New Asia Pacific* (Sydney: Allen and Unwin, 1997), 111–12.

8. Ibid., 111–13.

9. Ibid., 197–200.

10. Evans and Grant, *Australia's Foreign Relations*, 116–18.

11. Evans's account of these communications with Baker and subsequently with the Clinton administration are to be found in ibid., 117–18.

12. Greg Sheridan, "PM's Doctrine Under Siege," *The Australian*, September 25, 1999.

13. Greg Sheridan, "The Lure of Asia," *The Australian*, December 10, 2005.

14. Greg Sheridan, "We Might as Well Sign This Treaty," *The Australian*, April 14, 2005.

15. A detailed account of the Bush-Howard dialogue and disagreement over China policy is provided in Greg Sheridan, *The Partnership: The Inside Story of the US-Australian*

Alliance Under Bush and Howard (Sydney: University of New South Wales Press, 2006), 188–205.

16. For example, an interesting contribution to the Australian debate comes from Allan Gyngell, a former senior diplomat and foreign-policy adviser to Paul Keating and now the executive director of the Lowy Institute for International Policy. Gyngell takes a straightforward and rational approach to redesigning regional architecture. He argues that APEC should be refocused on trade liberalization and its leaders' meeting severed from APEC itself. He proposes a regional leaders' meeting, but not one connected to APEC. He suggests that East Asian community building should be carried out within the APT grouping and that a new security dialogue body should be established, based on either an expansion of the Six-Party Talks or the existing Shangri-la Dialogue organized by the London-based International Institute for Strategic Studies. Gyngell's plan is clean and neat, in some ways matches form to function, and is a useful contribution to the debate, but it is completely unrealistic because it contradicts the national interests of numerous players, not least Australia. See Allan Gyngell, *Design Faults: The Asia Pacific's Regional Architecture*, Lowy Institute Policy Brief (Sydney: Lowy Institute for International Policy, July 2007), http://www.lowyinstitute.org/Publication.asp?pid = 638.

8. The Strong in the World of the Weak

SOUTHEAST ASIA IN ASIA'S
REGIONAL ARCHITECTURE

Amitav Acharya

Southeast Asian countries, despite living in the shadow of their more powerful neighbors India, China, and Japan, have exerted a major influence on the development of Asian regional approaches to regional architectures. Not only is Southeast Asia the birthplace of Asia's first viable multilateral organization concerned with security, the Association of Southeast Asian Nations (ASEAN), but other parts of Asia and the wider region as a whole have adopted the principles and mode of regional interaction developed in Southeast Asia. This influence is an important paradox for both theorists and practitioners of international relations. It is also a convenient point of departure for understanding and analyzing elements of continuity and change in Southeast Asia's role in forming Asia's regional architecture.

What explains ASEAN's influence and "leadership" over Asian institutions?[1] Among international-relations theories, the realist view sees international institutions as marginal forces in world politics. To the extent international institutions matter at all (the North Atlantic Treaty Organization, for example), they must have the direct sponsorship or at least the active backing of great powers. As a group of essentially weak and small nations, ASEAN from a realist perspective faces a serious structural limitation in providing "regional solutions to regional problems" and in playing a "leadership" role in building wider Asian

institutions.[2] Although liberal and constructivist theories take international institutions far more seriously, they often stress the role of materially powerful
actors in institution building[3] and norm diffusion.[4] ASEAN as a group of weak
and small powers would seem incapable of developing institutional structures
to attract and bind great powers (as opposed to the great powers "self-binding"
themselves through institutions) or to propagate its own norms and identity in a
larger region, as would be necessary for it to acquire and hold onto its leadership
role.

An "eclectic" approach is more promising in explaining why ASEAN has
been able to "lead" Asian regionalism. Instead of testing "the relative explana-
tory power" of individual theories, such as realism, liberalism, and constructivism, the eclectic approach pulls "selectively from all three in the effort to
establish the interconnections between the various processes."[5] Here, the interconnections between realism (a softer version) and constructivism are most
pertinent.[6] Viewed from a soft realist lens, individual ASEAN members lack
structural power, but collectively they acquire (as its founding members would
have rationally calculated) enough bargaining clout to command the attention
of great powers and even to socialize them through its regional institutions.
Developing multilateral institutions to engage great powers is part of this game.
Assisting ASEAN's quest for institutional leadership is the fact that the
great-power claimants to such leadership in Asia cancel each other out because
of their mutual rivalry. Because ASEAN's ability to "lead by default" depends
on its ability to hang together,[7] ideational factors such as regionalist norms as
well as identity and socialization processes stressed by constructivism are extremely important. Southeast Asia may be a diverse region, but it is less culturally heterogeneous than Asia or the Asia Pacific. Moreover, Southeast Asia's regional identity is easier to articulate than the identity of other subregions: it
derives substantially from a "natural" and shared desire not to be seen as a cultural or geopolitical appendage to either India or China. Although ASEAN
countries were initially pushed to accept regionalism in the face of a common
fear of externally backed communism, this threat-driven initial unity (which is
not inconsistent with the pathways of other security communities, including
the European Union) was sustained and reinforced by decades of interaction
and socialization. The latter led to a reduction in intramural conflict and to a
capacity for managing conflicts in the Southeast Asian neighborhood, such as
the Cambodia conflict during the 1980s. This habit of hanging together and
avoiding intramural problems created a favorable international image for
ASEAN that attracted other nations in the Asia Pacific and motivated them to
take it seriously. It also meant that regional institutions sponsored by ASEAN
have more "soft power" and are deemed more credible than those created by
the region's greater powers.[8] Another logic of soft realism can also be added to

the mix: institutions controlled by weaker states are generally deemed to be less threatening and hence enjoy more legitimacy than institutions created by stronger powers. Taking these points together, one gets the picture of why ASEAN has been able to assume leadership of regional groups in the Asia Pacific.

Starting from this perspective, this chapter examines how ASEAN's role in Asia-Pacific regional institutions has evolved. After offering a brief history of regionalism to underscore ASEAN's role as a hub of regionalist interactions, the chapter examines perspectives from Southeast Asia on a number of issues pertaining to the evolving regional architecture of Asia, such as the nascent East Asian regionalism, the relevance and role of other regional organizations, the role of the United States and its alliances in the region, attempts to reform and reinvent ASEAN itself, and the principles and norms underpinning Southeast Asian and Asian regionalism.

ASEAN's central role in Asia's regional architecture will face growing challenges from the rise of Chinese and Indian influence and the emergence of wider frameworks of regionalism, such as the ASEAN Regional Forum (ARF) and the East Asian Summit (EAS). But ASEAN's ability to sustain its crucial role in Asia's regional architecture will likely persist until and unless other actors, such as China, acquire substantial legitimacy through soft-power resources. The ASEAN leadership role will also depend on its members' continued ability to hang together, especially in overcoming internal differences regarding the purpose and scope of Asian regional institutions.

EVOLVING PERSPECTIVES

Asia has historically never truly been a region of institution building.[9] Since the end of World War II, the center of gravity of regional institution building or architectural work has shifted. Thus, Asian regionalism has assumed a variety of forms: pan-Asian, Afro-Asian, subregional (Southeast Asian), trans-Pacific (Asia Pacific), and East Asian. These regionalisms have not been distinct or mutually exclusive, but overlapping and often, if not always, complementary.[10] But Asian regionalism has traditionally not been centered in Southeast Asia.

Southeast Asia was a relatively unimportant actor in the early stages of Asian regionalism. India and to a lesser extent China led the major efforts in the direction of regionalism. India's Jawaharlal Nehru was instrumental in organizing the first Asian regional conference in the post–World War II period, the Asian Relations Conference, held in 1947 and 1949. The fact that the second conference focused on Indonesia's liberation from Dutch colonial rule but was held in New Delhi rather than in a Southeast Asian capital is telling. Apart from the fact that Malay was still under British colonial rule, the conference location attests to India's leading role in Southeast Asian regionalism at the time. Indeed, insofar as regionalism was concerned, there was no clear separation between South Asia and Southeast Asia. The official sponsors of the historic Asia-Africa Conference in Bandung, Indonesia, in 1955 were called the "Colombo Powers," although they preferred to describe themselves as the Conference of South East Asian Prime Ministers.

These early interactions among Asian countries were driven by some (but not a great deal of) pan-Asian sentiment. More important, there was a clear congruence between nationalism and regionalism. The latter was seen as a useful device to press for the end of colonial rule in the region,[11] but it did not aspire to any form of supranationalism. Sovereignty and nonintervention were the hallmarks of early Asian regionalism. Although Southeast Asia's role was limited, Burma and Indonesia did provide some of the initial regionalist (pan-Asian) concepts. Burma's Aung San envisioned a regional federation, and Indonesia's premier Ali Sastroamidjojo was the man behind the Bandung conference idea.[12] Nevertheless, Southeast Asian countries were wary of a regional organization that might be dominated by "outside" regional powers such as India and China. As one Burmese individual put it, "It was terrible to be ruled by a Western power, but it was even more so to be ruled by an Asian power."[13]

With neither India nor China acceptable as a regional leader and a still-recovering Japan yet to develop the economic muscle to underwrite regional cooperation, Southeast Asia came to occupy the center stage of Asian efforts to develop a regional organization. After two short-lived experiments, the Association of Southeast Asia and Maphilindo (Malaysia, the Philippines, and Indonesia), failed, ASEAN was set up in 1967 with five original members (Indonesia, Malaysia, the Philippines, Singapore, and Thailand). The emergence of ASEAN paralleled the decline of the Southeast Asia Treaty Organization (SEATO). ASEAN also proved more viable that the Asian and Pacific Council, which had been established in 1966 with Australian and Japanese participations as an "indigenous" Asian alternative to SEATO. But it was ASEAN that provided the only viable alternative, underscoring the importance of small-state indigenous regionalism over regionalism sponsored by bigger powers, whether Asian or other.

After a shaky start due to intramember squabbles, ASEAN recovered following the U.S. withdrawal from Indochina; the fear of Communist takeovers inspired ASEAN to overcome internal squabbles and to focus on domestic stability and economic growth. The organization came of age in the 1980s when it resisted Vietnam's occupation of Cambodia and sought a political settlement of the conflict. The Vietnamese withdrawal from Cambodia and the Paris Peace Agreement settling the conflict marked the high point of ASEAN-led regionalism. The ASEAN experience and its model of informal, nonlegalistic, and sovereignty-enhancing cooperation proved attractive to South Asian leaders, inspiring them to establish the South Asian Association for Regional Cooperation (SAARC) in 1984, but with far less success.

With the establishment of the Asia-Pacific Economic Cooperation (APEC) forum and the ARF, ASEAN and its approach to regional institutions moved closer to center stage. Both APEC and the ARF embraced the core elements of the ASEAN model of soft institutionalism, avoiding intrusive or binding measures, relying on voluntary concessions and compliance, and practicing organizational minimalism (APEC set up a secretariat, the ARF did not). But these institutions' credibility, as well as ASEAN's, suffered a major setback with the 1997 Asian financial crisis. The stage was then set for regionalism to develop on an East Asian basis, with ASEAN Plus Three (APT, adding China, Japan, and South Korea), which seemingly vindicated Malaysia's 1990 proposal for the East Asia Economic Caucus as Asia's response to the European common market and the North American Free Trade Agreement.[14] East Asian regionalism has subsequently evolved into the EAS, with the long-term objective of creating an East Asian community.

Nevertheless, in spite of setbacks and changes in how the region perceives regionalism, Southeast Asia and ASEAN have remained at center stage in this process. This is not to say that ASEAN members have always acted as a single cohesive entity or offered a single perspective on regionalism. There have been elements of agreement and difference. During the Cold War, Singapore, Thailand, and the Philippines resisted Indonesia and Malaysia's preference to create a more exclusionary framework for regional security. This division reflected Cold War realities, the former basing their security strategy largely on the U.S. military presence and strategic access to their own territories. Differences also existed over the necessity, pace, and scope of regional economic integration, with Singapore's neighbors particularly concerned that such cooperation would benefit the republic more than them. In addition, with the more recent expansion of ASEAN to include Burma (Myanmar), Cambodia, Laos, and Vietnam, the gap has widened between the new and older members in terms of levels of economic development. In the post–Cold War period, intra-ASEAN differences are less about foreign military bases and more about the necessity and scope of collective regional action in areas such as peacekeeping and on issues such as human rights and democracy, with particular reference to Burma. ASEAN's weak leadership has also been blamed for the ARF's lack of further progress. But no major player is demanding that ASEAN give up its role as the driving force behind key regional institutions such as the ARF because no other driver would be acceptable.[15]

In sum, since the formation of ASEAN, the history of Southeast Asia's involvement in Asian regional cooperation has evolved, expanded, and entered a new phase. With the end of the Cold War, ASEAN lost some of its earlier reluctance to enter into security dialogues both within its own membership and with outside powers such as Australia, China, Japan, and the United States. This shift was in part a response to new ideas and proposals for cooperative security circulating at the time, but the practical implementation of these ideas, such as APEC and the ARF, was undermined by the Asian economic crisis of 1997. This crisis was the single most important factor in stirring the call for reform and reinvention of ASEAN's approach to regionalism. The crisis directly sparked emergent differences on the issues of interventionism, greater institutionalization and legalization, movement toward security and economic communities, and the establishment of an ASEAN charter. Even a decade after the financial crisis, debates about regional architectures have become more intra- and extra-ASEAN in nature, reflecting both domestic and external challenges to the member states, drawing them into playing a major role in the emergence of *East* Asian regionalism, and thus challenging ASEAN's identity and centrality.

DEBATES ABOUT REGIONAL ARCHITECTURE

In Southeast Asia, the debate about regional architecture is seldom over whether ASEAN is necessary or desirable. ASEAN members reached a consensus in the 1970s on the necessity or the inevitability of increasing regionalist sentiments. Then as now, regionalism is seen as a crucial element to the survival of small states facing larger and more powerful neighbors, a bulwark against great-power intervention (both during the Cold War and after), a useful framework for reducing intraregional tensions that may undermine economic growth and domestic political stability, and a means of expressing the identity of Southeast Asian nations to the international community. Southeast Asian nations continue to hold the view that through regional cooperation they enjoy greater international clout than might be possible through singular national existence and effort.

Although isolationist Burma and neutralist Cambodia chose to stay out of ASEAN during the Cold War and Vietnam expressed hostility toward ASEAN (which it viewed as another U.S.-backed misadventure like SEATO), today none of ASEAN's members question its legitimacy and hence participation in it. The haste with which Burma, Cambodia, Laos, and Vietnam grabbed the opportunity to join ASEAN in the 1990s attests to this commitment. Burma might stage a walkout on ASEAN if ASEAN decides to impose sanctions against the regime for not implementing political reform, but this event is not very likely.

Rather, the most important Southeast Asian debates about regionalism and regional architecture today revolve around two major issues: the direction of

ASEAN itself, including the need for reform or reinvention; and the role that ASEAN should play in the establishment of broader regionwide institutions. The first debate—the direction ASEAN should take—has intensified since the 1997 economic crisis, particularly over the issue of nonintervention. The most serious controversy about ASEAN's direction occurred in 1998 and 1999 over Thailand's idea of "flexible engagement," which called for ASEAN members to tackle challenges that may originate from a member's domestic sphere (and hence are subject to the noninterference principle) but carry regional implications—such as human rights in Burma, forest fires in Indonesia, or economic mismanagement in member states that might invite a national collapse and regional instabilities.[16] Indonesia and Singapore openly opposed the Thai proposal because it was vague about how or with what sort of action flexible engagement should be carried out.

But instead of disappearing, the notion of flexible engagement has persisted in recent years, particularly with the downfall of Suharto in Indonesia, the East Timor massacres, the Bali bombings, outbreaks of severe acute respiratory syndrome and avian influenza, and the worsening political situation in Burma. With these developments, Indonesia moved to the reformist camp, proposing the idea of an "ASEAN security community," which in its earlier iteration was to include such unorthodox ideas as creating a regional human rights mechanism and enshrining democracy as a basic norm of ASEAN.[17] These bold ideas did not survive ASEAN's consensus-building process, however, with the main opposition (if less vocal than Singapore's previous stance against "flexible engagement") coming from Burma and Vietnam.[18] Yet Singapore's strong advocacy of political sovereignty is tempered by its passion for regional economic integration. It proposed the idea of an ASEAN economic community that will create a nearly borderless regional economy and pushed for an ASEAN charter that would make ASEAN's hitherto informal regionalism considerably more institutionalized and legalized. Some of the ideas for this charter include more frequent summit-level meetings, a stronger ASEAN Secretariat with more bureaucratic authority, provisions for majority voting in selected areas (thus departing from the consensus principle), and greater accountability for compliance with ASEAN treaties and obligations.[19] But it is quite likely that the more intrusive measures will encounter stiff resistance from some members, especially Burma (which is a candidate for "punishment").

Debates over the reform of ASEAN in recent years, in both the economic and the security spheres, were driven by leading member states' domestic and external imperatives. Democratic transitions were one crucial determinant. Just as Thailand's advocacy of flexible engagement was underpinned by the emergence of a more democratic regime in the 1990s, the impact of the democratic transition on Indonesia's attitude toward and role in ASEAN can be seen in its advocacy of a very liberal notion of an "ASEAN security community." Conversely, the opponents of institutional reform were the region's illiberal and authoritarian regimes. At the same time, the imperative for economic liberalization and globalization in the face of competition from China and India influenced Singapore's drive for closer ASEAN economic integration (although Singapore also pushed for bilateral trade agreements with China, India, the United States, and other major economic players).

The second area of debate over broader regional architecture centers on the question of who should take part in Asia's emergent regionalism. There are two main perspectives in ASEAN. The narrower one, aggressively championed by Malaysia (and supported by China), sees a future East Asian community confined exclusively to East Asian nations (ASEAN plus China, Japan, and South Korea). This move toward a narrower East Asian institution can be traced to 1990, when Malaysian prime minister Mahathir bin Mohamad proposed the East Asia Economic Group (later renamed the East Asia Economic Caucus). His proposal was spurred by a fear of regional trade blocs emerging in Europe and North America and the crisis over the Uruguay Round of the General Agreement on Tariffs and Trade (GATT), which was facing a breakdown. The proposal remained dormant in the face of open U.S. opposition and Japan's resulting reluctance to back it. Following the Asian financial crisis, the concept found a new legitimacy among ASEAN members and Japan, leading to the formation of the APT.[20]

The other position on East Asian regionalism, held by Singapore and Indonesia (and now strongly supported by Japan), would keep East Asian regionalism "open" and nonexclusionary. This approach would be consistent with evolving regional norms and practice, including the norms of open regionalism and cooperative security, both of which stress nonexclusionary frameworks. It also underlies these nations' strategic imperative, which rests on close U.S. involvement in regional affairs. The greater Chinese enthusiasm for an exclusionary East Asian regionalism is, the stronger this group's resistance will be to keeping its membership confined to East Asian nations.

A related area of debate involves Southeast Asian countries' attitude toward other regional institutions. Views in Southeast Asia vary according to the other institutions' functions and roles. ASEAN countries have been traditionally nervous about U.S. dominance of APEC and its push for turning APEC into a vehicle for trade liberalization on terms that favor Washington's agenda. They have also been concerned about the possibility that APEC may overshadow ASEAN itself. Because APEC has stalled, these fears have dissipated considerably. Since 1997, APEC has been seen as in decline, although its annual summit is regarded as useful and worth retaining. It is also a convenient vehicle for those opposed to Washington's participation in the EAS to argue that trans-Pacific architecture is already covered. In general, ASEAN countries would support a revival of APEC, but perhaps mainly as an instrument of trade facilitation rather than trade liberalization.[21] Within ASEAN, there is no serious advocacy of turning APEC into the region's premier economic or security institution, although ASEAN members recognize and value APEC's contribution in addressing transnational security issues, especially terrorism, transnational crime, supply-chain security, and environmental degradation.

The ARF, once the proud achievement of ASEAN and a forum where ASEAN member states remained in the "driver's seat," has stalled. It has made less than expected progress in moving from a confidence-building stage to a preventive diplomacy stage. Even its confidence-building agenda remains modest, with none of the transparency and constraining measures found in the Organization for Security and Cooperation in Europe or even in the Shanghai Cooperation Organization. Nor has the ARF played a role in resolving or mitigating regional conflicts. ASEAN has gone along with China's insistence that the ARF avoid any discussion of the South China Sea dispute and the Taiwan issue. The two Koreas' membership in the organization has not led to any discernable ARF impact on the Korean Peninsula. Instead of dealing with interstate or regional conflicts, the ARF has turned its attention to transnational issues, including terrorism and transnational crime.[22] This development brings us full circle back to the first debate concerning how and to what extent ASEAN and ASEAN-centered institutions can reform and reinvent themselves to meet these new challenges.

THE U.S. ROLE AND U.S. ALLIANCES

Southeast Asian governments continue to view the U.S. role and its approach to Asian community building with some ambivalence. ASEAN members fully recognize that the United States has historically viewed the need for multilateralism in Asia to be less pressing than that in Europe because its bilateral alliances in the region, part of the so-called San Francisco system, have worked well since their inception at the onset of the Cold War. Moreover, from the early 1990s to the present, there has been a general preference in Washington for ad hoc or à la carte multilateralism that comprises a limited number of actors most relevant to a specific issue area (on this point, see chapter 2 in this volume).

From the perspective of Southeast Asian states, the limited U.S. interest and engagement in broader, longer-term regional institutions is a mixed blessing. On the one hand, it has worked to the advantage of the lesser powers, especially

ASEAN itself, which does not want great-power dominance in the regional order-building process. But a lack of U.S. support has meant fewer resources for Asian regional organizations. Also, without active U.S. participation, Asian regional organizations have suffered from a credibility problem, especially given the fact that the United States is seen as a de facto Asian power.

For ASEAN members, the greatest challenge in developing regional institutions is to strike a balance between U.S. indifference and U.S. dominance (the same can be said about China and Japan as well). APEC's experience in the early 1990s serves as a reminder that an aggressive push by Washington to steer a regional organization's agenda may generate suspicion and undermine its prospects. The U.S. emphasis on trade liberalization did not accord with Japan's preference for using APEC for developmental purposes. It also generated misgivings in the region about U.S. dominance. Washington's interest in using APEC as a vehicle for its trade-liberalization agenda waned with the successful conclusion of the Uruguay Round of GATT and with the backlash from Asian nations.

In addition, Washington's own regional friends and allies did not enthusiastically embrace its participation in the EAS. Malaysia is firmly opposed to it. Even Singapore's former prime minister Goh Chok Tong, himself no critic of America, believed that "East Asia cannot be extending to countries in the Pacific, for then even the political definitions would get stretched beyond belief." In Goh's view, the East Asia region's "engagement with the United States could be through the APEC and the ARF."[23] Singapore, supported by Indonesia, has sought to compensate for the exclusion of the United States by securing the entry of Australia and New Zealand into the EAS; Japan's role in the EAS also helps to fill in for the United States.

Intra-ASEAN differences over the role of the U.S. military presence and alliances in the region have narrowed compared to the situation during the Cold War period. Under ASEAN's "ZOPFAN" concept (Zone of Peace, Friendship, and Neutrality), put forward in 1971 and backed by Indonesia and Malaysia, foreign military bases were viewed as temporary. Thailand and the Philippines, formal alliance partners with the United States, went along with this arrangement because ZOPFAN was more the expression of an ideal than a plan of action toward a concrete regional security arrangement. In the post–Cold War period, the role and presence of U.S. alliances in Southeast Asia dramatically changed, especially with the removal of U.S. bases from the Philippines and Washington's increasing shift toward a "places not bases" approach (see chapter 11 in this volume). These changes made a virtue out of necessity by reducing the political and security problems associated with large, fixed military bases, even while retaining Washington's strategic access to Southeast Asia. The shift in U.S. position, along with the end of the Cold War (which also entailed the removal of Soviet military bases from Vietnam and thus a further obsolescence of ZOPFAN), has in turn removed a source of internal friction in ASEAN regarding the U.S. military presence in the region. For example, it makes Singapore's offer of military facilities to the United States more legitimate from the collective ASEAN standpoint. In any case, the Singapore offer, designed to help offset the loss of U.S. bases in the Philippines, caused a degree of tension with Malaysia, but the fact that Malaysia had developed close security ties with the United States took the sting out of its protestations.

The realization is growing that the tension between the U.S. security approach centered on its bilateral alliances and the emergence of multilateral principles and institutions might be further reduced.[24] There was never any clear sense within ASEAN that U.S. bilateralism and regional ASEAN-led multilateralism were necessarily incompatible. If and when there was such a sense, ASEAN was able to bypass or at least obscure it through diplomatic formulas and compromises, as in the case of ZOPFAN, which disallowed foreign intervention but considered foreign military bases in the region to be "temporary" (without any timetable, however). Increasingly, the United States has allowed its bilateral alliances to become platforms for multilateral activities. Admiral Dennis Blair, commander of the U.S. Pacific Command, proposed the idea of a regional "security community" to offer such pathways for reconciling bilateralism with multilateralism.[25] Examples of this approach include the opening up of the initially bilateral (United States and Thailand) Cobra Gold exercises to other regional states, even China (which has participated as an observer), and the undertaking of multinational naval exercises and operations, such as the humanitarian operations in the wake of the December 2004 Indian Ocean tsunami. ASEAN members have not only gone along with this trend, but welcomed it, which reduces the political costs of their own *bilateral* defense ties with the United States. The approach has its limits, however, because Washington will not push too far in "multilateralizing" the San Francisco system, which is still geared for the most part to deterring large and powerful enemies (China being the most apparent candidate). ASEAN countries—especially those that are formal treaty allies of the United States, such as the Philippines and Thailand, or those that are nearly formal treaty allies, such as Singapore—will be hard pressed to decide their course of action should war break out between the United States and China (over Taiwan, for example). In such a case, they would face overwhelming expectations from the United States to open their territory for use by U.S. operations against China, but doing so would undermine decades of multilateralist efforts to engage China. Their course of action would depend on the specific circumstances and causes of the U.S.-China confrontation. There is little doubt, however, that such a scenario, if it ever materializes, will pose one of the greatest tests of Asian regionalism, a primary goal of which is to soften the U.S. containment policy toward China and to foster an alternative approach centered on the socialization and engagement of China at a time of its rapid ascendancy.

CONCLUSIONS: PRINCIPLES AND PROSPECTS

The basic organizing principles of Asian regionalism have undergone little change, even in an era of rapid geopolitical and economic shifts, and will continue to shape Southeast Asian approaches to the future regional security architecture. They are fairly conservative, designed to preserve regional order by reducing the likelihood of interstate wars, enhancing domestic stability, and, at least from a Southeast Asian perspective, preventing any single outside power's dominance of the region.

These principles deserve some further elaboration. Preventing the dominance of Southeast Asia or of Asia more generally by any single power is the objective of any traditional balance-of-power approach. All great powers at work in Asia, the United States included, place great value on this goal. But as in any balance-of-power system, such an objective may not conflict with a great power's desire to assert its own influence, even at other nations' expense. Hence, the United States can speak of maintaining a balance of power in the Pacific even when that notion has merely been a fig leaf covering U.S. primacy and military dominance. Similarly, China's acclaimed goal of ensuring global and regional multipolarity does not mean Beijing wishes to see its influence wane in Southeast Asia.

ASEAN countries have generally accepted U.S. military dominance of the Pacific, including Southeast Asia, despite their ostensible commitment to avoiding dominance by any single power. They have done so because some of them, such as Singapore, see the United States as a "benign" superpower. They also see it as an off-shore balancer, with an over-the-horizon presence that does not intrude into the regional political space on any obvious day-to-day basis. But it is unlikely that China, Japan, or India would be acceptable in this role. Despite China's growing clout in the region, thanks largely to its "charm offensive," there is little possibility of a Chinese sphere of influence over ASEAN.[26] Hence, if U.S. regional military dominance is diluted (due to either distraction in the Southwest Asia or China and India's growing power), then ASEAN's desire for a region free from the dominance of any single power will have a better chance of being realized. In the meantime, this approach will remain a critically important principle in ASEAN's approach to developing Asia's regional architecture.

The other principles that mark ASEAN's approach to regional architecture include an open and nonexclusionary regionalism, noninterference in the internal affairs of states (except in some qualified and context-dependent possibilities), no regional military pacts or overarching suprabureaucracy along the lines of the European Union, and ASEAN leadership in regional institutions. Some of these principles are not ASEAN's invention, but they have survived powerful challenges and are likely to continue to do so because of ASEAN's fierce resistance to any outside effort to dilute them. ASEAN has also embraced the notion of cooperative security, the essence of which is "security with" rather than "security against" the adversary, although this notion was not an ASEAN principle to start with. The principle of open regionalism was challenged when the EAS was initially conceived as a gathering exclusively of East Asian nations, but the EAS ended up embracing the notion of "open and nonexclusionary regionalism." ASEAN has resisted proposals to disconnect some of the ARF's institutions and processes from its control, such as holding the annual ARF ministerial meeting in non-ASEAN member states. A Chinese proposal to host the second EAS in China was rebuffed. Hence, there seems to be an emerging principle in Southeast Asia for handling regional financial cooperation through the APT process rather than through APEC or the EAS. In general, ASEAN will adhere strongly to the principle that outside powers should not dictate the terms of regional cooperation, but can be fully engaged in economic and political dialogues if they are friendly to ASEAN members.

The future of the noninterference principle is more difficult to assess. It has faced powerful challenges, both from within and from without ASEAN. Although this principle is still upheld in theory, it is increasingly being compromised in practice. Moreover, ASEAN countries are coming to the view that giving up a degree of sovereignty to some extent is itself an exercise of sovereignty. Without this realization, there can be no meaningful action against the many new transnational challenges that Southeast Asia faces. On the political side, the debate over the new ASEAN Charter (detailed in chapter 10 in this volume) indicates some member states' readiness to begin considering increased attention to individual states' internal human rights or political affairs, but this proposal is still contested and will almost certainly not lead any time soon to an overt campaign on human rights or clear-cut requirements for democratization as a condition for membership in ASEAN (in the way that it is a condition for membership in the European Union, for example).

With these principles as a foundation, the future regional architecture of Asia is likely to retain many of the core elements of the past and the present. It will remain multilayered (or "multiplex" as some would put it), featuring a number of different and overlapping (both functionally and geographically) institutions. Although some analysts predict that East Asian regionalism will overtake or supplant Asia-Pacific institutions, this scenario is unlikely given the multiple and serious challenges the former faces, especially over its geographic scope, membership, and the Sino-Japanese rivalry. The EAS's functional role is uncertain, although it is useful for brainstorming and symbolic interaction. It is unlikely to develop institutional machinery for cooperation unless and until it becomes part of an overarching East Asian community (which will then combine APT and the EAS). In the meantime, the EAS's future direction will remain contested. As noted, Malaysia has backed China's desire to build an East Asian community through the APT process, which is narrower in membership than the EAS. Although Singapore and Indonesia have not openly opposed this move, they are unlikely to go along with a policy of excluding Australia, India, and New Zealand from the East Asian community while keeping them involved in the summit, especially if these three non–East Asian nations refuse to accept their "second-class status" in the EAS. Overall, the East Asia community ideal remains ill defined enough as a blueprint for institution building. As a result, there will be continuing confusion as to different institutions' mandates. Duplication rather than division of labor will be evident and will present a major obstacle in building the region's overall institutional architecture.

That said, Southeast Asia, or ASEAN, will remain the hub of Asian regionalism, not least because other possible contenders will either lack legitimacy (as applies to the United States, Australia, or Canada) or be too divided among themselves to stake a leadership claim successfully (as applies to China and Japan or China and the United States). For the time being, ASEAN looks to keep its leadership role in East Asian institutions, and other major powers are unlikely to challenge that role for now out of fear of undermining the whole process. But ASEAN's prominent role is likely to come under increasing challenge from the rising influence of China and India. A key challenge for ASEAN would be to engage these powers without courting their dominance. ASEAN has had some success in this area in the past, but sustaining it in the future will require that ASEAN, as the hub of regional socialization, remain a cohesive organization.

The region's soft institutionalism will gradually give way to bureaucratization and legalization, but only gradually and limitedly. Initiatives such as the ASEAN Charter will give ASEAN a new look, but any mechanisms for regional conflict resolution or collective peacekeeping should not be expected. Similarly, ASEAN will not create regional mechanisms for the protection of human rights and democracy. Internal domestic problems will be left out of its mandate unless they pose a direct and serious threat to regional stability (as of this writing, 2007, the current political situation in Burma does not qualify). ASEAN will not embrace regional humanitarian intervention under the "responsibility to protect" formulation. ASEAN countries will try their best to ensure that the wider regional institutions continue to reflect these principles and preferences.

In sum, the trajectory of regional institutions in Asia will remain evolutionary. No dramatic changes can be expected in the mandate, decision-making styles, or leadership of these major institutions, such as ASEAN, the ARF, and the EAS. The most promising stimulus for change may be the need to cope with transnational crises such as terrorism, pandemics, and major natural disasters.[27] These issues seem to be less divisive and more amenable to collective responses than traditional intrastate or interstate conflicts, over which Asian regional institutions have had little impact.

During its formative years (the 1960s and 1970s), ASEAN was an inward-looking organization concerned with regime survival and state-building objectives. It came of age by managing the regional conflict in Cambodia in the 1980s. But at the dawn of the twenty-first century, it is increasingly challenged by transnational threats that defy national boundaries and national remedies. Indeed, separating the internal from the external is increasingly meaningless in the face of such transnational dangers as terrorism, pandemics, and economic downturns. In the face of these challenges, ASEAN's state-centric and inward-looking regionalism faces considerable pressure to become a transnational regionalism. Yet ASEAN still remains a state-centric and sovereignty-bound grouping of nations. There is a serious mismatch between its traditional institutions geared to preserve state sovereignty and the new challenges its faces. How it adapts to this new environment will be a crucial test of its future leadership role in Asian regionalism.

NOTES

1. The term *ASEAN's leadership* is meant to capture four dimensions: (1) ASEAN as the "origin" or the first viable regional grouping in Asia; (2) ASEAN as the "model" for other subregional groupings in the region, especially SAARC; (3) ASEAN as the institutional "platform" for wider Asia Pacific and East Asian regional institutions; and (4) ASEAN as the "hub" of Asian regionalist debates and interactions over changing norms and mechanisms for regional cooperation in Asia, such as debates about non-interference and legalization.

2. Michael Leifer, *ASEAN and the Security of South-East Asia* (New York: Routledge, 1989), 24–28; Michael Leifer, "Regional Solutions to Regional Problems?" in *Towards Recovery in Pacific Asia*, ed. Gerald Segal and David S. G. Goodman (New York: Routledge, 2000), 108–18.

3. Robert Keohane, "Hegemonic Leadership and U.S. Foreign Economic Policy in the 'Long Decade' of the 1950s," in *America in a Changing World Economy*, ed. David

Rapkin and Avery William (New York: Longman, 1982), 49–97; Robert O. Keohane, *After Hegemony: Cooperation and Discord in the World Political Economy* (Princeton, N.J.: Princeton University Press, 1984); G. John Ikenberry and Charles A. Kupchan, "Socialization and Hegemonic Power," *International Organization* 44, no. 3 (1990): 283–315; G. John Ikenberry, *After Victory: Institutions, Strategic Restraint, and the Rebuilding of Order After Major Wars* (Princeton, N.J.: Princeton University Press, 2001).

4. One constructivist argument is that norms promoted by powerful actors have many more opportunities for diffusion. See Ann Florini, "The Evolution of International Norms," *International Studies Quarterly* 40, no. 3 (1996): 363–89. See also Alexander Wendt, *Social Theory of International Politics* (Cambridge: Cambridge University Press, 1999), 331; Martha Finnemore and Kathryn Sikkink, "International Norm Dynamics and Political Change," in *Exploration and Contestation in the Study of World Politics*, ed. Peter Katzenstein, Robert Keohane, and Stephen Krasner (Cambridge, Mass.: MIT Press, 1999), 266.

5. Peter J. Katzenstein, *A World of Regions: Asia and Europe in the American Imperium* (Ithaca, N.Y.: Cornell University Press, 2005), 39.

6. I leave liberalism out of the picture. Liberalism views the emergence of international institutions in terms of efficiency considerations and functional links, and it stresses the pacific effects of economic interdependence and shared democratic politics. It is of little relevance in explaining ASEAN's role not only because ASEAN countries share little economic interdependence, but also because they are markedly different from each other in terms of domestic political systems (bearing in mind that liberalism requires not just a shared political system, but a shared democratic political system and culture as a condition for successful institution building). Moreover, ASEAN hardly behaves like an institution whose functions have been described by neoliberal institutionalist theory, a recent variant of traditional institutionalism that incorporates the realist notions of anarchy but considers it to be manageable. These functions include reduction of transaction costs, sharing of information, and prevention of cheating through provision of collective sanctions. Of these functions, ASEAN might fulfill some of the transaction and information roles, but hardly the cheating/compliance function. Hence, liberalism is out of place in considering ASEAN's emergence and leadership; the view of ASEAN as an illiberal regional grouping is closer to reality.

7. Khong Yuen Foong and Helen E. S. Nesadurai, "Hanging Together: Institutional Design and Cooperation in Southeast Asia: AFTA and the ARF," in *Crafting Cooperation: The Design and Performance of Regional Institutions in Comparative Perspective*, ed. Amitav Acharya and Alastair Iain Johnston (Cambridge: Cambridge University Press, 2007), 32–82.

8. Sarah Eaton and Richard Stubbs, "Is ASEAN Powerful? Neo-realist Versus Constructivist Approaches to Power in Southeast Asia," *Pacific Review* 19, no. 2 (2006): 135–55.

9. In this chapter, I focus on institutions, but fully recognize that regionalism is a much broader notion than institutions and that the latter capture only a small part of the former.

10. T. J. Pempel, "Introduction: Emerging Webs of Regional Connectedness," in *Remapping East Asia: The Construction of a Region*, ed. T. J. Pempel (Ithaca, N.Y.: Cornell University Press, 2005), 1–28.

11. Amitav Acharya, *The Quest for Identity: International Relations of Southeast Asia* (Singapore: Oxford University Press, 2000).

12. Roselan Abdulgani, *The Bandung Connection: The Asia-Africa Conference in Bandung in 1955* (Jakarta, Indonesia: Gunung Agung, 1981).

13. Quoted in William Henderson, "The Development of Regionalism in Southeast Asia," *International Organization* 9, no. 4 (1955): 466.

14. Richard Stubbs, "ASEAN Plus Three: Emerging East Asian Regionalism?" *Asian Survey* 42, no. 3 (2002): 440–55.

15. Johan Garafano, "Power, Institutions, and the ASEAN Regional Forum: A Security Community?" *Asian Survey* 42, no. 3 (2002): 502–21.

16. Amitav Acharya, "Realism, Institutionalism, and the Asian Economic Crisis," *Contemporary Southeast Asia* 21, no. 1 (1999): 1–29.

17. Department of Foreign Affairs, Indonesia, "Towards an ASEAN Security Community," paper presented at the ASEAN Ministerial Meeting, Phnom Penh, Cambodia, June 16–18, 2003.

18. Barry Wain, "Jakarta Jilted: Indonesia's Neighbours Are Not Very Supportive of Its Vision of a Regional Security Community," *Far Eastern Economic Review*, June 10, 2004. Singapore opposed the ASEAN proposal for a peacekeeping force. See Barry Wain, "ASEAN Apathy: Indonesia Proposes a Regional Peacekeeping Force, but Neighbours Show Little Interest," *Far Eastern Economic Review*, May 6, 2004.

19. "The ASEAN Charter will set the framework and lay the legal foundation for ASEAN to restructure its existing mechanisms and improve its decision-making process to enhance efficiency and ensure prompt implementation of all ASEAN agreements and decisions. The Charter will also provide ASEAN with a legal personality" (ASEAN Secretariat, "The ASEAN Charter: Frequently Asked Questions," February 2, 2007, http://www.aseansec.org/Fact%20Sheet/ASC/2007-ASC-001.pdf). See also Ministry of Foreign Affairs, Singapore, *Report of the Eminent Persons' Group (EPG) on the ASEAN Charter*, http://www.mfa.gov.sg/internet/press/16012007/ReportOfThe EminentPersonsGroup(EPG)OnTheAseanCharter.pdf.

20. China has joined Malaysia as the major proponent of this narrower conception of an East Asian community. This position is ostensibly linked to perceptions of regional identity: East Asia is seen as culturally more homogenous than Asia or the Asia Pacific. An alternative explanation suggests that China might see East Asian regionalism as its preferred approach to regional engagement because it excludes the United

States and other Western nations and thus might allow China to exercise greater influence over regionalism's agenda and direction, especially in keeping it beholden to state sovereignty. See chapter 3 in this volume.

21. John Ravenhill, "Mission Creep or Mission Impossible: APEC and Security," in *Reassessing Security Cooperation in the Asia Pacific*, ed. Amitav Acharya and Evelyn Goh (Cambridge, Mass.: MIT Press, 2007), 135–54.

22. Amitav Acharya, "The Role of Regional Organizations: Are Views Changing?" paper presented at the Pacific Symposium 2004, National Defense University, Washington, D.C., April 22–23, 2004, http://www.ndu.edu/inss/symposia/pacific2004/acharya.htm.

23. S. Narayan, "High Stakes at the Kuala Lumpur Summit," *Financial Express*, November 9, 2005, http://www.financialexpress.com/archive/story0-108042-High -stakes-at-the-Kuala-Lumpur-summit.html.

24. William T. Tow, *Asia-Pacific Strategic Relations: Seeking Convergent Security* (Melbourne: Cambridge University Press, 2001).

25. Dennis Blair and John Hanley, "From Wheels to Webs: Reconstructing Asia-Pacific Security Arrangements," *Washington Quarterly* 24, no. 1 (2001): 7–17.

26. Amitav Acharya, "Will Asia's Past Be Its Future?" *International Security* 28, no. 3 (2003–2004): 149–64, and "Asia-Pacific: China's Charm Offensive in Southeast Asia," *International Herald Tribune*, November 8, 2003, http://www.iht.com/articles/2003/11/08/edacharya_ed3_.php.

27. See, for example, Ong Keng Yong, secretary-general of ASEAN, "ASEAN's Efforts in Combating Terrorism and Transnational Crime," remarks at the Second Asia-Pacific Homeland Security Summit and Exposition, Honolulu, Hawaii, November 16, 2004, http://www.aseansec.org/16557.htm.

PART II

The Functional Challenges

9. Emerging Economic Architecture in Asia

OPENING OR INSULATING THE REGION?

Amy Searight

Economic regionalism in Asia has surged in recent years. Nearly a decade after the Asian financial crisis brought several regional economies to their knees, Asian countries have rebounded with vibrant and stable growth, while dramatically deepening mutual economic ties. Regional production networks have expanded and diversified, spurred in large part by China's rapid economic rise. Intraregional flows of trade and investment have increased steadily. These growing economic linkages have been accompanied by rising aspirations for regional political cooperation, and governments have responded by creating new institutional architectures, ranging from informal governmental networks to legalistic and binding agreements, in order to facilitate and deepen economic cooperation.

However, regionalism has followed different paths in trade and finance. Trade integration has been primarily market driven, fueled by low tariffs, expanding production networks, and China's rapid economic rise. Unlike other regions, Asia did not embrace free-trade agreements until quite recently. Asian countries are now pursuing them enthusiastically, but they are only beginning to take effect, and they are likely to matter primarily at the margins. By contrast, financial regionalism has been driven by governmental cooperation rather than by markets. Capital markets remain small, fragmented, and relatively closed to outsiders. Yet governments have taken steps to reduce the risks of another financial crisis by providing a safety net of emergency credit and strengthening bond markets. These efforts are aimed primarily at strengthening and stabilizing regional financial systems, but they also reflect a desire to integrate regional financial markets and to lessen their dependence on global capital flows.

This chapter has two aims. First, it describes the key features of emerging regional economic architecture in both trade and finance. Second, it seeks to assess these new institutional structures' impact on regional economies in terms of shaping both their interaction with each other and their engagement with the rest of the world. To what extent is the emerging economic architecture opening the regional economies to global economic opportunities, and to what extent is it promoting regional integration at the expense of outsiders? In particular, the chapter seeks to address the implications of new regional economic cooperation and institution building for U.S. economic interests and policy options. As the chapter describes, the implications of the new regional economic cooperation are decidedly mixed. On balance, the regional trade and financial architecture appears relatively benign. Bilateral agreements in trade and multilateral regional cooperation in finance tend to promote the opening of markets and the building of institutional rules, and they are broadly supportive of global trade and financial regimes anchored by the World Trade Organization (WTO) and the International Monetary Fund (IMF).

REGIONAL INTEGRATION AND THE FREE-TRADE AGREEMENT BOOM

Regional integration in East Asia has accelerated considerably over the past decade. Regional production and distribution networks have flourished as multinational firms have fragmented their operations and spread them across many borders. China's economic ascendance has fueled regional economic growth and intensified production and trade linkages. More than half of all East Asian trade now occurs within the region, a level of intraregional trade that is higher than in any region except the European Union (figure 9.1).

Despite rising levels of intraregional trade, however, East Asia remains strongly tied to the global economy. Rising regional trade shares are partially accounted for by China's rapid trade growth and East Asia's growing levels of worldwide trade. As China and other Asian countries grow, they trade more with the entire world as well as with regional partners. Yet regional trade has also grown in intensity, outpacing growth in gross domestic product and growth in trade with the world. Rising trade integration in East Asia is being driven by

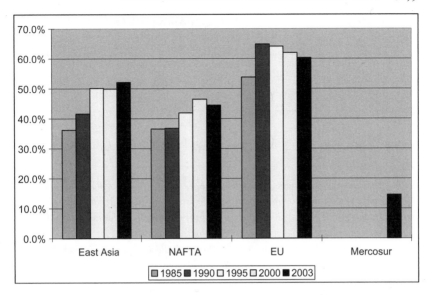

FIGURE 9.1 RISING INTRAREGIONAL TRADE IN EAST ASIA.
*Note: East Asia includes the ten Association of Southeast Asian Nations (ASEAN)
countries plus China, Hong Kong, Japan, South Korea, and Taiwan.*
*Source: Ministry of Foreign Affairs, Japan, "Growth and the Share of the Intra-regional
Trade Among East Asian Countries," http://www-mofa.mofa.go.jp/region/asia-paci/growth
.pdf.*

regional production networks, which manufacture components and send them
across borders in ever-expanding multinational production chains. Consequently, regional trade integration has been much more pronounced on the
import side than on the export side (table 9.1). Whereas the share of intraregional trade in imports has risen 43.5 percent over the past decade and a half,
the share of intraregional exports has risen more slowly at 32 percent. Regional
trade has surged in imports of components and other intermediate goods, especially in the electronics and nonelectrical machinery industries. At the end of
the production chain, however, the finished consumer goods continue to be
exported at high levels to the United States, Europe, and other global markets.

Although this deepening integration has been largely market driven, countries have recently embraced formal institutional agreements, in the form of
bilateral and plurilateral trade agreements, to facilitate further economic integration. Virtually every country in the region has jumped on the bandwagon,
and most are actively pursuing trade deals with several different regional partners. These arrangements are generally referred to as free-trade agreements
(FTAs), although Japan prefers to call them economic partnership agreements
(EPAs) to highlight areas of economic cooperation that go beyond traditional

TABLE 9.1. SHARE OF INTRAREGIONAL EXPORTS AND IMPORTS
IN THE APT REGION, 1990–2005

	1990	1995	2000	2005	Increase, 1990–2005
Intraregional export share	26.8%	34.9%	33.7%	35.4%	32.0%
Intraregional import share	30.6%	39.3%	41.8%	43.9%	43.5%

Note: Intraregional export share is the percentage of exports going to regional partners out of the region's total exports to the world. Intraregional import share is the percentage of imports from regional partners to total imports of the region from the world. A higher share indicates a higher degree of integration between partner countries.
Source: Asia Regional Integration Center, Integration Indicator Database, Asian Development Bank, available at http://aric.adb.org/indicator.php.

tariff liberalization and perhaps to deflect attention from the exceptions carved out in agriculture and other sensitive sectors. However, Japan is not alone in exempting sensitive sectors from FTA coverage. Indeed, most so-called FTAs emerging in the region are far less comprehensive than the term *free trade* implies. The lack of purity in Asian FTAs and indeed in FTAs around the world helps to fuel the debate over whether FTAs are "building blocks" or "stumbling blocks" to broader liberalization in multilateral trade.

THE ECONOMIC DEBATE: BUILDING BLOCKS AND NOODLE BOWLS

Economists have long argued that nondiscriminatory multilateralism always trumps the partial liberalization achieved in bilateral free-trade accords. From an economic perspective, renewed effort toward successful conclusion of the Doha Round is clearly the first-best policy because a WTO accord would lower trade barriers on a most-favored nation (MFN) basis and provide broader and less-distorting trade benefits than would a patchwork of regional FTAs. Yet in recent years policymakers and even many economists have come to appreciate the benefits of FTAs for a host of practical and economic reasons. FTAs are easier to conclude than WTO agreements because they involve a small number of countries as opposed to the large and diverse WTO membership. The bilateral or minilateral nature of the talks makes it easier for governments to tackle complex regulatory issues that affect trade between them. Accordingly, governments can tailor such agreements to meet the particular needs of their bilateral economic relationship. FTAs therefore provide them with an opportunity to go "beyond multilateralism" by reaching deeper into domestic trade regimes than is currently possible at the WTO.

The fact that trade liberalization under an FTA is restricted to only one or a handful of trade partners also makes it easier for governments to overcome domestic opposition to liberalization because the impact of trade concessions is more limited. The downside of the small-number negotiating dynamic is that it also makes it easier for governments to carve out sensitive sectors as exemptions from trade liberalization, which is more difficult to do in the face of multilateral peer pressure at the WTO. This tendency has been quite noticeable in East Asian FTAs, which often exclude sensitive products in agriculture and other sectors.

The optimistic view of FTAs holds that various accords can be negotiated sequentially, gradually adding new partners and new areas of coverage to a network of interlinked FTAs. Furthermore, FTA reforms can be multilateralized by bringing the issues covered in bilateral accords to the WTO or to a regional forum such as Asia-Pacific Economic Cooperation (APEC) for multilateral agreement. In this way, FTAs can serve as "building blocks" for regional and global free trade. Skeptics dismiss the "building block" view as unrealistic and misguided. As they see the situation, not only do FTAs divert energy away from multilateral negotiations, but their proliferation creates a "spaghetti bowl" of overlapping agreements with ad hoc and mutually inconsistent rules and procedures.[1] FTAs that create different standards and establish separate dispute-settlement mechanisms increase the complexity of the trade system and may make it more difficult for governments to coordinate around issues of economic integration. Of particular concern is the creation of a tangle of restrictive and highly complex rules of origin, which complicates and raises the cost of exporting and sourcing products in different markets.

In Asia, the proliferation of overlapping and inconsistent FTAs has been dubbed the "Asian noodle bowl." Whether this mixed bowl of trade deals helps to build or serves to reduce freer trade in the region hinges on the specific content of these agreements as well as on key players' underlying motivations. It also depends on key participants' ability and willingness to expand and consolidate bilateral FTAs into larger regional groupings or to find ways to harmonize rules and mitigate the welfare-reducing "noodle bowl" effects. I return to these issues later in the chapter.

REGIONALISM AND THE NEW BILATERALISM IN ASIA AND THE ASIA PACIFIC

Regional initiatives in Asia began as defensive moves against regionalism in Europe and North America. In the early 1990s, the European Union was consolidating its single market, and the United States launched negotiations for the North American Free Trade Agreement (NAFTA). In response, Malaysian prime minister Mahathir bin Mohamad proposed forming an East Asian economic bloc to counter these emerging regional blocs. He advocated the East Asia Economic Group, which would incorporate the countries of the Association of Southeast Asian Nations (ASEAN) plus China, Hong Kong, Japan, South Korea, and Taiwan. The prospect of an Asia-only economic bloc triggered a swift response in Washington, and U.S. officials called on Japan and other Asian governments to resist the idea. Washington countered Mahathir's vision by pushing for the APEC forum, which had been established under Japanese and Australian initiative in 1989 as a loose consultative forum. The United States inaugurated APEC's annual summit when it hosted the meetings in 1993 in Seattle, and it forged a vision for an Asia-Pacific FTA that was then ratified in the Bogor Goals in 1994, committing developed APEC countries to eliminate barriers to trade and investment by 2010 and developing countries by 2020.

Concerned with being overshadowed by trans-Pacific regional integration and a rapidly opening Chinese economy, ASEAN governments set up the ASEAN Free Trade Area (AFTA) in 1992 to initiate a process of tariff reduction that would create an enlarged internal market in fifteen years. In its early years, the AFTA project stagnated as member governments continually failed to reach target dates and insisted on maintaining lengthy exceptions list. AFTA's stagnation kept APEC in the spotlight during much of the 1990s as the main vehicle for regional integration. However, in the late 1990s AFTA gained momentum, and the target date for full liberalization by the original five members was moved up to 2002. The five core ASEAN countries—Indonesia, Malaysia, the Philippines, Singapore, and Thailand—have now reduced tariffs to between 0 and 5 percent, although the exceptions list remains long, and implementation has been uneven.

APEC set forth a vision of regionalism that was distinctly nondiscriminatory and outward oriented. Member economies would engage in coordinated but voluntary liberalization based on enlightened mutual self-interest. However, confidence in APEC's ability to promote liberalization began to wane in the mid-1990s when efforts at sectoral liberalization provoked bitter disagreement, primarily between the United States and Japan. APEC's perceived failure to play any constructive role in the 1997/1998 Asian financial crisis dealt the organization another severe blow, and by the end of the decade countries were openly questioning its relevance.

APEC's decline and a growing disenchantment with the WTO opened the door to bilateralism. Outside of Asia, the 1990s witnessed a dramatic proliferation in FTAs, led by the European Union, the United States, and several Latin American countries. Asian governments initially resisted the trend. Apart from the AFTA set up in 1992, no major Asian country had a bilateral or plurilateral trade pact in place prior to 2000. Japan and South Korea remained staunch defenders of multilateralism well into the late 1990s and thus found themselves alone among Organization for Economic Cooperation and Development members that had not signed any bilateral trade accords. However, they began to grow concerned about economic isolation as liberalization efforts stalled in the WTO and APEC continued to lose momentum. South Korea opened talks with Chile for an FTA in 1999, and discussions at the quasi-governmental level began between South Korea and Japan on forging an FTA. When Singapore approached Japan with a proposal to launch an FTA, the Japanese government decided that it would be an excellent test case, and the two countries signed an agreement in January 2002. Japan then turned its focus toward negotiating an FTA with Mexico to mitigate NAFTA's adverse effect on Japanese business.[2]

A new burst of negotiating activity was sparked by China's proposal to ASEAN in November 2001 to establish an ASEAN-China FTA (ACFTA) by 2010.[3] The two sides began negotiations soon, with China offering "early harvest" trade deals to open farm trade with interested ASEAN members, Thailand being the first in October 2003.[4] Negotiations on trade in goods were complete by late 2004, and an agreement on services was signed in January 2007. China's activism took Japan by surprise, and Japan scrambled to keep pace by coming up with its own initiative for a Japan-ASEAN economic alliance. Within two months of China's proposal, Japanese prime minister Koizumi Junichiro toured the region and proposed a Japan-ASEAN comprehensive economic partnership, which would include an FTA.[5] However, Japan decided to deploy a two-track strategy for FTAs with ASEAN. First, building on the recently signed Japan-Singapore FTA, it would negotiate bilateral FTAs with the most advanced ASEAN countries prior to ASEAN-wide negotiations. In 2002, it approached Thailand, Malaysia, and the Philippines for bilateral FTAs, judging these countries more ready for FTA negotiations that would entail broad coverage of trade and significant domestic policy reforms in areas such as services, investment, and intellectual property rights (IPR). It hoped that precedents set in these bilateral accords would become the standard for a Japan-ASEAN FTA, which would include the less-developed ASEAN members.[6] Ideally, this "high-standard" FTA would then serve as the foundational building block for a broader regional FTA that would incorporate China. Accordingly, if Japan's strategy plays out, China will then be brought into an agreement with strong disciplines in the key areas of IPR, services, and investment protections.

By mid-2005, Japan finalized negotiations with Thailand and Malaysia and launched talks with Indonesia, and it began active negotiations with ASEAN as a whole. However, to date, Japan's two-prong strategy has been only partially successful. Although Japan wrapped up bilateral FTAs with the key ASEAN countries, it faced strong resistance in the areas of IPR and government procurement. Individual ASEAN countries did not want to step out ahead of their less-developed members, and they simply refused to agree to obligations in these areas. Japan was more successful in gaining commitments in services and investment provisions.[7]

Meanwhile, South Korea approached ASEAN for an FTA in late 2004, and a deal was signed in mid-2006. Thailand, however, opted out of the deal because South Korea refused to include rice. South Korea then took the dramatic step of approaching the United States for an FTA, indicating that it was willing to make bold moves to achieve a deal.[8] The two sides completed negotiations successfully in March 2007, and both are optimistic about ratification. Other countries in the region, notably Australia, Singapore, and Thailand, have been actively pursuing FTAs with a wide range of trade partners.

The result of this flurry of FTA activity can be seen in table 9.2 and figure 9.2.

Figure 9.2 illustrates the rapidly expanding network of trade deals taking shape in the region. ASEAN lies at the center of this activity, signing "plus one" free-trade pacts with China and South Korea,[9] and conducting ongoing negotiations for deals with Japan, Australia–New Zealand, and India. These "plus one" deals create somewhat of a hub-and-spokes structure, with the ASEAN "hub" locking in deals, while the "spoke" countries (China, Japan, South Korea, and perhaps India) remain some distance away from negotiating bilateral FTAs between themselves. At the same time, China, Japan, South Korea, and the United States are vying to form competing "hubs" by forging FTAs with multiple regional and trans-Pacific partners. The advantage of being a "hub" is twofold. First, hub countries tend to reap larger economic gains from preferential liberalization in an FTA network than do "spoke" countries.[10] Second, hubs are often able to set standards for agreements. Just as the European Union and the United States have promoted their own distinct "model" of FTAs, Japan, China, and ASEAN all hope to promote their own priorities in the regional FTA game.

Another notable and perhaps more surprising feature clearly visible in figure 9.2 is the strong trans-Pacific dimension of the emerging FTA architecture. In addition to the Japan-Mexico and South Korea–Chile FTAs mentioned earlier, several East Asian countries have reached across the Pacific to negotiate trade accords, including Singapore (with the United States, Chile, Canada, and Mexico), South Korea (with the United States, Canada, and Mexico in addition to

TABLE 9.2 FREE-TRADE AGREEMENTS (FTAS) IN THE ASIA PACIFIC

Completed (Date in Effect)	Finalized (Date Finalized)	Under Negotiation (Date Started)	Proposed
NAFTA[1] (January 1994)	U.S.-Peru (December 2005; signed April 2006)	U.S.-Thailand (June 2004)	FTAAP[2]
U.S.-Chile (January 2004)		U.S.-Malaysia (March 2006)	
U.S.-Singapore (January 2004)		U.S.-South Korea (July 2006)	
U.S.-Australia (January 2005)			
Japan-Singapore (November 2002)	Japan-Philippines (signed September 2006; in effect in 2007)	Japan-Vietnam (January 2007)	
Japan-Mexico (April 2005)	Japan-Thailand (signed April 2007)	Japan-ASEAN (April 2005)	
Japan-Malaysia (July 2006)	Japan-Chile (September 2006)	Japan-South Korea (December 2003)	
	Japan-Indonesia (November 2006)	Japan-India (January 2007)	
	Japan-Brunei (December 2006)	Japan-Australia (April 2007)	

(continued)

TABLE 9.2 *(continued)*

Completed (Date in Effect)	Finalized (Date Finalized)	Under Negotiation (Date Started)	Proposed
AFTA[3] (1993)		Australia–New Zealand–ASEAN (February 2005)	ASEAN Plus Three[4]
ASEAN-China (July 2005)		ASEAN-India (January 2004)	ASEAN Plus Six[5]
ASEAN–South Korea[6] (June 2007)			
South Korea–Chile (April 2004)		South Korea-India (March 2005)	South Korea–Australia[7]
South Korea–Singapore (March 2006)		South Korea-Canada (July 2005)	
		South Korea–Mexico (February 2006)	
Singapore–New Zealand (January 2001)		Singapore-Mexico (July 2000)	
Singapore-Australia (July 2003)		Singapore-Canada (October 2001)	
Singapore-India (August 2005)		Singapore-Pakistan (August 2005)	
Singapore–Chile–New Zealand–Brunei (May 2006)		Singapore-Peru (February 2006)	
		Singapore-China (October 2006)	

Australia–New Zealand (January 1983)		Australia-Malaysia (May 2005)	Australia-Chile[8]
Australia-Thailand (January 2005)		Australia-China (May 2005)	
New Zealand–Thailand (July 2005)		New Zealand–Hong Kong (2001)	
		New Zealand–China (November 2004)	
		New Zealand–Malaysia (March 2005)	
China–Hong Kong (January 2004)			
China-Macau (January 2004)			
China-Chile (October 2006)			
Chile-Canada (July 1997)	Chile-Peru (signed August 2006)	Chile-Malaysia (November 2006)	Chile-Thailand[9]
Chile-Mexico (August 1999)		Peru-Thailand (January 2004)	
		Peru-Mexico (May 2006)	
		Peru-Canada (2007 soon to start)	

(continued)

TABLE 9.2 (continued)

Completed (Date in Effect)	Finalized (Date Finalized)	Under Negotiation (Date Started)	Proposed
India–Sri Lanka (March 2000)	SAFTA[10] (signed January 2004)	India-Thailand (January 2004)	
	India-Chile[11] (signed March 2006)		
	India-Malaysia (signed December 2005)		

Notes: List includes members of the Asia-Pacific Economic (APEC) forum plus India.

[1] The North American Free Trade Agreement (NAFTA) consists of Canada, Mexico, and the United States.

[2] The Free Trade Area of the Asia-Pacific (FTAAP) is an FTA among APEC member countries.

[3] The ASEAN Free Trade Area (AFTA) consists of Brunei, Cambodia, Indonesia, Laos, Malaysia, Myanmar, Philippines, Singapore, Thailand, and Vietnam.

[4] The countries included here are China, Japan, and South Korea, in addition to ASEAN member countries.

[5] The countries included here are Australia, China, India, Japan, New Zealand, and South Korea, in addition to ASEAN member countries.

[6] This agreement does not include Thailand.

[7] The two countries agreed in December 2006 to conduct a joint study on an FTA.

[8] The two countries agreed in December 2006 to launch a working group on an FTA.

[9] The two countries agreed in January 2006 to set up a joint study group on an FTA.

[10] The South Asia Free Trade Agreement (SAFTA) participating countries are Bangladesh, Bhutan, India, the Maldives, Nepal, Pakistan, and Sri Lanka.

[11] This is a limited-coverage agreement.

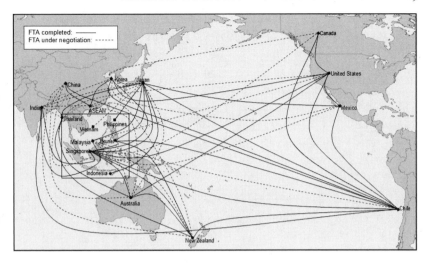

FIGURE 9.2 EMERGING FTA NETWORK IN EAST ASIA AND THE ASIA PACIFIC.

Note: NAFTA, North American Free Trade Agreement; EU, European Union; Mercosur, Mercado Común del Sur (Southern Common Market).

Chile), Japan (with Chile in addition to Mexico), Australia (with the United States), and Thailand and Malaysia (both of which are negotiating FTAs with the United States). Many of these countries are also negotiating trade accords with the European Union and European Free Trade Association countries (Iceland, Liechtenstein, Norway, Switzerland). These centrifugal moves underscore the continuing "open" nature of economic regionalism in Asia. With trans-Pacific and cross-regional trade deals flourishing, the region does not appear to be headed toward an Asia-only trade bloc.

ECONOMIC AND STRATEGIC MOTIVATIONS FOR ASIAN REGIONAL FTAS

It is important to consider the motivations underlying the new FTAs before analyzing their content and potential economic impact because such motivations may determine that impact as well as the future course of regional FTA management and coordination. Are countries motivated primarily by economic or strategic considerations when choosing FTA partners?

One notable feature of the emerging FTAs in Asia is the relatively modest size of the bilateral trade flows involved. As shown in table 9.3, Asian countries have chosen to negotiate FTAs with partners that are only moderately impor-

TABLE 9.3 FREE-TRADE AGREEMENT (FTA) PARTNER EXPORT
MARKETS, AS SHARE OF TOTAL EXPORTS AND RANK, 2005

FTA (Country A– Country B)	Share of Country A's Exports Absorbed by Country B	Country B's Rank as Country A's Export Market	Share of Country B's Exports Absorbed by Country A	Country A's Rank as Country B's Export Market
U.S.-Chile	0.6%	29	15.4%	1
U.S.-Singapore	2.3%	11	10.4%	2
U.S.-Australia	1.7%	14	6.7%	4
Japan-Singapore	3.1%	8	5.5%	6
Japan-Mexico	1.2%	19	0.7%	6
Japan-Malaysia	2.1%	11	9.4%	3
Japan-Philippines	1.5%	14	18.1%	2
Japan-Thailand	3.8%	7	13.7%	2
South Korea– Chile	0.4%	37	5.4%	5
South Korea– Singapore	2.6%	8	3.5%	11
Singapore–New Zealand	1.4%	18	0.5%	20
Singapore- Australia	3.7%	9	2.9%	10
Singapore-India	2.6%	13	5.2%	4
Australia–New Zealand	6.4%	5	21.4%	1
Australia- Thailand	3.0%	9	2.9%	8
China-Chile	0.3%	40	10.8%	3
Chile-Canada	2.6%	11	0.1%	36
Chile-Mexico	3.9%	8	0.3%	13
ASEAN-China	8.1%	4	7.3%	4
ASEAN–South Korea	3.8%	7	9.6%	3

tant or, in some cases, relatively insignificant in terms of bilateral trade. Japan's FTA partners—Singapore, Mexico, Malaysia, and the Philippines—rank as its eighth-, nineteenth-, eleventh-, and fourteenth-largest export markets, respectively. South Korea has concluded FTAs with its thirty-seventh-, eighth-, and third-largest export markets (Chile, Singapore, and ASEAN, respectively). Of course, there are some notable exceptions to this trend. NAFTA linked the United States to two of its largest export markets and tied Canada and Mexico to their largest trade partner, the United States.[11] The ASEAN "plus one" deals are also potentially more commercially significant because ASEAN represents the third-largest export market for both South Korea and Japan, the fourth-largest market for China, and the second-largest market for India. A South Korea–U.S. FTA, if successfully concluded, would represent the most commercially significant FTA not only for South Korea, but also for the United States outside of NAFTA. Nevertheless, the majority of trade agreements remain between countries that are not major trade partners.

Why are countries channeling their energy toward negotiating trade accords with medium- and small-size trading partners? First, some countries have deliberately sought out smaller, less trade-relevant partners to initiate FTAs as a learning process and as a way to ease domestic opponents to trade liberalization into the FTA game. The hope is that liberalization can unfold through successive FTAs as an incremental process, which will allow domestic constituencies to adjust to relatively small steps in trade liberalization until they are ready to accept take larger steps with larger reforms.[12] South Korea selected Chile as its first FTA partner precisely because the two countries had such low levels of bilateral trade. Chile's exports to South Korea were heavily dominated by raw materials, mainly copper, and its agricultural exports had a relatively small share of the Korean market. The South Korean government hoped that limited concessions to Chilean farm goods would not provoke too much opposition from domestic farmers.[13] Moreover, Chile was already an experienced FTA negotiator. Japan selected Singapore as a "test case" for similar reasons. Singapore has virtually no agricultural exports to Japan, so negotiations could focus on establishing high-quality rules for trade between the two advanced economies.

Second, the selection of smaller-size trade partners for FTAs underscores a general point many observers have made about the trend toward FTAs in today's global economy: tariff reduction is not their primary goal or even their main effect.[14] Tariffs in many countries are relatively low after decades of multilateral tariff liberalization in the General Agreement on Tariffs and Trade (GATT) and WTO. Furthermore, economic integration and rising competition with China has led ASEAN countries to lower applied tariff rates substantially over the past decade.[15] Of course, tariff peaks remain and distort trade, and they become motivating targets in FTA negotiations. However, other policy considerations are often equally important. To some extent, concern over tariffs and trade in goods has been replaced by a focus on nontariff and nonborder issues that affect trade and that can often be more easily dealt with in bilateral negotiations. Singapore, for example, has made services liberalization a top priority in its FTAs.[16] Japan, in its FTA negotiations with ASEAN countries, has also stressed expanding trade in services and improving protections of IPR and investment.[17] These nontariff policy goals reflect Japanese business priorities. When Japan's Ministry of Economy, Trade, and Industry (METI) surveyed Japanese businesses about the most important problems they face in operating in ASEAN, only 7.6 percent mentioned high tariffs. Business respondents were more concerned about issues that affected a rule-based, stable business environment, including legal systems (11.4 percent), human resources (12.9 percent), labor problems (12.9 percent), and political and social instability (13.6 percent). When asked about problems in China, the contrast is even starker, with only 3.6 percent of Japanese businesses mentioning tariffs, but 26.5 percent pointing to the legal system, 18.7 percent to IPR infringement, and 10.8 percent to investment restrictions.[18]

An exclusive focus on trade objectives also fails to capture the importance of investment relations in motivating FTAs and shaping negotiation outcomes. The investment link has been particularly strong for Japan and its FTA partners. Japan has targeted countries that heavily depend on Japanese foreign direct investment to fuel their manufacturing export industries. In many cases, these countries rely on Japan as their largest or second-largest source of inward direct investment (table 9.4). Signing an FTA with Japan serves to lock in these investment flows and perhaps to augment them relative to competing states, which are primarily fellow ASEAN members. Japanese trade negotiators have successfully used this investment incentive as leverage in FTA talks.[19] They persuaded Malaysia to liberalize its domestic automobile sector substantially by pointing to the recently finalized FTA with Thailand, arguing that equivalent reforms were needed to place Malaysia in a more competitive position for Japanese business investment in the electronics and auto sectors. These arguments were born out when Japanese foreign direct investment to Malaysia jumped fivefold in the six months following the implementation of the FTA in July 2006, marking the highest level of Japanese foreign direct investment in more than a decade.[20]

Finally, and perhaps most important, countries are often motivated less by commercial reasons and more by political and strategic considerations. China's FTA outreach to ASEAN was grounded in a desire to build political trust with its Southeast Asian neighbors and to create a regional framework that enhances its influence. As Sheng Lijun notes, "[F]or China, the process of working for an FTA with its Southeast Asian neighbors is just as important as the outcome it-

TABLE 9.4 INVESTMENT FLOWS BETWEEN FREE-TRADE AGREEMENT (FTA) PARTNERS

FTA (Country A–Country B)	Share of Country A's Outward FDI Absorbed by Country B	Country B's Rank in Country A's International Investment Market	Share of Country B's Inward FDI Funded by Country A	Country A's Rank in Country B's Inward FDI Market
U.S.-Chile	0.5%	17	26.3%	2
U.S.-Singapore	2.3%	8	15.1%	2
U.S.-Australia	5.5%	3	25.0%	1
Japan-Singapore	3.0%	5	13.5%	3
Japan-Mexico	0.9%	15	3.1%	4
Japan-Malaysia	1.2%	14	14.0%	3
Japan-Philippines	0.9%	16	25.6%	1
Japan-Thailand	3.0%	6	32.2%	1
South Korea–Chile	0.1%	48	0.1%	32
South Korea–Singapore	2.1%	8	0.7%	>7
Singapore–New Zealand	0.7%	>16	1.7%	>5
Singapore-Australia	4.9%	9	1.5%	7
Singapore-India	0.7%	>17	3.4%	5
Australia–New Zealand	19.0%	3	46.7%	1
Australia-Thailand	0.1%	14	1.3%	>5
China-Chile	0.1%	>10	0.1%	30

(continued)

TABLE 9.4 (continued)

FTA (Country A–Country B)	Share of Country A's Outward FDI Absorbed by Country B	Country B's Rank in Country A's International Investment Market	Share of Country B's Inward FDI Funded by Country A	Country A's Rank in Country B's Inward FDI Market
Chile-Canada	14.2%	3	1.2%	14
Chile-Mexico	1.4%	11	0.1%	>15
ASEAN-China	1.4%	10	1.5%	>10
ASEAN–South Korea	1.6%	9	12.3%	4

Note: Due to the high annual variation, data in foreign direct investment (FDI) are examined over a longer period of time, the stock either at year end or between periods. EU-25 is taken as one economy. ASEAN is taken as one economy only in calculating ASEAN-China and ASEAN–South Korea investment flows (the last two rows). In the remainder of the table, ASEAN countries are treated individually. Rankings for FDI may not include all countries, depending on the availability of data.

self."[21] Although China stands to gain relatively little in terms of commercial benefits in the short run, it has gained enormous diplomatic credit for its FTA activism with ASEAN and other countries in the region. ASEAN, for its part, has courted several countries for FTAs as a strategy to remain center stage and act as the standard setter for regional integration. Japan and South Korea have accelerated their own FTA diplomacy to keep pace with China and compete for regional influence. The current spate of FTA negotiations include surprising pairings, such as Japan and India, and Japan and Australia, which will raise difficult sectoral trade issues. However, these agreements are part of Japan's broad strategy to counter China's growing regional influence and to bolster the institutional linkages of the East Asia Summit (EAS) countries, which Japan favors over ASEAN Plus Three (APT) as a venue for regional integration.

The prevalence of strategic and nontrade objectives in the current flurry of FTA negotiations may have negative implications for the quality of the FTAs that emerge. Countries driven by strategic and political considerations in their FTA initiatives may be more willing to negotiate trade deals with relatively soft coverage, long phase-in periods, and generous exemptions for sensitive sectors. These less-desirable features are more likely to tangle the "noodle bowl" even further and in turn make it more difficult to harmonize or aggregate FTAs in a broader regional trade arrangement that will liberalize trade.

ASSESSING THE EMERGING FTA ARCHITECTURE

FTAs are designed to promote selective liberalization between participating countries and are therefore inherently discriminatory. Discriminatory liberalization contradicts the basic norms of both the global and regional trade regimes, potentially undermining nondiscriminatory multilateral liberalization at the WTO as well as the "open regionalism" and "concerted unilateral" liberalization envisioned by APEC. At the same time, however, the specific provisions of some FTAs may serve to bolster the rules and norms of these broader trade regimes. Whether they act as "building blocks" or "stumbling blocks" depends on their content and how they are managed and perhaps coordinated in the future.

To date, the economic impact of the emerging FTA architecture in Asia is limited because FTAs in the region are still quite new. Most of the existing FTAs were implemented in the early 2000s, and their lengthy phase-in periods will delay the impact of trade liberalization, particularly on sensitive sectors. Preferential liberalization has only begun to occur.[22] Instead, market forces continue to drive the process of regional economic integration. Business firms are fragmenting operations across the region to take advantage of local efficiencies. The dynamic regional division of labor that drives "Factory Asia" continues to advance as China moves to higher-technology assembly and as lower-end processes shift to less-advanced ASEAN economies. Tariffs are already relatively low in the region because ASEAN countries have moved unilaterally to lower their tariffs and other barriers in order to remain competitive. For these reasons, the ACFTA, the ASEAN–South Korea FTA (AKFTA), and other FTAs will matter only at the margins for some time to come.

Nevertheless, the FTAs' economic effects will grow over the next decade, and their political significance will likely continue to rise. The question then becomes whether the emerging FTA architecture will undermine or reinforce global and regional trade norms. Here the picture is rather mixed. On the one hand, the discrimination inherent in the preferential liberalization of FTAs violates the most basic WTO principal, unconditional MFN treatment, which is enshrined in Article I of the GATT. Yet the GATT also established rules, subsequently incorporated into the WTO, that permit countries to liberalize selectively in customs unions and FTAs, provided that they eliminate tariffs on "substantially all the trade" between the partner countries (GATT, Article XXIV).[23] This requirement has been left vaguely defined, leaving it open to interpretation and controversy. The standard interpretation, advanced by the European Union and others, holds that at least 90 percent of trade between participants should be covered, with no major sectors excluded. In addition, tariff liberalization should be implemented in a reasonable period of time, which GATT and the WTO define as ten years.

As seen in table 9.5, existing accords in Asia generally meet the quantitative benchmark of 90 percent trade coverage, with a few notable exceptions (e.g., Japan's FTA with Mexico covers only 86 percent of Japan's imports, and India's FTA with Singapore covers only 80 percent of India's imports). However, many fall short of the qualitative standard of not excluding any major sectors. Asian FTAs tend to have significant carve-outs of tariff lines in particular sectors, especially agriculture. Moreover, many of these FTAs have lengthy and complicated phase-in periods for tariff reductions. Both the ACFTA and the AKFTA have adopted the ASEAN approach of dividing tariff lines into a "normal track" and a "sensitive track." Tariff lines on the "normal track" are further divided into different categories subject to gradual reductions until they are supposed to be eliminated by 2010 (for AKFTA) or by 2012 (for ACFTA).[24] Sensitive-list items, which can make up to 10 percent of total trade value, are supposed to be reduced only 20 to 50 percent over a lengthy time frame. South Korea's decision to exclude rice from its liberalization commitments led Thailand to opt out of the AKFTA. In addition to rice and other agricultural items, South Korea placed industrial items in chemicals, textiles, and automobile sectors on the sensitive list. China and ASEAN have placed many important industrial prod-

TABLE 9.5 EXISTING FREE-TRADE AGREEMENTS (FTAS), COVERAGE, AND EXEMPTIONS

Partners	Date in Effect (or Signed)	Trade Coverage (Total)	Trade Coverage (Each Side)	Exceptions	Rule Coverage
NAFTA[1]	January 1994	99%[2]		Agricultural goods subject to three separate bilateral agreements. Exemptions include (for Canada) dairy products, poultry, and eggs; (for the United States) dairy products, sugar, cotton, and peanuts. Numerous side agreements for agricultural exemptions between the United States and Mexico, and lengthy phase-in period for tariff eliminations.[3]	Extensive coverage in services (negative list approach).
U.S.-Chile	January 2004	100%[4]		None[5]	Broad coverage in services (negative list approach).

(continued)

TABLE 9.5 (continued)

Partners	Date in Effect (or Signed)	Trade Coverage (Total)	Trade Coverage (Each Side)	Exceptions	Rule Coverage
U.S.-Singapore	January 2004		Export to Singapore: 100% Export to the United States: 92% Liberalized immediately, with remaining phased in within ten years	None[6]	Broad protections for investment, including MFN, and for national treatment, including dispute settlement; chapter on movement of persons includes steps to implement APEC Mutual Recognition Agreement for conformity assessment of telecommunications equipment.
U.S.-Australia	January 2005		Industrial goods: 99%[7] Agricultural goods: 75% duty free in	U.S. side: sugar; tariffs on dairy products and beef phased out over eighteen years.	Extensive services coverage.

Japan–Singapore	November 2002	98%[9]	Export to Singapore: 100% Export to Japan: 94%[10]	Singapore: none. Japan: all agriculture (other than goods already duty free under WTO); leather and leather goods.[11]	Service commitments beyond GATS; mutual-recognition provisions, including for professional services and movement of persons; investment fully covered; builds on and expands WTO TRIPS; builds on WTO Government Procurement; rules of origin fairly complex and product specific.[12]
Japan–Mexico	April 2005	96%[13]	Export to Japan: 87% Export to Mexico: 98%[14]	Rice and wheat, dairy products, cassava starch, sago starch, plywood, tuna, and mackerel.[15]	Complex and product specific ROO.[16] negative list approach in services (financial services excluded). *(continued)*

four years, with remaining tariffs removed in ten to eighteen years[8]

TABLE 9.5 (continued)

Partners	Date in Effect (or Signed)	Trade Coverage (Total)	Trade Coverage (Each Side)	Exceptions	Rule Coverage
Japan-Malaysia	July 2006	97%[17]	Export to Malaysia: 99% Export to Japan: 94%[18]	Rice and wheat, beef, pork, sugar, pineapple, cassava starch, and sago starch.[19]	Services coverage beyond GATS, with standstill and transparency provisions.
Japan-Philippines	Signed September 2006	94%[20]	Export to Philippines: 97% Export to Japan: 92%[21]	Japan: rice and wheat, dairy products, sago starch, and fishery products;[22] gradual tariff reduction on bananas, frozen tuna, dried pineapple, textiles, and clothing. Philippines: moderate tariff reductions in automotive sector, subject to renegotiations in 2009.	Service commitments beyond GATS, including standstill and transparency provisions.
AFTA[23]	1993	90%[24] (number of items)		Thailand, Malaysia, Philippines: rice. Indonesia: sugar, garlic, and meat.[25]	Simple and straightforward ROO (40% cumulative content); services agreement but limited value added beyond GATS.
ASEAN-China	July 2005	90%[26]	Export to China: 93%	Items placed on highly sensitive list can be protected by high tariffs, subject to	Abides by WTO provisions on IPR,

			Export to ASEAN: 90%[27]	50% reduction by the end of 2014 (2017 for CLMV). These items include (for China) numerous tariff lines in chemicals, automobiles, and agriculture; (for Indonesia) autos, grain, plastics, sugars, chinaware, and so on; (for Malaysia) iron and steel, autos, tobacco, glass products, chinaware, and so on; (for the Philippines) plastics, meat, vegetables, glass products, autos, and so on; (for Thailand) autos, coffee and tea, fat and oil, stone materials, general machines, and so on; (for Brunei) autos; (for Singapore) beer.[28]	TBT,[29] antidumping, sanitary, and phytosanitary measures.
ASEAN–South Korea[30]	July 2006	90%[31]		Rice, poultry, frozen and live fish, garlic, onion, hot peppers, and most fruits.[32]	No investment clause; complicated, product-specific ROO.
South Korea–Chile	April 2004	96% (number of items)[33]	Export to Chile: 96.5% Export to South Korea: 96.2%[34]	South Korean side: rice, apples, pears, and wheat flour; most other agricultural products subject to seven- to sixteen-year phase-out period. Chilean side: refrigerators and washing machines.	Services coverage moderate; builds on WTO protocols in IPR, antidumping, sanitary, and phytosanitary measures, TRIMs,[35] and TBT; complicated rules of origin.

(continued)

TABLE 9.5 (continued)

Partners	Date in Effect (or Signed)	Trade Coverage (Total)	Trade Coverage (Each Side)	Exceptions	Rule Coverage
South Korea–Singapore	March 2006		Export to Singapore: 100% Export to South Korea: 91.6%[36]	South Korea: agricultural products such as meat, vegetables, fruits, cereals, and frozen and live fish.[37]	Extensive services coverage (Singapore offers 95.6% coverage); national treatment for investment.
Singapore–New Zealand	January 2001	100%[38]		None[39]	National treatment and MFN for investment; positive list approach in services.
Singapore-Australia	July 2003	100%[40]		None[41]	Extensive services coverage (negative list approach); IPR builds on WTO TRIPS; national treatment for investment (but not for MFN).
Singapore-India	August 2005		Export to Singapore: 100% Export to	India: CD and DVD players, auto parts, high-speed diesel, shampoos, deodorants, yarn and fiber, cigarettes, condensed milk, edible oils, chocolate and cocoa	

Singapore–Chile–New Zealand–Brunei	May 2006	90%[44]	Chile: dairy products (to be eliminated on January 2017). Brunei: alcohol, tobacco, and firearms. New Zealand: textiles, apparel, footwear, and carpet products (to be eliminated in January 2015).[45]	Extensive coverage in services with significant improvements on WTO commitments; government procurement builds on WTO and APEC protocols; builds on TRIPS and WIPO treaties on IPR; open-accession clause.[46]
Australia–New Zealand	January 1983	100%[47]	None (original 1983 agreement had limited coverage, but 1988 protocol led to complete elimination of tariffs by 1990).	
Australia–Thailand	January 2005	98%[48]	Extremely long phase-in periods (tariffs eliminated by 2020 or 2025) for beef, beef innards, pork, and processed dairy products such as powdered skim milk.[49]	Broad protections for investment, including MFN, national treatment, and dispute settlement; services coverage reflects existing GATS commitments.

(continued)

TABLE 9.5 (continued)

Partners	Date in Effect (or Signed)	Trade Coverage (Total)	Trade Coverage (Each Side)	Exceptions	Rule Coverage
New Zealand–Thailand	July 2005	100%[50]	Thailand: immediately eliminates tariffs on 52% of imports; 85% by 2020. New Zealand: 85% in July 2005; 97% by 2010; remaining tariffs will be phased to zero by 2015.[51]	Extremely long phase-in periods for dairy products (tariffs eliminated by Thailand by 2025), textiles, apparel, footwear, and carpets (tariffs eliminated by 2015 by New Zealand).[52]	
China-Chile	October 2006	97%[53]		China: iodine, rice, forest products, and TVs. Chile: sugar, oats, wheat flour, tires, textiles, home appliances (e.g., microwaves, washing machines), and metal products.[54]	

Chile-Canada	July 1997	99.8%[55]	Canada: dairy products, poultry, and eggs.[56] Chile: rice, vegetable oil, sugar, and nondurum wheat and flour (phase-out periods of ten to eighteen years).[57]
Chile-Mexico	August 1999		Chile: barley, wheat flour, and seed oil. Mexico: fisheries, dairy products, and tobacco.[58]

[1]The North American Free Trade Agreement (NAFTA) consists of Canada, Mexico, and the United States.

[2]Committee on Regional Trade Agreements (CRTA), Draft Report on the Examination of the North American Free Trade Agreement (Geneva: World Trade Organization CRTA, 2000).

[3]Japan External Trade Organization, International Economic Research Division, "Nihon no Norin Suisanbutsu Yunyu to Shuyo FTA no Reigai Hinmoku," WTO/FTA Column 10 (August 9, 2002), 1, http://www.jetro.go.jp/biz/world/international/column/pdf/010.pdf.

[4]U.S. Trade Representative, "Free Trade with Chile: Summary of the U.S.-Chile Free Trade Agreement," December 11, 2002, http://www.ustr.gov/Document_Library/Fact_Sheets/2002/Free_Trade_with_Chile_Summary_of_the_US-Chile_Free_Trade_Agreement.html.

[5]Ibid.

[6]Tony Sitathan, "FTA Gives Singapore Trans-Pacific Benefits," Asia Times, May 21, 2003, http://www.atimes.com/atimes/Southeast_Asia/EE21Ae07.html.

[7]U.S. Trade Representative, "U.S.-Australia FTA Summary of the Agreement," July 15, 2004, http://www.ustr.gov/Trade_Agreements/Bilateral/Australia_FTA/US-Australia_FTA_Summary_of_the_Agreement.html.

[8]Austrade, "The Australia–United States Free Trade Agreement: In Brief," 6, http://www.fta.gov.au/default.aspx?FolderID=246&ArticleID=193.

[9]Ministry of Foreign Affairs, Japan, "Nihon-Shingaporu Shinjidai Keizai Renkei Kyotei (gaiyo)" [The Japan-Singapore Economic Agreement for a New Age Partnership (summary)], January 2003, http://www.mofa.go.jp/mofaj/area/singapore/kyotei/html.

[10]Ibid.

[11]Customs and Tariff Bureau, Ministry of Finance, Japan, "Nihon Shingaporu shinjidai keizai renkei: Kyotei kosho no jisshitsu daketsu no gutaiteki naiyo" [Japan-Singapore economic partnership in the new era: Specifics for the negotiation], October 31, 2001, 24, http://www.mof.go.jp/singikai/kanzegaita/siryou/kanc13031c.pdf. WTO is the World Trade Organization.

(continued)

TABLE 9.5 (continued)

[12] GATS is the General Agreement on Trade in Services; TRIPs is the Agreement on Trade-Related Aspects of Intellectual Property Rights.

[13] Hiroyuki Kato, "Viva Free Trade! Japan-Mexico FTA Approaches," Daily Yomiuri, March 31, 2005.

[14] Economic Affairs Bureau, Ministry of Foreign Affairs, Japan, "Nihon no Keizai Kyotei (EPA) kosho: Genjo to kadai" [EPAs of Japan: Status and issues], June 2008, 30, http://www.mofa.go.jp/mofaj/gaiko/fta/pdfs/kyotei_0703.pdf.

[15] International Affairs Department, Secretariat, Ministry of Agriculture, Forestry, and Fisheries (MAFF), Japan, "Keizai Renkei Kyotei (EPA) Jiyu Boeki Kyotei (FTA) wo meguru jokyo" [Status of EPAs and FTAs], January 2007, 6, http://www.maff.go.jp/sogo_shokuryo/fta_kanren/fta-1.pdf.

[16] ROO is "rules of origin."

[17] Economic Affairs Bureau, Ministry of Foreign Affairs, Japan, "Nichi Mareshia Keizai Renkei Kyotei" [The Japan-Malaysia EPA], January 2006, 2, http://www.mofa.go.jp/mofaj/gaiko/fta/j_asean/malaysia/pdfs/renkei_g.pdf.

[18] Ibid.

[19] MAFF, "Status of EPAs and FTAs."

[20] Economic Affairs Bureau, Ministry of Foreign Affairs, Japan, "Nichi-Firipin Keizai Renkei Kyotei no gaiyo" [Summary of Japan-Philippines economic partnership], September 2006, 2, http://www.mofa.go.jp/mofaj/gaiko/fta/j_asean/philippines/pdfs/gaiyo.pdf.

[21] Ibid.

[22] MAFF, "Status of EPAs and FTAs."

[23] AFTA (ASEAN FTA) consists of Brunei, Cambodia, Indonesia, Laos, Malaysia, Myanmar, Philippines, Singapore, Thailand, and Vietnam.

[24] ASEAN, "Southeast Asia: A Free Trade Area," 2002, 2, http://www.aseansec.org/viewpdf.asp?file=/pdf/afta.pdf; Asian and Oceanian Affairs Bureau Regional Policy Division, Ministry of Foreign Affairs, Japan, "AFTA (ASEAN Jiyu Boeki Chiiki) ni tsuite" [On the ASEAN Free Trade Area (AFTA)], June 2003, 5, http://www.mofa.go.jp/mofaj/area/asiakeizai/pdfs/afta.pdf.

[25] Peter D. Garrucho, "A Look Back at a Decade of AFTA," http://www.aseansec.org/peter_garrucho.htm.

[26] "Agreement on Trade in Goods of the Framework Agreement on Comprehensive Economic Co-operation Between the Association of Southeast Asian Nations and the People's Republic of China, Vientiane, November 29, 2004, ANNEX II. Modality for Tariff Reduction/Elimination for Tariff Lines Placed in the Sensitive Track," 1, http://www.aseansec.org/accfta%20tif/annex%202.zip.

[27] ASEAN, "Do Business with China Under the ASEAN-China Free Trade Area (ACFTA)," http://www.aseansec.org/acfta-brochure.doc; Mizuho Sogo Kenkyu Sho (Mizuho Research Institute), "Kaishi go ichinen no ASEAN-Chugoku FTA: ACFTA no koka to wagakuni kigyo ni yoru katsuyo" [One year after the ASEAN-China FTA: ACFTA's effectiveness and its application to Japanese firms], Mizuho Report, August 3, 2006, http://www.mizuho-ri.co.jp/research/economics/pdf/report/report06-0803.pdf.

28 "Agreement on Trade in Goods of the Framework Agreement," 24–33. CLMV is "Cambodia, Laos, Myanmar, and Vietnam."

29 IPR is "intellectual property rights"; TBT is "technical barriers to trade."

30 This agreement does not include Thailand.

31 "Agreement on Trade in Goods Under the Framework Agreement on Comprehensive Economic Cooperation Among the Governments of the Member Countries of the Association of Southeast Asian Nations and the Republic of Korea, Annex 2. Modality for Tariff Reduction/Elimination for Tariff Lines Placed in the Sensitive Track," 1, http://www.aseansec.org/AKFTA%20documents%20signed%20at%20in%20rok,24aug06,KL-pdf/Annex%202%20to%20TIG%20(Sensitive%20Track)%20-%20ASEAN%20Version%20-%20august%2006.pdf.

32 Ministry of Foreign Affairs and Trade, Republic of Korea, "Conclusion of the Agreement on Trade in Goods of the Korea–ASEAN Free Trade Agreement (FTA)," April 29, 2006, http://www.fta.go.kr/english/resources/resources_view.php?page=5&board_id=1204&country_id=1.

33 The 96 percent figure refers to the number of trade items rather than to the trade volume covered by the agreement. See "FTA with Chile to Boost Korea's Global Image," Korea Times, April 1, 2004; "S Korea–Chile Trade Agreement to Boost Exports to Latin America," Asia Pulse, March 31, 2004.

34 "S Korea–Chile Trade Agreement to Boost Exports to Latin America."

35 TRIMs is the Agreement on Trade-Related Investment Measures.

36 Ministry of Foreign Affairs and Trade, Republic of Korea, "Korea-Singapore FTA Ratified by the National Assembly," December 2, 2005, http://www.mofat.go.kr/me/me_a005/me_b022/1195140_1020.html.

37 Development Research Center (China), National Institute for Research Advancement (Japan), and Korea Institute for International Economic Policy (KIEP, South Korea), Joint Report and Policy Recommendations Concerning a Free Trade Agreement Among China, Japan, and Korea (Seoul: Development Research Center, National Institute for Research Advancement, and Korea Institute for International Economic Policy, 2006), December 11, 2006, 10, http://www.nira.go.jp/newse/paper/joint6/houko_E.pdf.

38 "Prime Ministers Sing Singapore Free Trade Deal," New Zealand Herald, November 14, 2000; Customs and Tariff Bureau, Ministry of Finance, Japan, "Chiiki boeki kyotei ni okeru kanzei seidojo no shuyo ronten" [Main issues concerning the regional trade agreements and tariff systems], August 10, 2001, 9, http://www.mof.go.jp/singikai/kanzegaita/siryou/kanc1308roc2.pdf.

39 "Prime Ministers Sing Singapore Free Trade Deal."

40 Austrade, "The Singapore-Australia Free Trade Agreement: In Brief," 4, http://www.fta.gov.au/ArticleDocuments/272/SAFTA_in%20brief.pdf.

41 International Enterprise Singapore, "Singapore-Australia Free Trade Agreement: Media-Info Kit," http://www.iesingapore.gov.sg/wps/wcm/connect/resources/file/ebfe95427/82404/FTA_SAFTA_Mediakit.pdf?MOD=AJPERES.

42 Sanjeev Sharma and Nandini Sen Gupta, "India, Singapore FTAs Ready to Get off Ground," Economic Times, April 16, 2005.

(continued)

TABLE 9.5 (continued)

43 Amiti Sen and G. Ganapathy Subramaniam, "S'pore Asks India to Widen Import List, Relax Origin Rules," Times News Network, August 4, 2006, http://economictimes.indiatimes.com/articleshow/1849879.cms.

44 "Singapore, New Zealand, Chile, Brunei Conclude Economic Partnership Agreement," AFX-Asia, June 3, 2005; "Singapore, Chile, Brunei, and NZ Sign Trade Agreement," Asia Pulse, June 3, 2005; "Brunei, Chile, New Zealand, Singapore Reach Trans-Pacific Agreement," Xinhua General News Service, June 3, 2005.

45 Ministry of Foreign Affairs and Trade of New Zealand, "The New Zealand–Singapore–Chile–Brunei Darussalam Trans-Pacific Strategic Economic Partnership," October 2005, 17–24, http://www.mfat.govt.nz/downloads/trade-agreement/transpacific/trans-pacificbooklet.pdf.

46 Government of Singapore, "Media Info Note: Trans-Pacific Strategic Economic Partnership Agreement," June 2, 2005, http://www.bilaterals.org/article.php3?id_article=2016. WIPO is "world intellectual property rights."

47 Ministry of Foreign Affairs and Trade, New Zealand, "The Australia New Zealand Closer Economic Relations (CER) Trade Agreement: 1983–2003 Backgrounder," http://www.mfat.govt.nz/Trade-and-Economic-Relations/o--Trade-archive/o--Trade-agreements/Australia/o-trade-agreement.php.

48 Austrade, "The Thailand-Australia Free Trade Agreement: In Brief," http://www.fta.gov.au/ArticleDocuments/260/TAFTA_In%20brief.pdf.

49 Department of Foreign Affairs and Trade, Australia, "Australia-Thailand CER FTA: Trade in Goods, Principal Outcomes for Australia," http://www.dfat.gov.au/trade/negotiations/aust-thai/goods_outcome_benefits_03003.html.

50 Ministry of Foreign Affairs and Trade, New Zealand, "Summary of Key Outcomes for New Zealand Exporters to Thailand," December 2004, http://www.mfat.govt.nz/Trade-and-Economic-Relations/o--Trade-archive/o--Trade-agreements/Thailand/o-key-outcomes-exporters.php#overall_outcomes.

51 Ibid.

52 Ibid.

53 "China, Chile Start New FTA Talks as One Goes Into Effect," Business Daily Update, November 30, 2006.

54 Japan External Trade Relations Organization, "Chugoku tono FTA kosho goi: Saicho 10 nenkan de kanzei teppai" [FTA negotiation with China reached agreement: Tariff elimination in 10 years], Tsusho Koho, November 7, 2005, http://www5.jetro.go.jp/jet-bin/pro1.cgi/news.html?%2043661%5d1115dc.

55 Committee on Regional Trade Agreements Seventeenth Session, World Trade Organization, "Examination of the Free Trade Agreement Between Canada and Chile," June 11, 1998, 2, http://www.sice.oas.org/geograph/south/wto_ca-ch.doc.

56 Foreign Affairs and International Trade, Canada, "Canada-Chile Free Trade Agreement: Legend for Use with Canadian Tariff Schedule," 9, http://www.international.gc.ca/tna-nac/cda-chile/cdasched/menu-en.asp.

57 Thomas Andrew O'Keefe, "The Evolution of Chilean Trade Policy in the Americas: From Lone Ranger to Team Player," Southwestern Journal of Law and Trade in the Americas 5 (1998), http://www.sice.oas.org/geograph/south/okeefe1.asp#III.

58 "Free Trade Agreement Between Chile and Mexico," Annex 3-04(4), http://www.worldtradelaw.net/fta/agreements/chilmexfta.pdf.

ucts on the sensitive track, including automobiles, appliances, chemical products, iron and steel, and textiles, in addition to many farm goods such as rice and palm oil.[25] South Korea targeted mostly agricultural products for sensitive-track treatment in AKFTA, but also included items in the chemicals, textiles, and automobiles sectors.[26]

The exceptions built into these bilateral FTAs may make subsequent liberalization at the regional or multilateral level more difficult. Domestic lobbies that have successfully resisted FTA reforms may further dig in their heels against multilateral liberalization at the WTO.[27] Some export sectors, in contrast, may feel they have gained sufficient access to key markets through regional FTAs and thus are unwilling to expend the necessary political capital to defeat domestic resistance to WTO accords in their home political economies. FTAs, in other words, may weaken the "pro-WTO" coalition at home.

Restrictive rules of origin are potentially an even larger problem. Rules of origin are at the heart of the "spaghetti bowl" problem, which Jagdish Bhagwati describes as "preferences like noodles criss-crossing all over the place."[28] Rules of origin are designed to provide protection for domestic producers by limiting an FTA's effects to producers in partner countries, but they can pose high administrative costs on business and exacerbate trade and investment diversion. Perhaps worst of all, stringent rules of origin can impede regional integration by discouraging businesses from using a regional network of suppliers. Rules-of-origin codes in Asia-Pacific FTAs vary considerably, ranging from relatively simple 40 percent cumulative content requirement in AFTA and ACFTA to the highly restrictive code negotiated by the United States in NAFTA. Japan and South Korea have tended to follow the U.S. and European Union model of negotiating relatively complex, product-specific rules of origin; in the Japan-Singapore FTA, for example, the rules-of-origin protocol is more than two hundred pages long.[29] Singapore, Australia, and other Asian countries have favored looser rules of origin in their FTAs.

In other ways, however, Asian FTAs conform to a "building block" approach that may serve to reinforce and extend WTO and APEC norms. Most are comprehensive in coverage, going beyond trade in goods to include trade in services as well as provisions for investment, government procurement, competition, IPR protection, dispute settlement, and technical barriers to trade. Perhaps the most noteworthy feature of Asian FTAs is their broad coverage of services trade. Services liberalization ranges from moderate to substantial, with ASEAN FTAs on the low end and FTAs by Australia, Japan, and Singapore on the high end.[30] Indeed, a recent study by researchers in the WTO Secretariat found that countries are often willing to go well beyond their WTO commitments in services when they negotiate FTAs.[31] Not only do countries sometimes improve on their existing commitments in the General Agreement on Trade in Services (GATS), but they typically make "new and improved" offers in FTAs that go beyond their current GATS offers in the Doha Round negotiations. Moreover, many FTAs adopt the negative-list approach in services and have thus created deeper commitments and greater actual market-opening results than achieved at the WTO.[32] Researchers at the World Bank concur that the relatively liberal provisions on services, such as liberal rules of origin, are likely to boost services trade and can serve as "building blocks" for multilateral liberalization. At the same time, they point to the danger that FTAs may deflate the appetite for Doha Round negotiations among the major service exporters, including the United States, the European Union, and Japan. "If the demanders of services are able to advance their offensive interests through FTAs, important bargaining chips may be removed from the multilateral negotiating table."[33]

Investment is another area in which Asian FTAs have made concrete progress over WTO talks. Most FTAs in the region have provisions for protecting foreign direct investment, including national treatment and MFN treatment for foreign investors. Many FTAs go beyond these general commitments to include provisions regarding expropriation, compensation, and, in some cases, repatriation of earnings. Economists O. G. Dayaratna Banda and John Whalley argue that these substantive commitments on investment found in many Asian FTAs are similar to those proposed in the failed Multilateral Investment Agreement, which was an attempt to go beyond the relatively weak provisions achieved at the GATT/WTO in the Uruguay Round (in the Agreement on Trade-Related Investment Measures). In this regard, they contend that "regional negotiations clearly seem to be fulfilling the role of a partial substitute for a wider multilateral agreement between countries who were not (in the main) forces of resistance to an agreement on multilateral disciplines eventually emerging from the WTO."[34]

Coverage in other areas also tends to reinforce or build on WTO agreements. In the area of IPR, many Asian FTAs build on the WTO Agreement on Trade-Related Aspects of Intellectual Property Rights, with the Japan-Singapore and U.S.-Singapore agreements setting an advanced standard. Likewise in government procurement, FTAs have enabled many countries to go beyond their WTO commitments. The United States and Japan tend to build on the WTO government procurement protocol in their FTAs, even when their partners are not signatories to the WTO agreement.[35] Australia has included government procurement in most of its FTAs even though it is not a signatory to the WTO protocol. The New Zealand–Singapore FTA makes explicit reference to APEC's Nonbinding Principles on Government Procurement. The trans-Pacific FTA among Singapore, New Zealand, Chile, and Brunei extensively covers government procurement, even though the parties are not signatories to the WTO protocol. Richard Baldwin makes the more general point that "it is remarkable to see how developing nations are willing to accept disciplines in FTAs on intellectual property rights, investment measures, government procurement and agricultural that they reject at the WTO level."[36]

What emerges from this brief assessment of regional FTAs is a complex picture with mixed implications. Asian FTAs vary widely in quality and coverage. They contain elements of concern, in particular sectoral carve-outs and restrictive rules of origin, but they also feature areas of substantive commitment that may well serve to facilitate deeper integration and outward-oriented trade. They tend to reinforce WTO (and APEC) rules and norms, and they allow countries to go beyond WTO commitments in areas where they desire deeper integration. These countries may subsequently find it easier to offer these commitments in the broader multilateral setting of the WTO or APEC. But, alternatively, the gains achieved through these FTAs may reduce major players' incentives to take up these issues at the WTO. And there is growing concern that the FTA fervor has drained energy from APEC. Furthermore, not everyone benefits equally from the emerging FTA architecture. Taiwan in particular has been virtually excluded from the regional and cross-regional network of FTAs. Consequently, it perhaps has the most to lose from the shift of negotiating activity away from the WTO and APEC into FTA bilateral channels. Other small countries that fail to become FTA "hubs" may lose out as well.

On balance, however, the emerging FTA architecture will most likely produce relatively benign effects both for the region and for the United States. Rather than government-negotiated preferences, market-driven forces, fueled by China's burgeoning growth, will continue to dominate the shaping of trade and investment flows. The largest bilateral trade flows in East Asia—between Japan and China, China and South Korea, South Korea and Japan—remain uncovered by FTAs. And significantly, the United States, far from being excluded from a regional network of FTAs, is a central player in the emerging architecture, which is more trans-Pacific and cross-regional than exclusively Asian. The U.S.–South Korea FTA, if implemented, will solidify the trans-Pacific dimension of the network and may serve as an important building block for a broader trans-Pacific trade agreement.

Another key question is whether the multiple and overlapping FTAs emerging in the region can be brought together by aggregating them into a broader regional FTA or at least by harmonizing some of their provisions. Several competing proposals for broader FTAs have been advanced by countries in the region. South Korea, China, and ASEAN have been advocating an APT FTA, which would perhaps be the most easily attainable because ASEAN is already negotiating "plus one" agreements with its three Northeast Asian partners. Japan, however, is concerned that an APT FTA would be relatively "soft" and lack coverage in key areas of importance to Japanese business. Consequently, it has countered with a proposal for an ASEAN Plus Six FTA among the EAS countries (which includes India, Australia, and New Zealand as well as the thirteen APT countries). The United States, growing concerned that it might get left out of a regional FTA, recently began pushing the Free Trade Area of the Asia-Pacific (FTAAP) proposal as a long-term goal for APEC.

Econometric analysis of different regional FTA scenarios show clearly that the broader the grouping, the greater the benefits to member countries.[37] Thus, an APEC-wide FTA would generate the highest benefits, followed by ASEAN Plus Six and then APT (with worldwide free trade under the WTO offering the greatest benefits of all). Despite the economic payoffs of a broader FTA, however, the political realities may make a smaller grouping more viable. Nevertheless, progress on negotiating a regional arrangement will likely be slowed considerably by rivalry between China and Japan over their preferred regional groupings, which mirrors their rivalry over APT and the EAS as institutional venues for building an East Asian community. The FTAAP proposal, meanwhile, is hampered by the strong skepticism in the region regarding whether an APEC-wide FTA is realistic given all of the difficult bilateral combinations it would require. Among other difficulties are the fact that in the foreseeable future, the United States will probably not consider entering into an FTA that includes China, and China will resist an FTA that includes Taiwan.

The United States has sought to advance the FTAAP proposal in APEC by suggesting a building-block approach, in which a subset of countries form a "coalition of the willing" and forge a high-standard regional FTA, with a relatively open invitation for others to join when they are ready. With this in mind, the United States announced in September 2008 that it was launching negotiations to join the Trans-Pacific Agreement, a comprehensive FTA between Brunei, Chile, Singapore, and New Zealand (known as the P4). Australia, Peru, and Vietnam have also signaled their interest in joining the agreement.

An alternative route would be to seek harmonization of key provisions in regional FTAs. Of particular importance in untangling the "noodle bowl" would be to converge rules of origin to a common standard, one that is as low as possible and symmetrical. However, the problems facing such a move are both practical and political. In practical terms, the diversity and complexity of current FTA rules-of-origin codes would make harmonizing them extremely difficult. The political problem runs even deeper. Rules of origin are negotiated for a specific reason—to protect domestic producers and to offer an advantage to domestic exporters by limiting the trade opening of FTAs to partner countries. Thus, countries that negotiate complex and restrictive rules of origin are unlikely to want to relinquish them.

APEC has advanced collective work on developing "best practices" and model chapters for regional FTAs, designed to promote "building-block" features such as comprehensiveness in coverage, transparency, open accession provisions, and strong disciplines in government procurement and dispute set-tlement. In APEC style, these guidelines are nonbinding and voluntary, but perhaps they can serve as a basis for dialogue and consensus building for more concrete collective action in the future.

FINANCIAL AND MONETARY COOPERATION

In contrast to the rampant bilateralism that characterizes trade initiatives in Asia and the Asia Pacific, efforts to promote monetary and financial coopera-tion have been distinctly regional and have been anchored in regional multilat-eral institutions. In large part, these characteristics stem from the initiatives' connection to the Asian financial crisis of 1997/1998. The "contagion" effects of the crisis created a heightened sense of mutual interdependence rooted in Asia. Regional solidarity was further strengthened by the widely shared disappoint-ment with the passive U.S. response to and the IMF's perceived failure to man-age the crisis. Japan's offer to establish an Asian monetary fund, which was re-buffed by the United States, and its subsequent bilateral assistance to affected countries through the Miyazawa Initiative, were seen as signs of emerging re-gional leadership. China's decision to refrain from devaluing its currency dur-ing the crisis was likewise viewed as a demonstration of solidarity and responsi-ble leadership. These actions spurred regional confidence that Asian countries could work together to find solutions to strengthen their financial systems and reduce vulnerability to volatile global financial markets.

The financial crisis also fueled momentum toward establishing a new re-gional framework for economic cooperation—the APT. The ten ASEAN coun-tries began meeting with their three Northeast Asian dialogue partners—China, Japan, and South Korea—as a group in 1995 in preparation for the first Asia Eu-rope Meeting. In early 1997, they decided to hold a meeting of heads of state, but by the time this summit was convened in December 1997, the financial crisis had erupted and was sweeping the region. Dealing with the crisis took center stage at the summit, and the APT quickly became the central institu-tional venue for regional discussions of cooperation in financial markets.

The searing experience of the Asian financial crisis left countries in the re-gion desiring regional "self-help" mechanisms to monitor and stabilize financial flows and to prevent future financial crises. APT provided an institutional mech-anism to pursue these goals. Finance ministers of APT countries began conven-ing regular meetings in 1999, and they worked quickly toward creating a common vision for financial regionalism. This vision includes mechanisms for collective self-defense as well as measures to strengthen regional financial markets and deepen financial integration. The three pillars of functional cooperation that have emerged are a regional financing arrangement for emergency liquidity provision; regional bond markets; and institutionalized networks for policy dialogue, surveillance, and information exchange.

REGIONAL FINANCING ARRANGEMENT: THE CHIANG MAI INITIATIVE

The signature achievement of Asian financial regionalism is the creation of a regional financing mechanism known as the Chiang Mai Initiative (CMI). Meeting on the sidelines of an Asian Development Bank meeting in Chiang Mai, Thailand, APT finance ministers agreed to set up a network of bilateral swap arrangements between their central banks to provide emergency liquidity in the event of a crisis. The CMI allows a country under attack to swap its "soft" home currency for hard currency (primarily U.S. dollars) held by other central banks in order to obtain short-term liquidity and fend off against speculative attacks. The hope is that this debt-swap arrangement will create greater stability in the face of another financial shock to the region by providing collective defense against speculative attacks on regional currencies. The debt-swap network was fully in place by 2003 with total funds amounting to about $40 billion, although individual countries would have access to only a small portion of that total pool. In a meeting in Istanbul in May 2005, APT finance ministers agreed to double the size of available funds, which has expanded the total pool to $80 billion (figure 9.3).

The CMI was designed to supplement rather than compete with IMF lending. It is explicitly linked to the IMF through a provision that holds that only 10 percent of funds can be disbursed automatically in a crisis, and the remaining disbursement is conditional on an IMF loan and the associated program of macroeconomic or structural policy adjustments. The May 2005 Istanbul Agreement doubled the automatic disbursement to 20 percent of funds, but maintains the IMF linkage for the remaining 80 percent of the money. A country hit by a liquidity crunch thus has rapid and unconditional access to a considerable amount of funding to help it weather the first few weeks of the crisis while it is in the process of negotiating a stand-by agreement with the IMF. The IMF link ensures that the IMF retains a central role in macroeconomic management. It also helps to ward against the economic and political moral hazard that might tempt vulnerable countries into unnecessarily risky behavior. Japan and China, which are by far the largest potential creditors in the CMI swap network, thus have a strong incentive to maintain this IMF link.[38] Nevertheless, Williams Grimes observes that the CMI gives regional countries considerably more leverage over the IMF because it serves as an implicit exit threat. If the IMF linkage were dropped, the CMI would in effect be transformed into an Asian monetary fund, which would

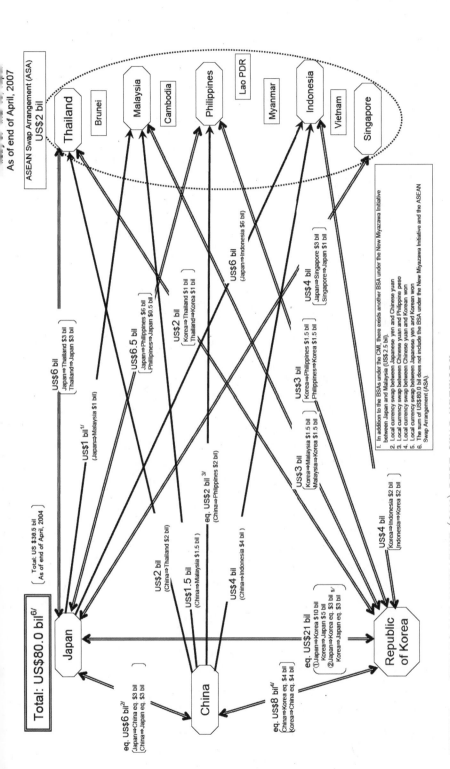

FIGURE 9.3 CHIANG MAI INITIATIVE (CMI) DEBT-SWAP NETWORK.

Source: Ministry of Finance, Japan, April 2007, http://www.mof.go.jp/english/if/CMI_0704.pdf.

supplant rather than supplement the IMF. Although Japan and China have no current incentive to change the status quo, the possibility that they can do so may well influence IMF lending policies toward Asian countries.[39]

Scholars and financial analysts debate the CMI's financial significance. Some point to the relatively modest size of funds that would be available to an individual country through the swap agreements—funds that are well below the speculative positions taken against individual foreign-currency markets in the 1997/1998 crisis and well below the amounts of the original rescue financing these countries received. Doubts exist whether the system can serve as a credible and effective line of defense against speculative attacks on regional currencies. On the other side, proponents and many scholars argue that the available funds are considerable and likely to grow. Thailand, for example, has access to $6 billion though the CMI, which is more than four times its IMF quota.[40] Moreover, the CMI represents a first line of defense against a speculative attack. APT countries may decide to come up with a rescue package of additional short-term lending to restore the financial stability of a member economy under attack. Finally, now that the CMI legal and policy framework is in place, the size of the swap agreements can easily be expanded over time. The May 2005 Istanbul Agreement demonstrated the ease of augmenting the size of swaps. It also aimed to strengthen the CMI's institutional framework by taking some steps toward multilateralizing the networks to coordinate the activation of swaps.[41] On the one hand, this aim points to the potential expansion and consolidation of the CMI into a full-fledged regional monetary institution, which can more easily seek independence from the IMF. On the other hand, surveillance and monitoring mechanisms in the CMI remain weak, leaving countries dependent on the far more robust surveillance of IMF Article V.[42] This operational weakness, combined with Japan and China's current interest in retaining the IMF linkage, make it less likely that a regional fund will seek autonomy from the IMF in the foreseeable future.

Finally, it is important to note that East Asian governments have taken unilateral steps to guard against another financial crisis by dramatically increasing their foreign-exchange reserves in the decade following the Asian financial crisis. East Asian countries now account for two-thirds of global reserve holdings, with eight Asian countries ranking among the top ten holders of foreign exchange (figure 9.4).[43] This massive exchange accumulation suggests that Asian countries strongly prefer unilateral ammunition to deploy as self-insurance in a currency crisis, rather than the collective defense provided by the CMI. Massive stockpiles of foreign reserves also secure greater room to maneuver in maintaining stable and competitive exchange rates, thereby providing some insulation from volatility in global currency movements, in particular against the U.S. dollar.

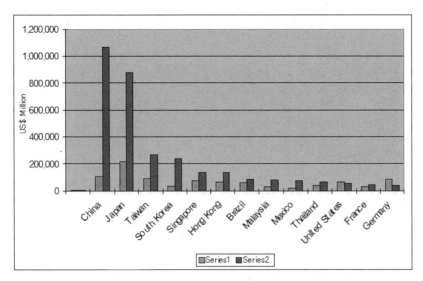

FIGURE 9.4 FOREIGN-EXCHANGE RESERVES, 1996 AND 2006.
Note: *These data include Special Drawing Rights (SDRs), reserve position in the International Monetary Fund (IMF), and foreign exchange. It does not include gold.*
Source: *IMF, "International Financial Statistics Online," http://www.imfstatistics.org/imf/ logon.aspx, available through the Gelman Library, George Washington University. The data on Taiwan are from Central Bank of the Republic of China, "Foreign Exchange Management," http://www.cbc.gov.tw/EngHome/Eeconomic/Statistics/FS/Release/ ERESERVE-N.xls.*

PROMOTING REGIONAL BOND MARKETS: THE ASIAN BOND MARKET INITIATIVE AND THE ASIAN BOND FUND

The second area of financial cooperation involves efforts to promote regional bond markets. These initiatives grew out of the strong regional interest in the postcrisis years to strengthen local capital markets in order to attract investment and to recycle the region's high domestic savings, which would in turn provide some insulation from volatility in global financial markets. The underdevelopment of local capital markets has led central banks and regional investors to channel their savings into foreign-currency assets, primarily U.S. treasuries and other dollar-denominated assets. Regional borrowers tend to borrow heavily in dollar-denominated loans and bonds, often on a short-term basis, to fund projects that generate local currency over the long-term. This flow of the region's excess savings through New York or London creates liquidity and exchange risks, making the region more vulnerable to cyclical downturns and fluctuations of the U.S. dollar. The heavy reliance on domestic bank lending in APT econo-mies is viewed as an additional problem because it often leads to maturity mis-matches and regulatory failures; it may have been a major contributing factor to the Asian financial crisis. APT governments have sought to reduce these vul-nerabilities by promoting the development of strong, well-functioning local-currency bond markets that will encourage local and regional financial intermediation, channel more regional savings into local capital markets, re-duce the excessive reliance on banks, reduce borrowing and transaction costs, and generate more financial stability.

The Asian Bond Market Initiative (ABMI) launched by APT governments in August 2003 seeks to strengthen the infrastructure of local bond markets by improving and harmonizing regulation. The ABMI is wrapped in rhetorical aspirations of creating a regional bond market, but at present it is focused more concretely on addressing structural impediments to the development of strong local-currency bond markets within countries. The ABMI created several work-ing groups to research and discuss ways to develop better infrastructure in areas such as accounting standards, disclosure rules, settlement systems, the estab-lishment of regional credit-rating agencies, and regulatory and supervisory pro-cedures. A similar APEC initiative was launched in September 2003 to promote securitization and credit-guarantee markets to enhance the efficiency of local bond markets.

A second project to increase liquidity in local bond markets is the Asian Bond Fund (ABF). This initiative was launched by the central bankers group in the region, the Executives' Meeting of East Asia Pacific Central Banks (EMEAP), which includes the financial authorities from the core APT coun-tries as well as Australia, Hong Kong, and New Zealand. EMEAP launched the first ABF (ABF 1) in June 2003. The fund, managed by the Bank for Interna-tional Settlement, pooled $1 billion in exchange reserves from the APT central banks and invested them in U.S. dollar–denominated bonds issued by sover-eign and quasi-sovereign issuers in the emerging market economies of EMEAP (which excludes Australia, Japan, and New Zealand). The second ABF (ABF 2), launched in July 2005, invests $2 billion of central-bank reserves in local-currency-denominated public-sector bonds. Unlike the first fund, ABF 2 thus involves the actual creation of local-currency bond funds. It is also passively managed and traded against a predetermined set of benchmarks

It is too early to assess whether these regional bond-market initiatives will achieve their goals of creating robust local-currency bond markets and, more broadly, boosting intraregional financial intermediation. Many observers do credit these initiatives with several tangible achievements already, though. First, the initiatives put central-bank cooperation into practice, generating high-quality policy dialogue and joint learning. For example, although the impact of the

ABF 1 was limited because it invested only in U.S. dollar–denominated bonds, at the same time it provided a "learning by doing" exercise that enabled the EMEAP central banks to launch the ABF 2.[44] The ABF process also improved the quality of central-bank discussion and helped the banks jointly identify market impediments to bond-market development in the region.[45] Central banks' involvement is also significant because they are often key regulatory agencies in home governments, giving them an important role in spearheading and coordinating domestic regulatory reform at home.[46]

Second, these bond-market initiatives, according to several analysts, have had a significant impact on strengthening domestic regulatory frameworks. The ABF 2 in particular promotes benchmarks for regional bonds and a variety of incentives for governments to remove impediments to domestic markets.[47] As part of the negotiations, China agreed to allow the Pan-Asian Bond Index Fund, a private fund set up as part of ABF 2, to purchase interbank bonds on mainland China. This fund thus became the first foreign institutional investor granted direct access to the Chinese interbank bond market. Beyond China, the ABF initiative seems to be promoting a broad range of policy reforms, from capital-control liberalization in Malaysia to tax and legal reforms in several ASEAN countries. A study by Bank for International Settlement researchers found that "[f]or such relatively small sums, the ABF2 initiative has apparently been unusually effective in promoting the reform of local bond markets."[48]

NETWORKS FOR POLICY DIALOGUE
AND INFORMATION EXCHANGE

An important spillover effect from the ongoing functional cooperation described in the previous sections has been the creation of institutionalized networks for policy dialogue and information exchange. As countries engage in concrete policy discussions on issues such as ongoing negotiations over debt-swap agreements and collaboration on launching ABFs, they build shared expertise and deepen linkages between themselves. A variety of dialogues between APT finance ministers and the central banks in EMEAP contribute to this process. These dialogues foster greater transparency and build trust by creating networks of officials that come to know each other and exchange information on a regular basis. Japanese finance and central-bank officials report that these networks have been especially valuable for improving transparency of and access to China's financial policymaking.[49] The hope is that in a time of financial instability or crisis, these networks can be used for information exchange and closer coordination.

More concrete efforts to establish a strong regional surveillance mechanism have met with limited success. In the wake of the Asian financial crisis, there has been strong interest in setting up a "self-help" surveillance mechanism to detect problems and preempt financial crises through policy adjustments. The first system put in place was the Manila Framework Group, which the United States helped to set up after it vetoed Japan's proposal for an Asian monetary fund in November 1997. The group included APT countries as well as Australia, Canada, New Zealand, and the United States, and was designed to strengthen the IMF's role in regional surveillance, but it lacked a clear focus and strong peer review and so was dissolved in November 2004.[50] In May 2000, APT instituted its own process, the Economic Review and Policy Dialogue, which monitors short-term capital flows and is linked to the CMI. These regional surveillance efforts are not as effective as they would need to be to prevent another financial crisis. To be effective, the economic analysis and peer review functions will have to be strengthened considerably, which would probably require the creation of a secretariat that can take the lead in interrogating, analyzing, and making tough recommendations to participating countries. Most important, countries would have to accept much more intrusion into their domestic policymaking domain than they have been willing to accept so far.

IMPLICATIONS FOR THE UNITED STATES

The rise of regionalism in East Asian economic relations is driven by both market forces and government initiatives. Regional integration is far more advanced on the trade and investment side of the East Asian economy, but capital markets remain small, fragmented, and largely tied to the U.S. dollar. However, in contrast to trade, financial cooperation among East Asian governments has been marked by strong regionalism and multilateral institution building.

Although the term *regionalism* connotes inward-looking and insular integration, Asian regionalism in trade and finance has remained largely outward oriented and market opening. On the trade side, the strong triangular pattern of trade and the openness of Asian economies to both trade and investment make it highly unlikely that Asian countries will seek to create a closed economic bloc. Instead, emerging bilateral FTAs link Asian countries across regions and, to some extent, broaden trade and investment relations by widening the scope of liberalization efforts beyond the global standards upheld by the WTO. Moreover, the United States plays a central role in this cross-regional, trans-Pacific FTA network. Nonetheless, U.S. interests might be damaged by the creation of a "noodle bowl" of overlapping and restrictive rules and regulations, which may promote inefficiency and trade discrimination. Even more damaging to the United States would be a narrowly Asian FTA, composed of either the APT or ASEAN Plus Six countries. Such a trade grouping would create substantial trade diversion away from U.S. goods. It would also potentially marginalize the U.S. interests in subsequent negotiations and initiatives on regional trade.

On the financial side, Asian regionalism to date has involved cooperation in the CMI debt-swap network and bond-market initiatives. These efforts have contributed to substantial growth in regional financial groupings and networks that exclude the United States. Moreover, these initiatives are wrapped in the rhetoric of "self-help" and regional autonomy. The ABMI touts the creation of regional (rather than just local) bond markets, and both the CMI and bond-market efforts proclaim the goal of promoting regional autonomy from the global financial system. In practice, however, all of these efforts have for the most part promoted openness and transparency, market access, and efficiency. They have emphasized the necessity of adhering to global standards, such as those laid down in the Basel Accords, in order to improve the efficiency of local capital markets. These goals, in addition to promoting financial stability in the region, are broadly in accord with U.S. interests. As cooperation deepens, however, Asian countries may be tempted to provide preferential treatment to each other on market-access issues and deny nondiscriminatory access to outsiders, such as the United States. Resentment against the United States on financial matters remains strong ten years after the financial crisis. Because the United States will likely not have a seat at the table for many of the discussions by regional groupings on market-access issues, U.S. financial interests may potentially suffer.

The CMI framework, meanwhile, has developed as a complement to the IMF rather than as a substitute or competitor, as envisioned by some proponents of the original Asian monetary fund proposal. Although it is possible that the CMI may eventually be transformed into a regional monetary fund that seeks autonomy from IMF conditionality, there are few signs that the key countries are interested in and capable of moving in that direction any time soon.

LOOKING AHEAD

The emerging economic architecture in East Asia reflects growing regional aspirations for economic integration and community building. However, the regional economy remains strongly anchored in the global economic system, and key regional players have taken steps to ensure that the benefits of market-oriented institutional rules and global regimes are strengthened rather than undermined. In finance, under the auspices of APT, East Asian countries have made impressive progress in building cooperative institutional frameworks for strengthening financial sectors, reducing the region's vulnerability to financial shocks, and fostering information exchange and policy dialogue. Although financial cooperation has been motivated in large part by the desire for financial integration and greater insulation from global capital volatility, in practice it has promoted financial reforms and strengthened global standards and regimes.

In trade, countries have embraced bilateral FTAs to facilitate trade and investment integration, but these new Asian FTAs are strongly linked to cross-regional and especially trans-Pacific partners. Although the FTAs vary considerably in quality and coverage, many of them have building-block features in areas such as services and investment, which may well contribute to broad economic liberalization at the multilateral level. It is also possible, however, that this emerging FTA architecture will ultimately lock in protection of sensitive domestic sectors, reduce incentives to pursue accords at the WTO, and lead to a noodle bowl of inefficient regulations and trade diversion. These FTAs have not been in effect long, and it is too soon to judge whether their market-opening elements will outweigh their noodle bowl effects. On balance, their effects will most likely be relatively benign, in large part because the economies of Asia are already open and highly integrated into global trade and investment flows. Much will depend on how these FTAs are implemented.

Another key question, of particular importance for U.S. interests, is whether these new bilateral FTAs will create a domino effect leading to an APEC-wide FTA or, alternatively, whether Asian countries will seek to create a regional trade accord among APT or ASEAN Plus Six countries. An Asian FTA might intensify regional trade preferences to the detriment of the United States and other outsiders. Moreover, if based on low standards of coverage and quality, it may potentially exacerbate the negative noodle bowl effects of inefficient regulation. In the most likely scenario, however, rivalry between China and Japan and other negotiating difficulties are likely to impede progress toward an Asian FTA. An APEC-wide FTA faces even more political difficulties, not least the likely anti-free-trade political mood in the United States. It seems likely that markets rather than regional institutions will continue to drive trade and investment flows, and "open regionalism" will remain a central feature of the emerging economic architecture.

NOTES

1. Jagdish Bhagwati, testimony before the House Committee on Financial Services, *Opening Trade in Financial Services—The Chile and Singapore Examples: Hearing Before the Subcommittee on Domestic and International Monetary Policy, Trade, and Technology,* 108th Cong., 1st sess., April 1, 2003, http://financialservices.house.gov/media/pdf/108–16.pdf.

2. Japanese business felt disadvantaged by NAFTA as well as by a European Union–Mexico trade deal that was spurred by NAFTA.

3. The ACFTA calls for zero tariffs on trade to come into force in 2010 for China and the ASEAN Plus Six countries: Brunei, Indonesia, Malaysia, the Philippines, Singapore, and Thailand. Cambodia, Laos, Myanmar, and Vietnam will have until 2015 to comply. China first broached the idea of an FTA with ASEAN at the China-ASEAN Summit in November 2000; a year later, in November 2001, China formally proposed an FTA to be completed by 2010.

4. The Early Harvest Program went into effect in January 2004, with participating countries offering preferential tariffs on a package of mostly agricultural products.

5. Prime Minister Koizumi toured the five core ASEAN nations from January 9 to January 13, 2002, proposing a Japan-ASEAN economic agreement in each country. See "Koizumi Seeks Japan-ASEAN Talks with FTA in Mind," Jiji Press Ticker Service, January 9, 2002; Koizumi Junichiro, "Japan and ASEAN in East Asia—A Sincere and Open Partnership," speech, Singapore, January 14, 2002, http://www.kantei.go.jp/foreign/koizumispeech/2002/01/14speech_e.html.

6. METI officials, interview by author, August 18, 2005, Tokyo; December 17, 2005, Tokyo; and September 18, 2006, Washington, D.C.; Naoko Munakata, *Transforming East Asia* (Washington, D.C: Brookings Institution Press, 2006), 121.

7. METI officials, interview by author, February 19, 2007, Washington, D.C.

8. The first step South Korea took was eliminating its screen quota system, which the United States had made a precondition to the talks.

9. Thailand has opted not to sign the AKFTA because of South Korea's exclusion of rice and other agricultural products.

10. Dean DeRosa and John Gilbert, for example, find that U.S. gains are much larger if the United States acts as a "hub" and negotiates multiple FTAs with several partners. "Spoke" countries, in contrast, gain relatively more if "hub" countries negotiate fewer FTAs. See Dean DeRosa and John Gilbert, "Technical Appendix Quantitative Estimates of the Economic Impacts of U.S. Bilateral Free Trade Agreements," in *Free Trade Agreements: U.S. Strategies and Priorities*, ed. Jeffrey Schott (Washington, D.C.: Institute for International Economics, 2004), 397.

11. When NAFTA was implemented in 1994, Mexico was the third-largest export market for the United States; it now ranks second, after Canada.

12. Munakata, *Transforming East Asia*.

13. Republic of Korea Ministry of Foreign Affairs and Trade official, e-mail message to author, March 5, 2007. South Korea also selected Chile because of its experience negotiating FTAs. See Chung Hae-kwan, "The Korea-Chile FTA: Significance and Implications," *East Asian Review* 15, no. 1 (2003): 74.

14. Fukunari Kimura, "Bilateralism in the Asia-Pacific: An Economic Overview," in *Bilateral Trade Agreements in the Asia-Pacific*, ed. Vinod K. Aggarwal and Shurjiro Urata (New York: Routledge, 2006), 157–90.

15. According to Richard Baldwin, Indonesia's average applied tariffs dropped from 16 percent in 1995 to 9 percent in 2003; the Philippines' tariffs fell from 19 percent in

1995 to 4 percent in 2003; Thailand's tariffs fell from 40 percent in 1992 to 14 percent in 2003. Richard Baldwin, "Multilateralising Regionalism: Spaghetti Bowls as Building Blocs on the Path to Global Free Trade," *World Economy* 29, no. 11 (2006): 5.

16. Hadi Soesastro, "Dynamics of Competitive Liberalization in RTA Negotiations: East Asian Perspectives," paper presented at the Pacific Economic Cooperation Conference and Latin America Economics and Business Association Conference "Regional Trade Agreements in Comparative Perspective," Washington, D.C., April 22, 2003, http://www.pecc.org/trade/papers/washington-2003/soesastro.pdf; Martin Roy, Juan Marchetti, and Hoe Lim, *Services Liberalization in the New Generation of Preferential Trade Agreements (PTAs): How Much Further Than the GATS?* World Trade Organization (WTO) Staff Working Paper no. ERSD-2006–07 (Geneva: WTO, September 2006), http://www.wto.org/english/res_e/reser_e/ersd200607_e.pdf.

17. METI official, interview by author, 2005, Tokyo, and February 19, 2007, Washington, D.C.

18. METI, *Higashi Ajia Kigyou Senryaku wo Kangaeru Kenkyuukai* [*Study group on corporate strategy in East Asia*], interim report (Tokyo: METI, September 2003), 47, http://www.meti.go.jp/kohosys/press/0004463/2/030905higashiajia-h.pdf.

19. METI trade officials, interview by author, August 2005, Tokyo.

20. Rupa Damodaran, "Japanese FDIs into Malaysia Stage Strong Comeback," *New Straits Times*, February 2, 2007.

21. Sheng Lijun, "FTA with ASEAN a Safety Cushion for China," *Korea Herald*, November 9, 2002.

22. Baldwin, "Multilateralising Regionalism," 13.

23. An enabling clause gives looser restrictions for agreements between developing countries, but it does not apply when developing countries enter into agreements with developed countries.

24. These deadlines apply to China and South Korea and to the ASEAN Plus Six countries; the less-developed ASEAN members (Cambodia, Myanmar, Laos, and Vietnam) are permitted longer phase-in periods and more-sensitive list exclusions.

25. Ishikawa Koichi, "Higashi Ajia FTA no genjou to tenbou" [Current situation of East Asian FTA and its outlook], *Toa*, no. 462 (2005): 26–34, http://www.kazankai.org/essay_list.html?id = 2&file = 43.

26. Chang Jae Lee, Hyung-Gon Jeong, HanSung Kim, and Ho-Kyung Bang, *From East Asian FTAs to an EAFTA: Typology of East Asian FTAs and Implications for an EAFTA*, Policy Analysis no. 06-01 (Seoul: Korea Institute for International Economic Policy, December 2006), http://www.kiep.go.kr/eng/std_data_view.asp?scate = 013001&num = 177169#.

27. John Ravenhill, "The Political Economy of the New Asia-Pacific Bilateralism: Benign, Banal, or Simply Bad?" in *Bilateral Trade Agreements in the Asia-Pacific*, ed. Vinod K. Aggarwal and Shurjiro Urata (New York: Routledge, 2006), 27–49.

28. Bhagwati, *Opening Trade in Financial Services*, 61.

29. Antoni Estevadeordal and Kati Suominen, "Rules of Origin in the World Trading System," paper presented at a seminar on regional trade agreements and the WTO, Geneva, November 14, 2003, http://www.wto.org/English/tratop_e/region_e/sem_novo3_e/estevadeordal_paper_e.pdf; Chang et al., *From East Asian FTAs to an EAFTA*, 64–65.

30. Michael G. Plummer, *Toward Win-Win Regionalism in Asia: Issues and Challenges in Forming Efficient Trade Agreements*, Asian Development Bank Working Paper Series on Regional Economic Integration no. 5 (Tokyo: Asian Development Bank, October 2006), table 4, http://aric.adb.org/pdf/workingpaper/WP5%20Plummer%2001106.pdf.

31. Roy, Marchetti, and Lim, *Services Liberalization*.

32. Ibid.

33. Carsten Fink and Martín Molinuevo, "East Asian Free Trade Agreements in Services: Roaring Tigers or Timid Pandas?" working manuscript, January 2007, 70.

34. O. G. Dayaratna Banda and John Whalley, *Beyond Goods and Services: Competition Policy, Investment, Mutual Recognition, Movement of Persons, and Broader Cooperation Provisions of Recent FTAs Involving ASEAN Countries*, National Bureau of Economic Research (NBER) Working Paper no. 11232 (Cambridge, Mass.: NBER, March 2005), 17.

35. Plummer, *Toward Win-Win Regionalism in Asia*, 26.

36. Richard Baldwin, *Managing the Noodle Bowl: The Fragility of East Asian Regionalism*, Discussion Paper no. 5561 (Washington, D.C.: Center for Economic Policy Research, January 2006), 39, http://www.bwl.uni-kiel.de/phd/files/paper_baldwin.pdf.

37. Robert Scollay and John Gilbert, *New Regional Trading Arrangements in the Asia-Pacific?* (Washington, D.C.: Institute for International Economics, 2001); Michael G. Plummer and Ganeshan Wignaraja, *The Post-crisis Sequencing of Economic Integration in Asia: Trade as a Complement to a Monetary Future*, Asian Development Bank Working Paper Series on Regional Economic Integration no. 9 (Tokyo: Asian Development Bank, May 2007), 16–23, http://aric.adb.org/pdf/workingpaper/WP09_Plummer&Wignaraja.pdf; Edward J. Lincoln, *East Asian Economic Regionalism* (New York: Council on Foreign Relations; Washington, D.C.: Brookings Institution Press, 2004); Kimura, "Bilateralism in the Asia-Pacific," 64–69.

38. William W. Grimes, "East Asian Financial Regionalism in Support of the Global Financial Architecture? The Political Economy of Regional Nesting," *Journal of East Asian Studies*, no. 3 (2006): 367; Jennifer Amyx, "Japan and the Evolution of Regional Financial Arrangements in East Asia," in *Beyond Bilateralism: U.S.-Japan Relations in the New Asia-Pacific*, ed. Ellis S. Krauss and T. J. Pempel (Stanford, Calif.: Stanford University Press, 2004), 198–220; C. Randall Henning, *East Asian Financial Cooperation*, Policy Analysis in International Economics no. 68 (Washington, D.C.: Institute for International Economics, October 2002), 76. Malaysia, Thailand,

and some other ASEAN countries have long opposed the IMF linkage and have pushed for its removal or reduction.

39. Grimes, "East Asian Financial Regionalism in Support of the Global Financial Architecture?" 367.

40. Ibid., 359; Henning, *East Asian Financial Cooperation*, 20–22.

41. APT finance ministers announced at their meeting in Kyoto in May 2007 further details of their plan to multilateralize swap networks by pooling reserves and managing them under a single contractual arrangement, although "the agreement lacked specifics, including a timeline for realization, how much money should be committed and, most importantly, how the pool would be managed" (Eric Johnston, "Asia Finance Chiefs Agree on Foreign Reserves Pool," *Japan Times*, May 6, 2007).

42. Grimes, "East Asian Financial Regionalism in Support of the Global Financial Architecture?" 361; Yung Chul Park and Yunjong Wang, "The Chiang Mai Initiative and Beyond," *World Economy*, no. 1 (2005): 96.

43. East Asia (ASEAN, South Korea, Japan, China, Hong Kong, Macau, and Taiwan) accounted for 66.5 percent of global reserves at the end of 2006. Calculated by the author based on data from IMF, "International Financial Statistics Online," http://www.imfstatistics.org/imf/, 33–35, a proprietary resource available at the Gelman Library, George Washington University; the data on Taiwan are from Central Bank of the Republic of China, "Foreign Exchange Management," http://www.cbc.gov.tw/EngHome/Eeconomic/Statistics/Category/Foreign.asp.

44. Guonan Ma and Eli M. Remolona, "Opening Markets Through a Regional Bond Fund: Lessons from ABF2," *Bank for International Settlement Quarterly Review*, June 2005, 86.

45. EMEAP Working Group on Financial Markets, "Review of the Asian Bond Fund 2 Initiative," June 2006, 5, http://www.emeap.org/ABF/ABF2ReviewReport.pdf.

46. Ibid., 32; Grimes, "East Asian Financial Regionalism in Support of the Global Financial Architecture?" 365.

47. Jennifer Amyx, "Linking China Strategy with a Broader Asia Strategy," remarks to the Congressional Study Group on the Asia Pacific Economy, Washington, D.C., December 4, 2006, 4.

48. Ma and Remolona, "Opening Markets Through a Regional Bond Fund," 88.

49. Bank of Japan official, interview by author, June 2002, Tokyo; Japanese Ministry of Finance official, interview by author, August 2005, Tokyo; Japanese Ministry of Finance official, interview by author, May 2006, Japanese Embassy, Washington, D.C.

50. Hadi Soesastro, "Regional Integration in East Asia: Achievements and Future Prospects," *Asian Economic Policy Review* 1 (2006): 221.

10. Norms and Regional Architecture

MULTILATERAL INSTITUTION BUILDING IN ASIA AND ITS IMPACT ON GOVERNANCE AND DEMOCRACY

William Cole and Erik G. Jensen

Beginning with the People Power movement in the Philippines and the establishment of democracy in South Korea in the mid-1980s, the past two decades have seen a wave of democratization movements sweeping across most of Asia and the rest of the world. In the early 1980s, there were about only 40 democracies; today there are 125. This dramatic political transformation parallels and to a certain extent overshadows the equally important but less headline-grabbing process of restructuring, capacity building, and decentralization that has also taken place in governing institutions in most countries. Both democratization and broader governance reform have been occurring in tandem with and have been necessitated by the tremendous national and local changes resulting from the rapid globalization of markets and of communication and information flows. In part, advances in democracy and governance reform are driven by factors within countries—the creation and release of new forces with new expectations through rapid economic growth, the demand for redress of perceived injustices as old tensions are exacerbated and new ones emerge, and the general rise in expectations about what one should expect from political leaders and from government institutions as electronic media become accessible for even the poorest communities in the world.

But external influences, long a dimension of local change, have become increasingly important: the European Union sets rigorous standards of democratic governance for new entrants; two presidential administrations since the end of the Cold War have seen the United States placing democracy promotion near the center of its foreign policy; Japan is contemplating a more proactive role in support of governance reform; and even the Association of Southeast Asian Nations (ASEAN)—once the champion of the principle of "noninterference in internal affairs"—hints that it is gravitating toward universal norms in redrafting its charter.

These examples suggest that multilateral institution building may be able to reinforce norms of governance and democracy, even within a region as diverse as Asia. However, the evidence is still incomplete. Indeed, governance reform both as a contested issue within ASEAN and as an element in Japanese foreign policy dates back a decade and is still hotly contested by many ASEAN governments and in the region more broadly. Moreover, the debate over the broader causal connection between democracy and governance reform and economic development among developing countries remains unresolved.

Nevertheless, the debate about the normative dimension of institution building, indicated in the country chapters in this volume (particularly in the chapters on Japan and China), strongly suggests that questions of governance (now) and democracy (more gradually) will increasingly be inseparable from the process of "community building" in Asia and that the multilateral process may have a significant impact on how states govern themselves internally. To assess these issues, this chapter begins with a discussion of why governance reform actually matters in Asia and should matter to successful Asian governments. It then focuses on the case of ASEAN, where multilateral institutionalization among diverse governments has begun yielding new standards with respect to governance. Next, the chapter examines the external influences on governance reform emanating from North America and Europe as well as within Asia (Japan) in the form of pressures, assistance, and models for emulation. Finally, it considers the prospects for a more ambitious inclusion of standards of governance and democracy in the region's emerging architecture.

WHY GOVERNANCE REFORM MATTERS

Does governance reform actually matter in Asia? Relevance can be safely assumed in the other functional areas covered by this book—traditional security threats, nontraditional security threats, and economic growth are all self-evidently important concerns. Although the pace and nature of reforms related to democracy, human rights, rule of law, and good governance clearly have concrete implications for growth and security, researchers and practitioners' interests are typically driven by a complex mix of realism and idealism, with the two sometimes painfully muddled. This debate cannot be fully sorted out here, but it is useful to provide a general sense of why governance and democracy reform as well as the pace and sequence of that reform are increasingly important components in the ongoing dialogue about the evolution of Asia's regional architecture.

Despite many scholarly and policy claims to the contrary, there is much we do not know about the process of change—the specific causal connections between political and economic liberalization that move a country from developing to developed.[1] The analysis that follows comports closely with the modernization theory articulated by the late Seymour Martin Lipset.[2] That is, as countries experience economic growth and the middle class expands, citizens will demand more political liberalization. The democratic breakthrough in South Korea in 1987 is one of the best examples of modernization theory in practice. Taiwan and, to a more limited extent, Singapore are also examples.[3] Granted, global experience over the past two decades shows that the causal arrows between economic and political liberalization are not as simple as modernization theory predicted. It shows that tight sequencing from economic development to political development is not possible, nor are specific institutional arrangements by any means inevitable. Nonetheless, modernization theory still holds more salience and resonance for Northeast and Southeast Asia than for any other region of the developing world. The critics of sequencing in modernization theory have argued that East Asia represents a "small set" of countries.[4] That is true, but it also represents the most successful cluster of developing (some now developed) countries in the world. With regard to the future resilience of modernization theory, the biggest question is whether China will follow the modernization path of South Korea and Taiwan. If current rates of growth and social transformation continue, this change will happen within a generation, but we do not have empirical tools with sufficient predictive capability either to confirm or to challenge this speculation.[5]

As a general matter, policymakers are not driven by empirical evidence. Nonetheless, in the domain of democracy, governance, and the rule of law, three empirical insights are most salient to what has motivated East Asian democratization in the past and might motivate a more robust regional agenda in the future. The first two insights should motivate democratic reform; the third insight should motivate governance and rule-of-law reform.

First, the evidence shows that authoritarian regimes do not grow more slowly than democratic regimes, but rather that democratic regimes enjoy more *stable* growth with less volatility than do authoritarian regimes. *Sustained* economic growth is an important objective. Just focusing on mean growth ignores the important developmental benefit of *steady* growth.[6] (Variation in growth over time among developing countries is six times greater than among developed countries.)

Second, a more contested view is that democratic regimes do not militarily attack one another. This view may be generally true, but it does not mean that nondemocratic regimes are perforce more belligerent simply because of regime type. Witness ASEAN's own experience in which members have not had violent state-sanctioned interstate conflict for forty years despite the fact that only a minority of its members have been democracies. Feeding into the traditional ASEAN concern for stability and economic growth, these two empirical insights suggest that ASEAN members should be motivated to engage in political reform to maintain stability and security.

Third, a push for better governance and rule of law is justified because "in the *long run* countries that have attained high levels of income are those with high-quality institutions."[7] As Dani Rodrik points out, high-quality institutions are not necessary either to start the process of economic growth or to achieve high growth rates. Neither India nor China had such institutions in place at the onset of their remarkable growth runs that started more than twenty years ago. Even today, governing institutions in both countries are improving only slowly. The nouveau high-growth club in the region that includes Vietnam does not have such institutions. And certainly Cambodia, a recent entrant into the high-growth club, does not have such institutions. The empirical evidence suggests, then, that although economic growth may require investments in advanced governance and law institutions as developing countries become more mature economies (for example, Indonesia and Thailand today), there is little evidence that much more than basic and often informal institutions are needed at earlier stages of market-based development.

In short, there is no clear consensus that the full package of governance, democracy, human rights, and the rule of law is indispensable to economic development or flows naturally therefrom, but strong empirical evidence suggests that certain elements, such as high-quality institutions, do become critical to sustainable economic growth as countries move up the development chain.[8] These domestic institutions also become important for more advanced economies (Japan, Singapore, and even China) as they seek to protect their investments and exposure in the less-developed countries. A strong external constituency for governance reform is therefore needed as Asian economic integration proceeds. Finally, although the causal link between human rights/political liberty and sustainable economic growth remains blurred, there is increasing evidence that more-advanced democracies have constituencies within or national-identity incentives for reinforcing universal norms in the process of regional institution building, even if the implementation is not as clear as the articulation. All of this becomes particularly evident in the case of ASEAN.

THE CASE OF ASEAN

For several reasons, this chapter focuses on ASEAN. First, considering the full range of regional architecture in Asia, ASEAN is perhaps the only institution that has begun to edge toward inclusion of at least some elements of democratic governance and human rights in the range of issues with which it is grappling. Second, through the ASEAN Regional Forum (ARF), ASEAN Plus Three, ASEAN Plus Six, and other regional mechanisms in which ASEAN is playing a central role, what happens within ASEAN has potential implications for the region as whole. Third, given the strikingly broad range of regime types in the region—from thriving democracy to managed semidemocracy to Leninist market socialism to military dictatorship—ASEAN is in some ways a microcosm of the region as a whole. To an important extent, what works and does not work in terms of integration efforts to advance domestic-governance reform through ASEAN may tell us something about what is possible through other international mechanisms that start with regional community building rather than with common ideology and similarity of political institutional arrangements. Fourth, the ASEAN region consists of a cluster of some of the most dynamic nations in the world in terms of both sustained rapid economic growth and relatively peaceful social transformation. Thus far, each has succeeded in making the adjustments to policy and governing institutions needed to maintain growth, even in the face of occasionally severe shocks, including the 1997 Asian financial crisis. To this extent, given its success in helping to build and maintain the community of nations in the region, ASEAN does serve as a potential model for other regions.

And finally, another reason for focusing our analysis on ASEAN is that forty years after its founding, it is at a critical crossroads. By the mid-1990s, the leadership of several ASEAN member states had begun to embrace the idea of a tighter Southeast Asian community of nations that would help to strengthen members domestically and advance the interests of the region as a whole in an increasingly uncertain world. In December 1997, the leaders released *ASEAN Vision 2020*. This document envisions a concert of Southeast Asian nations with tighter economic integration, closer cooperation, and coordination in a range of areas, including poverty reduction, increased food security, and the narrowing of the development gap among members. Among other aspirations, ASEAN *Vision 2020* states: "We envision our nations being governed with the consent and greater participation of the people with its focus on welfare and dignity of the human person and the good of the community."[9] Although not in any way an endorsement of democratic institutions, the statement seems to open the door to consideration of norms addressing the outcomes of governance structures, if not the specific character of those structures themselves. Ten years later, in January 2007, the ASEAN Eminent Persons Group (EPG) issued a report building on *ASEAN Vision 2020* to recommend the contents of a new charter to guide ASEAN into the next century. This time, the EPG made an explicit statement of support for inclusion of universal values of democracy, human rights, and rule of law into the ASEAN Charter and a clear shift on the principle of noninterference in internal affairs. The ten ASEAN governments watered down some of the recommendations to maintain consensus among the diverse range of member states, but the EPG report serves as a barometer of the shift in thinking among some of ASEAN's leading states about the need to be more proactive in advancing standards for democracy, human rights, good governance, and rule of law through regional institutions.

THE EVOLUTION OF THINKING ABOUT GOVERNANCE IN ASEAN

How did ASEAN come to this point? As one would expect, given its long-standing goals and its behavioral and procedural norms, its efforts related to domestic-governance issues have been limited, and progress to date has been slow. However, given the organization's initial goals and aspirations, activities occurring under the overall ASEAN umbrella have dramatically increased over the years: there have been some two hundred ASEAN agreements to date, and both dialogue and cooperation on a striking range of areas now occur through this regional mechanism.

Current and past ASEAN engagement with member states in areas related to governance (broadly conceived) cover a range of topical areas. In some of these areas, significant dialogue and cooperation occur, but in some the dialogue is politically sensitive and just beginning. The former type of engagement involves primarily mutual support, capacity building, policy adjustments, and institutional development in certain technical areas of common concern, particularly in those that affect economic growth and involve human security. The latter type of engagement includes aspects of democracy and human rights that may be more threatening to the political systems of some members and where there are fewer grounds for consensus. On the whole, prospects for progress are greatest in "lowest-common-denominator" areas: that is, areas of dialogue and cooperation on which all members can find common ground or even common cause. Although a degree of standard setting is possible, lowest-common-denominator activities do not require binding commitment on the part of participating countries, nor is there any expectation of (or capacity for) enforcement. These activities fit comfortably within ASEAN's traditional noninterference and consensus model. In an important sense, in fact, the workings of this model tend to "filter out" anything that is too overtly political. The definition of what is "too politically sensitive" has of course evolved very slowly over time in ASEAN, but the long-term evolution appears to be toward emergence of a wider set of binding cooperative norms that relate to democracy, human rights, governance, and rule of law in the region. (We discuss later the issues of democracy, human rights, and rule of law as undertaken by the EPG and show how this works in practice.)

It is useful to provide a brief overview of ASEAN activities that relate generally or specifically to democracy, human rights, and the rule of law. In a high number of cross-border issues, ASEAN has initiated measures (either formal agreements or looser cooperative undertakings) that urge members to alter their domestic policies. In general, this set of measures—the lowest common denominators—promotes very basic rights and minimum institutional capacities that can underpin economic development and quality of life. These measures can be categorized under rule of law, human rights, democracy, and governance.

For example, regarding the rule of law, ASEAN has two committees, the ASEAN Law Ministers Meeting and the ASEAN Senior Law Officials Meeting, which work toward the "gradual harmonization of national laws to catch up with the level of cooperation and integration amongst ASEAN Member Countries." The goal of these bodies appears to be directed primarily at bringing different nations' domestic laws into closer conformity in order to aid economic integration. Most of what ASEAN has done in this area lacks teeth. One exception may be that member governments have signed the Treaty on Mutual Legal Assistance on Criminal Matters, which formalizes the process by which governments are to collaborate on information sharing and investigation.[10]

On human rights, certain member countries have been pushing ASEAN to take a more assertive stance. The Philippine government historically has been the principal human rights advocate in the group. The push gained momentum at the tenth ASEAN Summit in November 2004, which produced the Vientiane Action Plan, promoting greater human rights and a more open dynamic and resilient ASEAN community. In January 2007, ASEAN heads of state signed the Cebu Declaration, which focused on migrant-worker issues.[11] The Cebu Declaration is just that: declaratory. It is strong on general principles to which the sending and receiving states should adhere, but short on enforcement. Indeed, one provision abundantly illustrates the weakness of the declaration's binding effect: in resolving disputes about migrant workers, it provides that *national law* shall apply.

On questions of democracy, various collective and individual measures proposed by ASEAN members speaking out against the suppression of Burmese political leader Aun San Suu Kyi—particularly when she was once again placed under house arrest in 2002—were noteworthy. Much of the international conversation about Suu Kyi has focused on democracy, but the ASEAN dialogue and action vis-à-vis Burma is more about the outer limits of tolerance of an authoritarian regime's behavior than it is about democracy. The collective challenge by members against Burma's right to chair ASEAN in 2006 was an extraordinary snub given the deeply embedded norm of consensus and the "ASEAN way." Neither of these acts—the 2002 condemnation of Suu Kyi's rearrest and the 2006 denial of Burma's ASEAN chairmanship—adds up to an endorsement of democracy, but together they show that Burma's membership has forced ASEAN to confront its norms of noninterference and consensus.

On issues of governance, ASEAN has taken up a number of measures on civil-service capacity, transparency, the environment, and public health. For example, the ASEAN Resource Centers, operated in member countries, help spur the development of and information sharing about "activities on e-Government, capacity-building, information exchange, performance management, case studies for the civil service, career executive service examinations, public sector leadership and new generation leadership programs."[12] Although a promising start, these activities have not yielded much in terms of tangible accomplishment.

In the wake of the 1997 Asian financial crisis, transparency and financial-sector reform dominated the discourse.[13] As ASEAN weighs its relationship with East Timor, however, it should promote the Extractive Industries Transparency Initiative. To date, only East Timor is a formal member, though Indonesia has a presence, too.[14] One of the most important rule-of-law measures to reduce corruption and improve economic growth is the credible and transparent management of a country's natural resources—a form of economic justice. If East Timor manages its oil and gas reserves responsibly, it will have a greater positive effect on strengthening the rule of law in the country, enhancing citizen security and stability, and aiding economic growth and development. And, of equal importance, it will demonstrate effective and legitimate government by protecting against bureaucratic caprice and corruption.[15]

Environmental issues have also been prominently featured in ASEAN meetings since the early 2000s as the organization tries to develop a coherent strategy for limiting transborder pollution and promoting regional energy sustainability. Again, ASEAN members have undertaken obligations to develop alternative energy sources and build bureaucracies to implement reforms.[16] Since 1997, ASEAN has had to deal extensively with forest-clearing fires and haze emanating most prominently from Indonesia. In response to the terrible fires of 1997, ASEAN signed the Agreement on Transboundary Haze and Pollution, which came into force near the end of 2003. The fires of 2006 in Indonesia were the worst since 1997 and forced Indonesian president Susilo Bambang

Yudyohono to apologize and promise action. The Haze Agreement was the first regional agreement binding a group of states to address haze pollution. It does not provide for either sanctions or third-party dispute-resolution mechanisms. "This absence is particularly worrying given that the Agreement is probably one of the few multilateral treaties in existence that relies, almost exclusively, on *one* state party for meaningful compliance and effectiveness."[17] With billions of dollars of loss (one estimate puts the loss at more than $9 billion) over the past decade resulting from transborder haze, the pressure to address the problem is high. So far the Haze Agreement has not proved entirely effective in its implementation, but if Indonesia, as the principal violator, ratifies the agreement, it may well contribute to rule of law and the building of governance capacity in a regional sense.[18]

Similarly, ASEAN governments have been relatively proactive in forming agreements to share resources and information related to public-health crises that might affect the region. Outbreaks of avian influenza and severe acute respiratory syndrome (SARS), as well as the spread of HIV and AIDS have generated coordinated responses that impose individual obligations on member governments to change their policies and develop bureaucratic capabilities.[19] The SARS crisis in particular forced greater transparency even among countries with more closed political systems.

DIRECT INVOLVEMENT BY ASEAN IN MEMBER STATES' DOMESTIC AFFAIRS

The list of governance-related areas of dialogue and cooperation is promising. Aspiring to set norms and capacity building to institutionalize them is one thing, but establishing enforceable standards is quite another. The real import of these efforts will ultimately depend on ASEAN states' willingness to establish and abide by enforceable compliance mechanisms—in effect, the degree to which states are willing formally to relinquish aspects of sovereignty in certain limited areas to collectively determined regional governance mechanisms. This question is separate from consideration of either norm or standard setting for democracy, human rights, rule of law, and governance, but it bears obvious implications for progress in those areas. The idea that ASEAN might be able to enforce decisions in these areas has clearly gained momentum among some member states, though it has been opposed at key moments by other states such as Vietnam, Burma, and Laos, which have used the association's consensus rules to shield themselves from external pressures by other members.

In ASEAN's founding document, the Bangkok Declaration of August 1967, the principle of noninterference is firmly established, and it has been reiterated in many subsequent statements and agreements over the years. Remaining true to that principle, ASEAN has demonstrated a preponderant disinclination to get involved in member states' internal affairs. In essence, the principle of noninterference does not just reflect how member states would interact within the context of ASEAN, but represents the behavioral norm that defines appropriate interactions among member states in *all* official contexts. Given the history of regional conflicts, the diversity of regime types involved, and the substantial risk of external manipulation in the context of the Cold War, ASEAN's initial purpose was to reduce the risk of violent conflict among the nations of Southeast Asia, so taking the principle of nonintervention to such lengths was seen as necessary and perhaps essential.

Progress toward establishing an ASEAN community by 2015 will almost certainly require movement away from current interpretations and current practice related to noninterference and toward arrangements in which enforceable standards are set. To consider the prospects for such movement, it is useful to note instances in the recent past when ASEAN has shown some flexibility on the noninterference concept.

In July 1999, reflecting a level of concern among member states with developments in Burma, Thailand's foreign minister Surin Pitsuwan proposed a divergence from past practice such that member states would be able to raise critical questions about one another's domestic policies and practices. Other members immediately rejected the proposal, called "flexible engagement," though divergent views among Singapore, Indonesia, and Malaysia to some extent left the door open on this question. Philippine president Joseph Estrada and Indonesian prime minister B. J. Hababie's subsequent public criticism of the arrest of Malaysian deputy premier Anwar Ibrahim showed some leaders' willingness simply to ignore the established norm.

ASEAN, despite its overwhelming disinclination to intervene in member governments' affairs, used its stature to convene peace talks during the Cambodian war of the 1990s. To the degree that the ultimate effects of these peace-building efforts in Cambodia colored internal governance, ASEAN could be said to have played a role in internal affairs. Again, though, it should be stressed that such ASEAN involvement has been sporadic. ASEAN has organized several conferences with the United Nations on conflict prevention, conflict resolution, and peace building in Southeast Asia. In part, these conferences seek to develop strategies for identifying conflict trigger points and forestalling violence, but the meetings' goals are unambitious. The ASEAN Secretariat itself is quick to caution that "[at one of the meetings] no one pushed any specific steps at the official level. . . . The ASEAN Secretariat has only a minor role in political matters. . . . ASEAN organizations are not keen to add on to their already heavy agendas."[20]

The situation in Burma has spurred the most significant debate within ASEAN about its role in member states' domestic affairs. On the basis of standard noninterventionist arguments, ASEAN has traditionally been very reluctant to intervene directly in Burma's internal affairs and has resisted calls to expel it from ASEAN. But since the early 2000s, the organization has begun to take a firmer stand and has formally called on Burma to release political prisoners and "begin moves toward democracy." Individual ASEAN member governments have also taken advantage of the forums provided by ASEAN meetings to make their own statements pressuring Burma to reform.[21]

The Burmese case is an outlier, but its importance concerns how it demonstrates a willingness within ASEAN to cooperate in defining appropriate state behavior by its members. Establishing acceptable limits on state behavior is something quite different from establishing any proactive standards or models of what ought to be. Certainly, ASEAN's treatment of Burma is in itself no embrace of a standard of democratic practice for its members—a standard on which ASEAN members probably cannot fully agree, anyway. Nonetheless, ASEAN statements and measures regarding Burma represent a real departure from the noninterference principle. The Burmese case is also important in departing from the long-standing ASEAN principle of acting only on the consensus of all members. Criticism of Burma's behavior may have established the principle that a lowest-common-denominator standard can be established by consensus of all ASEAN members minus the state being criticized. Although this principle does not yet deal with the important question of sanctions, it is a significant step away from the old constraints under the principle of full consensus.

The ARF has been meeting since 1993 with the goal of "promoting peace and security through dialogue and cooperation." It includes not only members of ASEAN, but also members such as Australia, China, the European Union, Japan, and the United States (for a full discussion of the ARF, see chapter 8 in this volume). For all of its flaws, the ARF may serve to help in the development of new regional governance norms, although the presence of countries such as North Korea in the forum will ensure that the ARF follows the precedent set by ASEAN rather than setting its own.[22] Constructivists argue that the very process of ASEAN cooperation on economic and security issues will create a new set of accepted regional norms that will impact the domestic governance of member countries. One ASEAN document talks about "enlightened regionalism," the idea that ASEAN as an organization serves as a voice for reason and moderation in the region.[23] Participation in ASEAN's free-trade provisions has certainly required countries such as Vietnam and Cambodia to adopt a more Western-style view of the government's role in the economy. One possibility is that ASEAN may come to promote a more comprehensive "regional view" of governance (though there is not much concrete evidence that it has done so yet).

GRAVITATION TO UNIVERSAL NORMS:
THE DRAFTING OF THE ASEAN CHARTER

After almost forty years, ASEAN's relative success was clear in terms of both its original goals of fostering regional peace and its evolved role in fostering dialogue and cooperation. In these years, there was no war between members, most members became vastly more prosperous, and areas of cooperation under ASEAN expanded exponentially. Yet, despite past success, it was also clear that ASEAN's role would continue to be limited as long as the instruments to enforce compliance among members remained so weak. As noted, there have been more than two hundred ASEAN agreements, but most are voluntary and not legally binding. In the absence of mechanisms to get beyond the stark limitations imposed by adherence to consensus decision making and, even more important, in the absence of concrete sanctions for noncompliance, members can continue to be indifferent and simply ignore inconvenient decisions—Burma being the most important case in point.

For this reason, consistent with broad aspirations for the establishment of a vibrant, unified ASEAN community laid out in the 1997 ASEAN Vision 2020[24] and the 2003 Declaration of ASEAN Concord II (Bali Concord II) and its plans of action and roadmap,[25] ASEAN heads of state committed in December 2005 to establishing a formal charter by the end of 2007. The charter would establish ASEAN as a legal entity, helping to build a "concert of Southeast Asian nations, outward-looking, living in peace, stability and prosperity, bonded together in partnership in dynamic development and in a community of caring societies."[26]

Why did ASEAN choose to draft a charter that broadens the definition of security, makes ASEAN a legal entity, and contemplates an expanded role for ASEAN as a norm- and standard-setting regional institution active in the "promotion of democracy, human rights and obligations, transparency and good governance and strengthening democratic institutions"?[27] Five principal explanations stand out.

First, ASEAN's move is consistent with an international trend that makes sovereignty more conditional on meeting certain minimum standards of governance.[28]

Second, Burma's 1997 accession to membership in ASEAN forced the declining organization into an ongoing dynamic dialogue and internal struggle about its policy regarding constructive engagement. This position is contrary to common wisdom, which holds that ASEAN was duplicitous to have admitted Burma and to have allowed it to stay within the organization. Burma and to a lesser extent Laos are outliers even for ASEAN, which has traditionally tolerated a very wide bandwidth of regime types. It includes regimes that are categorized as authoritarian, but the region as a whole—with the exceptions of Burma and Laos—is liberalizing, economically and politically.[29] Burma's accession has forced an internal debate about human rights that ASEAN would probably prefer to avoid. Interestingly, Freedom House categorizes six of ASEAN's ten country members as "Not Free" (Brunei, Cambodia, Laos, Burma, Thailand, and Vietnam), but Burma is the least free of all, earning the maximum score of 7.[30]

Third, Indonesia's democratization opened new opportunities for movement on the charter. Indeed, Indonesia is the only ASEAN member ranked as "free" in the Freedom House Index.[31] Hints of Indonesia's influence are found in the text of the *Report of the Eminent Persons Group on the ASEAN Charter* (hereafter *EPG Report*).

Fourth, China's rise, with its classic dangers and opportunities, has created pressure on ASEAN to develop a deeper, more integrated, and more consolidated identity. On the opportunity side, the ASEAN-China Comprehensive Economic Cooperation Framework Agreement (2002) should provide ASEAN with an incentive to hasten work on mechanisms for trade in goods, rules of origin, services liberalization, investment cooperation, and dispute settlement.[32] However, according to some ASEAN members, China's relations with two ASEAN members—Burma and Cambodia—present particular challenges to the evolution of minimum standards of governance within ASEAN. For example, China and Burma just concluded a major oil pipeline deal,[33] and Cambodian prime minister Hun Sen has cultivated closer ties to China, and China is providing extensive foreign assistance to Cambodia in addition to extensive private Chinese investment.[34]

Fifth, Vietnam, with its strategy of *doi moi* (renovation) launched in 1986 and its attendant rapid economic growth and modicum of political openness over the past decade, has become a key swing state between the original five members and the "new" members. In a sense, Vietnam is today "more ASEAN than older ASEAN members."[35] Among other activities driving rapid modernization, Vietnam is sending five thousand students abroad every year, which over the next decade may radically transform the nation into an outward-looking country very active in regional fora and very different from its reserved and reticent past.

These and other impetuses in the region are likely to create increasing pressure for the revision of two of ASEAN's most sacrosanct principles: nonintervention and lowest-common-denominator consensus building.

THE EPG REPORT

In 2006, ASEAN convened the EPG to prepare a report that would provide key input to the new ASEAN Charter. The *EPG Report* was endorsed during the twelfth ASEAN Summit in Cebu, Philippines, in December 2006. A high-level task force made up of a group of senior ASEAN officials was then authorized to draft the actual text of the charter for ASEAN heads of state to review in November 2007. The ten authors of the *EPG Report* were drawn from the ten ASEAN member countries and included such prominent figures as Fidel Ramos (former president of the Philippines) and Ali Alatas (former Indonesian minister of foreign affairs). Released in December 2006, the report contains observations, recommendations, and recommended draft language for the charter; Ali Alatas initially drafted the charter, but the rest of the group revised and ultimately endorsed it. The *EPG Report* represents an ambitious effort to advance a vision of a future ASEAN substantially evolved along several important lines.[36]

First, the *EPG Report* contains language that is the clearest and strongest endorsement of democratic governance principles yet seen in a quasi-official ASEAN document. It advocates the "[p]romotion of ASEAN's peace and security through the active strengthening of democratic values, good governance, rejection of unconstitutional and undemocratic changes of government, the rule of law including international humanitarian law, and respect for human rights and fundamental freedoms."[37] These four points are recommended for inclusion in the new charter. Although civil-society organizations based in Southeast Asia have been aggressive in demanding movement along these lines, most observers expected the EPG to be far less ambitious in its recommendations. However, the mere submission of a jointly prepared document by persons of this status suggests that at least some ASEAN member states are becoming more comfortable with the prospect of including political norms among the statement of its members' expectations.

Second, the *EPG Report* goes further than previous efforts in proposing the establishment of specific new institutional mechanisms for overcoming the current requirement for full consensus of members on critical matters and for imposing sanctions for noncompliance with collectively established agreements and standards. On the first point, although traditional "consensus" would be used for undefined "important" decisions, voting in some form would be used to prevent one or two member states from standing in the way of key ASEAN decisions. On the second point, a new "dispute-resolution mechanism" would be put in place, which would have the power to impose sanctions on a member state for noncompliance with ASEAN decisions as a whole. Combining these two points, the report recommends that in imposing sanctions in important cases, the collective decision of all ASEAN members, minus the offending member, would be determinant. This recommendation seems to institutionalize the recent criticisms of Burma referred to earlier, where members were willing—in a stark departure from the original interpretations of noninterference—to isolate and jointly to criticize a single member. As the *EPG*

Report states, "ASEAN's problem is not one of lack of vision, ideas, and action plans. The problem is one of ensuring compliance and effective implementation." The report continues, "As ASEAN steps up its integration efforts, appropriate monitoring, compliance and dispute settlement mechanisms should be established. The EPG therefore recommends that Dispute Settlement Mechanisms (DSM) be established in all fields of ASEAN cooperation. . . . Failure to comply with decisions of the DSM should be referred to the ASEAN Council for possible measures to redress non-compliance."[38]

Third, the *EPG Report* also recommends that the organization be allowed to issue binding sanctions against members: "[T]he Charter should also include provisions for measures to redress non-compliance and serious breaches. Such measures may include, among others, the temporary suspension of rights and privileges for membership, such as withholding the right to participate in ASEAN activities, and to chair ASEAN bodies and their meetings."[39] The final charter will not include this possibility.

Fourth, the *EPG Report* recommends a major strengthening of the position of secretary-general, including a provision that the secretary-general would be empowered to sign certain legally binding agreements on member states' behalf. In addition, the number of deputies to the secretary-general would be increased from two to four, which though perhaps fully justified by the workload now involved in running ASEAN, would nonetheless substantially increase the scope and capacity of the ASEAN Secretariat.[40] Finally, as fully expected by all member states, the *EPG Report* recommends that ASEAN be incorporated as a legal person.

Although the *EPG Report* imagined a bold step forward for the organization, the ten diverse governments of ASEAN ultimately could not reach full consensus on implementing this forward-leaning set of recommendations. Cambodia, Laos, Burma, and Vietnam constituted enough of a unified bloc that more cautious bureaucrats in the remaining six member states pulled back from some of the report's institutional recommendations. After thirteen contentious meetings, ASEAN officials agreed that consensus and "family" were more important than imposing norms on the less-progressive members. In a document full of contradictions reflecting the diversity of its member states, the final November 2007 charter reaffirms the principle of noninterference in internal affairs. Yet it also asserts that a core mission for ASEAN will be to "strengthen democracy, enhance good governance and the rule of law, and to promote and protect human rights and fundamental freedoms" (Chapter 1, Article 1, Section 7).[41] The charter also establishes a human rights commission, but provides no authority for punishing offenders within the association's ranks. As Singapore's solicitor general explained, "[W]hat this means is [that] at some point—sooner, we hope, rather than later—we will have a human rights body in ASEAN."[42]

The ASEAN Charter disappointed those who had pushed for a legally bind-ing document that would move the ten member states closer to a European Union–style grouping. But the norms expressed in the charter did break new ground. Its democratic members are clearly struggling to find ways to institu-tionalize norms of good governance, democracy, and human rights within a consensus-oriented multilateral process that includes authoritarian govern-ments. In addition, it should be noted that there was equal disappointment on the economic side of the charter, which failed to grant the ASEAN Secretariat any authority to negotiate with outside powers any trade or other economic agreements on behalf of the member states or to impose punishments for fail-ure to adhere to agreements among the member states. The charter's language and the debates emerging out of the *EPG Report* suggest that the organization is still evolving and that even though progress may appear to be slow and epi-sodic given the charter's outcome, the overall trend lines are positive.

POINTS OF EXTERNAL INFLUENCE ON GOVERNANCE NORMS IN ASIA

The United States, the European Union, and other external champions of gov-ernance and democracy in Asia tend to focus on their own direct impact on in-dividual states rather than on the impact of institution building within the re-gion. That is why this chapter began with a focus on ASEAN. But, of course, the external actors do matter and will ultimately reinforce (but, it is hoped, not undermine) the prospect for regional institutions such as ASEAN to promote governance reform and democracy. We turn now to the most important exter-nal influences: the European Union, Japan, and the United States. We also highlight here the growing importance of civil-society networks in influencing governance norms in Asia. Finally, we consider the potential effects of alternate external visions being presented by China and Russia through the Shanghai Cooperation Organization.

THE U.S. ROLE IN THE EVOLUTION OF DEMOCRACY AND GOVERNANCE INSTITUTIONS IN ASIA

The March 2006 version of *The National Security Strategy of the United States of America* puts security first, but sees development and particularly advanced liberal democracy as the prerequisite to security in the world. The strategy states that "democracy is the most effective long-term measure for strengthening international stability; reducing regional conflicts; countering terrorism and terror-supporting extremism; and extending peace and prosperity."[43] Rapid progress on political reform is important and a high priority. When this report is read together with the stated priority areas of the U.S. Agency for International Development (USAID) in democracy and governance (elections and political process, rule of law, civil society, and good governance), it appears that the U.S. position on democracy treats it outside the context of development in general and is quite different from the ASEAN way. Although many Asian nations accept the overall direction of this idealism, many find it hard to embrace its sense of urgency and heavy footprint. They are more tolerant of variance in regime type among their neighbors, and peace, cooperation, and common ground are more important than democratic ideology. Most important, Asian nations do not seem to share the belief that liberal democracy is the *prerequisite* to security and development.

The past two decades have seen a relatively high and increasing level of engagement by Western countries in this regard, but particularly by the United States. This engagement comes in two forms: diplomatic dialogue (on the Asian side often viewed more as pressure) and foreign assistance aimed at strengthening key institutions such legislatures, elections, and the judicial system and at promoting human rights, often by working through local civil-society organizations.

Growing international pressures for advances in these areas are driven by three important arguments. First, there is the long-standing belief in the inherent moral ascendancy of democracy based on the rule of law as a form of government. Second, many within development circles are convinced that democratic institutions are essential prerequisites for rapid economic and social transformation. Third, the United States in particular makes the official argument that freedom and democracy better ensure peace and security. The research literature indicates that the links between regime type and economic growth and between regime type and security are more nuanced than these arguments imply.[44] Nevertheless, these different arguments for supporting democratic transformations are heavily intertwined in current U.S. foreign policy. In a speech to the National Endowment for Democracy in 2003, U.S. president George W. Bush made one of the most important articulations of a U.S. commitment to advancing freedom and democracy, particularly in the Middle East. That speech drew on all three arguments and indicated that the general commitment to supporting democratic, human rights, and rule-of-law reform would ensure that a ready pool of resources from the U.S. government would be available for this purpose.[45]

Almost all U.S. engagement in Asia, in the form of diplomatic pressure and foreign assistance, has over the years been bilateral in character and has been concentrated on certain countries in East and Southeast Asia. Diplomatic pressure has sometimes been sustained over very long periods—two decades of U.S. pressure on Burma being a case in point. Foreign assistance focused on democracy promotion tends to be concentrated on countries that are in moments of crisis or major transition: the Philippines in the late 1980s, Cambodia through the 1990s, Indonesia following the fall of Suharto in 1998, and East Timor beginning in 2002. Although foreign assistance to ASEAN in the past has not included funding for advancing governance reform, that policy may change. A USAID project begun in 2007 provides substantial resources to the ASEAN Secretariat and through the secretariat to member countries for a range of areas including rule of law and human rights should such assistance be requested.

THE EUROPEAN UNION'S ROLE IN THE EVOLUTION OF GOVERNANCE IN ASIA

The European Union's role as a promoter of democracy and good governance and human rights has grown rapidly in recent years. In 1989, it entered into a multilateral agreement (known as "Lome IV") with countries of Africa, the Caribbean, and the Pacific that wrote human rights, democracy, and the rule of law into its political conditionalities.[46] In 1999, it adopted the European Initiative for the Development of Human Rights (EIDHR) as a comprehensive strategy "in support of democratization, the strengthening of the rule of law and the development of pluralist and democratic civil society."[47] Since then, democracy promotion has become a centerpiece of the union's foreign policy. In 2001, for example, the European Union and its member states disbursed $900 million on democracy promotion compared to USAID's $633 million that same year.[48] Today, the European Union and its member states are by a wide measure the largest funders of democracy promotion in the world. Its operational style with accession countries is famously detailed and technocratic. With its development partners, however, an "open and constructive dialogue" on human rights and democracy is encouraged with "managed compliance" and more of a soft-diplomacy approach, though sanctions are not ruled out.

Because the European Union is outside Asia's neighborhood, it has been, according to Tanja Borzel and Thomas Risse, less effective in pushing political conditionality. Its Asia Strategy, adopted in 1994, "sought to intensify political dialogue with Asian countries but issues of human rights and democracy have been largely banned from the agenda of the Asia-Europe Meetings (ASEM)."[49] In 2003, the European Union issued a communication subtitled *A New Partnership with South East Asia* in which it highlighted an "essential element" clause. This clause stipulates that respect for fundamental human rights and democratic principles, as laid down in the Universal Declaration on Human Rights, underpins the internal and external policies of the parties and constitutes an "essential element" of the agreement.[50] The union's bilateral trade agreements with India, Sri Lanka, Nepal, Cambodia, Vietnam, Bangladesh, and Pakistan contain democracy and human rights clauses. But China, South Korea, Laos, the Philippines, and Malaysia have refused political conditionality on their sectoral trade agreements. The European Union and a number of its member states carry out annual human rights dialogues with countries in Asia, such as China.

Although the European Union precedent of requiring universal levels of governance and democracy will not apply to the Asian regional institution-building process any time soon, there are two reasons why Europe can have an influence on the diffusion of governance norms in Asia as the regional architecture takes shape. The first reason is the intensification of a European Union–Asian dialogue through forums such as the annual Asia Europe Meeting, which require the Asian members to negotiate Burma's participation and other sensitive issues on a regular basis, ultimately reinforcing those actors within ASEAN who seek greater adherence to universal norms and find comfort in non-U.S. pressure to conform. The second reason is the example that the European Union sets for Japan, which has increasingly come to champion the former's precedent (see chapter 5 in this volume).

"ARC OF FREEDOM OF PROSPERITY": JAPAN'S NEW APPROACH TO ASIAN GOVERNANCE REFORM

Where does "democracy" fit in the discourse *within Asia?* The comment made by India's foreign minister in 2005 in the context of India's relationship to Burma, "we don't do democracy promotion," is perhaps the most telling regarding where democracy can or will fit in any evolving Asian regional architecture.[51] India's deeply embedded democratic values are subordinate to, among other things, its oil and gas interest in Burma.

Japan, in contrast, is articulating a vision of its role and responsibility to freedom and prosperity in the region in increasingly bolder terms. In a major foreign-policy address in November 2006, Foreign Minister Aso Taro articulated two pillars of Japan's foreign policy relevant to democracy, human rights, governance, and the rule of law. The first pillar, "'value oriented diplomacy,'" . . . involves placing emphasis on the 'universal values' such as democracy, freedom, human rights, the rule of law, and the market economy as we advance our diplomatic endeavors."[52] This pillar introduces the idea that we have a dialogue with our neighbors on values that include democracy and human rights. It contrasts with current ASEAN views, but it also contrasts with the heavy-footprint approach taken by the United States.

The second pillar, the "arc of freedom," was outlined in an address by Foreign Minister Aso in which he compared the size of Japan's economy with that of the rest of the region and suggested a commensurate duty to support freedom and prosperity, given Japan's economic strength:

> If we take the combined GDP of the entirety of East Asia, including China, as well as that of the nations of the Pacific, the figure amounts to a mere 67.3 percent of the Japanese economy. Throw the GDP for the entirety of South Asia into the mix and all told it still reaches only 89.4 percent of the size of Japan's economy.
>
> In other words, as a country of this size, I would hold that Japan has a duty to support such things as freedom and prosperity. But it is better if whenever possible we undertake such efforts in cooperation with other nations with which we share the same values, such as the nations of Europe.[53]

With the forging of the U.S.-Japan "Common Agenda" in official development assistance in the 1990s, the Japanese have been developing an assistance program that—at least on the level of broad goals and objectives as they relate to democracy, governance, human rights, and the rule of law—mirrors in many ways those of the United States and the European Union. One can expect operationalization of the evolving Japanese assistance agenda to be much less adhesive than the U.S. carrots-and-sticks approach. As Foreign Minister Aso said, despite the great value that the Japanese place on democracy, "such deep feelings on this topic may perhaps best be left unsaid." This statement seems to suggest that the Japanese might be expected to continue to subordinate democracy and governance reform to the primacy of security and development. In this respect, the ASEAN way and the Japanese way seem very compatible:

> Japan, having cast off the peace and tranquility of the Edo era, joined the age of imperialism underway around the globe, finally settling on democracy after having wavered among a number of approaches. The fact that Japan had to go through so much to reach that point is why Japanese are second to no one in how greatly they value democracy.
>
> Yet, *such deep feelings on this topic may perhaps best be left unsaid.* Keeping those feelings inside, we want to think of the aspirations of Georgia or the Ukraine, or Laos or Vietnam—countries moving forward, heads held high—as

the path towards freedom and prosperity. We also want to run the race to-gether with them, sometimes *sharing our water* with them. That is our funda-mental stance on creating this Arc of Freedom and Prosperity.[54]

"Sharing our water," especially in the context of the countries mentioned (Laos, Cambodia, and even Burma), presumably means that foreign assis-tance will be made available even to nondemocratic countries. We can cer-tainly expect Japan to approach democracy, human rights, and governance with more emphasis on engagement and a greater tolerance for the evolutionary na-ture of progress.

THE GROWING ROLE OF CIVIL SOCIETY

Over the past few decades, increasing numbers of nongovernmental organiza-tions (NGOs), both international and domestic, have become engaged in a great variety of humanitarian, development, and rights-related activities in East and Southeast Asia. In part, this engagement has been made possible by many East and Southeast Asian governments' growing openness to such activities, but it also reflects the substantial financial support provided since the early 1980s by Western assistance programs, an increasing share of which is focused on local NGO development. This assistance is often passed through international NGOs. Well more than six thousand international NGOs, the large majority with secretariats based in the United States and Europe, are active in East and Southeast Asia. Most are engaged in humanitarian or direct development ef-forts, but some focus on issues that have at least some impact on governance reform, including democratization, human rights, legal reform, and the envi-ronment.[55] To what extent, then, are these international NGOs directly or indi-rectly helping to shape emerging architecture at the regional level in East Asia?

In terms of direct impact, although some international NGOs are focused on influencing the security-related regional architecture in East Asia, very few seek a direct role in shaping regional architecture in areas of governance re-form. What role they do play is primarily through encouragement and financial and technical support to national-level civil-society organizations and regional NGO networks. Advocacy by domestic civil society is one of many factors af-fecting direction and pace of governance reforms at the national and local lev-els in less-restrictive East Asian countries, but particularly in Thailand, the Philippines, and Indonesia. Some nationally based NGOs in certain important areas of reform—including human rights, women's empowerment, and the environment—are seeking greater influence in establishing regional norms and

shaping regional architecture. This connection was seen clearly in the assertiveness that Asian NGOs showed in support of strong positions on democracy and
human rights in the ASEAN Charter. The trend will almost clearly be toward
greater engagement and influence by Asian NGOs and Asian NGO networks in
determining the direction and formalization of regional norms, with critical
support from international NGOs. To the extent that international NGOs become greater proactive allies of Asian NGOs in transnational networks seeking
to influence regional governance reform in areas such as democracy, human
rights, and environment, we may see the emergence of a soft or epistemic form
of multilateral architecture that complements the more formalized meetings
among governments.[56] How influential this multilateral architecture might become in the establishment of regional norms has yet to be seen. The trend explains at least some of the sensitivity to international NGOs in less-open states
such as China and Vietnam

AN ALTERNATIVE VISION: THE SHANGHAI
COOPERATION ORGANIZATION

The potential influence of Westernized models of good-governance norms may
be counterbalanced in the region by the emergence and growth of other, potentially alternative models of governance in the region. The Shanghai Cooperation Organization (SCO) may stand out in this regard. The SCO traces its roots
to a series of regularized working-level contacts in the early to mid-1990s to
settle and introduce military confidence-building measures along the seven-
thousand-kilometer border between China and four of its Central Asian neighbors: Kazakhstan, Kyrgyzstan, Russia, and Tajikistan. On the basis of these
agreements, the "Shanghai Five" process of summitry began in the late 1990s,
and at the June 2001 summit the grouping formally established the SCO, with
Uzbekistan added as a sixth member at that time. The SCO evolved to issue
numerous key documents and statements, establish a permanent secretariat, set
up a regional counterterrorism center in Tashkent, Uzbekistan, and expand its
activities to include—in addition to annual heads-of-state summits—a full range
of political, economic, trade, energy, military, law enforcement, health, educa-
tional, sports, and cultural exchanges and cooperation at both working and
ministerial levels.[57]

The SCO's founding documents provide some insight into its aims. At the
June 2001 summit establishing the SCO, two important documents were is-
sued. The first, the Shanghai Convention on the Fight Against Terrorism,
Separatism, and Extremism, set the fight against what the group termed "the

three evils" as a high priority for the organization. The second document was the Declaration on the Creation of the Shanghai Cooperation Organization. Of particular relevance to this chapter, Article 5 of the declaration states that the group will "abide by strictly the purposes and principles of the Charter of the United Nations, mutually respect independence, sovereignty and territorial integrity, not interfere in each other's internal affairs, not use or threaten to use force against each other, adhere to equality and mutual benefit, resolve all problems through mutual consultations and not seek unilateral military superiority in contiguous regions."[58]

In June 2002, the SCO issued its twenty-six-article charter.[59] Here, too, the organization stresses a wide-ranging set of principles, with a strong emphasis on mutual trust, good neighborliness, and cooperation. In particular, the group aims to promote "a new democratic, fair and rational political and economic international order" while encouraging "efficient regional cooperation in such spheres as politics, trade and economy, defense, law enforcement, environment protection, culture, science and technology, education, energy, transport, credit and finance, and also other spheres of common interest" (Article 1). The charter sets out certain principles for pursuing these goals, including "mutual respect of sovereignty, independence, territorial integrity of States and inviolability of State borders, non-aggression, non-interference in internal affairs, non-use of force or threat of its use in international relations, seeking no unilateral military superiority in adjacent areas" (Article 2).

Interestingly, however, in spite of the familiar declarations concerning non-interference, the charter does go on to lay out some stipulations for intervening against member states that are seen by fellow members to be in violation of the charter. For example, Article 13 states, "SCO membership of a member State violating the provisions of this Charter and/or systematically failing to meet its obligations under international treaties and instruments, concluded in the framework of SCO, may be suspended by a decision of the Council of Heads of State adopted on the basis of a representation made by the Council of Ministers of Foreign Affairs. If this State goes on violating its obligations, the Council of Heads of State may take a decision to expel it from [the] SCO as of the date fixed by the Council itself." Article 16 states that SCO decisions will be taken by consensus, "except for the decisions on suspension of membership or expulsion from the Organisation[, which] shall be taken by consensus minus one vote of the member State concerned." It is too early to say at this point whether those provisions against a fellow member state would actually be implemented within the SCO, but it is interesting nonetheless to note that the organization included such a procedure in its foundation document.

Current indications suggest that the SCO will strongly retain its "noninterference" principles and that in the wake of "color revolutions" in the mid-2000s

in such locations as Georgia and Ukraine and within member states Uzbekistan and Kyrgyzstan, its members may actually have found even deeper common cause to adhere all the more strictly to these principles. In 2005, the
SCO's calls for the U.S.-led coalition carrying out antiterrorist activities in Afghanistan to provide a timeline for its eventual withdrawal from bases in Central Asia and the admission of Iran to the SCO as an observer in 2006—even as
the international community was seeking to isolate Iran to constrain its nuclear ambitions—certainly raise a host of concerns about how dedicated the
SCO will be to broader global norms regarding counterterrorism and nonproliferation. Made up of authoritarian and semiauthoritarian states, the SCO is
not likely to act as a catalyst for fostering norms of democracy and good governance among its members. Indeed, because the SCO is led by the emergent
and increasingly confident states China and Russia, it may itself pose as a viable alternative for multilateral organizations in Asia, focusing little if at all
on governance and democratic norm building, and far more on mutual security and economic gain—all built on traditional principles of sovereignty and
noninterference.

In June 2006, Chinese president Hu Jintao clearly enunciated the "Shanghai
Way" and sent a message of noninterference to the United States: "We hope the
international community can respect the social system and road of development independently chosen by SCO member countries and observer countries,
respect their internal and external policies of peace, friendship, and cooperation based on their own domestic situation, and create a harmonious and easy
environment for their development."[60] Emboldened by enormous oil revenue
windfalls, international reluctance to intervene because of the war in Iraq, and
a domestic backlash against extraordinary international pressures that force-fed
economic reform in Russia in the 1990s, President Vladimir Putin is on the
same page with his Chinese counterpart regarding the primacy of sovereignty
and noninterference. Putin's advancement of the idea of "sovereign democracy"
is in lockstep with the "Shanghai Way."[61]

For the time being, membership in the SCO is closed. On August 13, 2007,
just ahead of the SCO's summit in Bishkek, Kyrgyzstan, the Russian deputy
minister of foreign affairs Alexander Losyukov announced that SCO members
have agreed to suspend the organization's expansion. "The SCO Charter allows
new admissions, but the organization has yet to work out criteria and algorithm
of such [a] procedure."[62] Losyukov underscored that the agreement does not
turn the SCO into a "closed club," but the suspension of expansion is tanta-
mount to a de facto rejection of the United States and any other nonmembers.
This suspension of membership expansion presumably also applies to the SCO's
three observers: India, Iran, and Pakistan.

HOW EFFECTIVE IS EXTERNAL ASSISTANCE FOR GOVERNANCE AND DEMOCRATIC REFORM?

In general, most of the research on foreign-funded democracy and rights promotion seems to suggest that it is either not very effective at all[63] or might be effective, but minimally so because it is usually insufficiently nuanced or poorly targeted.[64] Very recent research, however, suggests that the problem with this view is the research methods it has used and that, in fact, democracy promotion (though not human rights promotion) has generally been more effective than indicated in previously evaluative work.[65] Scholars of comparative politics have conducted long-running debates over the relative importance of short-term "human agency" factors (i.e., the targets of democracy-promotion aid) versus long-term structural preconditions for democratic reform, which economic development assistance might effect but democracy aid cannot.[66] Taken as a whole, the literature (and our own decades of direct experience with governance reform in Asia) suggests that assistance for democracy, rule-of-law, and good-governance reform is most likely to be effective where it is sustained over time and carefully targeted based on substantial knowledge of domestic dynamics, and where powerful domestic interests, either inside or outside government (preferably both), are driving in the same direction as outside diplomatic pressure and donor assistance. Where all these conditions were in place in Southeast Asia, even limited foreign assistance, combined in some cases with nuanced diplomatic pressure, was quite effective—for example, in the transitions from authoritarian to democratic rule in the Philippines in 1986 and in Indonesia in 1998, in the introduction of positive law institutions in China over the past decade, and in constraints on human rights abuse in Cambodia since the late 1990s. Clearly, however, external interventions rarely have either the nuanced sophistication or the scale to move countries in directions that they are fundamentally predisposed not to go in for internal reasons—again, Burma illustrates the point.

Because the evidence suggests that official assistance for democracy promotion and governance reform is more effective when it is sustained and carefully targeted, there is obvious merit in increasing coordination among the United States, Japan, and the European Union. Democracy and governance assistance will ultimately be most effective, however, when it is reinforcing the norms and patterns of cooperation already in place within the region. That is why the example of ASEAN's evolution on governance reform is so important and why it is worth considering how broader institution building in Asia can reinforce those positive trends.

THE WAY AHEAD

It is not clear whether the ASEAN Charter itself will ultimately have an impact on strengthening governance reform and democracy within the region, but the trend lines from the *ASEAN Vision 2020* of 1997 to the *EPG Report* in 2007 suggest that the norm of noninterference in internal affairs is steadily being replaced by a new consensus around the need to emphasize progress on governance, democracy, and rule of law. Moreover, to the extent that liberal democracy and rule of law are seen as long-term goals to be held up but not accepted as prerequisites to sustainable high growth and rapid developmental transformation, the new ASEAN Charter suggests a convergence with the thinking in Japan, as reflected in the Arc of Freedom and Prosperity initiative. That approach toward democracy, human rights, and governance places more emphasis on engagement and a greater tolerance for the evolutionary nature of progress, in contrast to the European Union or U.S. approaches. At the same time, it suggests increasing convergence with the latter approaches in terms of placing universal norms as an explicit target and increasing pressure on member states (if often quietly and behind the scenes) to improve governance and democracy. This emerging approach also stands in contrast to other mechanisms in the region, such as the SCO, which is distinctly on the nonprogressive side on this set of issues and a great deal less willing to consider placing democracy and human rights or even governance and the rule of law on its agenda.

This is not to suggest that there are distinct and immutable "camps" within Asia on the broad issues of governance, human rights, and democracy. In many of the areas of governance reform outlined at the beginning of this chapter, in particular those that might have a direct impact on the region's economic integration and competitiveness, at least some degree of support within ASEAN can be expected—enthusiastic from some members, more tepid from others, but enough to ensure that such changes in the charter are implemented. At a minimum, this support means that inclusion of some areas related to rule of law, such as legal harmonization and civil-service reform, will find broad acceptance, as will governance reforms addressing key areas related to nontraditional security threats and possibly areas related to countercorruption. To the extent that reforms related to good governance can be more clearly defined—for example, in technical efforts to curb corruption—there is likely to be acceptance as well. In all of these areas, cooperation is already strong and increasing. A more proactive ASEAN with greater capacity to lead cooperation and harmonization efforts and even the authority to impose some level of sanctions on it members for noncompliance is not likely to be overly threatening. There may also be a willingness to increase cooperation in a few, fairly limited human right areas, such as women's and children's rights, human trafficking, and possibly migrant-laborer rights (which is controversial but also in line with the Vientiane Action Plan and the Cebu Declaration signed in January 2007).[67] These norms associated with good governance will also possibly resonate in Beijing, where there is an increasing concern about fragile states on China's periphery and a recognition of the need to fight corruption and improve economic governance at home.

Where ASEAN members diverge, however, is on those parts of the *EPG Report* and the final charter that emphasize advancing democracy and human rights. This divergence, of course, mirrors broader divisions within the region as a whole. Two difficulties with the *EPG Report* and the charter stand out: one is definitional; the other involves permanence. The *EPG Report* and the ASEAN Charter lack clear definition of the elements of democratic governance. The *EPG Report* tries to introduce the notion of compliance and sanctions, a move away from consensus-based decision making and noninterference. It raises the specter of sanctions for noncompliant members. Specifically, it states, "Consensus decision making is especially appropriate for decisions in more sensitive areas of security and foreign policy. . . . [M]ajority voting can be used in less sensitive and noncontroversial areas."[68] The member states ultimately put off the sanctions question in composing the final charter, but the establishment of a human rights commission is likely to reopen this question at some point in the future. Although Indonesia, the Philippines, Singapore, Malaysia, and Thailand would likely find the potential for intrusion in their internal affairs only minimally threatening, Cambodia, Laos, Brunei, and even Vietnam at this stage cannot be expected to embrace policies based on the democracy and human rights clauses in the charter, and Burma and Vietnam will be particularly nervous about any move in that direction. Burma's political leadership would obviously wish to avoid future sanctions, but the primary problem for moving in this direction is not Burma. Within ASEAN, Burma is already in a weak position in this regard. In resisting the assumption of Burma as chair of ASEAN in the organization's rotating system, other ASEAN members have already demonstrated their willingness to put significant pressure on the Burmese government regarding its domestic politics. Although this pressure occurred in a back channel for the most part and was ultimately self-imposed by Burma itself, the outcome was nonetheless a de facto punishment in denying the ASEAN chairmanship to Burma. Burma would presumably not be quite so compliant with respect to the democracy, human rights, and good-governance clauses in the ASEAN Charter, but other members might at least to some extent disregard those objections.

Vietnam is an entirely different matter. Despite strong and increasing commonality of interest among ASEAN members, the fact remains that Vietnam in particular is pursuing rapid economic development by a political path that is fundamentally different from the one taken by its neighbors. Vietnam is not willing to allow itself to be railroaded into endorsing democracy and human rights standards simply by the threat of possible future sanctions for noncompliance. Perhaps even more important, it will not risk providing leverage for local dissidents to pressure the government and the Communist Party of Vietnam on matters that cut so close to the party's fundamental interests. Under ASEAN in its current form, "ASEAN way" norms provide a strong check against collective movement toward anything related to democracy and human rights that would be fundamentally threatening to any members. The charter's commitment to loosely defined democratic values and human rights may have a significant impact within member states such as Vietnam, but without the compliance mechanisms originally envisioned by the *EPG Report* it is not clear how great that impact will be.

Consequently, ASEAN may continue sticking with a lowest-common-denominator approach, which has relatively fewer mechanisms for advancing the EPG's democracy and human rights recommendations and relatively more mechanisms for issues associated with the rule of law, countercorruption, and governance related to economic policy. At the same time, a subset of democratic ASEAN states—possibly Indonesia, Malaysia, the Philippines, Singapore, and Thailand—may take the initiative to establish joint standards for themselves in areas such as elections or basic legal rights, probably in the form of "guidelines" on "best practices" rather than anything like rigid standards. However, these member states will likely take care not to go so far as to undermine the traditional "solidarity" that has been so central to ASEAN's overall strategic outlook.

For democratic governance norm setting, some ASEAN members might join a broader group of non-ASEAN advanced democratic states, either within East Asia (i.e., Australia, Japan, New Zealand, South Korea) or outside East Asia (Europe and the United States) to press for global standards in areas of democracy beyond the Universal Declaration of Human Rights—such as electoral standards. Japanese prime minister Shinzo Abe and U.S. vice president Richard Cheney floated this possibility in late 2006 and April 2007, respectively, and met a mixed response, although subsequent meetings at the undersecretary level among Australia, India, Japan, and the United States to explore the concept suggest that it will evolve over time.

This "concert of democracies" approach would resemble in some ways the evolution of economic institutions such as the World Trade Organization and the European Union in which the advanced nations, as the first movers, set the bar high. New entrants, though treated officially as equal partners, are forced to comply with norms and standards that they have not been a party in establishing. It is important to recognize that this approach lies in stark contrast to that which has shaped and animated ASEAN from the outset. The ASEAN approach starts with bringing as many actors as possible into the tent based on the core goal of peaceful coexistence, and tolerance of diversity of regime type is inherent in this approach. From there, ASEAN moves forward slowly and carefully based on consensus in areas in which least-common-denominator agreement can be made. For this reason, ASEAN democracies would meet this broader "concert of democracies" with caution if it appeared to draw a firm line between democratic and nondemocratic Asian and ASEAN states.

It is striking that despite the domestic trend toward increasing democratization in many countries and growing collective interest in governance reforms that will make the region safer and more competitive, so little of this trend has moved up to the regional level in the form of official standard setting. Dialogue on such issues occurs to some extent, but it is still limited. In part, this characteristic reflects the diversity of regime types within the region and ASEAN's original raison d'être—to reduce the likelihood of violent conflict between members. Hence, the group emphasizes the pragmatic need to tease out and stick with lowest-common-denominator approaches to cooperation on all fronts, especially concerning governance reforms that are sensitive and even potentially threatening to some states. But this characteristic also reflects the firm embrace of a similar pragmatism over ideology in the evolution of domestic politics in most states in the region, at least over the past three decades. Peace, security, and above all rapid improvements in the quality of life have been the foundations of the legitimacy of government. Democratic governance reform has proceeded slowly and partially in most cases, in fits and starts in others. But unlike in many other regions of the world, in East and Southeast Asia political reform has not been allowed to outpace or disrupt the capacity to deliver rapid developmental transformation. It is not surprising that the tolerance of diversity among neighboring states and a pragmatic approach to political reform at home have played out the way that they have at the level of regional architecture, where the desire for everyone to embrace human rights, democracy, and rule of law has remained sharply in check.

However, that same pragmatism will ensure that the more successful democratic states in Asia will continue pushing the region to take steps to strengthen good governance and democracy without breaking the momentum toward "community building." Thus, the normative trends in the region are generally on the side of the American-led neoliberal order, but the United States and other external actors will achieve more effective results if they allow these norms to be institutionalized in an Asian way, even if that way proves to be more incremental and evolutionary than the American way of democracy promotion.

NOTES

1. In a forthcoming book, *A Conceptual Framework for Interpreting Recorded Human History,* Douglass North, John Wallis, and Barry Weingast develop what they call the "theory of double balance": "The double balance implies that sustaining fundamental changes in either the economic or political system cannot occur without fundamental changes in the other. Understanding the forces maintaining a balance between political and economic institutions is critically important to our understanding of both the stability of various orders and to the transition from [developing to developed]." For a synthesis of the authors' argument, see *A Conceptual Framework for Interpreting Recorded Human History,* National Bureau of Economic Research (NBER) Working Paper no. 12795 (Cambridge, Mass.: NBER, December 2006), http://emlab .berkeley.edu/users/webfac/cromer/e211_sp07/wallis.pdf. In the context of this chapter's subject, never mind all that we do not know about specific causality in political and economic development. We know that there is a "double balance" between the two. That ASEAN members historically have been motivated by economic growth thus bodes well for increased movement on more political issues such as governance as countries in the region pay close attention to the gap between economic and political liberalization.

2. Seymour Martin Lipset, "Some Social Requisites of Democracy: Economic Development and Political Legitimacy," *American Political Science Review* 53, no. 1 (1959): 69–105.

3. Some argue that Singapore proves Lipset wrong because of the enduring gap between economic liberalization and political liberalization. We assert, however, that economic liberalization has had and continues to have a political liberalizing effect in Singapore, and the gap between the two in Singapore is really due to a variety of historical, geographical, and demographic characteristics that make the city-state sui generis.

4. Thomas Carothers, "How Democracies Emerge: The 'Sequencing' Fallacy," *Journal of Democracy* 18 (2007): 12–27.

5. For a canvassing of speculation among scholars, see Patricia Cohen, "An Unexpected Odd Couple: Free Markets and Freedom," *New York Times,* June 14, 2007. For another recent example of the growth industry in speculation among scholars, see Azar Gat, "The Return of Authoritarian Great Powers," *Foreign Affairs* 86, no. 4 (2007): 59–69.

6. On this point, see, for example, Ahmed Mushfiq Mobarak, "Democracy, Volatility, and Economic Development," *Review of Economics and Statistics* 87, no. 2 (2005): 348–61.

7. Dani Rodrik, "Development Lessons for Asia from Non-Asian Countries," *Asian Development Review* 23 (2006): 1, 12, emphasis in original.

8. For example, some believe that China will eventually experience its own version of the 1997 Asian financial crisis if it does not improve the quality of its institu-

tions. See, for example, Kenneth Dam, *The Law-Growth Nexus: The Rule of Law and Economic Development* (Washington, D.C.: Brookings Institution Press, 2006). Note that such views with respect to China's trajectory remain in the realm of speculation.

9. ASEAN Secretariat, *ASEAN Vision 2020* (Jakarta, Indonesia: ASEAN, 1997), http//www.aseansec.org/1814.htm.

10. See, for example, ASEAN Secretariat, "Joint Communiqué of the 6th ASEAN Law Ministers Meeting (ALAWMM)," Hanoi, Vietnam, September 19–20, 2005, http://www.aseansec.org/17738.htm; "Joint Press Statement of the 9th ASEAN Senior Law Officials Meeting (ASLOM)," Bandar Seri Begawan, Brunei Darussalam, August 23–24, 2004, http://www.aseansec.org/16335.htm; "Treaty on Mutual Assistance on Criminal Matters," Kuala Lumpur, Malaysia, November 29, 2004, http://www.aseansec.org/17363.pdf.

11. ASEAN Secretariat, "ASEAN Declaration on the Protection and Promotion of the Rights of Migrant Workers," Cebu, Philippines, January 2007, http://www.aseansec.org/19264.htm, and "Social Development" Web page, http://www.aseansec.org/8558.htm and http://www.aseansec.org/21218.htm. For more on the Cebu Declaration, see http://www.pia.gov.ph/asean/?m = 2&r = &fi = p070119.htm&no = 01.

12. ASEAN Secretariat, "ASEAN Cooperation on Civil Service Matters (ACCSM): Overview," http://www.aseansec.org/12950.htm.

13. See, for example, Yoshihiro Iwasaki, "At the Roots of the Asian Crisis: Governance and Transparency," speech, Phnom Penh, Cambodia, March 14–15, 2000, http://www.asiandevbank.org/Documents/Speeches/1999/Transparency/cam_speech.pdf.

14. "EITI [Extractive Industries Transparency Initiative]: Timor Leste," http://www.eitransparency.org/section/countries/_timorleste, updated February 22, 2008.

15. Erik Jensen, "Justice and Rule of Law," in *Building States to Build Peace*, ed. Charles T. Call and Vanessa Wyeth (Boulder, Colo.: Reinner, 2008), 119–42.

16. Gloria Macapagal-Arroyo, "One Sharing and Caring Community," chairperson's statement at the twelfth ASEAN Summit, Cebu, Philippines, January 13, 2007, http://www.aseansec.org/19280.htm; ASEAN Secretariat, "Cebu Declaration on East Asian Energy Security," Cebu, Philippines, January 15, 2007, http://www.aseansec.org/19319.htm; Alan Khee-Jin Tan, "The ASEAN Agreement on Transboundary Haze Pollution: Prospects for Compliance and Effectiveness in Post-Suharto Indonesia," *New York University Environmental Law Journal* 13 (2006): 647–722; ASEAN Secretariat, "Third ASEAN State of the Environment Report 2006: Executive Summary," Indonesia, November 2006, http://ekh.unep.org/files/Summary.pdf.

17. ASEAN Secretariat, "Third ASEAN State of Environment Report 2006."

18. Among other factors complicating Indonesia's ratification, Indonesia would like reciprocal agreements from Singapore that prevent Singaporeans from taking sand from Indonesia's islands near Singapore. On the sand dispute in general, see Richard Lloyd Parry, "Singapore Accused of Land Grab as Islands Disappear by Boat-

load," *Times Online*, March 17, 2007, http://www.timesonline.co.uk/tol/news/world/asia/article1527751.ece.

19. Macapagal-Arroyo, "One Sharing and Caring Community"; ASEAN Secretariat, "ASEAN Commitments on HIV and AIDS," Cebu, Philippines, January 13, 2007, http://www.aseansec.org/19322.htm; William Onzivu, "Globalism, Regionalism, or Both: Health Policy and Regional Economic Integration in Developing Countries, an Evolution of a Legal Regime?" *Minnesota Journal of International Law* 15 (2006): 118–88.

20. ASEAN Secretariat, "Third ASEAN/UN Conference on Conflict Prevention, Conflict Resolution, and Peace Building in Southeast Asia: ASEAN/UN Experiences in Anticipating and Mediating Conflicts," Singapore, February 18–19, 2003, http://www.aseansec.org/un_singapore.htm.

21. Macapagal-Arroyo, "One Sharing and Caring Community"; ASEAN Secretariat, "Politics and Security: Overview," n.d., http://www.aseansec.org/92.htm; South Center, *Analytical Note: The ASEAN Experience: Insights for Regional Political Cooperation* (Geneva: South Centre, 2007), http://www.southcentre.org/publications/AnalyticalNotes/GlobalPoliticalGov/2007Feb_ASEAN_Regional_Political_Integration.pdf; ASEAN Secretariat, "Third ASEAN/UN Conference on Conflict Prevention, Conflict Resolution, and Peace Building in Southeast Asia: Narrative Report on the Seminar on Conflict Prevention and Peace-Building in Southeast Asia: Regional Mechanisms, Best Practices, and ASEAN-UN Cooperation in the 21st Century," Manila, Philippines, February 19–22, 2002, http://www.aseansec.org/un_manila.htm; ARF, "Concept and Principles of Preventive Diplomacy," July 25, 2001, http://www.aseansec.org/3571.htm; "Asian Group Raps Burma on Rights," BBC News, December 12, 2005, http://news.bbc.co.uk/2/hi/asia-pacific/4520040.stm; "Myanmar: ASEAN's Thorn in the Flesh," *Asia Times*, July 25, 2003, http://www.atimes.com/atimes/Southeast_Asia/EG25Ae01.html; "ASEAN Pursues EU-Style Regional Integration," *International Herald Tribune*, January 15, 2005, http://yaleglobal.yale.edu/display.article?id = 8619; Sueo Sudo, "Regional Governance and East and Southeast Asia: Towards the Regulatory State?" *Japanese Journal of Political Science* 4, no. 2 (2003): 331–47 (on the possible increasing willingness to participate in domestic affairs, see 344).

22. ASEAN Secretariat, *Report of the Eminent Persons Group on the ASEAN* (Jakarta, Indonesia: ASEAN, December 2005), http://www.aseansec.org/19247.pdf; "ASEAN Regional Forum (ARF) Concept and Principles of Preventive Diplomacy," July 25, 2001, http://www.aseansec.org/3571.htm; "ASEAN Pursues EU-Style Regional Integration."

23. ASEAN Secretariat, "Politics and Security: Overview."

24. ASEAN Secretariat, *ASEAN Vision 2020*.

25. ASEAN Secretariat, "ASEAN Concord II (Bali Concord II)," Bali, Indonesia, October 7–8, 2003, http://www.aseansec.org/15159.htm.

26. ASEAN Secretariat, "Kuala Lumpur Declaration on the Establishment of the ASEAN Charter," Kuala Lumpur, Malaysia, December 12, 2005, http://www.aseansec.org/18030.htm.

27. Ibid.

28. But note the countertrend particularly in the Sino-Russia pole, where emphasis is on security and "sovereign democracy," implying that external democratic forces cannot trump sovereignty.

29. For example, Vietnam's rapid economic liberalization and growth in recent years has contributed to a more favorable environment in which to consider this set of issues.

30. Freedom House, *Freedom in the World 2007* (Boston: Freedom House, 2007). Country combined average ratings are available at http://www.freedomhouse.org/template.cfm?page = 366&year = 2007. Thanks to Don Emmerson for this point.

31. Ibid.

32. During a conference in April 2007 at Stanford University under the auspices of the Southeast Asia Forum, Termsak Chalermpalanupap, director and head of research, Office of the Secretary General, ASEAN, noted that ASEAN has entered into similar agreements with India (2003), Japan (2003), and Australia and New Zealand (2004).

33. In late April 2007, Chinese oil giant Sinopec announced that construction of the China-Burma oil pipeline was expected to start that year. At the beginning of April, China's National Development and Reform Commission approved the Sino-Burmese oil pipeline linking Burma's deep-water port of Sittwe with Kunming, the capital of China's southwestern Yunnan Province. See the China Knowledge Web site, April 23, 2007, http://www.chinaknowledge.com.

34. For example, in April 2006 China's prime minister, Wen Jiabao, and Burma's president, Hun Sen, signed eleven agreements to support a Chinese aid package to Cambodia of $600 million. Details are available at http://news.bbc.co.uk/2/hi/asia-pacific/4890400.stm.

35. Termsak Chalermpalanupap, interview by author, May 23, 2007, Stanford University.

36. ASEAN Secretariat, *Report of the Eminent Persons Group on the ASEAN Charter.*

37. Ibid., 2.

38. Ibid., 4, 21.

39. Ibid., 17.

40. Ibid., 34–35.

41. ASEAN Secretariat, "The ASEAN Charter," Jakarta, Indonesia, January 2008, http://www.aseansec.org/ASEAN-Charter.pdf.

42. Quoted in Jeremy Au Yong, "Charter Drafter: Sense of Family the Driving Force: Signing Caps Months of Debate and Negotiation," *Straits Times*, November 25, 2007.

43. White House, *The National Security Strategy of the United States of America* (Washington, D.C.: Government Printing Office, 2006), 3, http://www.whitehouse.gov/nsc.nss/2006/.

44. See, for example, Albert O. Hirschman, "The On-and-Off Connection Between Political and Economic Progress," *American Economic Review* 84, no. 2 (1994): 343–48; Adam Przeworski, Michael E. Alvarez, Jose Antonio Cheibub, and Fernando Papaterra, *Democracy and Development: Political Institutions and Well-Being in the World, 1950–1990* (Cambridge: Cambridge University Press, 2000); Philippe Aghion, Alberto F. Alesina, and Francesco Trebbi, *Democracy, Technology, and Growth*, National Bureau of Economic Research (NBER) Working Paper no. W13180 (Cambridge, Mass.: NBER, June 2007); Torsten Persson and Guido Tabellini, *Democracy and Development: The Devil in the Details*, Innocenzo Gasparini Institute for Economic Research (IGIER) Working Paper Series no. 302 (Milan: IGIER, January 2006), ftp://ftp.igier.uni-bocconi.it/wp/2006/302.pdf.

45. The president's speech was given on the occasion of the twentieth anniversary of the National Endowment for Democracy and can be found at http://www.ned.org/events/anniversary/20thAniv-Bush.html.

46. Background on Lome IV is available at http://www.acpsec.org/en/conventions/cotonou/cotonou_historical_note_e.htm.

47. Council Regulation 976/1999, adopted on April 29, 1999. Tanja A. Borzel and Thomas Risse, "One Size Fits All! EU Policies for the Promotion of Human Rights, Democracy, and the Rule of Law," paper presented at the Workshop on Democracy Promotion, Center for Development, Democracy, and the Rule of Law, Stanford University, October 4–5, 2004, http://iis-db.stanford/edu/pubs/20747/Risse-Borzel-stanford_final.pdf. Background on the European Initiative for the Development of Human Rights is available at http://www.delarm.ec.europa.eu/en/programmes/europeaninit.htm.

48. For an excellent discussion of the European Union's role in democracy promotion, see Borzel and Risse, "One Size Fits All!"

49. Ibid., 18.

50. European Commission, "Communication from the Commission: A New Partnership with Southeast Asia," COM (2003) 399/4, http://ec.europa.eu/external_relations/asia/doc/com03_sea.pdf.

51. Termsak Chalermpalanupap recalled this statement in a comment made at the workshop "Conflicting Priorities? Security and Democracy as Challenges to Regionalism in South East Asia," convened by Don Emerson and the Southeast Asia Forum of the Asia Pacific Research Center, Stanford University, May 22–23, 2007, http://seaf.stanford.edu/events/4880/. See C. Raja Mohan, "Balancing Interests and Values: India's Struggle with Democracy Promotion," *Washington Quar-*

terly 30 (2007): 99–115. Contrast this statement with India's strong support of the democracy movement during the coup of the Burmese generals in 1988.

52. Aso Taro, "Arc of Freedom and Prosperity: Japan's Expanding Diplomatic Horizons," speech at the Japan Institute of International Affairs, Tokyo, November 30, 2006, http://www.mofa.go.jp/announce/fm/aso/speech0611.html.

53. Aso Taro, "On the 'Arc of Freedom and Prosperity,'" address given on the twentieth anniversary of the founding of the Japan Forum on International Relations, Tokyo, March 12, 2007, http://www.mofa.go.jp/policy/pillar/address0703.html.

54. Ibid., emphasis added.

55. Boagang He, "Transnational Civil Society and the National Identity Question in East Asia," *Global Governance* 10 (2004): 228.

56. See, for example, Becky Shelley, "Political Globalisation and the Politics of International Non-governmental Organizations: The Case of Village Elections in China," *Australian Journal of Political Science* 35, no. 2 (2000): 225–38.

57. For more information on the SCO, see its Web site, http://www.sectsco.org.

58. "Declaration on the Creation of the Shanghai Cooperation Organization," Shanghai, China, June 15, 2001, http://www.sectsco.org/news_detail.asp?id = 88& LanguageID = 2.

59. An English version of the SCO Charter can be found at http://www.scosum mit2007.org/en/docs/47/. The quotations are from this source.

60. Quoted in "Hu Proposes Convention for Neighborly Relations," *Xinhua*, June 15, 2006, http://www.chinadaily.com.cn/china/2006-06/15/content_617773_2.htm.

61. Masha Lipman, "Putin's 'Sovereign Democracy,'" *Washington Post*, July 15, 2006, http://www.washingtonpost.com/wp-dyn/content/article/2006/07/14/AR2006071401534.html.

62. Xinhua News Agency, "SCO to Suspend Admitting New Members," *People's Daily Online*, August 14, 2007, http://english.people.com.cn/90001/90777/6238830.html.

63. Peter J. Burnell, "Democracy Assistance: State of the Art," in *Democracy Assistance: International Co-operation for Democratization*, ed. Peter Burnell (Portland, Ore.: Cass, 2000), 339–61. For the entirely negative view, see Steven Knack, "Does Foreign Aid Promote Democracy?" *International Studies Quarterly* 48 (2004): 251–66.

64. See the following works by Thomas Corothers: *Aiding Democracy Abroad: The Learning Curve* (Washington, D.C.: Carnegie Endowment for International Peace, 1999); *Assessing Democracy Assistance: The Case of Romania* (Washington, D.C.: Carnegie Endowment for International Peace, 1996); and "How Democracies Emerge: The 'Sequencing Fallacy,'" *Journal of Democracy* 18, no. 1 (2007): 12–27.

65. Steven E. Finkel, Anibal Perez-Linan, and Mitchell A Seligson, "The Effects of U.S. Foreign Assistance on Democracy Building, 1990–2003," manuscript under review for publication, March 2007.

66. See, for example, Dankwart Rostow, "Transitions to Democracy: Toward a Dynamic Model," *Comparative Politics* 2, no. 3 (1970): 337–59; Lipset, "Some Social Requisites of Democracy."

67. ASEAN Secretariat, "ASEAN Declaration on the Protection and Promotion of the Rights of Migrant Workers," Cebu, Philippines, January 13, 2007, http://www.12thaseansummit.org.ph/innertemplate3.asp?category = docs&docid = 23.

68. ASEAN Secretariat, *Report of the Eminent Persons Group*, para. 63.

11. Defense Issues and Asia's Future Security Architecture

Michael E. O'Hanlon

This chapter explores several specific and immediate security challenges in Asia and considers existing as well as improved mechanisms for addressing them. Few subjects are more important. As former U.S. assistant secretary of defense Joseph Nye underscored during the Clinton administration, security is like oxygen—easy to take for granted until it is lost. East Asia is a region that has a Stalinist regime building nuclear weapons in the North, elements of jihadist extremism in the South, and a rapidly rising major power in the form of China. Given these historic developments, together with the region's raw economic power and its huge demands on natural resources, the potential for significantly disruptive and dangerous events is clear. Yet properly managed, Asia's security challenges can continue to be contained, and its remarkable economic and human development can continue to make this region perhaps the most exciting on the planet.

This chapter is divided into three main parts—a discussion of security challenges facing the region, an assessment of existing mechanisms for addressing them, and thoughts on what future arrangements are still needed. The chapter focuses primarily on traditional military activities and issues, whereas chapter 12 in this volume focuses on the crucial "new security agenda" and the subject of transnational dangers, on nontraditional security issues (though I do explore how traditional militaries can contribute to mitigating the latter in their own right), and chapter 13 looks at the challenges ahead for building a multilateral "security architecture" in the region.

PRINCIPAL SECURITY CHALLENGES IN EAST ASIA

The Asia-Pacific region faces three main types of challenges and potential dangers today. The most immediate and obvious is North Korea, with its nuclear weapons program, its fragile society, and the possibility of state collapse. The second and probably most important challenge for the longer term is the rise of China, juxtaposed with the unresolved issue of Taiwan and the troubled Sino-Japanese relationship in particular. The last challenge is the most diffuse and includes matters such as terrorism and civil conflict. These last two challenges are difficult enough on their own terms, but each also risks complicating attention to the other because development of more capacity to address terrorism and civil conflict in places such as Japan and China can—if handled badly—reinforce worries about militarism and remilitarization and thus contribute to security dilemmas.

Other possible challenges, such as the fears of a rising Japan in some quarters or a weakening of the U.S.–South Korea alliance in recent years, require attention. They are not insignificant, but a fundamental premise of this chapter is that as long as America's alliances in the region remain strong, their internal dialogues and workings remain transparent to the region, and organizations such as the Association of Southeast Asian Nations (ASEAN) and the ASEAN Regional Forum (ARF) further codify the importance of sharing and discussing information publicly, such matters can be successfully addressed.

NORTH KOREA

When North Korea began to develop a clandestine uranium-enrichment program in the late 1990s, it violated not only the 1994 Agreed Framework with the United States, under which it pledged not to develop or possess nuclear weapons, but also the Nuclear Non-Proliferation Treaty (NPT) and the 1991 North-South denuclearization pact with Seoul. When the George W. Bush administration in the United States rightly challenged Pyongyang after discovering the full scope of the highly enriched uranium program in 2002, North Korea then claimed its right to withdraw from the NPT, but only after violating it—an action of questionable legitimacy. Pyongyang also expelled International

Atomic Energy Agency inspectors, putting itself further into contravention of its NPT obligations and removing necessary transparency.[1] In addition to keeping its secret uranium-enrichment program (which is probably not yet producing enough uranium for a weapon), it subsequently reprocessed the plutonium in the spent fuel at the Yongbyon site and thus increased the estimated size of its likely nuclear arsenal from one or two bombs to perhaps eight or even more. In 2006, it tested a nuclear device, albeit one with a small yield that likely reflected imperfections in the weapon's design (and even if the imperfections are correctly diagnosed and repaired, there will be ambiguity about whether it can be launched successfully atop a North Korean missile). Initial agreements in 2007 led to a revival of the stalled Six-Party Talks and the prospect of controlling one piece of the North's program (the plutonium-based facilities at Yongbyon), but left little room for optimism that North Korea would soon abandon its newfound status as a nuclear-armed state.

North Korea's nuclear arsenal poses a grave risk for several reasons, each of which reflects more generic concerns described earlier. First, North Korea might sell some nuclear technology or even materials to terrorists or other states. Second, if North Korea someday collapses, its nuclear materials may fall into the hands of those who would sell them to the highest bidder. Third, the deterrent provided by the U.S.–South Korea or U.S.-Japan alliance might be weakened if North Korea thought it had a nuclear trump card. Should war then result, the more bombs North Korea possessed, the greater its odds of successfully delivering a nuclear warhead against Seoul or another population center (even in the United States, probably by means other than missile attack). And fourth, North Korean nuclear weapons have the potential to start a nuclear domino effect in Northeast Asia, possibly provoking Japan, South Korea, and Taiwan, which in turn would weaken global nonproliferation more broadly.

One might be tempted to argue that with North Korea possibly now in possession of a small nuclear arsenal, the international community will accept this reality as a fait accompli, and the issue will recede as a matter of strategic or political significance. However, this argument is both too fatalistic and too optimistic. It is fatalistic because it surrenders to North Korean nuclearization without testing the possibility that a combination of pressure and diplomacy might yet convince Pyongyang to abandon its nuclear weapons. This prospect is increased by the historical facts that the international community ultimately convinced South Africa, Ukraine, Belarus, and Kazakhstan to denuclearize. The argument is too optimistic because accepting North Korea's nuclear power status as if it were a tolerable development on the world stage ignores the associated dangers. In addition to the arguments noted earlier, North Korea has been considering resumption of construction on two large reactors with the theoretical capacity to produce enough plutonium for dozens of bombs a year. If that construction progresses substantially, the same types of questions about pre-emptive strikes (actually, in this case, preventive strikes) will be raised as are currently being forced to the policy table by Iran. The highly enriched uranium program is even more problematic because its location is hidden underground and its signature is difficult to detect. The February 13, 2007, agreement negoti-ated by U.S. ambassador Chris Hill gives hope that at least the new reactor problem will be kept in check because it requires North Korea to shut down nuclear facilities in exchange for fuel oil. But it would be seriously premature and fly in the face of past experience to assume that this interim deal truly points to any definitive end to the nuclear standoff.

STATE FAILURE AND TERRORISM

Many scenarios in Asia can involve either terrorism or state collapse or some com-bination of the two. In general, the attacks on the United States on September 11, 2001, demonstrated that the United States has at least some limited national-security interest in many if not most places where states may fail, given the constant dan-ger that terrorist groups such as Al Qaeda will find safe haven in such states. It would not take much of a shock to the international system or the internal politics of states such as Indonesia or Bangladesh to create the specter of this scenario. Even more dangerous would be instability in a nuclear-armed Pakistan; there is a chance that someday it will teeter on the brink of dissolution. The combination of Islamic extremists and nuclear weapons in Pakistan is extremely worrisome: were parts of Pakistan's nuclear arsenal ever to fall into the wrong hands, Al Qaeda might conceivably gain access to a nuclear device, with terrifying results.[2] Augur-ing against the Pakistani collapse scenario is that country's relatively pro-Western and secular officer corps.[3] But the intelligence services, which created the Tali-ban and have condoned if not abetted Islamic extremists in Kashmir, are less de-pendable, and the country as a whole is sufficiently infiltrated by fundamentalist groups—as the attempted assassinations of President Pervez Musharraf as well as other evidence make clear—that this threatening scenario of civil chaos cannot be dismissed.[4] Were such civil chaos to occur in Pakistan, it is unclear what the United States and like-minded states would or should do.

CHINA'S RISE

Structural realists have argued that any time a great rising power encounters an established one, war is likely as they sort out their relative places in a new inter-national order. Historians have noted that China will inevitably seek a hegemonic position once it reestablishes its historic position as the "Middle King-dom" following years of suppression and shame at the hands of other great powers. China's willingness to play by the rules of today's international system is, in its eyes, just a means of playing for time. These assessments are determin-istic predictions based on broad power trends and historical realities. Still other analysts focus on the specifics of today's world. They argue that war will likely occur as the United States and China compete for diminishing Persian Gulf oil supplies or increasingly depleted ocean fisheries. Or they think China will at-tack Japan or Korea or even Russia over disputed resources (and over disputed views of their respective histories), dragging the United States into war indi-rectly through alliance relations and friendships. Put differently, for one reason or another, many scholars have concluded that the world is not big enough for both a United States that has become accustomed to global military dominance and economic leadership *and* a China of at least 1.3 billion people that finally has gained the type of power and stature that its people and rulers have long considered its proper due.[5]

Taiwan is the one big issue dividing the two sides. China views the issue as a matter of sovereign pride and territorial integrity, whereas the United States views it as a matter of regional stability as well as of commitment to fellow de-mocracies and to a dependable network of military alliances and friendships. It is the one big subject where both sides explicitly view the use of force as a pos-sible tool in resolving the issue. And it is the one fundamental problem involv-ing the United States and China in which the actions of a third party largely beyond their control can have an unpredictable and incendiary effect on their interactions with each other. The United States will almost certainly continue with its complex policy of balancing its interests in promoting Taiwan's emer-gence on the world stage as an important market-oriented democracy against U.S. interests in restraining leaders in Taipei from pursuing policies that would unilaterally change the status quo in the Taiwan Strait and possibly lead to war.

Beyond Taiwan, and contrary to some of the thinking outlined earlier about the inevitability of U.S.-China conflict, there are very good reasons to think that such a confrontation between China and the United States can be avoided. The world is in many respects different today from what it was in situations of great-power rivalry in the past. The constraints on conflict are probably more significant today than they were in August 1914, though it must be admitted that few if any European leaders at that time expected the resulting millions of casualties and trauma to the international system. A century later, the interna-tional community has demonstrated greater wisdom about the risks of total war,[6] a wisdom reinforced by the deterrent effect of nuclear weapons. In addi-tion, wealth and power no longer depend nearly as much on the direct physical control of large land masses as they once did. Indeed, China's national power rests almost entirely on integration into the global economy, even though the rules of that economy were established largely by the United States and its allies. Chinese leaders' recognition of this reality is clear in the decision to join the World Trade Organization (WTO) in 2001 and the continued efforts to open the economy to outside investment. Integration with the international economy is an indispensable source of job creation, stability, and popular support for the Communist Party leadership. Although a rising power in one sense, China is also a status quo power in that its rise (and the Communist Party's rule) is facilitated by the current international economic and political system, making it highly doubtful that China would seek to challenge the prevailing international order even once it becomes strong enough to do so.[7] Furthermore, China's rise is happening in a much more benign international environment than the rise of Germany or Japan in the first half of the twentieth century, thanks to continued U.S. hegemonic stability based on economic strength and the U.S.-led alliance system, whose member states compose roughly 75 percent of global gross domestic product and military strength.[8]

The question still remains whether a rising China might challenge a regional power for leadership in the regional context, with Japan being the obvious source of rivalry or confrontation. The legacy of Japanese imperialist aggression in the 1930s and 1940s will continue to animate Chinese nationalism in ways that cannot be fully predicted. Both Japan and China are demonstrating an increased political sensitivity to territorial issues, even over uninhabited islands, and to the military capabilities to defend those perceived interests and sources of national pride. Of course, both are also highly codependent countries with leaders who recognize the devastating economic fallout from conflict, not to mention the military risks. Both nations therefore remain quite pragmatic. For Japan in particular, the continued constraints on security practices are still stark.[9] For example, even though the government of Prime Minister Junichiro Koizumi deployed forces to Iraq, it placed them under such restrictive rules of engagement that other foreign troops were needed to protect them. Japan's recent moves toward a more normal and unencumbered security posture are therefore better interpreted as a form of "reluctant realism" than any form of latent militarism.[10] And as Japan expert Mike Mochizuki and I have noted, whatever Japan's enduring problems with "the history question," allegations that it has whitewashed its own history ignore the reality that an overwhelmingly high percentage of Japanese textbooks accurately describe the atrocities that Japanese forces committed in China in the 1930s and 1940s.[11]

Can tension over huge trade deficits or over China's effects on the global environment spin out of control and lead to conflict? China's acquisition of foreign companies—not just in Asia, but in Africa, Latin America, and the United States itself—also raises questions about whether it intends to gain geostrategic influence in the Western Hemisphere, which has possible security implications. Again, however, what is theoretically possible seems practically implausible. Most communities in both China and the United States have an interest in maintaining their strong economic relationship. This assessment is not meant to trivialize the risk of serious economic disputes. As Ted Fishman writes, "As China's new economic might helps it acquire geopolitical clout, its growing political power and strategic presence also hinder the rest of the world's ability to force China to compete on a level playing field."[12] Even in the event of trade tensions, however, the more likely approach is to reduce trade ties or impose penalties, not to fight. The countries are likely to need each other's markets and to value their economic relationship even if one of them seeks to curtail that relationship somewhat. This change might create serious tension, but probably not induce war. And given the nature of modern economic interdependencies, it is also hard to see what the goals of such a war would realistically be—to force the other side to buy one's goods or invest in one's country?[13]

This generally optimistic assessment rests, however, on the premise that the U.S., Chinese, Japanese, and other regional governments will remain strategically sensible and rational in their decision making. That assumption seems fair considering the recent past, but in the broader course of regional history it is hardly a given. Any security architecture for the region will have to do what it can to ensure that such good governance continues and in fact improves further. One key is to promote enough frequent diplomacy that, as Churchill admonished, regional powers continue to "jaw jaw jaw" rather than "fight fight fight." Such an approach places a continued premium on summitry and regional meetings, at least in a certain number. It also places a premium on military confidence-building measures in the region. These measures have been slower to develop in Asia than in Europe or the Western Hemisphere, particularly in China's case; nonetheless, there have been some developments in Asia. China has been issuing defense white papers for several years now and inviting foreign military attachés to observe exercises as well. ASEAN is beginning a defense ministerial for the first time, with an expectation that there may be a higher level of participation in the ARF as a result. Japan and China exchanged surface combatants for port calls for the first time in 2007 and 2008 (a Chinese destroyer to Japan in 2007 and a Japanese training destroyer to China in 2008). And U.S. Pacific Command continues expanding cooperative engagement through joint exercises and training at the Asia Pacific Center for Security Studies in Honolulu. This growing norm for transparency has not yet led the People's Liberation Army to reveal any details about its missile or nuclear forces—including its antisatellite test of early 2007—or established the kind of maritime military agreement between Japan and China or China and Taiwan necessary to avoid unintended military incidents at sea, but it does help to mitigate against the security dilemma in a region where traditional balances of power continue to matter for peace and stability.[14]

This chapter, focused as it is on regional security institutions rather than on diplomacy, makes only passing note of such activities, vital as they are.

ASSESSING EXISTING MECHANISMS FOR HANDLING ASIA'S CHALLENGES

How well are Asia-Pacific powers prepared to prevent or respond to these widely varied dangers? This is a complicated question. The very fact that serious challenges like those outlined earlier can arise demonstrates clearly that not all problems in Asia have been solved. However, that fact is not necessarily an indictment of existing regional security architectures. Even if one has the right institutional basis for tackling a problem, solutions may prove elusive because the right ideas have not yet been conceptualized or used as the basis for negotiation or because the problem is so large and daunting that it is unrealistic to expect *any* one mechanism to address it entirely. In any assessment of existing structures, therefore, the question is not whether they are perfect or omnipotent—they clearly are not—but whether a better structure or set of mechanisms can be imagined in theory and then put into practice.

On balance, the mechanisms in place to handle China's rise seem sound. Bilateral alliances, particularly with Japan, anchor the United States in the region. The United States is the only country militarily capable of deterring China, not only from actual use of force, but from any overly ambitious military buildup (as impressive as improvements in the People's Liberation Army have been of late, China might certainly move even faster if it had major motivation to do so). And these alliance systems are being updated. For example, the global posture review initiated under the current Bush administration moves ten thousand American GIs out of South Korea and reconfigures those who remain in regions south of Seoul, where they should cause less strain on the alliance. Guam will now have several U.S. attack submarines stationed in its waters, greater capacity for sustaining combat air operations, and over the next decade seven thousand Marines relocated there from Okinawa. Once the wars in Iraq and Afghanistan are over, or at least scaled back, the ground-force weaponry previously stored on Guam will be returned there.[15]

Japan is strengthening its military capabilities in areas such as missile defense (managed and coordinated through the bilateral alliance) and is expanding the security dialogue with U.S. allies such as South Korea through the Trilateral Coordination and Oversight Group and Australia through the Trilateral

Security Dialogue. The U.S. Pacific Command is placing greater focus on helping create a broader security community designed to address the new security agenda and to reassure nonallies even as it maintains traditional partnerships. The bottom line is that as long as the United States remains firmly committed to its Asian allies, it is far more likely to dissuade and deter China from attacking these states than to be dragged into conflict. China would not be able to seize any substantial amount of territory or cause any notable amount of damage to these countries without making a war against the United States nearly inevitable. And a half-century of American presence in the region has largely conveyed this message. Moreover, bilateral alliances seem a sound approach because they pose a lower risk of being weakened by partners that may be more inclined to take a soft approach on China. Having the U.S.-Japan alliance at the core of the U.S. strategy of hedging against China's rise is particularly reassuring in this regard, provided it does not give rise to excessively nationalistic or provocative American or Japanese behavior.

Meanwhile, China is engaged positively through strong multilateral global institutions such as the WTO that facilitate constructive relations among major countries, while also engaging actively in a range of regional multilateral security mechanisms (see chapter 3 in this volume). Using international structures for these purposes embeds China more deeply in international and regional stability and gives the maximum number of countries a positive stake in China's rise.

There are perhaps two caveats to this analysis. One is that if China succeeds in building stronger bridges to most Asian states than the ones the United States can maintain, it may succeed in gradually creating two blocs of states, forcing the United States to rely excessively on military and diplomatic partnership with just Japan and perhaps Australia. Such a situation may embolden China to risk a crisis, believing that the ensuing economic embargoes and similar measures would hurt the United States and Japan as much as they damaged China itself. Specifically, China may doubt America's commitment to Taiwan, where Beijing asserts its sovereign claims and with which the United States has no formal security treaty or even official diplomatic relations. This danger does not seem acute; the United States has since the mid-1990s made it appear rather clear that it would indeed come to Taiwan's defense if need be. But the situation requires ongoing attention given the lack of formal structures in place to ensure deterrence.

What about challenges such as possible state collapse in Pakistan or an Indonesia engulfed in civil strife or a more limited threat by regional terrorists? In these cases, it is not the policies that are presently lacking so much as the mechanisms for rapid cooperation. The United Nations provides a legitimating mechanism for the use of force in some situations, but little beyond that. Military means of addressing such crises quickly and effectively are of little present value. In the case of a collapsing, nuclear-armed Pakistan, for example, it is very unlikely that "surgical strikes" can be conducted to destroy the nuclear weapons before extremists make a grab for them. It is doubtful that the United States would know the weapons' location and at least as doubtful that any Pakistani government would countenance such a move, even under duress. If a surgical strike, series of surgical strikes, or commando-style raids were not possible, the only option might be to try to stabilize the situation before the weapons were taken by extremists and transferred to terrorists. But stabilization operations, even if invited by the Pakistani government, would be an enormous undertaking in a country the size of Pakistan (with a population of 150 million, six times that of Iraq).

The global community spends about a trillion U.S. dollars a year on military forces and keeps more than twenty million men and women under arms. But only modest numbers of those dollars and only a very small fraction of those troops translate into a military force that can be projected over substantial distances. Leaving aside the United States, the rest of the world combined cannot muster more than a couple hundred thousand military personnel for such purposes. Most countries, even those with strong militaries, are like caged tigers: fierce if fought on their home turf, but relatively harmless beyond. The United States has a limited willingness to engage in humanitarian military interventions and peace operations. It also has limited capacity at present to engage even in strategically crucial interventions (such as helping to stabilize a fraying Pakistan), given its commitments in Iraq and Afghanistan.

Nor is there any reason to think that military missions motivated principally by humanitarian rather than traditional strategic interests should be primarily a U.S. responsibility. All of the world's countries—especially democracies, but other states as well—presumably share the same values about the sanctity of human life and the importance of protecting it. The United States should do its fair share, but there is no reason to assign it a special burden. Other countries can and should do more than they do at present. Better mechanisms also need to be created to allow these militaries to practice and play war games together in peacetime so that they can operate in a timely and effective way when crises occur.

On North Korea policy, too much has been made of the multilateral versus bilateral dichotomy. For one thing, there is no dichotomy; the Bush administration conducted some bilateral contacts even within a six-party framework. Second, given North Korea's many needs, multiple regional actors would indeed be needed in any major effort to improve the situation by helping North Korea to reform, modernize, and join the international system. So the six-party framework makes general sense as a structure for cooperative diplomatic efforts to end North Korea's nuclear weapons programs.

This is not to say that existing policy as pursued within that six-party frame-work has always made sense. North Korea successfully outmaneuvered and split the other five parties at key junctures and in the process bought time and space to create a substantial nuclear arsenal while paying little cost for doing so. It is remarkable that successful countries such as China, Japan, Russia, South Korea, and the United States allowed the world's last Stalinist regime to accomplish this objective. A fundamentally new approach is needed, but it should be carried out largely within the six-party framework established in recent years. Some enhanced bilateral contact that allows North Korean to save face and that works out narrowly bilateral issues might be acceptable as long as it does not weaken the broader multilateral effort.

FUTURE REGIONAL SECURITY ARCHITECTURES AND POLICIES

The assessments given so far suggest several ideas for the future. First, the framework for conducting policy on North Korea is generally sound. The strategy employed within that framework has failed, but a different strategy does not require an alternative mechanism for negotiation or for implementation of any deal that can be reached. Second, existing bilateral alliances are probably the most effective mechanism for hedging against the negative outcomes associated with China's continued rise, but further coordination across these alliances may be useful, and ongoing changes in the technical characteristics of key bilateral alliances will continue to be needed. Third, for handling the new security agenda and the problems posed by weak or potentially failing states, new mechanisms are indeed important. It is in this area where architecture is most in need of redesign and augmentation. In the next few sections, I address the architecture requirements to deal with each challenge.

NORTH KOREA

As noted, the crux of the North Korea problem seems conceptual, not procedural, but there is no reason why a better approach cannot be pursued within the six-party framework (with possible complementary bilateral sessions to jumpstart things and help the North Koreans save face if it turns out that they are otherwise prepared to negotiate seriously). In this sense, the issue says little about the need for new security systems. Rather, a new policy is needed that at its core would involve forcing North Korea to choose between greater economic and diplomatic engagement, on the one hand, and nuclear weapons, continued isolation, and internal difficulties, on the other. The goal should be to make the status quo untenable for Pyongyang, compelling it to choose a better relationship with the outside world as well as more trade, investment, and assistance, rather than the prospect of pressure and coercion being applied against it. In short, it should try to induce and pressure North Korea to adopt what might be called the Vietnam model of reform.[16]

This analysis is admittedly my own specific sense of how the North Korean problem should be addressed. Others will disagree, viewing such a broad negotiating agenda as too ambitious or the idea of complete North Korean denuclearization as unrealistic. The spirit of my proposal, therefore, is less to make a definitive case for one approach and more to suggest the kind of fresh thinking that will be useful as a recently inaugurated President Lee Myong-bak seeks a new approach in South Korea and as a new U.S. president prepares to enter the White House in 2009. There are of course other possible approaches. They include Victor Cha's concept of "hawk engagement," in which diplomacy is attempted in large measure in the expectation it will fail, but also in the expectation that such failed negotiations will reveal North Korea as the main culprit in any diplomatic breakdown, making it easier to organize a coalition to punish the North Korean regime thereafter. They also include Leon Sigal's argument, made in reviewing the Agreed Framework of 1994, that North Korea has in effect been looking for a better relationship with the United States for years and might be induced with consistent positive U.S. diplomacy to pursue it. Yet another approach such as the "Perry process" of the late 1990s would offer North Korea a step-by-step roadmap to better relations, promising inducements for cooperative behavior and reprisals for uncooperative or threatening behavior, and employing bilateral talks as well as other diplomatic tools in the process. This approach would be unremarkable and commonsensical, but it would be pursued diligently and consistently.[17]

For most of these possible approaches, military options would not be totally off the table, especially if North Korea either threatened to sell nuclear materials abroad or if it continued construction on its large reactors. One possibility, though hardly a panacea, would be a "surgical" military strike against the larger reactors. Such a strike would, at a minimum, require consultation between Washington and Seoul (with notice to Tokyo and perhaps Beijing), but no need for a larger security grouping to plan or conduct it. In fact, operational secrecy would be important.

All-out war would run too high a chance of causing the very outcome that it was designed to prevent: detonation of at least one nuclear weapon in a major city, be it Seoul or Washington or Seattle. That said, the United States and South Korea would have to be braced for possible war after any limited use of airpower because they would not be able to predict how North Korea might re-spond.[18] But the undesirability of the military option and the undesirability of a nuclear North Korea make the case for a serious phased negotiation strategy that has a chance to unify the other five participants in the Six-Party Talks around a common approach toward Pyongyang.

One more contingency requires attention with regard to North Korea: the possibility of state collapse. The likelihood of such a scenario is probably still less than the conventional wisdom would have it, but it is hardly zero. On this matter, there is reason for concern: the proposed dissolution of the U.S.–South Korea unified command structure makes little sense, probably weakens deter-rence, and certainly complicates the coordinated operation of U.S. and South Korean forces in the event of any major scenario, including that of collapse. But the good news is that the bilateral alliance mechanism still allows for very close planning and training, and in fact has already produced new variants of war plans (often referred to as 5029 plans in contrast with the more traditional 5027 plan). If the fraying of the U.S.–South Korea alliance can be stopped and the command issue resolved, there is every reason to think that existing mecha-nisms would be able to handle the full range of challenges North Korea might pose.

There is also little reason to think that a security alliance broader than the U.S.–South Korea alliance should be responsible for military operations. Given Japan's history on the peninsula, any role for its self-defense forces should be extremely circumscribed in any such operation. And although close consulta-tion and coordination with China would be imperative (possibly including some limited role for Chinese forces in an operation in northern North Korea), the idea that such an operation can be planned and implemented through a U.S.–South Korea–China team does not begin to reach the threshold of plausi-bility given China's ties to North Korea.

DEALING WITH A RISING CHINA

Two kinds of major security challenges are associated with China's rapid rise. One is the possibility of direct threat to friends and allies of the United States. The other is a more subtle, gradual increase in Chinese influence that, together with a decline in American influence, will ultimately leave the United States and its allies less well positioned to deal with the possible negative implications of China's rise over the longer term. In other words, the first threat is more blunt and immediate, whereas the second is more subtle and gradual—though in the end both threats may ultimately involve many of the same types of stakes and thus require serious attention and focused strategies.

With regard to the second set of more subtle challenges, the good news is that U.S. officials tend to know the tools to employ in maintaining a strong U.S. influence in the Asia Pacific. Strong and healthy bilateral alliances are key. Those alliances, however, must be healthy not only in their internal operations, but in the face they present to the broader region (which is why the United States must be concerned about such issues as Japanese prime ministerial visits to the Yasukuni Shrine, which alarm Beijing, suggest to many that an unrepentant Japan may again become a threat, and weaken the political capacity of the U.S.-Japan alliance in the region).[19] In addition, broader regional security dialogues are important because most countries in the region are not U.S. allies, and even those countries that are U.S. allies do not interact with each other very much through bilateral mechanisms.

Americans should not be overconfident that their generally good instincts on these matters will guarantee success. The global war on terror has sometimes distracted U.S. officials from paying sufficient heed to regional concerns (which are generally *not* about jihadism, some issues in Southeast Asia notwithstanding). Meanwhile, China's security diplomacy has become much more sophisticated. China has been downplaying territorial disputes in places such as the South China Sea, improving relations with Russia through a 2001 bilateral friendship treaty, developing new security organizations of its own through efforts such as the Shanghai Cooperation Organization, working to solve or at least defuse territorial disagreements and other bones of contention with India, strengthening political and economic ties in Southeast Asia, and striking deals with authoritarian governments in the region (and beyond) in situations where the United States would feel the need to constrain relationships due to such governments' internal practices.[20] Other chapters in this volume—especially chapters 3 through 8—detail these shifts in Chinese policies around the region.

But if engaged intelligently, these Chinese practices should in general be relatively benign and nonthreatening to the United States; indeed, it is clearly preferable that China be conciliatory and cooperative with its neighbors rather than the alternative. Existing institutions and mechanisms do not seem to prejudice American interests. Of course, the messages that U.S. officials send through these various dialogues matter as well. Americans need to remain pragmatic about helping with the near-term problems on regional leaders' minds, such as piracy and other forms of crime. They also need a broader, longer-term goal for the region—not as an actionable plan, but as a vision to share with others and use to explain and inspire near-term policy. For example, keeping strong bilateral alliances might hold even more appeal to some if the United States and its current alliance partners envisioned a formal security community that would eventually include countries such as China should those countries be inclined to participate—and should their security behavior prove sufficiently cooperative. Leaders in Seoul, Tokyo, and Washington should use bilateral contacts and regional forums such as the Shangri-la gatherings and the annual Asia-Pacific Economic Cooperation and ASEAN summits to tell Beijing that they do not rule out an alliance with China if it satisfies conditions similar to those demanded of new North Atlantic Treaty Organization (NATO) members—more civilian control of the military, agreement not to settle disputes with neighbors by force, and democratic and economic reforms.[21] However, the day when this might happen is clearly a long way off.

As for the more classic, blunter type of possible threat posed by China, many of the relevant questions crystallize when one is thinking about South Korea's situation. Very close geographically and economically to China, yet a longstanding and important ally of the United States, it understands the dilemmas of a hedging strategy better than perhaps any other country. A major overland Chinese threat to South Korea appears highly improbable. To the extent that China may cause other countries in the region concern in the future, it seems less likely to put direct military pressure on South Korea—a longstanding independent country with a clear ethnic, linguistic, and cultural identity that makes it a poor candidate for invasion—and to use force to gain resources or territory it considers its own. Taiwan and the South China Sea are the most notable examples of where China might use force, although disputes regarding overlapping economic zones at sea might also arise between South Korea and Japan. In other words, to the extent that China may pose a threat to its neighbors, it seems more likely to act as an irredentist power seeking to back up claims to specific localized regions, most of them at sea, than to pursue empire or regional hegemony. This conclusion is reinforced by the fact that China has resolved a number of territorial disputes with neighbors and demilitarized several borders in recent years.[22]

However, international relations being what they are, it is not implausible that someday China may appear seriously threatening to South Korea's core interests. Having U.S. forces in South Korea would therefore give future Chinese leaders who might contemplate making any such threats further reason for pause. It is not so much that a small U.S. presence in South Korea, together with Korean forces, might confidently stop any hypothetical Chinese military action, but they would perhaps slow it down. In addition, the presence of U.S. forces would immediately involve the United States in any such conflict, with the associated near certainty that U.S. military reinforcements would subsequently be deployed. That fact may strengthen deterrence. Knowing in advance that this dynamic might operate, South Korean leaders would probably be less inclined to develop a nuclear arsenal as a hedge against Chinese pressure. If a continued U.S. presence in South Korea were able to reduce the prospects of nuclear proliferation in the region, that accomplishment in itself would be very important.

A U.S. force presence in South Korea would also be beneficial for Japan–South Korea relations. First, it would reassure the Koreans, who would not have to wonder if they were a second-class ally of the United States in the event of a major dispute with Japan over disputed territories or maritime resources. Second, the Japanese government might also prefer this arrangement. With U.S. military facilities also in South Korea, Japan would avoid becoming singularized as the only country in the region hosting U.S. forces, and Tokyo would probably find it easier to sustain the support of the Japanese people and regional neighbors for the security alliance.

Also, keeping forces in the two countries would help Washington retain influence with both South Korea and Japan in a way similar to how it has ensured its influence with even more quarrelsome neighbors, such as Greece and Turkey or Israel and Egypt: by forging close military relations with both sides. In this way, the United States can also help facilitate the tightening of a trilateral network of military officers and officials—complementing other steps to introduce confidence-building measures and expand military-to-military exchanges in the region. It does not seem likely that countries in Southeast Asia will generally wish to formalize or tighten their security partnerships with the United States given their desire to avoid antagonizing China and their own historical backdrops and political cultures. But existing alliances do make sense for the reasons noted earlier, and it would be ideal if they can be retained, even strengthened. In the end, however, the idea of a long-term U.S.–South Korea alliance makes sense only if the South Korean people support it. Given the strategic implications and diplomatic sensitivity of any such alliance and its potential impact on South Korea–China relations in particular, it would be inappropriate for Americans to assume that Koreans will favor such a formal security partnership in the future, even though they hope that the Korean people will in the end do so.

Developments of the past ten years—including the updates to the U.S.-Japan basing arrangements (with Japan playing a greater role in supporting U.S. forces on its territory), ongoing efforts to streamline U.S. forces in South Korea and move them southward, and other "transformation" activities ranging from missile defense to greater use of precision-strike systems to more pre-positioning of advanced U.S. systems in the Asia-Pacific theater—have generally made sense. They remain crucially important to convey a sense of dynamism, commitment, and modernity to the U.S.-Japan and U.S.–South Korea alliances in particular. But it is important to avoid the sometimes breathless quality of the transformation agenda made popular in U.S. defense circles. None of these changes promises to make enemy missiles impotent or make war a quick and painless enterprise for U.S.-led coalitions or resolve ongoing strategic disagreements between the United States and certain regional partners (especially South Korea) about the nature of the future security environment. Defense modernization aimed at bolstering credible deterrence is critically important, but it is closer to a gradual workmanlike process than to a revolutionary enterprise. Similarly, a workmanlike attitude will be necessary to address the complications in the military alliance associated with the dissolution of the combined U.S.–South Korea command in the coming years. This idea is very questionable on military grounds because it weakens the simplicity and cohesiveness of unity of command among the allies and, as such, would seem to fly in the face of not only the Goldwater-Nichols reform process in the United States, but also basic military common sense in general. It was an unfortunate, if perhaps inevitable, decision. To make amends, the allies will have to think thoroughly about a wide range of possible military scenarios, including not just all-out war, but commando operations, limited air strikes, and other such activities, and anticipate the challenges that may arise due to an overly complex command-and-control arrangement. This problem is probably solvable, but it has not yet been solved, and it is significant.

Overall, far more subtle strategic thinking will be crucial to retaining America's role in the region and ensuring deterrence against possible Chinese assertiveness. Planning for contingencies that no one in the region expects even when the very act of doing the planning and preparing can worsen near-term relations with the region's most important rising power is a challenge of Bismarckian proportions. U.S. strategists and diplomats will need a subtlety, sensitivity, and ability to listen that has sometimes been lost in recent years if they are to strike this balance successfully. This challenge is, of course, one more reason why they will also need to stay heavily engaged in regional dialogues and summits. At such meetings, U.S. officials must do more than warn of the threat of global terrorism or the specter of China's rise. They must also listen well to regional security concerns and try to tailor their aid packages, joint military exercises, and other policy interventions to local needs and desires. To put it differently, they should compete with the more sophisticated modern brand of Chinese security diplomacy by using a sophisticated approach of their own.

NEW SECURITY STRUCTURES FOR THE PROBLEMS OF FAILED STATES AND OTHER NONTRADITIONAL THREATS

The nontraditional security agenda can be couched in the language of threats and anxieties, but it can also be viewed as a cooperative vision for regional players' joint action. A formal collective security arrangement or regionwide alliance is inappropriate for the region because several key players see threats in a fundamentally different light and in some cases themselves pose risks or at least create anxieties for each other. But a common agenda that aspires to help the region lift its remaining poor out of poverty, manage strains on the environment, and contain nontraditional, nonstate security problems can also help breed confidence and a spirit of cooperation among the major powers that moderates the more traditional types of security dilemmas. It can also provide mechanisms to address broader regional problems that may intensify in coming years, such as instability in certain Central or South Asian states of fairly immediate interest to the major powers of East Asia. (Such an agenda may not be the way to handle conflict in places such as Congo or Sudan, although these hotspots are also worthy candidates for potential deployment of any additional regional capacity for peacekeeping and humanitarian response.)

To address other kinds of security threats besides the prospect of traditional war, the United States, its regional allies, and other friendly states should increase collaboration on certain security tasks among themselves. These types of efforts can cover everything from training for peacekeeping and humanitarian relief to search-and-rescue exercises to counterpiracy and counterdrug operations to joint preparations for counterterrorist operations.[23] Such activities can also be done in conjunction with neutral states in the region, such as Russia and China (as well as with several Southeast Asian countries, some of them U.S. allies and some not). Such activity is already under way, in fact. The United States has conducted peacekeeping exercises with Russia and search-and-rescue exercises with China; Japan has conducted search-and-rescue exercises with Russia and joined with South Korea to deliver humanitarian assistance.[24] Much, much more needs to be done, however. To be sure, the degree of collaboration depends in part on the reciprocity of the countries cooperating in such activities and on transparency about some of their military operations. That said, the stated goals of this type of coalition building matter for shoring up political support, so the declared policy should be ambitious even as the implementation is gradual.

Some analysts would agree with the need for multilateralism, but argue for looser and more inclusive structures, perhaps patterned after the Organization for Security and Cooperation in Europe, as well as a dissolution of formal alliances in the region. But hinging everything on relatively weak institutions, confidence-building measures, and security dialogues also seems unwise. Although such measures and dialogues are very worthwhile, they are better for preserving a widely endorsed status quo than for solving fundamental disputes between countries.[25] They do not reflect a solemn commitment by countries to defend each other's security the way that formal alliances do. Because some fairly fundamental issues still remain to be addressed in the Asia-Pacific region and the status quo is not universally accepted, much more than confidence-building measures and dialogues will be needed to assure stability. Even if capacity building is done largely within alliance structures, countries can still make individual and ad hoc decisions about which contingencies they wish to participate in. This is very much the norm in NATO, for example.

To have meaningful military capacity and the capability for rapid and coordinated response to major disasters (such as large-scale strife or the risk of state failure in a place such as Pakistan or Indonesia), regional collaboration should build from as strong a base as possible. Existing bilateral alliances are the right starting point. Exercises should also be demanding and be done less to demonstrate political goodwill than to uncover weaknesses in possible coalition response to various serious scenarios, permitting remedial action to be identified and adopted.

Because the U.S.-Japan and U.S.–South Korea alliances have considerable credibility at present, it makes sense to keep them, as most countries in the Asia-Pacific region recognize. Working military alliances help ensure high and uniform standards in military equipment and training. It is hard enough for one country to achieve good military readiness—witness the difficulties of the U.S. military in the late 1970s, most memorably exemplified in the failed hostage rescue mission in Iran. Getting coalitions to a high state of joint readiness is remarkably difficult and cannot be done at the last minute through some improvised process; strong working alliances are needed. For this type of future security community, it makes sense to maintain a wide range of U.S. forces in the region. For example, Marines can conduct routine patrols and expeditionary missions of various types. They can also train with Korean, Japanese, and perhaps someday also Russian and Chinese forces for peacekeeping or counterterrorist missions. U.S. Army forces might play a role in such joint training, too; they have the advantage of sharing doctrine and basic operational concepts with other countries' militaries, which are generally dominated by ground forces. Moreover, the U.S. Army has gained considerable experience in counterterrorist operations in Afghanistan and elsewhere, so having a role in such efforts would be natural. Naval and air capabilities would clearly be important as well.

But more difficult than the question of enduring U.S. capabilities in the Asia Pacific is the challenge of how to get regional friends and partners to do more and to increase their capacities for doing more without disrupting their relations with each other. China's rise has already been addressed here, so consider the other tough case, that of Japan. The assessment in this section shows what Japan needs to obtain to be capable of helping significantly with tough scenarios, but it also shows that even a major expansion of certain types of capabilities should be achievable in a way that will limit Japan's neighbors' fears about its new military capabilities.

More than half a century after World War II and more than a decade after the fall of the Berlin Wall, it is time for Japan to do more in the international security sphere. It need not and should not mimic the United States or even Great Britain; unilateral power-projection capabilities would unsettle some neighbors and displease many Japanese themselves. Nor need it even increase defense spending very much. But it should reexamine the basic way in which it structures and equips its military. It should also regain the momentum it began to establish in the early 1990s when it sent about seven hundred personnel to Cambodia in 1992 and 1993 for peacekeeping and then four hundred to Zaire in 1994 for humanitarian relief after the Rwanda genocide, but largely lost in subsequent years. Despite its limited deployment of several hundred soldiers to Iraq, that mission was just as notable for what Japanese troops would *not* do in the way of risking casualties and employing weaponry as for what they would do. Many Asian countries oppose such Japanese security policies, fearing latent Japanese militarism. Many Japanese worry as well, but the alternative force structure outlined in the next paragraph would be designed to help with the new security agenda and as such would involve far too few troops to threaten countries such as China, South Korea, the Philippines, and Vietnam. Yet the new capabilities would be quite substantial for the demands of global humanitarian, peacekeeping, peace enforcement, and stabilization missions.

Japan has many options besides becoming a "normal" power or remaining a civilian and largely pacifist power. The basic idea would be to expand the country's physical capacities for operations abroad, but keep legal, diplomatic, and military checks on these new capacities so as to reassure Japan's neighbors and the Japanese people about the nature of the effort. The goal would expressly *not* be that Japan become an independent, global military power. Under such a framework, Japan would consider projecting power only in the context of multilateral security missions, preferably if not exclusively those approved by the United Nations Security Council. It would not develop the physical capacity for doing more than that. It would also be transparent about its plans, encourage other countries to develop capacities of their own, and pledge not to exceed certain ceilings on its capacities for the foreseeable future. The parallel situation in Germany can serve as an inspiration for Japan and as reassurance that a formerly aggressive country can become a responsible international military actor. Not only has Germany sent combat forces to Bosnia and Kosovo for peace implementation, but it recently dropped bombs on Serbia—a former World War II victim of Nazi aggression—in NATO's 1999 Operation Allied Force against Serbia. (It has also sent forces to Afghanistan, though there are some questions about the degree of risk German troops have been willing to accept there.) All things considered, if Germany can go so far without still being hamstrung by the past, why not Japan? Granted, multilateral security structures comparable to NATO do not now exist in Asia, and Germany would not have acted as it did outside a NATO context, so the pace of change may wind up being slower in the case of Japan.

If Japan chooses to move toward an alternative national-security policy and force posture, it will probably do so out of the recognition that its home islands are now much more secure against possible invasion than was the case during the Cold War. Current levels of active-duty ground forces for territorial defense may not be needed. Reservists can be used in greater numbers for this purpose if necessary, as in the case of Switzerland and the Scandinavian nations. The Japanese army can reorient itself to a smaller, more mobile organization, including an expeditionary ground capability of some twenty-five thousand individuals. This size of force would allow sustained deployment of at least two brigades as well as numerous other personnel such as military police and translators. Soldiers would be equipped for sustained operations abroad and trained for missions ranging from humanitarian relief to armed, forcible intervention to stop genocides and other civil conflicts, and to hostage rescue and counterterrorism. The Japanese navy and air force might acquire the long-range transport assets needed to move the ground self-defense forces. They might also help move other countries' forces; at present, among major regional powers, only the United States and to a much lesser extent Australia, Russia, and China have meaningful capacity for strategic transport throughout the Asia Pacific. These changes can be made without increasing Japan's annual level of defense expenditure. Under this proposal, its maritime self-defense forces would need to add only a modest amount of dedicated, roll-on/roll-off sealift. They might, for example, purchase enough to transport roughly one heavy division of ground forces—that is, their equipment and supplies for several weeks of operations, costing perhaps U.S.$1 billion to U.S.$2 billion in investment. Modest annual operating costs of U.S.$50 million to U.S.$75 million would result thereafter.[26]

In June 2006, U.S. secretary of the navy Donald Winter advocated a "1,000-ship Navy," a concept in which the United States would work with "other like minded nations" to integrate capacities to meet with new and global challenges.[27] In the Asia-Pacific region, the Japanese Maritime Self-Defense Force is well suited to support this initiative given its significant maritime capabilities and interoperability with the U.S. Navy, but a multilateral framework would ultimately be necessary for an effective 1,000-ship navy concept. Multilateral naval cooperation in Asia has been increasing recently. For example, the United States, Japan, and India conducted their first joint naval exercise in April 2007. The Indian navy demonstrated its prowess to the world in responding to the 2004 tsunami. India has 58 principal surface combatants, 19 patrol and coastal combatants, 14 mine warfare/mine countermeasures, 27 logistics and support vessels, and 16 submarines; and the Indian government appears ready to participate in expanded exercises with like-minded states in the region. Another country that has been active in enhancing regional security cooperation is Australia, whose navy comprises 13 surface combatants, 13 patrol/coastal ships, 7 mine sweepers, 18 logistics vessels, and 6 submarines. U.S.-Japan-Australia trilateral security cooperation has grown significantly in recent years, as has the Japan-Australia bilateral security cooperation, highlighted by a recent joint declaration on security cooperation. Although trilateral cooperation among the United States, South Korea, and Japan has slowed somewhat because of the political tensions between Seoul and Tokyo over history as well as over North Korea policy issues, there is also continued potential for expanding the South Korean navy's contributions to a regional security. South Korea is modernizing its military, and its navy has recently received additional resources in the national defense budget to build on its current fleet of 43 principal surface combatants, 75 patrol and coastal combatants, 10 mine ships, 14 logistics ships, and 20 submarines. Among ASEAN member states, Thailand has a solid navy with 20 surface combatants, 89 patrol vessels, 19 mine countermeasures, 19 logistics and support ships, and an alliance relationship with the United States. Singapore's forces were active in response to the 2004 tsunami and even to Hurricane Katrina in 2005 (Singapore's navy has 7 surface combatants, 17 patrol craft, 4 mine sweepers, 2 logistics vessels, and 4 submarines). Vietnam has also increased military-to-military interaction with the United States and has the potential to contribute more to regional capacity as well.[28] The future of the People's Liberation Army Navy causes some anxiety within the region, but the U.S. Navy and Pacific Command began expanding military exchanges with the Chinese army in the current Bush administration, and there is merit in encouraging Beijing to consider the need for greater transparency and confidence building by joining in multilateral efforts. The Chinese navy's capabilities might make a significant contribution to the one-thousand-ship navy concept. In short, the U.S.-Japan alliance might form the core of an increased naval capacity for responding to crisis in the region, but the goal should be to expand that responsibility to other like-minded states.

A commensurate amount of airlift for Japan might imply purchase of thirty to sixty C-17s. For its refueling needs, Japan might purchase ten to twenty DC-10-like aircraft. It might also do what the United States does and purchase some planes usable for either refueling or transport (i.e., variants of the DC-10 known as KC-10s). All in all, Japan might purchase twenty C-17 lift aircraft and thirty KC-10 lift/refueling dual-purpose aircraft under this initiative. Total investment costs would approach U.S.$10 billion, with operating costs of U.S.$300 million to $500 million per year thereafter. Assuming a ten-year acquisition period, that expenditure translates to U.S.$1 billion a year in investment and one-third to half as much after the ten years, which would amount to less than 10 percent of the annual cost of the Japanese air forces.

The capacity of these assets would be significant but hardly threatening. A large military transport aircraft might hold 40 to 50 tons of equipment, meaning that Japan might be able to transport up to 2,000 tons per sortie using its entire fleet. However, a single heavy division in the U.S. military weighs about 100,000 tons, and even light and airborne or air mobile divisions weigh 20,000 to 30,000 tons apiece. In rough terms, the 2,000 tons of supplies that Japan would be able to transport in a single voyage would not be enough to equip more than one thousand soldiers. This capability is very modest. It might be significant for peace operations, though, assuming secure airfields that permit rapid reinforcements with additional planeloads of supplies and people. It would not be significant against a hostile foe with a sizeable military, however—meaning that it should not incite real concern among Japan's neighbors. (The kind of specificity in force planning demonstrated here can be a useful model of the type of transparency that can mitigate security dilemmas and anxieties if nation-states communicate their own plans and intentions to each other.) Other countries can ask what types of similar capabilities they might provide as well. Not all would be in a financial position to provide much strategic lift, of course; some might focus on creating logistically self-sustainable forces while relying on Japan or the United States or Russia for initial transport to a theater of operations.

CONCLUSIONS

There is much still to do in East Asia, with many challenges ahead and many problems confronting the region. In most cases, however, we need creative new policy ideas for addressing individual problems and better national policies geared to key regional states more than we need new security communities or architectures. The two different approaches are not mutually exclusive, but we will mislead ourselves if we become obsessive about building new security organizations and ignore the potential that our existing tools already have for tackling many of the challenges of the Asia-Pacific region.

For example, Japan is poised to accomplish much more in the region, even if there are admittedly limits to what it can do anytime soon.[29] Doing more will require Tokyo to make two fundamental decisions, however. First, it would need to avoid stoking historical sensitivities and re-creating concerns about its long-term security intentions among its neighbors. The Koizumi and Abe governments have been too needlessly nationalistic on some issues, such as Yasukuni, an attitude that will have to change for Japan to play a greater role in stabilizing the region. Second, Japan would need to devote more resources to creating deployable military capabilities, and its leaders would need to run the domestic political risks of accepting Japanese casualties in some difficult multilateral peace operations. But Japan itself would have to make these decisions, not a regional forum:

Or consider South Korea. With a new president in 2008, it will have many opportunities for foreign-policy initiatives. Its instincts are naturally multilateralist in many ways.[30] But the question is, Can it work with the United States, its only ally, and key regional states such as China and Japan as well as ASEAN on matters such as expanded counterpiracy and counterterrorism missions, not to mention more muscular and effective peacekeeping? In doing so, it might benefit from new institutions to an extent. But many in South Korea and elsewhere already appreciate the basic nature of these challenges,[31] so more important now are concrete ideas on what to do about them—for instance, joint training missions or perhaps joint military training centers. These challenges require new institutions or forums less than they need pragmatic ideas on how institutions can work together. Thinking of the institutional architecture as the end in itself may actually slow movement toward such pragmatism, which can already be arranged with constructs such as ASEAN and the ARF.

Or consider a specific regional problem, such as North Korea's nuclear program. It is likely that when this book appears in print, we will have witnessed many years of frustration with bilateral as well as multilateral approaches to the problem. Reworking mechanisms for how to negotiate over the problem thus probably matters less than figuring out a new concept for what any deal with Pyongyang should look like. Again, institutions, although important, are not necessarily the main issue here.

Of course, policy choices in real life need not be "either-or" choices. There are undoubtedly opportunities to develop new methods of organizing the Asia-Pacific region or more likely better methods of using the institutions and forums we already have. But even more, the region needs to find better ways to use what mechanisms it possesses now and better policy ideas to address those key challenges it faces.

NOTES

1. For more on North Korea and the NPT, see Michael O'Hanlon and Mike Mochizuki, *Crisis on the Korean Peninsula: How to Deal with a Nuclear North Korea* (New York: McGraw-Hill, 2003).

2. Sumit Ganguly, *Conflict Unending: India-Pakistan Tensions Since 1947* (New York: Columbia University Press, 2001).

3. Stephen Philip Cohen, *The Idea of Pakistan* (Washington, D.C.: Brookings Institution Press, 2004), 97–130.

4. International Crisis Group, *Unfulfilled Promises: Pakistan's Failure to Tackle Extremism* (Brussels: International Crisis Group, 2004).

5. See, for example, John J. Mearsheimer, *The Tragedy of Great Power Politics* (New York: Norton, 2001); Aaron L. Friedberg, "Ripe for Rivalry: Prospects for Peace in a Multipolar Asia," *International Security* 18, no. 3 (1993–1994): 5–33. For a general discussion about the dangers whenever a new rising power emerges to challenge the existing balance of international power, see Robert Gilpin, *War and Change in World Politics* (Cambridge: Cambridge University Press, 1981).

6. China may have certain military advantages for any war on its territory, and the United States for any war at sea or over islands, but neither country is likely to perceive itself as having a systematic advantage for warfare in general. For related arguments, see Barry R. Posen, "Command of the Commons: The Military Foundation of U.S. Hegemony," *International Security* 28, no. 1 (2003): 5–46.

7. Nicholas R. Lardy, *Integrating China into the Global Economy* (Washington, D.C.: Brookings Institution Press, 2002), 1–28; Alastair Iain Johnston, "Is China a Status Quo Power?" *International Security* 27, no. 4 (2003): 5–56.

8. International Institute for Strategic Studies, *The Military Balance, 2005/2006* (London: Routledge, 2005).

9. For a good discussion, see Zbigniew Brzezinski, *The Choice: Global Domination or Global Leadership* (New York: Basic Books, 2004), 107–22.

10. Michael J. Green, *Japan's Reluctant Realism* (New York: Palgrave, 2001).

11. Mike Mochizuki and Michael O'Hanlon, "Calming the Japan-China Rift," *Washington Times*, April 21, 2005.

12. Ted C. Fishman, *China, Inc.: How the Rise of the Next Superpower Challenges America and the World* (New York: Scribner, 2005), 293.

13. See also C. Fred Bergsten, Bates Gill, Nicholas R. Lardy, and Derek Mitchell, *China: The Balance Sheet* (New York: Public Affairs, 2006), 73–161.

14. David Shambaugh, "China's Military Modernization: Making Steady and Surprising Progress," in *Strategic Asia, 2005–2006: Military Modernization in an Era of Uncertainty*, ed. Ashley J. Tellis and Michael Wills (Washington, D.C.: National Bureau of Asian Research, 2005), 70; International Institute for Strategic Studies, *The Military Balance, 2008* (London: Routledge, 2008), 359.

15. Douglas J. Feith, Under Secretary of Defense for Policy, "Strengthening U.S. Global Defense Posture: Report to Congress," U.S. Department of Defense, Washington, D.C., September 2004, 4–12; U.S. Department of Defense, "Active Duty Military Personnel Strengths by Regional Area and by Country," September 30, 2007, http://siadapp.dmdc.osd.mil/personnel/MILITARY/history/hst0709.pdf; Admiral William J. Fallon, United States Navy, Commander, United States Pacific Command, statement before the House Armed Services Committee, March 7, 2007, 110th Cong., 1st sess., http://armedservices.house.gov/pdfs/FCPACOM030707/Fallon_Testimony030707 .pdf; Yoshifumi Sugita, "Futenma Base Issue Still Stalled," *Daily Yomiuri*, May 22,

2007, 4; U.S. Department of Defense, "Eight United States Army Units," http://8tharmy.korea.army.mil/Eusapages/Units.htm; John A. Tirpak, "Comeback in the Pacific," *Air Force Magazine*, July 2007, 26–27; Christian Caryl, "U.S. Military Embraces Guam," *Newsweek International*, February 26, 2007, http://www.msnbc.msn.com/id/17202830/site/newsweek.

16. According to my proposal, developed in the book *Crisis on the Korean Peninsula*, the United States and its regional partners South Korea, Japan, China, and Russia should offer Pyongyang a set of inducements as well as a clear threat that the nuclear status quo, or worse, cannot and will not be accepted. In doing so, they should be careful not to set a precedent for rewarding illicit behavior by granting North Korea large benefits simply for undoing a nuclear program it should not have had in the first place. They should make more comprehensive demands—not only denuclearization, but reductions in conventional forces, elimination of chemical arms, structural economic reform, and the beginnings of human rights improvements—as conditions for substantial increases in aid. If Pyongyang is prepared to make such a deal, Washington and other capitals should be clear that they are prepared to help finance a transition to a Vietnam-style economy in North Korea. Total aid packages in the range of $2 billion to $3 billion a year for several years to help build infrastructure and revitalize agriculture and improve the public-health and even education systems might be acceptable if North Korea were to move verifiably and decisively in this direction. (More modest reforms can be met with more modest, yet still generous, aid packages.) American and other multilateral and national bans on trade and investment might also be lifted, provisionally at first and permanently; a temporary U.S. diplomatic presence might lead to full relations and a permanent embassy within several years. This admittedly ambitious vision would try to induce Kim Jong Il to follow the reform models of Vietnam and China. By making the status quo untenable through the threat of sanctions and reductions in trade and investment should North Korea not denuclearize, this approach would also attempt to force Kim to choose between reform and slow strangulation of his state. Of course, even if the basic deal were to have some appeal to Pyongyang, it might not be feasible to convince North Korea to give up all of its nuclear capabilities immediately. It might take several years to reach that final goal, but as long as any deal immediately and verifiably froze North Korea's nuclear activities and then quickly began to get plutonium out of North Korea, the United States and its partners should be able to accept it.

17. Victor D. Cha, "Response: Why We Must Pursue 'Hawk Engagement,'" in Victor D. Cha and David C. Kang, *Nuclear North Korea: A Debate on Engagement Strategies* (New York: Columbia University Press, 2003), 70–100; Leon V. Sigal, *Disarming Strangers: Nuclear Diplomacy with North Korea* (Princeton, N.J.: Princeton University Press, 1998), 207–18; Yoichi Funabashi, *The Peninsula Question: A Chronicle of the Second Korean Nuclear Crisis* (Washington, D.C.: Brookings Institution Press, 2007), 220–24.

18. For a similar view, see Gary Samore, "The Korean Nuclear Crisis," *Survival* 45, no. 1 (2003): 19–22.

19. For an explanation of the Yasukuni Shrine controversy, see chapter 4, note 29.

20. On China's more sophisticated diplomatic and security policy with its neighbors, see Bates Gill, *Rising Star: China's New Security Diplomacy* (Washington, D.C.: Brookings Institution Press, 2007); Joshua Kurlantzik, *Charm Offensive: How China's Soft Power Is Transforming the World* (New Haven, Conn.: Yale University Press, 2007); Kurt M. Campbell and Michael E. O'Hanlon, *Hard Power: The New Politics of National Security* (New York: Basic Books, 2006), 195–200.

21. For one possible approach, see Ashton B. Carter, William J. Perry, and John D. Steinbruner, *A New Concept of Cooperative Security* (Washington, D.C.: Brookings Institution Press, 1992), 64–65; for a related and more recent view, see Zbigniew Brzezinski, "A Geostrategy for Eurasia," *Foreign Affairs* 76, no. 5 (1997): 63–64.

22. M. Taylor Fravel, "Regime Insecurity and International Cooperation: Explaining China's Compromises in Territorial Disputes," *International Security* 30, no. 2 (2005): 46–83.

23. On the latter point, see Ashton B. Carter and William J. Perry, *Preventive Defense: A New Security Strategy for America* (Washington, D.C.: Brookings Institution Press, 1999), 106–11.

24. Dennis C. Blair and John T. Hanley Jr., "From Wheels to Webs: Reconstructing Asia-Pacific Security Arrangements," *Washington Quarterly* 24, no. 1 (2001): 7–17.

25. Marie-France Desjardins, *Rethinking Confidence-Building Measures*, Adelphi Paper no. 307 (Oxford: Oxford University Press for the International Institute for Strategic Studies, 1996), 60–63.

26. The basic cost data are from Rachel Schmidt, *Moving U.S. Forces: Options for Strategic Mobility* (Washington, D.C.: Congressional Budget Office, 1997), http://www.cbo.gov/ftpdocs/oxx/doc11/Stratmob.pdf.

27. Secretary of the Navy Donald C. Winter, remarks at the Current Strategy Forum, Naval War College, June 13, 2006, http://www.navy.mil/navydata/people/secnav/winter/SECNAV_Remarks_NWC_Current_Strategy_Forum.pdf.

28. For details on the military capabilities, see International Institute for Strategic Studies, *The Military Balance*, vol. 107, no. 1 (London: Routledge, 2007).

29. Michael H. Armacost, "The Future of America's Alliances in Northeast Asia," in *The Future of America's Alliances in Northeast Asia*, ed. Michael. H. Armacost and Daniel I. Okimoto (Stanford, Calif.: Asia-Pacific Research Center, 2004), 11–16.

30. David C. Kang, "South Korea's Embrace of Interdependence in Pursuit of Security," in *Trade, Interdependence, and Security*, ed. Ashley J. Tellis and Michael Wills (Seattle: National Bureau of Asian Research, 2006), 138–70.

31. See, for example, Martin N. Murphy, *Contemporary Piracy and Maritime Terrorism: The Threat to International Security*, Adelphi Paper no. 388 (London: International Institute for Strategic Studies, 2007).

12. Nontraditional Security and Multilateralism in Asia

RESHAPING THE CONTOURS OF REGIONAL
SECURITY ARCHITECTURE

Mely Caballero-Anthony

Over the past decade, the dynamics that define the strategic regional environment in Asia have changed dramatically. The hope of a more stable and peaceful environment after the end of the Cold War was short-lived. Instead, Asia
confronts both traditional and new security challenges emerging from a host of
transnational threats. Of late, there is growing recognition that new security
challenges are proving to be more severe and are more likely to inflict more
harm to a greater number of people than conventional threats such as interstate
wars and conflicts.

These newly emerging challenges are also known as nontraditional security
(NTS) threats. They are defined as challenges to the survival and well-being of
peoples and states that arise primarily out of nonmilitary sources, such as climate change, infectious diseases, natural disasters, irregular migration, food
shortages, smuggling of persons, drug trafficking, and other forms of transnational crime. Transnational in nature, these dangers defy unilateral remedies
and thus call for comprehensive political, economic, and social responses as
well as humanitarian use of military forces.[1] As a consequence, policymakers
in the region have had to rethink their security agendas and find new and in-
novative ways to address NTS challenges. These new ways of thinking in turn
have had and will continue to have profound implications for how govern-

ments and other players organize themselves in Asia to realize greater regional security.

With this brief introduction to NTS as background, this chapter aims to do two things: first, to examine how Asia is addressing new and emerging security challenges through its various regional institutions, mechanisms, and relevant security arrangements; and second, to analyze how these NTS threats are shaping the institutional architecture in East Asia. In covering these key points, the chapter seeks to address the following questions: Is the "new" regionalism able to mitigate the emergent instabilities and security challenges facing the region? Does this new regionalism provide other layers of governance that allow for shifts in patterns of inter- and intrastate relations through elite consensus, market regulation, and dissemination of norms?

In addressing these questions, the chapter argues that as NTS issues increasingly define states' security agendas, the emergence of new cooperative mechanisms and the recalibration of existing institutions to address these challenges are pushing regional actors for deeper institutional commitments, including the adoption of more rules-based regimes, to ensure more effective implementation of regional measures and to enhance security cooperation in East Asia. Moreover, as regional mechanisms open spaces for other actors such as nongovernmental organizations, civil-society organizations, international organizations, and other external actors to help cope with NTS challenges, the nature and focus of regional security cooperation are being redefined to pay more attention to issues of human security. These NTS issues create new tensions and challenges as states attempt to strike a tenuous balance between protecting state and regime security, on the one hand, and promoting human security, on the other.

The next section provides a brief review of the developments of regionalism in Asia and compares these evolving trends to other patterns of new regionalism found in other regions. The chapter then proceeds to examine the nature of emerging security challenges in Asia, particularly East Asia. It identifies some of the key NTS issues in the region and examines how regional institutions such as the Association of Southeast Asian Nations (ASEAN) and ASEAN Plus Three (APT, made up of the ten ASEAN states plus China, Japan, and South Korea) are addressing these issues. It also reviews how the other regional institutions within the Asia Pacific—such as the Asia-Pacific Economic Cooperation (APEC) forum and the ASEAN Regional Forum (ARF)—have responded to NTS issues and examines the extent to which they complement or compete with subregional efforts. The chapter concludes with observations regarding the impact of NTS challenges on the evolving institutional architecture in the region.

NEW REGIONALISM AND THE EMERGING
SECURITY ARCHITECTURE IN ASIA

Despite growing concerns about the effectiveness of multilateralism in responding to global and regional problems, multilateralism does matter to Asian states,
for three important reasons.[2] First, notwithstanding the daunting challenges
faced by a number of multilateral institutions, there remains a shared and
strong interest among Asian states to maintain and strengthen global institutions. This interest is clearly demonstrated in their commitment to the centrality of the United Nations in establishing a normative global order and their
support for United Nations–led conventions, treaties, and regimes. Underpinning this commitment is the realization of their lack of military power and their
inability to act unilaterally when their security is threatened.[3]

Second, as Asian states cope with emerging challenges of globalization, they
have become more vulnerable to a host of insecurities brought about by complex
global forces. These insecurities include the risks to international financial crises,
imbalances in the global economy, unregulated migration, transnational criminal
networks, pandemics, international terrorism, and other forms of NTS threats.

Third, with the emergence of NTS threats, the impetus for effective multilateralism has become more urgent, as demonstrated in the current trend to
strengthen cooperation and deepen the integration processes in Asia through
regional frameworks. For instance, since the Asian financial crisis of 1997/1998,
ASEAN has undertaken a number of institutional innovations to respond more
effectively to a host of regional challenges. A good example is the 2003 Bali
Concord II, which announced the aim to establish an ASEAN community
based on three pillars: an ASEAN security community, an ASEAN economic
community, and an ASEAN sociocultural community. Some observers have
posited that this ongoing development is ASEAN's attempt at moving beyond a
"nascent" security community to become a "soft" security community. Similarly, APT formalized the framework for forging closer economic linkages between ASEAN and its three East Asian neighbors, China, Japan, and South
Korea. One such linkage can be seen in its development of a regional financial
mechanism—the Chiang Mai Initiative (CMI), which is a liquidity-support facility meant to prevent another financial crisis, and a regional bond market (for
more details on the CMI, see chapter 9 in this volume). APT is also currently
studying the possibility of adopting a common currency over the medium to
longer term. Beyond East Asia, the ARF and the APEC forum have also introduced a number of measures to respond to different security challenges—for
example, cooperative measures initiated to fight transnational crimes and terrorism, pandemics, and other threats. In the case of APEC, this trend to strengthen

cooperation has resulted in the expansion of its mandate beyond economic issues to encompass security cooperation as well.

These initiatives are driven by the broader objectives of building more capacity and coherence in regional efforts to address new regional challenges and in the process to complement the global efforts by the United Nations and other international organizations to promote peace, human rights, and development. Indeed, if one were to go by the core definition of *multilateralism*, coordinated relations among three or more countries "on the basis of certain principles of ordering relations among states,"[4] then these emerging trends suggest movement toward greater regional multilateralism in the future and raise many new questions about how the Asian security architecture will evolve.

The scholarly literature on this topic highlights the emergence of a second-generation regionalism that is characterized as more robust and more participatory. More significant, the second-generation approach of "new regionalism" reveals expanded and multidimensional forms of interstate cooperation and integration, covering a wide range of economic, political, security, social, and cultural areas. According to the literature on new regionalism in Europe, this type of second-generation regionalism comes with the following characteristics: deeper economic integration with political elements; multilevel governance; devolution within states; strong international legal frameworks; and cooperation along many dimensions. Bjorn Hettne, András Inotai, and Osvaldo Sunkel have argued that these new patterns of interstate actions reflect regional players' compelling need to integrate noneconomic issues of justice, security, and culture with issues of trade and economics and that they are driven by the "political ambition of establishing regional coherence and identity."[5]

Similarly, another study on new regionalism describes it as a route that states can take to "mediate the range of economic and social pressures generated by globalization."[6] Given the weakening impact of state-centric responses, mediation in this sense refers to states and other actors' ability to organize themselves and to craft appropriate responses to mitigate the destabilizing impact of global forces.[7] In brief, the new regionalism is best understood as project(s) of "regional governance" that can be vastly diverse and that provide different models depending on the political, economic, and security context within which they take place.[8]

NTS THREATS AND NEW REGIONALISM IN ASIA

Much has been written about the nature of security challenges in Asia. In many studies on security in the region, most of the identifiable and likely threats fall under the NTS rubric.[9] Moreover, these NTS threats have common characteristics: they tend to be nonmilitary in nature and transnational in scope (neither purely domestic nor purely interstate); they arise at very short notice and are transmitted rapidly due to globalization; they are difficult to prevent (though coping mechanisms can be devised) and resistant to national solutions, thus requiring regional and multilateral cooperation; and they are characterized by the fact that the object of security is no longer just the state (state sovereignty or territorial integrity), but also the peoples within and across states (involving survival, well-being, dignity), at both the individual and the societal levels.[10] The gravity of the problem can be seen in the way these transnational threats are increasingly discussed not only in academic circles, but also among policy-makers. Officials also portray these issues as threats to their states' national sovereignty and territorial integrity, as well as to their respective societies' well-being. Four key and representative examples of NTS threats in Asia are infectious diseases, natural disasters, transnational crime/terrorism, and poverty/human security.

INFECTIOUS DISEASES

Since the Asia-wide outbreak of severe acute respiratory syndrome (SARS) in 2003, the threats from infectious diseases appear to have become more severe. As the SARS experience showed, in this era of globalization and regionalization such types of infectious diseases have the capacity to affect detrimentally the security and well-being of all members of a society and all aspects of its economy.[11] This point was well highlighted at the 2006 World Economic Forum with the release of the report *Global Risks 2006*. The report ranked pandemics and natural disasters among the highest in the list of risks confronting the international community. The study also concluded that despite the interplay of these multiple global risks and their combined ripple effects, "disaster planning and crisis management suffer from a number of shortcomings." Among these shortcomings are limited investments of resources in health systems and varying responses to different assessments of threats.[12]

How have regional institutions dealt with the problem? The record is mixed. Along with SARS and the looming threat of a new pandemic, possibly from the mutation of the H5N1 virus (a strain of avian influenza), it is disturbing to note that the World Health Organization (WHO) declared that Southeast Asia would be the "next ground zero" if the H5N1 virus mutates to become infectious to humans on a pandemic scale.[13] The WHO warning reminds ASEAN and other regional governments that they may well be the first line of defense in case of an outbreak, hence raising the critical urgency of putting in place emergency plans and effective surveillance systems in the region.[14] The question, however, is whether Asian governments are organized for such an eventuality.

Information is sketchy about emergency response capability for disease control among countries in the region.[15] In this regard, the SARS experience was instructive. Whereas Singapore and Hong Kong were able to deal with the health crisis in a reasonably effective manner, China, the Philippines, and Taiwan experienced challenges ranging from the lack of contingency planning for managing the health crisis to ineffective coordination among relevant government agencies. It should also be noted that prior to the SARS outbreak, there had been very little institutionalized regional cooperation in the area of public-health policy. It was only after the SARS outbreak that some regional mechanisms were proposed. Building a regional capacity for surveillance and disease control topped the list.

Since the SARS outbreak, regional governments have proposed and established a number of mechanisms intended to strengthen the monitoring of disease outbreaks at the national and regional level. In December 2004, ASEAN established a task force to respond to the spread of avian flu in the region. Responsibility was divided among the five original members of the group, with each country to take on a specific role: Indonesia was to harmonize vaccination and culling procedures; Malaysia to draft action plans to contain the disease, boost emergency preparedness, and establish disease-free zones within the region; the Philippines to increase public awareness about the problem; Singapore to establish an information-sharing system; and Thailand to create surveillance systems to detect the disease and ensure rapid exchange and analysis of virus samples. The ASEAN plan was reinforced in October 2005 with the establishment of a regional fund for avian flu and a three-year action plan.[16] One of the key areas targeted by this action plan is the development of a regional rapid containment plan to stem the first signs of a pandemic outbreak. An important agenda item indicates that periodic simulation exercises are to be conducted at the national and regional level to test countries' readiness to contain a possible pandemic. Singapore, for instance, has been running influenza pandemic drills since early 2006. These drills, code-named "Sparrowhawk," are aimed at enhancing a number of government agencies' preparedness to contain the first signs of a pandemic.[17]

Although these efforts reflect greater mobilization within the region, they are still quite limited. Much more needs to be done to include the less-developed members of ASEAN, which would benefit largely from a regionwide initiative given the current state of their health systems. The task force for combating avian influenza involved only five out of the ten members of ASEAN. There is also the issue of limited resources, a point that ASEAN officials have acknowledged. So far, a regional fund of U.S. $2 million has been set up for this purpose, but ASEAN countries are looking to their richer dialogue partners (Japan, South Korea, and China) to assist in supplementing the amount.[18] The regional agenda for combating avian influenza has therefore been elevated to the bigger forums—APT and the East Asia Summit (EAS).[19]

At APT, two major initiatives have been established: the APT Emerging Infectious Diseases Program and the Regional Framework for Control and Eradication of Highly Pathogenic Avian Influenza. At its inaugural meeting, the EAS adopted the Declaration on Avian Influenza Prevention, Control, and Response.[20] Some of the measures outlined include strengthening institutional capacities at national and regional levels to ensure effective and efficient implementation of measures to prevent avian influenza; putting in place control programs and pandemic preparedness and response plans; and enhancing capacity building to cope with pandemic influenza. The latter would include establishing information-sharing protocols among countries and multilateral organizations, as well as effective, timely, and meaningful communication before and during a pandemic influenza outbreak.[21]

The nature of pandemic threats, however, has compelled countries outside the region to get involved in order to address the complexities of the problem effectively. Hence, outside the East Asian regional framework, other ASEAN dialogue partners have also been forthcoming in providing more assistance in preventing the possibility of a pandemic outbreak. The United States, for instance, has been one of the major external actors to take a keen interest in this issue. It was one of the largest donors to the global avian influenza fund set up at the 2006 Beijing conference, having pledged $392 million toward the initiative's total funding of $1.9 billion.[22] Moreover, through the APEC framework, the United States has initiated in partnership with Singapore the establishment of the Regional Emerging Diseases Intervention (REDI) Center. Formally launched in 2003 after the SARS outbreak, the REDI Center is to assist Asian countries in "tracking, controlling, and researching emerging infections with appropriate resources and expertise."[23] It is open to participation by other countries in the Asia Pacific. APEC also convened a series of regional meetings to respond to threats of avian influenza. These meetings generated a number of initiatives such as the creation of the Health Task Force and the Task Force on Emergency Preparedness.[24] These task forces are similarly focused on developing capacity within the region to enable adequate, systematic, and well-coordinated plans for prevention of pandemic outbreaks.

It is important to note that despite the obvious need to stem the spread of deadly pandemics in the region, many of these proposed measures from ASEAN, APT, EAS, and APEC were still not fully implemented as of 2007. Countries in the region still face many challenges in confronting this regional and global NTS problem. Among the most obvious challenges is a lack of resources allocated to improving public-health systems at the domestic level and an inability to translate those resources to effective regional mechanisms. In this regard, the region needs to consider a broader and more comprehensive strategy to prevent and contain the outbreak of infectious diseases. This strategy would include focusing on key issues such as building capacity to establish a credible and effective regional surveillance systems for monitoring infectious diseases. There is also the critical need to improve the poor state of health infrastructure in less-developed countries and to address the politics of crisis health management in the region.[25]

Concerning capacity building for disease surveillance and control, a positive and critical step in the right direction would be to create mechanisms for effective production and distribution of vaccines and other medicines. Within ASEAN, steps to develop a regionwide mechanism in rapid disease control have begun with the first exercise held in Cambodia in late March 2007. The exercise, Panstop 2007, was coordinated by the ASEAN Secretariat with the help of the WHO, the Japanese government, and the Japan International Cooperation System. This simulation exercise involved test procedures to rush antiviral drugs and equipment to infected areas.[26] Panstop 2007 demonstrated that although several regional initiatives from different regional frameworks may be addressing an NTS issue such as infectious diseases, implementation is often more effective if it starts at the subregional level. Larger, regionwide frameworks work better at building political will and strategic agreement, and complementarities with similar initiatives from other regional bodies should be noted in order to identify gaps and undertake interregional coordination.

NATURAL DISASTERS

Asia is well known as a region prone to major natural disasters. The December 2004 massive earthquake and tsunami in the Indian Ocean and the Kashmir earthquake of early 2005 tragically illustrated the enormous devastation and loss of life caused by natural disasters, as well as the immense challenges involved in disaster-relief operations to provide humanitarian assistance and postdisaster reconstruction and rehabilitation. Natural disasters generate complex emergencies that require urgent and coordinated responses from a broad range of international, regional, state, and nonstate actors. Unfortunately, many states in Asia are ill prepared to cope with these complex emergencies. This gap was vividly revealed in the region's experience with the 2004 tsunami when the impact of the humanitarian emergency would have been far more catastrophic without the humanitarian assistance provided by external partners such as the United States, India, and Japan, together with a number of international aid agencies.

In the aftermath of the tsunami, ASEAN countries agreed to enhance cooperation in disaster relief, including prevention and mitigation.[27] Specifically, its member states agreed to mobilize additional resources to meet the emergency needs of tsunami victims. They also called on the international community through the United Nations to convene an international pledging conference for sustainable humanitarian relief efforts and explore the establishment of "standby arrangements" for other humanitarian relief efforts. ASEAN also called on donor countries, the World Bank, the Asian Development Bank, and other financial institutions to provide the necessary funds to support rehabilitation and reconstruction programs in disaster-stricken areas. In particular, ASEAN welcomed the initiative for a moratorium on affected countries' payments of external debts and at the same time urged private-sector participation and contribution to the ongoing rehabilitation efforts.

If another major disaster were to strike the region, would ASEAN and other Asian multilateral groups be prepared to protect human security? Aside from the initial demonstrations of regional solidarity, the region needs to do more in the areas of prevention and mitigation by developing more effective multilateral mechanisms such as an early-warning system. A shift in thinking is needed to institutionalize regional cooperation in disaster management. The ASEAN Regional Disaster Emergency Response Simulation Exercise, carried out in 2005, was a positive step in the right direction.[28] It was envisioned as an annual exercise to bring together several personnel and to mobilize light to medium equipment geared toward providing immediate humanitarian assistance to affected countries in times of natural disaster, and it was in fact held again in 2006 and 2007.

Beyond ASEAN, other ad hoc exercises in disaster management have been undertaken within the ARF framework. After the tsunami disaster in December 2004, the ARF ministers agreed to work together in providing emergency relief, rehabilitation, and reconstruction, as well as in developing prevention and mitigation efforts to address natural disasters.[29] More significant, at the July 2006 ARF Ministers' Meeting, officials from ARF countries—including major powers such as China, Japan, Russia, and the United States—discussed the possibility of developing guidelines to improve civilian and military cooperation in humanitarian operations in the wake of natural disasters. These guidelines would involve standard operating procedures for civilian-military cooperation in disaster-relief operations and a database of ARF members' military assets to be used for disaster relief.[30] APEC established the Virtual Task Force on Emergency Preparedness in 2005 to strengthen coordination efforts in disaster relief and to improve regional emergency and disaster-management capability.[31]

More can be done to integrate improved domestic preparedness into coordinated regional efforts. States in the region need not wait for calamity to strike before national and regional responses are switched to emergency mode. As images of natural disasters unfold, the unfortunate lag in response time often results in unnecessary loss of life and greater human misery. Although regional efforts are being considered to improve disaster management, attention also needs be focused on improving capacity at the national level. Countries in the region need to examine their own capacity and rethink their own national strategies for disaster mitigation or risk reduction as part of a comprehensive region-wide effort to improve preparedness.[32]

ASEAN member countries should also assess whether their regional mechanisms and strategies are sufficient (beyond simulation exercises) and whether these strategies complement national measures. ASEAN should expand these types of exercises to include more countries outside of ASEAN and thus tap into an extended Asian network of expertise in the prevention and mitigation of natural disasters. Such ideas have started to percolate in the region. At the Asian security summit conference held in Singapore in June 2006 (also known as the "Shangri-la Dialogue"), the Malaysian deputy prime minister and defense minister Najib Tun Razak proposed the idea of a disaster-relief center for the region. Under the proposal, ASEAN would initiate the project, and other countries such as the United States, Australia, and Japan would be invited to contribute later. It is also interesting to note that prior to this meeting, South Korea had also announced a plan to establish a comprehensive cooperative response system for regional and international disasters by "setting up a channel for information sharing and coordination of personnel, supplies, and equipment." Similarly, Japan proposed to develop strategies and procedures to facilitate a fast response by armed forces in the region in times of natural disasters.[33]

Given the interest that many actors are showing in disaster-relief operations, the task at hand is to draw up a mechanism that is able to coordinate all these initiatives—at the ASEAN, ARF, and APEC level—into a more coherent and effective regional response system. ASEAN might look to the experience of the Euro-Atlantic Disaster Response Coordination Center, which has served as the focal point of coordinating disaster-relief efforts in Europe.[34] The European experience in this regard can be shared through the ARF, where the European Union is a member, or through the Asia Europe Meeting. Given that a number of countries within and outside ASEAN are already able to provide immediate assistance in times of natural disasters, it is only logical for all these ad hoc arrangements to be coordinated into a wider and more integrated regional response that will have the capacity to anticipate many of the problems and security challenges that may arise in addressing the devastating impact of natural disasters that require large-scale humanitarian assistance efforts.

TRANSNATIONAL CRIME AND TERRORISM

The problem of transnational crime in Asia is severe and includes such challenges as illicit drug trafficking, money laundering, piracy, arms smuggling, and cybercrimes. These types of crimes constitute threats to state security by violating national borders, weakening national authorities, and undermining the rule of law. They also threaten the security and well-being of individuals and societies. Addressing these complex problems requires a transnational response, yet interstate cooperation in the region is often complicated by the fact that it touches on sensitive questions such as domestic jurisdiction, the sharing of information, extradition laws, and problems of corruption.[35]

Nevertheless, a number of regional efforts target transnational crime. For example, the ASEAN Ministerial Meeting on Transnational Crime evolved from the first ASEAN Conference on Transnational Crime held in Manila in December 1997. The meeting is headed by the respective ministers of home affairs and forms the core of ASEAN countercrime cooperation. Its activities focus on the exchange of information, legal and law enforcement cooperation, training, institutional building, and collaboration with extramural actors. Other institutional structures include the ASEAN Chiefs of National Police and the ASEAN Senior Officials on Drug Matters. ASEAN has also worked with its regional partners to enhance international cooperation in fighting transnational crime. One of the more significant regional arrangements in this area is the ASEAN-China Joint Declaration on Cooperation in the field of NTS, which was signed at the ASEAN-China Summit in 2002.[36] The agreement seeks to complement national and international efforts in combating such problems as trafficking in drugs, arms, and people; sea piracy; money laundering; cybercrime; and terrorism.

The ASEAN-China Joint Declaration dovetails with the ASEAN and China Cooperative Operations in Response to Dangerous Drugs (ACCORD) agreement. The ACCORD Plan of Action envisions a drug-free region, outlines work plans, and identifies priority projects and other cooperative measures.[37] The ACCORD is supported by the United Nations Office on Drugs and Crime, the United Nations International Drug Control Program, and individual countries with funding, technical cooperation, and joint programs. Although the ACCORD is a declaration of intent, it nevertheless addresses some of the limitations that have undermined previous collective efforts. For instance, it tackles the issue of supervision by establishing a regional coordination mechanism and by introducing measurable targets and dates. Moreover, it is also a good example of the kinds of soft mechanisms of cooperation that can be promoted to address NTS issues: the sharing of information and best practices, the creation of communication networks among specialized agencies, reciprocal cooperation, and the promotion of better regional coordination. In short, beyond the exhortatory injunctions about transnational crime, the ACCORD tries to complement domestic efforts against the illicit trafficking and abuse of drugs by establishing an institutional framework for cooperation. Its success will of course depend on the actual implementation and enforcement of its mandates.

During the seventh ASEAN Summit in 2001, member states issued the ASEAN Declaration on Joint Action to Counter Terrorism. This initiative aimed to deepen cooperation among front-line law enforcement agencies in combating terrorism and to share "best practices; enhancing information/intelligence exchange to facilitate the flow of information, in particular, on terrorists and terrorist organizations, their movement and funding, and any other information needed to protect lives, property, and the security of all modes of travel, and others."[38]

In May 2002, ASEAN states signed the Agreement on Information Exchange and Establishment of Communication Procedures in order to promote cooperation in combating transnational crime, including terrorism.[39] Similarly, ASEAN and the United States issued the Joint Declaration for Cooperation to Combat International Terrorism in August 2002, which committed the United States and all ASEAN members to improve intelligence-gathering efforts, strengthen capacity-building measures, and enhance mutual cooperation.[40] Aside from the United States, Australia has also developed a comprehensive network of bilateral counterterrorism arrangements with ASEAN states. It has provided substantial support in the establishment of the Transnational Crime Center in Jakarta, and its police force has worked very closely with its Indonesian counterpart in the monitoring, prevention, and prosecution of transnational crimes, including terrorism.[41]

Given the close linkages between transnational crime and terrorism, provision of mutual legal assistance in criminal matters and extradition agreements have been discussed within the framework of the ASEAN Ministerial Meeting on Transnational Crime. This framework has been expanded to the APT level with the first APT Ministerial Meeting on Transnational Crime held in Bangkok in January 2004. At the ARF level, member states have pledged to implement the United Nations recommendations on combating terrorist financing. Two important workshops were convened in this area in 2002: the first was on financial measures against terrorism, and the second was on prevention of terrorism. Meanwhile, ministerial meetings were held on counterterrorism and people trafficking, and, in the process, ad hoc working groups were formed to follow up on many of the issues raised during these meetings.[42] Moreover, as part of the continuing efforts to build capacity in fighting terrorism, three complementary institutions have also been established in Southeast Asia: the

Southeast Asia Regional Center for Counter-Terrorism, based in Kuala Lumpur, Malaysia; the Jakarta Center for Law Enforcement Cooperation; and the International Law Enforcement Academy in Bangkok.[43]

Piracy stands out as another example of transnational crime, the incidence of which has increased at an alarming rate. According to the International Maritime Bureau, the Straits of Malacca are the most piracy-infested channel in the world, and more than two-thirds of attacks reported to the bureau are in Asian waters.[44] In response to this growing threat, a trilateral arrangement among ASEAN's littoral states Malaysia, Indonesia, and Singapore was formed in 2004 to conduct joint coordinated patrols along the straits to beef up maritime security in the region. Since then, other ASEAN countries such as Thailand and the Philippines, together with Japan, have joined in many of the trilateral group's training activities in antipiracy, antiterrorism, and coast guard patrols.

Beyond Southeast Asia, the Regional Cooperation Agreement on Combating Piracy and Armed Robbery Against Ships in Asia was finalized in Tokyo in November 2004. It is the first government-to-government agreement to enhance the security of regional waters beyond ASEAN. The initiative, originally proposed by the Japanese prime minister in October 2001, aims to enhance multilateral cooperation among sixteen Asian countries: the ten members of ASEAN plus Bangladesh, China, India, Japan, South Korea, and Sri Lanka. Its goal is to combat sea piracy and armed robbery against ships in the region.[45]

POVERTY AND HUMAN SECURITY

Unlike the other three NTS issues just discussed, threats and insecurities brought on by poverty or sudden economic dislocation are less obvious and tangible, but the onslaught of the Asian financial crisis and its economic impact on many affected states were devastating. It also brought on a host of security-related problems for both states and societies, including ethnic conflict and violence. Yet, despite the discourse at the official level about building a regional community, far more needs to be done to "promote more inclusive and caring communities."[46] In a region where one finds some of the world's fastest-growing economies, it is also home to some 700 million persons who live on less than one dollar a day. Thus, the picture of a dynamic economic region is blighted by the fact that a majority of the world's poor are found in Asia. Although China and India are enjoying rapid economic growth rates, poverty levels remain significant, and there is rising income inequality. For example, the incidence of poverty in China and India are 13.4 percent and 30.7 percent respectively.[47] Meanwhile, Gini coefficients in China and India are 0.447 and 0.325, respectively.[48] Within Southeast Asia, concerns have been raised about the emergence of a "two-tiered ASEAN." Among ASEAN's older members, Malaysia's gross domestic product (GDP) is a distant third after Singapore and Brunei. At the same time, Indonesia's GDP per capita is only about one-third of Malaysia's, and the Philippines has the highest incidence of poverty among the original six ASEAN members.[49] With such levels of inequality affecting large sections of the population of developing countries, the experience of the 1997 financial crisis in Asia revealed that such inequality causes conflicts and instability. Very little provision for social safety nets makes the problem even more acute, unlike in developed states such as the United States and welfare states such as Sweden.

The greatest challenge to ASEAN economic integration and the security it can bring lies in addressing the development divide among its member countries. In recent years, regional efforts in addressing poverty and economic development have received more attention within the context of the ASEAN community and through the Vientiane Action Plan of 2004. For instance, ASEAN adopted the Vientiane Integration Agenda, which outlined specific areas and measures to narrow the development gap between the old and new members, albeit mainly in the economic sphere. These measures include the strengthening of the Initiative for ASEAN Integration, which explores modalities for more resource mobilization and programs on social development that will support the national poverty-reduction program with regional advocacy efforts.[50] Moreover, an important agenda item in the Bali Concord II provides for effective safety nets for marginalized groups especially in times of economic downturn. Many nongovernmental organizations and civil-society groups in the region are advocating this issue through their support for an ASEAN social charter. This development is significant, especially in the light of ASEAN's fledgling efforts at adopting a charter. So far, civil-society groups, such as the ASEAN Trade Union Council, have kept in step with official efforts in drafting the ASEAN Charter by also preparing their own draft of an ASEAN social charter, which it presented to ASEAN officials in December 2005. The social charter aims to promote common labor standards in ASEAN countries, including employment stability, health and safety measures, and just wages.[51]

To help prevent a repeat of the 1997 Asian financial crisis, APT set up the CMI in 2000. The CMI is basically a liquidity support facility for member countries to strengthen the region's collective capability to weather the effects of a liquidity crunch. In May 2005, APT finance ministers agreed to strengthen the CMI further by making it a more effective and disciplined framework through a number of measures, including enhancing and integrating the APT economic surveillance mechanism to enable early detection of financial irregularities and swift remedial policy actions; increasing the size of the available bilateral swap arrangement by up to 100 percent;[52] and improving the draw-down mechanism wherein the size of the swaps that can be withdrawn without the International Monetary Fund program can be increased to 20 percent from the current 10 percent.[53] These measures are important steps toward multilater-alizing the CMI to enable all countries to pool their financial resources. At the moment, the total reserve pool stands at U.S.$75 billion. An enhanced CMI can eventually create a regional mechanism such as an Asian monetary fund that can be used in the event of a financial crisis to prevent the devastating con-sequences of another sudden economic downturn.

CONCLUSIONS AND A LOOK AHEAD

Three key trends characterize Asian regional institutions' response to NTS challenges. First, despite the perceived inertia of Asian regional institutions in responding to security challenges, the picture has drastically changed. Since the 1997 financial crisis, institutions such as ASEAN have initiated numerous ad hoc mechanisms to address a range of transnational threats confronting the region, including infectious diseases, transnational crimes, terrorism, natural disasters, and environmental pollution. A "creeping institutionalism" has re-sulted within ASEAN, contributing to the creation of new institutional configu-rations such as APT and the EAS.

Second, this creeping institutionalism has generated different layers of bilat-eral and multilateral arrangements at subregional levels. Whether conceived within ASEAN or initiated by ASEAN arrangements such as APT and the EAS, a plethora of new cooperative efforts have emerged, geared mostly to ad-dressing different NTS threats. These subregional or minilateral arrangements bolster regional institutionalism. The extent to which these new regional struc-tures fit, complement, or compete with one another remains to be seen, al-though it should be noted that in some areas subregional responses either by ASEAN or by APT may be more effective because these subregional mecha-nisms are more institutionalized than the mechanisms set up by larger region-wide groupings such as the ARF and APEC. After almost twenty years, APEC still does not have a secretariat that can coordinate and monitor its many initia-tives. Serious discussions of establishing a secretariat began only in 2007. More-over, it is oftentimes easier to galvanize efforts at the subregional level when responding to certain issues pertinent to the region. In the case of maritime threats, for instance, it is faster to initiate coordinated maritime patrols, albeit modest, within ASEAN rather than through the ARF. The same is true regard-ing the initiation of processes within APT to monitor the spread of infectious diseases and to combat problems of drug trafficking and human smuggling.

Third, although these regional efforts are aimed essentially at building regional capacity to address different security challenges, the kinds of measures being adopted have gone beyond the usual process-oriented, confidence-building measures. Instead, they are now geared toward problem solving through sharing information; developing early-warning surveillance systems to prepare for the onset of infectious diseases and natural disasters; providing disaster-relief training, rehabilitation, and reconstruction; and, more significant, working toward coordinated procedures and even attempts at harmonizing legal frameworks to prosecute transnational crimes. Although many of these problem-solving efforts are at an inchoate stage and will require some time before they show more concrete results, the fact is that the institutions making the efforts are being built in response to new challenges.

In sum, institutional developments in Asia, particularly within ASEAN and APT, do exhibit characteristics of "second-generation regionalism" and reflect a qualitative change in interstate cooperation. These characteristics are seen not only in the widening of areas of functional cooperation, but also in the deepening of existing regional forms of cooperation. As the preceding discussion has noted, particularly in the case of ASEAN, the deepening of economic cooperation and integration is manifested in the realization of the ASEAN Free Trade Area, and through the APT process second-generation regionalism is seen in the progress of the CMI.

What do these trends tell us about the prospects for regionalism and the future security architecture in Asia? They point to a number of significant developments that define not just the shape, but the substance of regionalism in Asia as different actors—both state and nonstate—respond to new security challenges.

A first key aspect of the regional future will be the development of new norms. As states cooperate in many dimensions, the nature of interstate relations is bound to effect changes in state practices and pave the way for the development of norms such as the observance of a more rules-based regional framework. For instance, one of the main objectives in drafting the ASEAN Charter was to create an international legal personality for ASEAN and to provide the legal framework for incorporating ASEAN decisions, treaties, and conventions into member countries' national legislation (see the discussion of the ASEAN Charter in chapter 10 in this volume). In addition, with regard to deeper economic integration, much has already been done to facilitate the legal and institutional status of the ASEAN Free Trade Area and the CMI.

With this type of legal framework, however, there also comes the potential for more intrusive types of regional mechanisms. In the case of instituting a financial surveillance mechanism within the CMI, ASEAN member states as well as China, South Korea, and Japan appear prepared to accept more intrusive arrangements as and when certain threatening economic circumstances arise. A similar acceptance of greater intrusiveness appears in the regional response to transnational crimes such as terrorism, drug trafficking, and human smuggling. For example, under cooperative arrangements to counter the threat of terrorism, ASEAN countries will need to be more open to cross-border enforcement and extradition. Although limited, this development is significant given past arrangements among ASEAN members that abjured intrusions in order to protect domestic interests and maintain regime legitimacy. It appears that with the onset of greater NTS threats, ASEAN member countries and to some extent even ARF and APEC countries are more open to adopting more intrusive forms of regional cooperation if the issues at stake threaten national and regional security and the problems prove intractable to national solutions. Despite these regional institutions' perceived lack of institutional capacity, current trends in response to the widening range of new security threats support a deepening regionalism in Asia and in East Asia in particular.

In spite of a more robust regionalist spirit and practice, however, the problem of efficacy has arisen. For example, various ministers' and other officials' meetings within ASEAN, the ARF, and APEC reveal striking similarities and duplication across initiatives. To avoid superfluousness, far more serious coordination will be needed among these regional bodies. To ensure that regional efforts are not consigned to drawing boards and annual declarations, it will be important for smaller subregions to work within larger groupings to gain the coherence and localized implementation needed for a more effective response. For example, in one of the best cases, ASEAN turned to a larger grouping, APT, to create the CMI. It is significant that credible regional financial cooperative swap arrangements were adopted under the auspices of APT rather than ASEAN. ASEAN obviously did not have the institutional capacity to establish such an arrangement, whereas APT members such as Japan and China offered the much-needed financial resources required for effective regional liquidity. It should also be noted that although APEC did have the resources, it was not willing at that time to support a regional financing facility. APT has also provided a convenient framework for China to work with its ASEAN neighbors to institute a number of emergency measures to respond to an outbreak of SARS or avian influenza.

Nevertheless, even as Asian regionalism gains momentum to address some NTS issues, the importance of maintaining a more inclusive regionalism remains critical. In other words, when and where external help and expertise are required, countries outside the region should be welcome participants. The response to severe transnational security threats such as pandemics, terrorism, and natural disasters will require multilateral approaches. These threats inevitably require the involvement of extraregional powers such as the United States and Australia that have not only significant resources, but security interests that are compatible to and closely tied to the interests within the region. The United States does play an active role in helping individual states in the region cope with NTS issues, but there remains its ambiguity over promoting regionalism in Asia. The lukewarm U.S. response to the launching of the EAS raised concerns that Washington was increasingly less keen on Asian regionalism and might discourage the process.[54] There are also concerns that the United States is giving less and less attention to APEC and the ARF because of its preoccupation with challenges in the Middle East, the Persian Gulf, and Afghanistan.[55]

However, it is in East Asia where NTS issues are most critical and where regional cooperative modalities are being crafted. It was within ASEAN and APT that regional mechanisms were initiated to prevent the spread of infectious diseases such as SARS and avian influenza. It was in the EAS that regional modalities were deliberated to respond to the challenges of energy security. U.S. reticence toward Asian regionalism contrasts with China's activism and growing influence as well as with Australia and India's enthusiasm in wanting to be a part of these regional processes. Hence, in light of the new and complex security challenges brought on by NTS threats in Asia, the region would welcome a clarification of the U.S. position on regionalism and community building in Asia. Revitalizing U.S. interest in Asian regionalism need not compete with its interests in bilateral arrangements. As a prominent U.S. specialist argues, "[T]he time has come for the United States to take seriously the construction of new Asian [economic] arrangements since these arrangements could well have importance consequences for the United States itself."[56] The United States can begin to do so with greater engagement in responding to NTS threats. It gained much political mileage in Indonesia and the region as a whole with its prompt action in extending humanitarian assistance to victims of the 2004 tsunami. The U.S. gesture effectively turned the tables in its favor despite Indonesian Muslims' initial suspicions about American intentions in the region. As reflected in a national poll conducted by Terror Free Tomorrow, 65 percent of Indonesians viewed the United States more favorably after it provided extensive logistical and financial support during the tsunami disaster. Opposition to the U.S.-led war on terror also declined from 72 percent in 2003 to 36 percent in 2005.[57]

Finally, with the growing emphasis on NTS challenges, a more robust regionalism in Asia will place the human and comprehensive security agenda at the heart of each country's national policies. This trend may give rise to competing national priorities because addressing certain types of NTS challenges will also demand a level of (elite) consensus regarding certain values and norms. Tensions among members of regional institutions may rise as the push for a new normative framework gains momentum. The debate surrounding the drafting of the ASEAN Charter and ASEAN's response to the unrest in Myanmar in late 2007 reflected such tensions within the region (see chapter 10 in this volume). ASEAN's adoption of an ASEAN security community would be an opportune time for members to debate and review their norms and principles.

Creating an Asian security community will ultimately need to address the tensions inherent between the traditions of conservatism and noninterference, on the one hand, and the evolving necessity for flexibility for the sake of collective and effective regional governance, on the other. In looking ahead, one might perhaps take a leaf from the recent case of the haze (environmental pollution) in Southeast Asia. When certain capitals in the region had to confront (once again) the threats from the haze, Indonesia came under tremendous pressure to address the increasing severity of recurring forest fires that emanated from its provinces. The result was an unprecedented apology from President Susilo Bambang Yudhoyono to Indonesia's neighbors for the problems caused by the haze. The apology, however, did not stop Jakarta's neighbors from holding it accountable for this transboundary haze crisis—reflecting ASEAN officials and citizens' increasing intolerance of Indonesia's lack of action in stopping the haze from escalating into a major regional problem. But more important, regional leaders have called for Indonesia to ratify the Agreement on Transboundary Haze and Pollution adopted by ASEAN members in 2002. Regional pressures eventually resulted in Jakarta's announcement at the ASEAN ministerial meeting held in October 2006 that it would finally ratify and comply with the agreement.

Asia's new regionalism has reached a critical point where a collective will must address new security challenges. Declarations of intention and soft commitment have to give way to more common action in solving common problems, more binding commitments, and more credible enforcement of regional agreements or modalities adopted to address different types of NTS challenges. Many of these emergent commitments and initiatives are still at an early stage, and it may take some time to assess fully their results. Nevertheless, despite obvious institutional limitations and domestic constraints, the future regional security architecture in Asia will reflect a greater sense of cohesion and openness to explore and implement regional solutions.

NOTES

1. The Consortium of Non-Traditional Security Studies in Asia, otherwise known as NTS-Asia, has adopted this definition of the term *nontraditional security*. For more details, see the NTS-Asia Web site at http://www.rsis-ntsasia.org.

2. The following observations are drawn largely from the Council of Asia Europe Cooperation project on Global Governance as Challenge for Cooperation, in which I was involved. See also William Wallace and Young Soogil, eds., *Asia and Europe:*

Global Governance as a Challenge to Cooperation (Tokyo: Japan Center for International Exchange, 2004).

3. Wallace and Soogil, *Asia and Europe*, 1.

4. John Gerard Ruggie, ed., *Multilateralism Matters: The Theory and Praxis of an Institutional Form* (New York: Columbia University Press, 1993), 7.

5. Bjorn Hettne, András Inotai, and Osvaldo Sunkel, *Globalisation and the New Regionalisation* (London: Macmillan, 1999), xvi.

6. Jean Grugel, "New Regionalism and Modes of Governance—Comparing US and EU Strategies in Latin America," *European Journal of International Relations* 10, no. 40 (2004): 604.

7. Anthony Payne, "Globalisation and Modes of Regionalist Governance," in *Debating Governance: Authority, Steering, and Democracy*, ed. Jon Pierre (Oxford: Oxford University Press, 2000), 201–18.

8. Kanishka Jayasuriya, ed., *Governing the Asia Pacific: Beyond the "New Regionalism"* (London: Palgrave Macmillan, 2004).

9. See, for example, Mely Caballero-Anthony, Ralf Emmers, and Amitav Acharya, eds., *Non-traditional Security in Asia: Dilemmas in Securitisation* (London: Ashgate, 2006).

10. Ibid. See also Ralf Emmers, Mely Caballero-Anthony, and Amitav Acharya, eds., *Studying Non-traditional Security in Asia: Trends and Issues* (Singapore: Marshall Cavendish, 2006).

11. For more on SARS and its security impact, see Mely Caballero-Anthony, "SARS in Asia: Crisis, Vulnerabilities, and Regional Responses," *Asian Survey* 45, no. 3 (2005): 475–95; Melissa Curley and Nicholas Thomas, "Human Security and Public Health in Southeast Asia: The SARS Outbreak," *Australian Journal of International Affairs* 58, no. 1 (2004): 17–32; Elizabeth Prescott, "SARS: A Warning," *Survival* 45, no. 3 (2003): 162–77.

12. World Economic Forum (WEF), *Global Risks, 2006* (Geneva: WEF, 2006), 1–12, http://www.weforum.org/pdf/CSI/global_Risk_Report.pdf.

13. "WHO Says Attention Must Not Be Shifted from 'Ground Zero' in Southeast Asia," *Straits Times*, October 18, 2005.

14. Ibid.

15. In June 2005, the Singapore government put into place its avian flu plan. See Ministry of Health, Singapore, "Influenza Pandemic Readiness and Response Plan," June 29, 2005, http://www.fao.org/docs/eims/upload//221490/national_plan_ai_sin_en.pdf. Since February 2004, it has also established tight surveillance and control over the local poultry population.

16. Luz Baguiro, "Fund Set Up to Fight Flu in S-E Asia," *Straits Times*, October 1, 2005.

17. "Singapore Holds Large-Scale Flu Pandemic Exercises," July 21, 2006, http://www.chanelnewsasia.com/stories/singaporelocalnews/view/220482/htm.

18. Ibid.

19. ASEAN Secretariat, "Kuala Lumpur Declaration on the ASEAN Plus Three Summit," Kuala Lumpur, Malaysia, December 12, 2005, http://www.aseansec.org/18o936.htm.

20. ASEAN Secretariat, "East Asia Summit Declaration on Avian Influenza Prevention, Control, and Response," Kuala Lumpur, Malaysia, December 14, 2005, http://www.aseansec.org/18101.htm.

21. Ibid.

22. U.S. Department of Health, Bureau of Public Affairs, "United States International Engagement on Avian and Pandemic Influenza," September 22, 2006, http://www.state.gov/r/pa/scp/2006/72923.htm.

23. Claude Allen, Deputy Secretary of Health and Human Resources, remarks at the Regional Emerging Diseases Intervention (REDI) Center, Singapore, May 24, 2004, http://singapore.usembassy.gov/052404.html.

24. APEC Secretariat, "Joint Statement of the 17th APEC Ministerial Meeting," Busan, South Korea, November 15–16, 2006, http://www.apec.org/apec/ministerial_statements/annualmeeting/2005_17th_apec.

25. For more on this issue, see Mely Caballero-Anthony, "Combating Infectious Diseases in East Asia: Securitisation and Global Public Goods for Health and Human Security," *Journal of International Affairs* 59, no. 2 (2006): 105–27.

26. "WHO, Asian Partners to Simulate Bird Flu Outbreak to Test Readiness to Contain Pandemic," *International Herald Tribune*, March 27, 2007.

27. "Statement from the Special ASEAN Leaders' Meeting on Aftermath of Earthquake and Tsunami," Jakarta, Indonesia, January 6, 2005, http://www.aseansec.org/17067.htm.

28. ASEAN Secretariat, "ASEAN Agreement on Disaster Management and Emergency Response," Vientiane, Laos, July 26, 2005, http://http://www.aseansec.org/17587.htm.

29. ASEAN Secretariat, "Chairman's Statement of the Twelfth Meeting of the ASEAN Regional Forum (ARF)," Vientiane, Laos, July 29, 2005, http://www.aseansec.org/17642.htm.

30. "Asia to Strengthen Civilian-Military Disaster Cooperation," Agence France-Presse, July 28, 2006.

31. APEC Senior Officials Meeting Chair, "APEC Strategy on Response to and Preparedness for Emergency and Natural Disasters," Seoul, South Korea, March 3–4, 2005, http://www.apecsec.org.sg/apec/apec_groups/som_special_task_groups/emergency_preparedness.html.

32. For more on improving preparedness, see Mely Caballero-Anthony, "Will Asia Heed Warning of Jakarta's Katrina?" *Today*, February 7, 2007, http://www.todayonline.com/articles/170454.

33. "5th Shangri-La Dialogue Calls for More Practical Cooperation," Xinhua News Agency, June 9, 2006, http://www.china.org.cn/english/international/170409.

htm. See also "Japan Seeks to Lead in Asian Disaster Relief," Japan Economic Newswire, June 3, 2006.

34. Established in 1998, the Coordination Center comprises forty-six member countries, representing the North Atlantic Treaty Organization's Euro-Atlantic Partnership Council. It has been designed to be a regional coordination mechanism that supports and complements the United Nations in its efforts to provide immediate assistance and relief to disaster-affected countries within the Partnership Council's area.

35. See, for example, Alan Dupont, *East Asia Imperilled: Transnational Challenges to Security* (Cambridge: Cambridge Asia Pacific Studies, 2001).

36. ASEAN Secretariat, "Joint Declaration of ASEAN and China on Cooperation in the Field of Non-Traditional Security Issues," Phnom Penh, Cambodia, November 4, 2002, http://www.aseansec.org/13185.htm.

37. For more on ACCORD and its plan of action, see http://www.undoc.un.or.th/accord/default.htm.

38. "ASEAN Declaration on Joint Action to Counter Terrorism," Bandar Seri Begawan, Brunei Darussalam, November 5, 2001, http://www.aseansec.org/7424.htm.

39. "Joint Communiqué of the Special ASEAN Ministerial Meeting on Terrorism," Kuala Lumpur, Malaysia, May 20–21, 2002, http://www.aseansec.org/5618.htm.

40. "ASEAN Declaration on Joint Action to Counter Terrorism."

41. "Australia Raises Counter-terrorism Assistance to Indonesia," ANTARA News Agency, December 8, 2004.

42. ASEAN Secretariat, "Matrix of ASEAN Regional Forum Decisions and Status," updated annually, http://www.aseansec.org/18600.htm.

43. ASEAN Secretariat, "Co-Chairs' Statement on Bali Regional Ministerial Meeting on Counter-Terrorism," Bali, February 5, 2004, http://www.aseansec.org/16001.htm.

44. For a recent study in this area, see Sam Bateman, Catherine Zara Raymond, and Joshua Ho, *Safety and Security in the Malacca and Singapore Straits: An Agenda for Action*, policy paper (Singapore: Institute of Defence and Strategic Studies, Nanyang Technological University, May 2006).

45. For more on the Regional Cooperation Agreement, see http://www.recaap.org/html/.

46. "ASEAN Socio-cultural Community in the ASEAN Bali Concord II," http://www.aseansec.org/15159.htm.

47. Asian Development Bank, *Asian Development Outlook, 2006* (Tokyo: Asian Development Bank, 2006), http://www.adb.org.

48. In the Gini coefficient measure of income inequality, zero means that all persons in a given society have the same income, and 1.0 means that one person has all the income. China recently surpassed the United States in its Gini coefficient, reflecting a greater concentration of wealth in China than in the United States.

49. Mely Caballero-Anthony, "Bridging Development Gaps in ASEAN: Towards an ASEAN Community," *UNISCI Journal*, no. 11 (2006): 37–48.

50. ASEAN Secretariat, "Vientiane Action Programme," http://www.aseansec.org/VAP-10th%20ASEAN%20Summit.pdf.

51. "Charter to Protect Workers in ASEAN," *The STAR*, December 5, 2005.

52. In the bilateral currency-swap arrangement, each party can request the other to enter into a swap transaction to provide liquidity support to overcome balance-of-payment difficulties in the specified currency up to a specified amount. As of November 10, 2004, the total size of the arrangement was U.S.$36.5 billion. See ASEAN Secretariat, "The Joint Ministerial Meeting of the 8th ASEAN + 3 Finance Ministers' Meeting," Istanbul, Turkey, May 4, 2005, http://www.aseansec.org/17448.htm; Denis Hew, ed., *Roadmap to an ASEAN Economic Community* (Pasir Panjang, Singapore: Institute of Southeast Asian Studies, 2005).

53. ASEAN Secretariat, "The Joint Ministerial Meeting of the 8th ASEAN + 3 Finance Ministers' Meeting."

54. See, for example, "Challenges of Building an East Asian Community," *Jakarta Post*, April 7, 2005; Singapore Institute of International Affairs, "The US Should Not Ignore or Veto East Asian Summit," July 14, 2005, http://www.siiaonline.org/us_east_asian_summit.

55. Pacific Economic Cooperation Council, *Report on State of the Region: 2006–2007* (Singapore: Pacific Economic Cooperation Council, 2006), http://www.asiapacificbusiness.ca/peo/SOTR/SOTR2006_2007.pdf.

56. Fred Bergsten, *China and Economic Integration in East Asia: Implications for the United States*, Policy Brief in International Economics no. PB07-03 (Washington, D.C.: Peter G. Peterson Institute for International Economics, March 2007), 9.

57. Husain Haqqani, "Earthquake Relief Can Win Allies in the Muslim World," *Asian Wall Street Journal*, October 11, 2005.

13. Challenges to Building an Effective Asia-Pacific Security Architecture

Brendan Taylor and William T. Tow

As the previous chapters in this volume so clearly demonstrate, "security architecture" has emerged as the latest concept for describing emerging frameworks in regional security politics. However, as they also demonstrate, widespread agreement about just what constitutes a security architecture and how it can be best applied remains elusive despite its popular application to ongoing discussions about contemporary security. The stakes in coming to agreement are critical because the alternative to a stable and enduring Asia-Pacific security order are a far less prosperous and far more dangerous regional outlook.

Analysts focusing on security architectures have identified some key conditions for their formation and management. These conditions include the emergence of a leading actor (or set of actors) within a region (or throughout the world) that is able to define the "rules" or norms that shape an architecture's purpose and structure. Just as important, other states must accept such leadership to the extent that regional or international conflict is visibly reduced and tangible order building occurs.[1] Such objectives, however, can be—and have been—realized through different means, and therefore little consensus exists on what actually constitutes an architecture. Moreover, unanticipated and politically volatile domestic changes are increasingly generating panregional and transregional consequences that may supersede even the most intricately crafted security mechanisms.

A major roadblock to defining and cross-comparing architectural "models" applicable to the Asia Pacific is the sheer number of available options. One can argue, for example, that Beijing's current ascension to great-power status fore-shadows its establishment of a hierarchical system similar to the suzerainty exercised by dynastic China.[2] Others insist that a more complicated system of regional power balancing or bandwagoning is emerging in which China, the United States, and other great powers such as Japan, India, and Russia will vie for positionality through selective coalition building, and smaller powers will "hedge" against them.[3] A variant of this pattern would be the application of overlapping bilateral and multilateral security relationships to fashion a complex system of existing and nascent alliances, coalitions, and regimes designed to achieve and sustain a tacit regional balance of power as an intermediate phase to negotiating a more enduring pan-Asian security regime underwritten by common norms and interests that currently remain indefinable.[4] Still others anticipate that an East Asian concert will develop among the four or five great powers to neutralize balancing and hedging tactics that, if unchecked, might lead to miscalculation and war.[5] Those concerned with "nontraditional" or "alternative" security scenarios maintain that structural threats such as state-centric nuclear arms races or energy competition are less likely to destabilize the Asia Pacific than non-state-centric hazards such as pandemics, global warming, and international terrorism (for more on such hazards, see chapter 12 in this volume).[6] In each case, there is a powerful argument for creating structures or mechanisms to manage that particular circumstance more effectively, but no one model has yet commanded sufficient support to prevail as the architectural typology of choice. It is imperative for future regional stability that such a typology be identified and gradually implemented.

It is becoming increasingly important to understand the dynamics of Asia-Pacific security architecture and the factors that shape it. The need to design and implement effective architectural formulas is evident at a time when the future of U.S. global power and how it will be applied in the region are becoming more ambiguous. For example, many regional policymakers view the U.S. bilateral alliance network in the Asia Pacific—the region's predominant stabilizing or balancing instrument for more than half a century, commonly known as the "San Francisco system" in honor of the city where it originated as part of the Japanese peace treaty after World War II—as an insufficient and outdated mechanism for underwriting regional stability. As China's economic and strategic weight increases and as Washington's geopolitical preoccupations continue to be directed toward the Middle East and the long war against terrorism, Asia-Pacific security arrangements are being shaped by a greater sense of Asian identity and by intensified pressure to structure a future security architecture along more regionally exclusive lines. Yet, as we see from many of the chapters in this volume, widely trumpeted Asian collective institutional norms have thus far failed to take precedence over the sovereign prerogative motivations of new or reconstituted Asian states and do not at this stage appear likely to trump the hard-power realities of Asia-Pacific relations. Such states' legacies of conflicts and rivalries from decolonization and social revolution continue to condition their interstate relationships and necessitate an ongoing U.S. offshore balancing role to adjudicate the region's security politics.

This dichotomous condition suggests that the Asia-Pacific security environment may well be experiencing what Kent Calder and Ming Ye characterize as a "critical juncture" in geopolitical development: "a historical decision point at which there are clear alternative paths to the future."[7] The character and viability of Asia-Pacific security architecture beyond this juncture will hinge on whether regional "architects" can reach consensus over how power-balancing strategies can be reconciled with institutional approaches to best build order in the Asia Pacific. Arriving at an agreement over what norms and values are required to facilitate such order building and over what institutions can best shape this process will be critical. Comprehending "security architecture" is therefore important not only because it "tells us something of a region's underlying logic," but also because it provides insight into "the design which is in the minds of its leading architects."[8] In the final analysis, however, the visions of "security architecture" now competing for dominance in the Asia Pacific must ultimately be resolved if a credible and enduring regional security order is to be realized.

WHY "SECURITY ARCHITECTURE"?

One first-order impediment to building a security architecture is the fact that the very term itself remains ambiguous and has spawned a growing debate over its relevance and applicability. Skeptics are particularly concerned that the term *security architecture* implies a static trend as opposed to the term *security arrangements*, which implies growth and development due to the efforts of various "architects" rather than one "master builder." In an Asia-Pacific context, factors related to sovereign prerogatives and an absence of "socially reconstructed sovereignty" (such as that which has taken place in Europe) are also seen to have limited the architecture concept's applicability.[9] Others debate the connections between institutions and architecture, concerned that "hyperinstitutionalism" does nothing more than generate an overabundance of such groupings without reconciling the countervailing national interests that their members bring to the table. If so, they argue, there cannot be any grand design, as the term *architecture* implies, but just an amalgam of loosely constructed networks that come and go as issues change.[10]

In theory, the ecumenical qualities of the term *security architecture* can be seen as a positive asset. It effectively accommodates the rationalist (realist and liberal-institutionalist) insistence that institutions and other groupings must adjudicate their individual members' national interests. It also conforms to the constructivist or ideational expectation that regional security collaboration can be "cultivated" apart from national interests by broadening and deepening networks of bargaining and collaboration between key actors. Likewise, *security architecture* circumvents the problem of whether regional order building is best considered from a top-down (global or state-centric and hierarchical-based) or bottom-up (individual or nonstate and actor-based) perspective.[11] Architecture in all its forms can be approached as either a top-down or bottom-up process and often optimally as a combination of the two approaches.

The flexibility offered by the security architecture concept has also appealed to practitioners of Asia-Pacific security who for political reasons have regarded it as advantageous to retain at least some of the definitional ambiguity surrounding the term. The concept appropriately highlights the idea that policy approaches and mechanisms can be fashioned to modify existing security structures in order to meet evolving security challenges. During the Cold War, the United States and its Asian allies formed a bilateral security network to contain what they viewed to be relentless Communist expansionism and to provide a buffer for the economic reconstruction or development of regional polities under the U.S. umbrella of extended deterrence guarantees. More recently, the Association of Southeast Asian Nations (ASEAN) created the ASEAN Regional Forum (ARF) to enmesh both American and Chinese regional security behavior within an Asian-centric version of regional order. By doing so, Southeast Asian elites modified the politics of balancing in their subregion and facilitated the coordination of great-power support for their own enterprise of building a security community. Despite great-power tendencies to view multilateralism or institutionalism as impediments to their own national-security agendas, alliances and institutions in the Asia Pacific have thus far been flexible enough to coexist and occasionally even to complement each other within the evolving contemporary regional security environment.[12] Such flexibility has resulted in policymakers' and independent analysts' using the term *security architecture* in describing their visions for achieving the linkage between an acceptable power equilibrium and institutional growth.[13]

The task of reconciling the diverse and somewhat jumbled architectural visions remains a major policy challenge. The bland and at least superficially nonthreatening connotations associated with the security architecture concept—relative, at least, to terms with a more definitive ring, such as *arrangements* or *systems*—can and often do generate an image of structural legitimization that can facilitate regional security cooperation. Everyone is capable of imagining their own (preferred) community by favoring the interests and values that would underwrite it. However, hard choices and compromises must be made between competing state-centric interests and in response to challenges that transcend state boundaries, such as global warming and pandemics. A broader, inclusive, and trans-Pacific definition of the term *architecture* embraces a sufficient array of interests, institutions, and identities for those decisions and for those who make them to command sufficient recognition as integral to building order.

NEW ARCHITECTS, NEW CHALLENGES, NEW COMPETITION

Accepting that "security architecture" is a useful concept and an overarching goal toward which virtually all the key actors in the region can aspire, analysts and practitioners must consider the main features of a contemporary Asia-Pacific security architecture and those factors that are likely to be instrumental in determining its future identity and composition. At least five critical factors bear heavily on the future development of an effective, regionwide security architecture: (1) the expanding number of architects or "builders" who will either find new forms of consensus or exacerbate regional security anarchy by failing to do so; (2) the sheer number of institutions and mechanisms that if not carefully managed may dilute order building and by default lead to a hierarchical or unnecessarily competitive regional security order; (3) the intensified amalgamation of traditional and nontraditional security issues in the Asia Pacific; (4) the tension between "exclusive" and "inclusive" approaches to regional order building; and (5) the principal architects' competitive and contrasting visions of the future.

ASPIRING ARCHITECTS

Prior to the 1990s, a tangible Asia-Pacific architecture remained elusive. This elusiveness continued not for want of trying, though. Several ill-fated efforts were undertaken to establish regional groupings that over time provided the basis for a more substantial Asia-Pacific architecture. These efforts included the Southeast Asia Treaty Organization, an eight-member grouping established in 1954 that never gained a consensus among its members over its strategic purpose and was finally dissolved in 1977, and the Association of Southeast Asia, which gave way to the founding of ASEAN in 1967.[14] The more successful subregional ASEAN expanded via several avenues, including the ARF (created in 1994). But even ASEAN's initial collaborative functions were essentially economic, political, and cultural, and its latest manifestations—ASEAN Plus Three (APT) and the East Asia Summit (EAS)—focus more on these issues than on the more difficult and sensitive questions of strategy, geopolitics, and hard-security challenges.

The near dearth of Asia-Pacific security institutions during the Cold War largely explains why the so-called San Francisco system of U.S. bilateral alliances and other security relationships in the region is frequently described as an "architecture" in its own right. To be sure, U.S. Asia-Pacific alliances remain an integral component of the region's architecture, and—notwithstanding the process of "transformation" the system is undergoing to accommodate the dynamics of the strategic environment after the September 11, 2001, attacks in New York City (see chapter 11 in this volume)—some of these relationships (the U.S.-Japan and U.S.-Australia alliances) have actually strengthened during the period since the end of the Cold War, contrary to the expectations of conventional theories of alliance politics.[15]

Because the hierarchical aspects of the San Francisco system are giving way to more fluid processes of intra-alliance consultations, however, new "minilateral" mechanisms such as the U.S.-Japan-South Korea Trilateral Coordination and Oversight Group and the U.S.-Japan-Australia Trilateral Security Dialogue (TSD) have been formed to address emerging security issues at both the regional level and the global level. This "expansive bilateralism" has been supplemented since the early 1990s by a startling growth in regional institutions, arrangements, and structures. According to one recent estimate, more than one hundred such channels now exist at the official (track-one) level, including such leading regional security institutions as the ARF, the Shanghai Cooperation Organization (SCO), and the EAS, which, despite its largely economic focus, still has the potential to emerge over time as an influential East Asian security mechanism.[16] More ad hoc but still substantial multilateral initiatives have also been undertaken regarding specific issues—such as the Four-Power Talks and later the Six-Party Talks concerning security on the Korean Peninsula. The growth in institutions and dialogues at the unofficial (or track-two) level has been even more profound, with in excess of two hundred such channels now estimated to exist.[17] Some of these processes have had visibly positive or stabilizing effects on Asia-Pacific order building, such as the informal "Jakarta workshop" discussions that led to the forging of the Declaration on the Conduct of Parties in the South China Sea in 2002 to manage peacefully the territorial dispute between China and the ASEAN claimants to the Spratly Islands.

TOO MANY ARCHITECTS?

As the volume of regional security institutions and activities has grown, so too has the number of architects involved in their design and construction. ASEAN is now moving to transform its earlier (1976) Treaty of Amity and Cooperation (TAC) into a more comprehensive ASEAN charter that envisions how its member states will shape their own intrastate relations and how they will condition outside powers to relate to them collectively. China and Russia spearheaded the SCO initially to settle long-standing border disputes between China and its Central Asian neighbors and to confront terrorism, separatism, and extremism in their region, but they now seem to see the body as a potential instrument to counter the North Atlantic Treaty Organization's expanding strategic influence in Afghanistan and in other former member states of the old Soviet bloc. The Asia-Pacific Economic Cooperation (APEC) forum is moving aggressively to put its stamp on broader, nontraditional security politics relating to global climate change, the response to a pandemic, and the safeguarding of maritime commerce. All of this stands in marked contrast to the Cold War period, during which time the United States was very much regarded as the "master builder" of whatever regional security architecture could be said to exist. Indeed, most regional actors interpreted intermittent Soviet efforts to initiate an "Asian collective security system" precisely for what they were: ill-founded tactics to isolate the region from U.S. or Chinese power, to compromise those powers within the region, and to compensate for the Soviet Union's singular lack of politicoeconomic appeal outside of North Korea, parts of Indochina, and perhaps India.[18]

A related feature of the contemporary expansion of security architects is that U.S. allies such as Australia, Canada, and Japan that accepted the U.S. hierarchy during the Cold War have emerged as increasingly direct contributors to the growth in Asia-Pacific (and international) security cooperation (see, for example, chapter 5 on Japan and chapter 7 on Australia in this volume). Australia has elevated its status within the U.S. alliance hierarchy by supporting U.S. military operations in Afghanistan and Iraq with its own force deployments in those countries and by assuming a leading role in stabilizing potential failed states throughout the South Pacific's so-called arc of instability. Canada has become a major force in developing and advancing human-security agendas. Japan is "normalizing" its strategic identity by supporting U.S. global strategy with modest force deployments abroad in noncombat roles and by gradually intensifying its security ties with India and peninsular ASEAN states.

The proliferation of security architects has not been limited to just U.S. security allies. Since the late 1990s, in an apparent embrace of multilateralism,

China has played a leading role in the establishment of a number of high-profile regional institutions, including the SCO, the Boao Forum for Asia, and the Network of East Asia Think Tanks (see chapter 3 in this volume).[19] The potential for India to become a leading regional security architect is also growing (see chapter 6 in this volume). The United States remains a qualified player in the intensification of multilateral regional politics, and concerns are rising in Washington that its once firm monopoly over core security trends may be dissipating. It increasingly recognizes, however, that it cannot afford to be seen as a marginal force in what appears to be an increasingly predominant trend for Asia-Pacific actors to seek security through dialogue and diplomatic instrumentalities.[20]

CONFLUENCE OF TRADITIONAL AND NONTRADITIONAL SECURITY

The rising diversity in the size and shape of the region's security institutions and activities is in part attributable to the Asia Pacific's strategic environment becoming more demanding and complex. As Mely Caballero-Anthony details in chapter 12, the persistence of traditional security concerns—such as the proliferation of weapons of mass destruction, regional flashpoints, and the prospect of a destabilizing arms race—has been complicated by an increasing range of nontraditional security challenges, including international terrorism, transnational crime, environmental issues, and potentially pandemic disease. As the continuing North Korean nuclear crisis and the plight of a perpetually starving North Korean population demonstrate all too well, there is also a growing awareness of the interdependence between the traditional and the nontraditional security agendas—a realization that has in turn fundamentally recast the dynamics of regional security cooperation. In the case of the U.S.-led system of bilateral alliances, for example, there is evidence of a shift (albeit intermittent at this stage) of focus toward nonmilitary security challenges, as demonstrated by the Indian Ocean tsunami relief effort of late 2004 and early 2005.

Hence, an emerging problem in reconciling traditional and nontraditional security paradigms is how key architects decide what should be "securitized" in the national interest. Such decisions all too often correlate more with sustaining the domestic political power base than with pursuing greater regional stability. After Chinese leaders initially denied that their country had a problem with the severe acute respiratory syndrome (SARS) virus in early 2003, for instance, they moved forcefully to implement quarantine measures, build or restructure hospitals to cope with the outbreak, sack local Communist Party officials to atone for covering up the outbreak, and collaborated with appropriate international organizations such as the World Health Organization (WHO) to check the epidemic. Yet they steadfastly opposed Taiwan's inclusion in WHO consultations as an independent participant, insisting that Taiwan, which was experiencing its own SARS outbreak, could interact with that institution only as a part of the People's Republic of China.[21] Upholding sovereign interests rather than pursuing greater regional stability has also been at the center of Australia's efforts in maintaining detention centers for the incarceration of undocumented migrants and of ASEAN member states' latent resistance to adopting common security responses to transnational crime. As long as these trends persist and prevail, striking a judicious balance between traditional and nontraditional functions within the Asia Pacific's architecture will remain difficult.

COMPETITIVE COMMUNITY BUILDING: EXCLUSIVITY VERSUS INCLUSIVITY

Another key characteristic of the Asia Pacific's architecture is a growing focus on East Asian community building. At the track-one level, this characteristic has been reflected in the establishment of a number of high-profile institutions, including the EAS. This trend is also being mirrored at the track-two level, as recently evidenced in the establishment of the Network of East Asia Think Tanks and its Japanese competitor the Council on East Asian Community. In recent years, community building appears to have evolved around giving greater credence to the TAC as a condition for participating in this process. This condition is not particularly onerous given that the document itself is somewhat uncontroversial and that ASEAN members have been accommodating toward those countries, such as Japan and Australia, that were initially concerned that the TAC might violate conditions underwriting their bilateral security alliances with the United States.[22] Yet as one respected analyst of Asia-Pacific regionalism has observed, Asians are now assigning greater importance to the need for regional cooperation in an era of intensifying globalization: "Regionalism . . . is a process for competently handling globalisation and interdependence. It is also a competitive issue among Asians, given parallel developments in Europe and the Americas."[23]

The proliferation of such groupings does not by itself necessarily constitute progress toward regional security. These entities tend to compete with each other for attention as much as to coordinate their purposes and functions. This trend is complicated by their divergent and often contradictory missions. The APT process, for example, was initiated largely by Asian economies that viewed the U.S.-dominated International Monetary Fund as an uncompromising creditor relative to their vulnerabilities exposed during the 1997 Asian financial crisis. Operating from this premise, the initial exclusion of the United States from membership in the EAS (which evolved from APT dialogues and norm building) was a foregone conclusion.

Washington and its regional security partners carry out an exclusionary approach to the perpetuation and expansion of alliance politics in the region. Intensification of the Australia-Japan leg of the increasingly prominent TSD in March 2007 was given further impetus with the idea that the TSD be expanded to a quadrilateral mechanism to include India—a move that official and unofficial Chinese commentators interpret as a containment initiative.[24] China, however, appears to be no less determined to shape its own architecture diplomacy along exclusionary lines. Convened in Shanghai during May 2006, the sixth SCO Summit declared that "[d]ifference in cultural traditions, political and social systems, values and model[s] of development formed in the course of history should not be used as a pretext to interfere in other countries' internal affairs. Models of social development should not be exported." This statement was nothing less than a rationale to counter perceived U.S. unilateralism and Washington's determination to force its version of democracy on other regional actors.[25] Until such zero-sum characteristics of institutional formation and operation are overcome, the prospects for achieving the regionwide building of order in the Asia Pacific remain questionable.

THE UNITED STATES AND THE ACCOMMODATION OF OTHER "ARCHITECTS"

It is useful when envisioning the future of Asia-Pacific architecture to weigh the competing architectural designs of the region's leading security architects. The United States is no longer the "master builder" it once was when it comes to Asian regional security architecture. Future American accommodation of indigenous order-building initiatives will depend largely on the level and extent of the involvement of (especially) China and other major regional powers in such ventures. This conclusion is consistent with the fact that regional institutions and activities are gradually being viewed as instruments of competitive influence. However, the unprecedented military power of the United States, its unrivalled capacity to deploy air and naval assets in the Asia-Pacific region, and its latent, if currently underutilized political and economic "soft power" suggest that it will remain a leading architect whose preferences and aspirations must be taken into account. To do so will not always be easy for other Asia-Pacific actors because, as Ralph Cossa observes, American politicians "are not famous for their ability to think long term, much less to plan or act in accordance with future visions."[26] That weakness conceded, it remains clear that Washington's greatest institutional priority within the context of regional order building will be to engineer the smooth transformation of its bilateral network of alliances into a form wherein the junior partners in that structure work together in ways that are congruent to U.S. interests.

Beyond the transformation of the U.S.-led bilateral alliance network, one of the most peculiar features of U.S. Asia-Pacific policy during the George W. Bush administration has been its distinctly sanguine response to the obvious resurgence of East Asian regionalism.[27] There is little historical precedent for this acquiescence, which stands in stark contrast to the historic U.S. quest to preserve a preponderance of power.[28] This trend might conceivably be rationalized as a product of material shifts in the Asia-Pacific balance of power, which now precludes any one actor from assuming the role of the region's leading "security architect." The U.S. ability to make an ideational shift that reflects a genuine acceptance of these new realities will be critical in determining the future shape and viability of an Asia-Pacific regional architecture and, indeed, the future of regional stability more generally.[29]

China stands out as an increasingly influential regional "architect," particularly in light of its growing interest and involvement in regional institutions and activities, as well as its obvious attempts to shape these arrangements in line with its own national interests. Chinese policymakers clearly favor an "exclusive" approach to regional architecture, which is apparent not only in their efforts to keep the United States out of such nascent regional forums as the SCO and the EAS, but also in their initial opposition to Indian and Australian membership in the EAS. Malaysia, which some might regard as an aspiring regional architect in its own right, has been the most outwardly supportive of the "exclusivist" vision. However, this vision has encountered sharp opposition from other regional players, including Japan, Singapore, and Vietnam. Statements out of Beijing indicating that the United States will not forever be excluded from the EAS might justifiably be interpreted as an acknowledgement from China that even it sees the limits to its ability to implement an exclusivist architectural approach.[30] Yet China's growing economic and strategic weight in the region will intensify the question of whether opposition to China's "exclusivist" architectural preferences and prescriptions will be sustainable.

The United States and China must also take into account the approaches of the Asia Pacific's other two leading security architects—Japan and India. Japan is likely to remain a key regional player for some time to come by virtue of its sheer economic weight. However, its capacity to shape Asia-Pacific architecture is likely to be circumscribed by continuing preoccupations surrounding its gradual yet inexorable transition to "normal" status.[31] India, in contrast, has become an increasingly involved and accepted player in such leading mechanisms as the EAS and the SCO, and as a preferred political partner of ASEAN.[32] It is being courted by the United States, Japan, and Australia as a potential collaborator in a proposed regional "alliance of democracies." As India's economic and strategic weight continues to grow, its willingness and potential ability to influence the shape and design of Asia-Pacific architecture will increase.

ASEAN's future role as an "architect" in any regional security order remains uncertain. As David Martin Jones and Michael Smith recently observed, the gap between the rhetoric and the reality of ASEAN's achievements at the panregional level remains substantial.[33] None of the ASEAN-led processes, for instance, have proven able to respond effectively to the major regional crises that have erupted over the past decade and a half. In part as a result of the consensual-style approach to decision making that is ASEAN's preferred modus operandi, the organization has moved slowly in implementing stated aims and objectives. The ARF, for example, has experienced real difficulties in moving from the confidence-building phase to the preventive diplomacy phase in its evolution, which has contributed to the perception that it is nothing more than a "talk shop." ASEAN's influence as an architectural entrepreneur may well diminish as the economic and strategic weight of the region's other leading architects increase and as the architectural environment consequently becomes increasingly crowded and competitive. However, because ASEAN may yet succeed in strengthening its identity as a security organization—a tangible benefit of the ASEAN Charter—it would be premature at this juncture to dismiss altogether its long-standing architectural ambitions and capacity to influence great-power behavior.

This tendency among the Asia Pacific's great powers—especially China and the United States—to view the politics of architecture as a process of mixed cooperation and competitive influence is likely to dominate the region's geopolitics for some time to come. As Barry Buzan has observed, "If one brings the global and regional-level dynamics together in assessing Asian security, a quite powerful case can be made that the main scenario is a slow working out of the existing patterns."[34] In an order-building context, the mixture of cooperation and competition means that the United States will contain China militarily while engaging with it economically and bind Japan to those alliance components of the architecture that the United States dominates in order to preclude strategic miscalculation in either Beijing or Tokyo. For China, the mixture means waiting until its growing material capabilities will enable it to intensify exclusivist strategies in institutional politics at U.S. expense, but not to a point where these strategies trigger an overreaction by Japan as the latter moves to become a more "normal state."[35] The quite deliberate exclusion of the United States from the EAS and the open bickering between China and Japan that dominated the first gathering of this group can be seen as strong evidence of this unfolding geopolitical pattern.

Although the United States has been relatively slow in responding to such developments, there are signs that it is finally doing so through its ongoing efforts to infuse new meaning into its traditional regional alliance network. It is injecting a greater security focus into APEC, exploring ways to build a new U.S.-ASEAN partnership, and reportedly "looking closely" at signing the TAC.[36] How successful this U.S. reengagement ultimately turns out to be is likely to be heavily conditioned by the willingness of many, if not most, Asia-Pacific governments to run the risk of antagonizing not only China, but also their own domestic constituents if they openly support future U.S.-led regional security initiatives.

CONCLUSIONS AND A LOOK AHEAD

This chapter began by drawing upon Calder and Ye's observation that the Asia-Pacific security environment is currently experiencing a "critical juncture" in geopolitical development. Competing architectural visions are vying for dominance. Although the outcome of this evolving contest and therefore the contours of the emerging Asia-Pacific security architecture remain unclear, one of two alternative architectural paths appears likely to prevail. The more pessimistic scenario is that a "competitive geometries" model—an essentially zero-sum approach to institutional formation and operation—will become entrenched as a result of the regional architects' inability to agree over how power-balancing strategies can be reconciled with broader and more inclusive institutional pathways to order building in this part of the world. The more optimistic scenario is that this competitive architectural mind-set will ultimately be transcended, thereby facilitating the emergence of a more inclusive "cooperative security" framework that is institutionally based, underwritten by mutually agreeable norms and values, and designed to confront effectively the region's profoundly difficult security challenges.

This latter outcome is obviously both desirable and necessary. The findings of this chapter, however, suggest that the challenges to realizing this structure remain formidable and that, on balance, the more pessimistic scenario is most likely to prevail. To be sure, competitive and cooperative dynamics can and often do coexist in international relations. Yet as Calder and Ye's "critical juncture" analogy makes clear, we must not become complacent over the capacity for tensions to persist indefinitely between the exclusive "competitive geometries" model and the more inclusive "cooperative security" approach to order building. Moreover, the "tipping point" whereby one of these models attains dominance over the other may be closer than we think. As Nick Bisley has recently observed, "[T]he present order is in a state of flux in which current security arrangements are likely to change over the medium and long term. Thus the next five years or so will be important in determining the shape of things to come."[37]

The collective magnitude of the range of potential security threats facing the region is substantial. If history does indeed serve as a reliable guide, however, the conclusions that can be derived from this chapter's observations are mixed. The Asia Pacific is a region not unfamiliar with architecture-building efforts, yet the vast majority of these efforts have fallen on barren ground. The two clear exceptions are ASEAN and the San Francisco system. Even these "success stories" are coming under strain, though, in an increasingly demanding and complex contemporary strategic environment. The U.S. alliance system, for instance, is being forced to adapt in the face of emerging transnational security challenges that it was never initially designed to confront—such as international terrorism, proliferation of weapons of mass destruction, and growing recognition of the security implications of natural disasters such as the 2004 Indian Ocean tsunami.[38] Meanwhile, ASEAN's track record remains shaky. Although it has shown some ability to adjust its agenda to incorporate a new crop of transborder security threats, its capacity to shape regional security outcomes may well diminish significantly as other aspiring architects bring their burgeoning economic and strategic weight to bear. In this context, the intermittent and overly euphoric sense of an impending regional community needs to be balanced against a clearheaded and candid recognition of the substantial challenges to building an effective and sustainable Asia-Pacific architecture.

The primary difference between the Asia Pacific of today and that of yesteryear is the sheer plethora of available channels for regional security dialogue, which constitutes some basis for optimism about the future of order building in the region. Somewhat ironically, however, the emergence of these channels has raised as many problems as it has potentially addressed. The multiplicity of multilateral institutions and activities in the Asia Pacific has afforded the region's great powers, in particular, the option of using these mechanisms as instruments of competitive influence. These regional heavyweights will occasionally square off against one another within institutional settings, as occurred between China and Japan at the inaugural EAS. Yet more often than not the broad menu of choice allows the region's great powers to make their presence felt within those institutions where they feel most comfortable and where they have the most influence—Beijing in APT and the SCO; Moscow in the SCO; Washington in APEC and through its own ad hoc mechanisms, such as the TSD and the Proliferation Security Initiative (PSI); and Tokyo in the ARF and increasingly the EAS as it strives to check China's growing influence in the APT process. That said, the fact that these structures have been established and persist arguably provides some cause for optimism, particularly given their capacity to curb the great powers' worst tendency to act solely in their own interests, or "anarchically."

None of these trends suggest, therefore, that the "competitive geometries" model must inevitably prevail. Architecture takes time to evolve—time for deepseated national and historical differences to be smoothed over, for compromises in architectural visions to be made, and for common understandings and norms to be agreed upon and implemented. It is important, of course, not to underestimate the potential and appeal of powerful concepts such as an East Asian community. Regionalism, too, is a painstakingly slow and gradual process, as the European process of architectural formation illustrates all too well. Yet time may not be kind to this process in the Asia-Pacific context given the sheer size, scope, and potential speed of many of the region's most pressing security challenges.

As the region negotiates this critical juncture in its geopolitical development, and regardless of whether the "competitive geometries" model or the more inclusive "cooperative security" approach to order building in this part of the world ultimately prevails, the U.S. role will remain critical, at least for the foreseeable future. Notwithstanding ongoing speculation about "community building" in the region, the United States still remains the only country with the material capabilities and assets to respond to a genuine regional crisis. As the protracted North Korean nuclear crisis demonstrates, however, the United States cannot always go it alone—not least because of its competing preoccupations in Southwest Asia and the Middle East.

Against that backdrop, if the "cooperative security" framework is to stand a chance, some accommodation by all parties will be required. The United States will need to become more comfortable with the notion that it cannot sustain its preeminence without accommodating and working with the interests of other major powers in the region. If it does not, the region will become less and less conducive to U.S. hegemony. Countries of the region in their turn also need to be mindful of the increasing marginalization of such a critical actor as the United States both from and within regional forums. A United States that senses its growing exclusion may ultimately opt to devote its energies to more temporary, ad hoc mechanisms that it can lead and engage on its on own terms. The PSI is already one such framework, as is the proposed Asia-Pacific "alliance of democracies." Countries of the region need to be careful about "what they wish for" because a Washington that further reinforces its traditionally heavy reliance on bilateral approaches to Asia-Pacific security, a Washington that seeks to apply the unilateral solutions to Asia-Pacific security problems, and a Washington that adds new mechanisms characterized by a heightened degree of expediency and informality to an already overcrowded regional security architecture is also a Washington that will generate numerous and potentially insurmountable "design faults" in the emerging regional architecture.[39]

Barring a shift in strategic mind-sets that appears improbable at the present time, however, it remains unlikely that the "cooperative security" framework and thereby a regionwide architecture that can effectively moderate state-centric rivalries, facilitate conflict avoidance, and respond to an ever wider array of security challenges will emerge. China is still determining its own regional security identity and appears caught between a preference for competing against residual U.S. power in the region and a growing receptivity to greater enmeshment by adopting the "responsible stakeholder" model. Its ultimate choice may well be guided by how effectively its leadership is able to check nationalist forces within China who are clamoring for the imminent annexation of Taiwan, to settle other irredentist and territorial disputes with its regional neighbors, and, ultimately, to avoid a confrontation with the United States to determine the future of global hegemony. It will also be influenced, however, by future U.S. administrations' success in checking anti-China lobbies and in controlling allied behavior in the region to the extent that Washington avoids becoming entrapped in a confrontation with Beijing by accident rather than by design. Until Sino-American bilateral relations are stable enough to produce and sustain reliable and permanent instruments for avoiding such miscalculation, the prospects for the "cooperative security" framework to prevail in the Asia Pacific will remain low.

In the absence of a Sino-American modus vivendi, multiple and competing architectural designs will continue to emerge. Such "competing geometries" may include the intensification of the SCO as a "de facto" anti-Western grouping, the further development of U.S.-led trilateral or other multilateral security dialogues as tacit instruments of containment against growing Chinese power, and even the globalization (or "Eurasianization") of various U.S. alliances and coalitions to check perceived competitors' geopolitical advances beyond traditional regional confines. China's expanding engagement in Africa and its cultivation of ties with Iran may be potential catalysts for this form of U.S.-led geopolitics to solidify over the next decade. Intensified Sino-Russian global strategic collaboration may also trigger a response from the United States and its allies to maintain what it would view to be an acceptable Asia-Pacific balance of power.

What, if anything, can be done to arrest these worrisome regional trends? First and foremost, regional security architects must boldly and as a matter of great urgency strive to develop and implement new approaches to overcome this seemingly intractable tendency of Asia-Pacific states to pursue sovereign interests and accrue geopolitical power at each other's expense. ASEAN leaders appear to have recognized the need for this approach by embracing the unmitigated liberal agendas reflected in the ASEAN *Vision 2020* document approved at their Hanoi summit in December 1998 and incorporated into the ASEAN Charter draft.[40] They also have "conditioned" great-power behavior by enmeshing these powers' cooperation in the "debalkanization" of the ASEAN region following the 1991 Cambodia peace accord and in the conflict-avoidance initiatives directed toward the South China Sea. The traditional "flashpoints" that remain as possible catalysts for war in the region loom in Northeast Asia and on the Indian subcontinent. In both instances, however, recent diplomatic efforts to defuse the potential nuclear crises on the Korean Peninsula and over the control of Kashmir extend the promise of emulating the ASEAN experience and are encouraging.

Second, nontraditional security issues such as infectious disease, terrorism, transnational crime, and disaster prevention and mitigation will not only be increasingly critical, but also provide genuine opportunities to develop the level of trust required, particularly among the region's great powers, to establish a genuine architectural consensus. Within a week following the December 26, 2004, South Asian tsunami, for example, U.S. military officials spearheaded the creation of the Regional Core Group, initially comprising the United States, Australia, Japan, and India, to establish military and civilian assistance programs to the victims of that natural disaster.[41] Likewise, in May 2006 the inaugural ASEAN Defense Ministers' Meeting in Kuala Lumpur identified disaster-relief cooperation as a priority issue on which to focus its future work. As part of its transition from confidence building to practical cooperation, the ARF has also been asked to adopt collaborative measures for addressing nontraditional security challenges, if only to demonstrate its continuing relevance in the increasingly crowded Asia-Pacific security agenda.[42]

Addressing these kinds of transborder challenges is easier than addressing traditional security issues not only because the former are becoming increasingly pressing and potentially affect the region as a whole, but also because they tend not to raise the same level of sensitivity that such traditional security issues generate. More centrally, they create precedents for cultivating habits of cooperation that, if given sufficient time and resource allocation, may "spill over" to affect positively the security cooperation in hard-security policy arenas. The Six-Party Talks well illustrate such a spillover effect. This process offers the greatest hope for overcoming the quandary resulting from the inherent tendencies of the region's great powers to discount the possibility of a regional institutional order that can address future security challenges.

Ultimately, however, state-centric factors related to both interests and values will still need to be faced and resolved if an effective architecture is to be implemented in the Asia Pacific. In this context, great-power politics will arguably remain the most crucial determinant, and the future of the U.S.-China relationship will be especially pivotal. The United States may well not have been excluded from the EAS, for instance, were it and China not potential strategic rivals. Likewise, the future of the Sino-Japanese relationship will be critical in defining the Asia-Pacific architecture, as the inaugural EAS demonstrated all too vividly. The extent to which great-power rivalries can be modified or finessed sufficiently to cultivate a longer-term sense of "community"—the tacit but widely understood vision underlying the need for a successful architecture in the region—remains unclear. Yet it is reasonable to conclude that such success will be elusive if traditional norms or means of securing state-centric interests remain unbending. The challenge posited by "architecture," therefore, is how much its alleged proponents will genuinely endeavor to fulfill its vision and work collectively to overcome the challenges embodied in realizing it.

NOTES

1. Joseph McMillan, Richard Sokolsky, and Andrew C. Winner, "Toward a New Regional Security Architecture," *Washington Quarterly* 26, no. 3 (2003): 161–75. In this article, a comparison of the Persian Gulf and the ARF security architectural factors addresses these two points.

2. David C. Kang, "Hierarchy in International Relations: 1300–1900," *Asian Security* 1, no. 1 (2005): 53–79.

3. Evan S. Medeiros, "Strategic Hedging and the Future of Asia-Pacific Stability," *Washington Quarterly* 29, no. 1 (2005–2006): 145–67.

4. William T. Tow, *Asia-Pacific Strategic Relations: Seeking Convergent Security* (Cambridge: Cambridge University Press, 2001).

5. Coral Bell, "The Twilight of the Unipolar World," *American Interest* 1, no. 2 (2005): 18–29.

6. See chapter 12 in this volume and Alan Dupont, *East Asia Imperiled: Transnational Challenges to Security* (Cambridge: Cambridge University Press, 2001).

7. Kent Calder and Ming Ye, "Regionalism and Critical Junctures: Explaining the 'Organization Gap' in Northeast Asia," *Journal of East Asian Studies* 4, no. 2 (2004): 198–99.

8. Joseph A. Camilleri, *Regionalism in the New Asia-Pacific Order: The Political Economy of the Asia-Pacific Region* (Cheltenham: Elgar, 2003), 2:14.

9. Hanns W. Maull, "The European Security Architecture," in *Reassessing Security Cooperation in the Asia-Pacific: Competition, Congruence, and Transformation,* ed. Amitav Acharya and Evelyn Goh (Cambridge, Mass.: MIT Press, 2007), 254, 273–74.

10. This question was considered in discussion of a preliminary draft of this paper at the exploratory workshop "Comparative Regional Security," conducted at Cambridge University, November 2–4, 2006. We are particularly grateful to Ole Waever for raising this point.

11. For further reading, see T. J. Pempel, "Introduction: Emerging Webs of Regional Connectedness," in *Remapping East Asia: The Construction of a Region*, ed. T. J. Pempel (Ithaca, N.Y.: Cornell University Press, 2005), 13, 19–28.

12. This argument is found in Tow, *Asia-Pacific Strategic Relations*, 221–23.

13. See, for example, Joseph R. Nunez, *A 21st Century Security Architecture for the Americas: Multilateral Cooperation, Liberal Peace, and Soft Power* (Carlisle, Pa.: U.S. Army War College, 2002); Gulnur Aybet, *A European Security Architecture After the Cold War* (London: Macmillan, 2000).

14. John S. Duffield, "Asia-Pacific Security Institutions in Comparative Perspective," in *International Relations Theory and the Asia-Pacific*, ed. G. John Ikenberry and Michael Mastanduno (New York: Columbia University Press, 2003), 248. See also Charles E. Morrison and Astri Suhrke, *Strategies of Survival: The Foreign Policy Dilemmas of Smaller Asian States* (St. Lucia, Australia: University of Queensland Press, 1978); Leszek Buszynski, *SEATO: The Failure of an Alliance Strategy* (Singapore: Singapore University Press, 1983).

15. See, for example, Stephen M. Walt, *The Origins of Alliances* (Ithaca, N.Y.: Cornell University Press, 1987).

16. Japan Center for International Exchange, "Overview Report: July–December 2005," *Dialogue and Research Monitor: Towards Community Building in East Asia*, dialogue, http://www.jcie.or.jp/drm/overview.html.

17. Desmond Ball, Anthony Milner, and Brendan Taylor, "Track 2 Security Dialogue in the Asia-Pacific: Reflections and Future Directions," *Asian Security* 2, no. 3 (2006): 174–88, http://rspas.anu.edu.au/gssd/analysis/Taylor_AsianSecurity_Track2.pdf.

18. The classical assessment of Soviet collective security politics in the Asia Pacific remains Arnold Horelick, "The Soviet Union's Asian Collective Security Proposal: A Club in Search of Members," *Pacific Affairs* 47, no. 3 (1974): 269–85.

19. On China's embrace of multilateralism, see, for example, Bates Gill, *Rising Star: China's New Security Diplomacy* (Washington, D.C.: Brookings Institution Press, 2007), esp. chap. 2.

20. This impression was confirmed in interviews with Department of State officials, March 2006, Washington, D.C., in the aftermath of a decision by Secretary of State Condoleezza Rice not to attend the ARF in Kuala Lumpur, Malaysia, the previous year.

21. "China-Taiwan Spat Bubbles Over at WHO Meeting," *Asian Economic News*, June 24, 2003.

22. Paul Kelly, "The Day Foreign Policy Won Asia," *The Australian*, August 6, 2005.

23. Simon Tay, "East Asian Community and the United States: An East Asian Perspective," in "The Emerging East Asian Community: Should Washington Be Concerned?" ed. Ralph A. Cossa, Simon Tay, and Lee Chung-min, special issue of *Issues*

and Insights 5, no. 9 (2005): 17, http://www.csis.org/media/csis/pubs/issuesinsights_v05n09.pdf.

24. Patrick Walters and Rowan Callick, "India's Inclusion in Security Pact Risks Alienating China," *The Australian*, March 16, 2007.

25. Quoted in National Institute for Defense Studies, Japan (NIDS), *East Asian Strategic Review, 2007* (Tokyo: NIDS, 2007), 48–49.

26. Ralph A. Cossa, "U.S. Security Strategy in Asia and the Prospects for an Asian Regional Security Regime," *Asia-Pacific Review* 12, no. 1 (2005): 72.

27. For further reading, see Michael Wesley, "The Dog That Didn't Bark: The Bush Administration and East Asian Regionalism," in *Bush and Asia: America's Evolving Relations with East Asia*, ed. Mark Beeson (London: Routledge, 2006), 64–79.

28. On the U.S. quest to retain the preponderance of power in the years since the ending of the Cold War, see Evelyn Goh, "The ASEAN Regional Forum in United States East Asian Strategy," *Pacific Review* 17, no. 1 (2004): 47–69.

29. Hugh White, "Great Power Gambits to Secure Asia's Peace," *Far Eastern Economic Review* 170, no. 1 (2007): 7–11.

30. See, for example, Zhai Kun, "China Pursues Open Regional Cooperation," *China Daily*, January 23, 2007.

31. Kenneth B. Pyle, *Japan Rising: The Resurgence of Japanese Power and Purpose* (New York: Public Affairs, 2007).

32. C. Raja Mohan, "India and the Balance of Power," *Foreign Affairs* 85, no. 4 (2006): 22–23.

33. David Martin Jones and Michael L. R. Smith, "Constructing Communities: The Curious Case of East Asian Regionalism," *Review of International Studies* 33, no. 1 (2007): 165–86, http://journals.cambridge.org/download.php?file = %2FRIS%2FRIS33_01%2FS0260210507007736Xa.pdf&code = 4138d6507e90d51150aadfcbedad50cd.

34. Barry Buzan, "Security Architecture in Asia: The Interplay of Regional and Global Levels," *Pacific Review* 16, no. 2 (2003): 171.

35. Ibid., 170–71. An alternative viewpoint is presented in Julie Gilson, "Strategic Regionalism in East Asia," *Review of International Studies* 33, no. 1 (2007): 145–63, http://journals.cambridge.org/download.php?file = %2FRIS%2FRIS33_01%2FS0260210507007358a.pdf&code = f99994ec791ee9f65e74d9e8bd98cb77. Gilson argues that the region's significance is increasing in the foreign-policy agendas of China, Japan, and the United States, which in turn is subsequently facilitating and encouraging a new form of regional joint leadership.

36. Derwin Pereira, "ARF = Asean Relief Force?" *Straits Times*, August 1, 2007.

37. Nick Bisley, "Asian Security Architectures," in *Strategic Asia, 2007–2008: Domestic Political Change and Grand Strategy*, ed. Ashley J. Tellis and Michael Wills (Seattle: National Bureau of Asian Research, 2007), 342.

38. An excellent account of alliance dynamics as they operated in the 2004 tsunami context is Brad Williams, "Why Give? Japan's Response to the Asian Tsunami Crisis," *Japan Forum* 18, no. 3 (2006): 399–416.

39. Allan Gyngell, *Design Faults: The Asia Pacific' s Regional Architecture*, policy brief (Sydney: Lowy Institute for International Policy, July 2007), http://lowyinstitute.org/Publication.asp?pid = 638.

40. ASEAN Secretariat, *ASEAN Vision, 2020* (Jakarta, Indonesia: ASEAN, 1997), http://www.aseansec.org/1814.htm.

41. "Bush Announces Int'l Coalition to Coordinate Relief," IndiaInfo.com, December 30, 2004, http://news.indiainfo.com/2004/12/30/3012tsunamibush.html.

42. Barry Desker, "Is the ARF Obsolete? Three Steps to Avoid Irrelevance," *PacNet*, no. 37A (July 27, 2006), http://www.csis.org/media/csis/pubs/pac0637a.pdf.

Appendix

SELECTED LIST OF PRINCIPAL
REGIONAL INSTITUTIONS IN ASIA

ASEAN Plus Three (APT)
Members: Brunei Darussalam, Burma, Cambodia, Indonesia, Laos, Malaysia,
    Philippines, Singapore, Thailand, and Vietnam; plus Japan, People's Repub-
    lic of China, and Republic of Korea
Founded: 1997

ASEAN Regional Forum (ARF)
Members: Australia, Brunei Darussalam, Burma, Cambodia, Canada, Demo-
    cratic People's Republic of Korea, East Timor, European Union, India, Indo-
    nesia, Japan, Laos, Malaysia, Mongolia, New Zealand, Pakistan, Papua New
    Guinea, People's Republic of China, Philippines, Republic of Korea, Rus-
    sian Federation, Singapore, Sri Lanka, Thailand, United States of America,
    and Vietnam
Founded: 1994

Asia Europe Meeting (ASEM)
Members: Brunei Darussalam, Burma, Cambodia, European Union, India, In-
    donesia, Japan, Laos, Malaysia, Mongolia, Republic of Korea, Pakistan, Peo-
    ple's Republic of China, Philippines, Singapore, Thailand, and Vietnam
Founded: 1996

Asian and Pacific Council (ASPAC)
Members: Australia, Japan, Malaysia, New Zealand, Philippines, Republic of
China (Taiwan), Republic of Korea, South Vietnam, and Thailand
Founded: 1966
Disbanded: 1975

Asia-Pacific Economic Cooperation (APEC)
Members: Australia, Brunei Darussalam, Canada, Chile, Chinese Taipei, Hong
Kong, Indonesia, Japan, Malaysia, Mexico, New Zealand, Papua New
Guinea, People's Republic of China, Peru, Philippines, Republic of Korea,
Russian Federation, Singapore, Thailand, United States of America, and
Vietnam
Founded: 1989

Asia-Pacific Partnership on Clean Development and Climate (APPCDC)
Members: Australia, India, Japan, People's Republic of China, Republic of
Korea, and United States of America.
Founded: 2005

Association of Southeast Asian Nations (ASEAN)
Members: Brunei Darussalam, Burma, Cambodia, Indonesia, Laos, Malaysia,
Philippines, Singapore, Thailand, and Vietnam
Founded: 1967

Bay of Bengal Initiative for Multi-Sectoral Technical and Economic Coopera-
tion (BIMSTEC)
Members: Bangladesh, Bhutan, Burma, India, Nepal, Sri Lanka, and Thailand
Founded: 1997

Central Treaty Organization (CENTO)
Members: Iran, Iraq, Pakistan, Turkey, United Kingdom, and United States of
America
Founded: 1955
Disbanded: 1979

Chiang Mai Initiative (CMI)
Established: 2000

Comprehensive Economic Partnership in East Asia (CEPEA)
Proposed: 2006

East Asia Economic Caucus (EAEC)
Members: Brunei, Indonesia, Japan, Malaysia, People's Republic of China, Philippines, Republic of Korea, Singapore, and Thailand
Proposed: 1990

East Asia Summit (EAS)
Members: Australia, Brunei Darussalam, Burma, Cambodia, India, Indonesia, Japan, Laos, Malaysia, New Zealand, People's Republic of China, Philippines, Republic of Korea, Singapore, Thailand, and Vietnam
Founded: 2005

Executives' Meeting of East Asia Pacific Central Banks (EMEAP)
Members: Bangko Sentral Ng Pilipins, Bank Indonesia, Bank Negara Malaysia, Bank of Japan, Bank of Korea, Bank of Thailand, Hong Kong Monetary Authority, Monetary Authority of Singapore, People's Bank of China, Reserve Bank of Australia, Reserve Bank of New Zealand
Founded: 1991

Free Trade Area of the Asia-Pacific (FTAAP)
Members: Australia, Brunei Darussalam, Canada, Chile, Chinese Taipei, Hong Kong, Indonesia, Japan, Malaysia, Mexico, New Zealand, Papua New Guinea, People's Republic of China, Peru, Philippines, Republic of Korea, Russian Federation, Singapore, Thailand, United States of America, and Vietnam
Proposed: 2006

Indian Ocean Rim Association for Regional Cooperation (IORARC)
Members: Australia, Bangladesh, India, Indonesia, Iran, Kenya, Madagascar, Malaysia, Mauritis, Mozambique, Oman, Singapore, South Africa, Sri Lanka, Tanzania, Thailand, United Arab Emirates, and Yemen
Founded: 1995

International Law Enforcement Academy (ILEA)
Established: 1995

Jakarta Center for Law Enforcement Cooperation (JCLEC)
Members: Indonesia and Australia
Founded: 2004

Korean Energy Development Organization (KEDO)
Members: Argentina, Australia, Canada, Chile, Czech Republic, European Union, Indonesia, Japan, New Zealand, Poland, Republic of Korea, United States of America, and Uzbekistan
Founded: 1995

Pacific Basin Economic Council (PBEC)
Members: Australia, Canada, Chile, Chinese Taipei, Colombia, Ecuador, Hong Kong, Indonesia, Japan, Malaysia, Mexico, New Zealand, People's Republic of China, Peru, Philippines, Republic of Korea, Russian Federation, Singapore, Thailand, and United States of America
Founded: 1967

Pacific Economic Cooperation Council (PECC)
Members: Australia, Brunei Darussalam, Canada, Chile, Chinese Taipei, Colombia, Ecuador, Hong Kong, Indonesia, Japan, Malaysia, Mexico, New Zealand, Pacific Islands Forum, People's Republic of China, Peru, Philippines, Republic of Korea, Singapore, Thailand, United States of America, and Vietnam
Founded: 1980

Proliferation Security Initiative (PSI)
Core Members: Australia, Canada, Denmark, France, Germany, Italy, Japan, Netherlands, Norway, Poland, Portugal, Russian Federation, Singapore, Spain, United Kingdom, and United States of America
Established: 2003

Regional Cooperation Agreement on Combating Piracy and Armed Robbery Against Ships in Asia (ReCAAP)
Members: Bangladesh, Brunei Darussalam, Burma, Cambodia, India, Indonesia, Japan, Laos, Malaysia, People's Republic of China, Philippines, Republic of Korea, Singapore, Sri Lanka, Thailand, and Vietnam
Founded: 2006

Shanghai Cooperation Organization (SCO)
Members: Kazakhstan, Kyrgyz Republic, People's Republic of China, Russian Federation, Tajikistan, and Uzbekistan
Founded: 2001

Six-Party Talks
Members: Japan, Democratic People's Republic of Korea, People's Republic of
    China, Republic of Korea, Russian Federation, and United States of America
Established: 2003

South Asian Association for Regional Cooperation (SAARC)
Members: Afghanistan, Bangladesh, Bhutan, India, Maldives, Nepal, Pakistan,
    and Sri Lanka
Founded: 1985

South Asian Economic Union (SAEU)
Proposed: 2007

Southeast Asia Regional Center for Counter-Terrorism (SEARCCT)
Established: 2002

Southeast Asia Treaty Organization (SEATO)
Members: Australia, France, New Zealand, Pakistan, Philippines, Thailand,
    United Kingdom, and United States of America
Founded: 1954
Disbanded: 1977

Trilateral Coordination and Oversight Group (TCOG)
Members: Japan, Republic of Korea, and United States of America
Founded: 2003

Trilateral Security Dialogue (TSD)
Members: Australia, Japan, and United States of America
Founded: 2002

Zone of Peace, Friendship, and Neutrality (ZOPFAN)
Members: Indonesia, Malaysia, Philippines, Singapore, and Thailand
Founded: 1971

CONTRIBUTORS

AMITAV ACHARYA is a professor of global governance and the director of the Governance Research Centre at the University of Bristol. Prior to joining the University of Bristol, he was a professor of international relations at Nanyang Technological University, Singapore, and deputy director of the Institute of Defense and Strategic Studies there. He specializes in multilateralism, regionalism, human security, international-relations theory, and Asian security. He previously taught in the Department of Political Science at York University, Toronto, where he was the associate director of the University of Toronto–York University Joint Centre for Asia Pacific Studies. His recent publications include *Constructing a Security Community in Southeast Asia* (2001) and journal articles in *International Organization, International Security, Pacific Review, Third World Quarterly,* and *Political Studies.*

MELY CABALLERO-ANTHONY is an associate professor at the Rajaratnam School of International Studies at Nanyang Technological University in Singapore and coordinator of the Asian Consortium on Non-Traditional Security Studies in Asia. She specializes in regionalism and regional security in the Asia Pacific, conflict prevention and management, nontraditional security, and human security. She is a member of the Council for Security and Cooperation in the Asia-Pacific in Singapore and its Working Group on Peace Operations, as well as an associate member of the ASEAN Institute of Strategic and International Studies.

WILLIAM COLE is the senior director of the governance, law, and civil-society programs and of program strategy and development at the Asia Foundation. He has held a range of foreign-aid and policy research positions focused on democracy and governance reform, economic policy reform, social change, strategic planning and management, and project design and evaluation. He is a frequent writer and speaker on topics related to Asian development, Afghanistan, democracy and governance, and the political economy of social and economic reform.

RALPH A. COSSA is the president of the Pacific Forum, affiliated with the Center for Strategic and International Studies. He is a senior editor of the forum's quarterly electronic journal *Comparative Connections*. He is also a member of the ASEAN Regional Forum Experts and Eminent Persons Group and a founding member of the Steering Committee of the Council for Security Cooperation in the Asia Pacific. He cochairs the council's study group aimed at halting the proliferation of weapons of mass destruction in the Asia-Pacific region and serves as the executive director of the council's U.S. Member Committee.

AKIKO FUKUSHIMA is a senior fellow at the Japan Foundation. She received her M.A. from the Paul H. Nitze School of Advanced International Studies at Johns Hopkins University and her Ph.D. from Osaka University. She serves as a member of a number of committees, including the Japanese Defense Ministry's Council on Defense Facilities and the Asia-Pacific Economic Cooperation Study Group. Her publications include *Japanese Foreign Policy: The Emerging Logic of Multilateralism* (1999) and *A Lexicon of Asia Pacific Security Dialogue* (2003).

BATES GILL is director of the Stockholm International Peace Research Institute in Stockholm, Sweden. He previously held the Freeman Chair in China Studies at the Center for Strategic and International Studies (2002–2007) and was the inaugural director of the Center for Northeast Asian Policy Studies at the Brookings Institution (1998–2002). A specialist in East Asian foreign policy and security issues, he is a member of the Council on Foreign Relations and the International Institute for Strategic Studies. His most recent book is *Rising Star: China's New Security Diplomacy* (2007).

MICHAEL J. GREEN is associate professor of international relations at Georgetown University, as well as senior advisor and Japan chair at the Center for Strategic and International Studies in Washington, D.C. He served on the National Security Council staff from 2001 through 2005, first as director for Asian affairs responsible for Japan and Korea and then as special assistant to the president and senior director for Asia. Prior to joining the National Security Council, he held positions at the Council on Foreign Relations, the Institute for Defense Analyses, and the Paul H. Nitze School of Advanced International Studies at Johns Hopkins University. His publications include *Japan's Reluctant Realism: Foreign Policy in an Era of Uncertain Power* (2001), *The U.S.-Japan Alliance: Past, Present and Future* (coedited with Patrick M. Cronin, 1999), and *Arming Japan: Defense Production, Alliance Politics, and the Post-war Search for Autonomy* (1995). He is a member of the Council on Foreign Relations and the Aspen Strategy Group and serves on several advisory boards, including for the Center for a New American Security and the Australian-America Leadership Dialogue.

ERIK G. JENSEN is a senior law adviser at the Asia Foundation; the codirector of the Rule of Law Program at Stanford Law School; and a research scholar for the Center on Democracy, Development, and the Rule of Law at Stanford University. He also advises the World Bank and the Asian Development Bank on empirical research design and evaluation. He is the coeditor (with Thomas C. Heller) of *Beyond Common Knowledge: Empirical Approaches to the Rule of Law* (2003).

LIM WONHYUK is a fellow at the Korea Development Institute. He received B.A.S. degrees in physics and history and a Ph.D. in economics from Stanford University. He previously taught at the Korea Military Academy and worked as a consultant for the World Bank and the Asian Development Bank Institute. He also served as an advisor for the Presidential Transition Committee after the 2002 election in South Korea. Most recently, he was at the Brookings Institution as the Center for Northeast Asian Policy Studies Fellow from South Korea for 2005/2006.

C. RAJA MOHAN is a professor at the S. Rajaratnam School of International Studies at Nanyang Technological University in Singapore and the strategic affairs editor of the *Indian Express* (New Delhi). He previously was a professor of South Asian studies at the Jawaharlal Nehru University in New Delhi. He also serves as the diplomatic editor and Washington correspondent of *The Hindu*. He has an M.A. in nuclear physics and a Ph.D. in international relations. He was a member of India's National Security Advisory Board from 1998 to 2000 and from 2004 to 2006. He was a Jennings Randolph Peace Fellow at the U.S. Institute of Peace in Washington, D.C., from 1992 to 1993. His recent books include *Crossing the Rubicon: The Shaping of India's New Foreign Policy* (2004) and *Impossible Allies: Nuclear India, United States, and the Global Order* (2006).

MICHAEL E. O'HANLON is a senior fellow of foreign-policy studies at the Brookings Institution. He specializes in national security. His previous works on East Asia include volumes coauthored with Richard Bush and Mike Mochizuki.

AMY SEARIGHT is the Gaston Sigur Memorial Assistant Professor of Political Science and International Affairs at George Washington University. She received her B.A. in political economy from Williams College and her Ph.D. in political science from Stanford University. Before joining George Washington, she served on the faculty at Northwestern University and was an advanced research fellow at the Program on U.S.-Japan Relations at Harvard University. She also has been a visiting scholar at the Institute of Monetary and Fiscal Policy at the Ministry of Finance in Japan. In 2003/2004, she was the Council on Foreign Relations International Affairs Fellow at the U.S. State Department, where she worked on Asia-Pacific Economic Cooperation policy in the Bureau of East Asia and Pacific Affairs and on Asian multilateral architecture with the Policy Planning Staff. Her research focuses on Japanese trade policies, U.S. and Japanese regional diplomacy in Asia, U.S.-Japan relations, and multilateral trade organizations.

GREG SHERIDAN is the foreign-affairs editor of *The Australian*. He is the most influential foreign-affairs and strategic commentator in the Australian media. He has authored five books covering different aspects of Asian culture and politics, Australian foreign policy, and the U.S.-Australia alliance. His work has been widely anthologized and translated into several Asian languages. His journalism has appeared in newspapers around the world, including the *Wall Street Journal*, the *Sunday Times* of London, and the *Jakarta Post*. He is a contributing editor to the *National Interest* and a visiting fellow at the Australian Land Warfare Studies Center, and has twice been a visiting fellow at the Center for Strategic and International Studies in Washington, D.C.

BRENDAN TAYLOR is a lecturer at the Strategic and Defense Studies Center of Australian National University. His research interests include Asia-Pacific security, alliance politics, U.S. foreign policy, and economic statecraft and sanctions. He is the editor of *Australia as an Asia-Pacific Regional Power: Friendships in Flux?* (2007).

WILLIAM T. TOW is a professor of international security in the Department of International Relations at Australian National University and the chief investigator at the Australian Research Council's Center of Excellence in Policy and Security. He has authored or edited eighteen books and numerous articles on

Asian security and U.S. alliance politics in the Asia-Pacific region. His latest works include *Asia-Pacific Security: U.S., Australia, and Japan and the New Security Triangle* (coedited with Mark J. Thomson, Yoshinobu Yamamoto, and Satu P. Limaye, 2007), *Asia-Pacific Strategic Relations: Seeking Convergent Security* (1991), and recent articles in such journals as *Asian Security, Australian Journal of International Affairs, Contemporary Southeast Asia, Current History, International Relations of the Asia Pacific,* and *Pacific Review.*

WU XINBO is a professor and the deputy director at the Center for American Studies and an associate dean at the School of International Relations and Public Affairs of Fudan University, Shanghai, China. He teaches China-U.S. relations and U.S. Asia-Pacific policy, and writes widely on China's foreign policy, Sino-American relations, and Asia-Pacific issues. He has published two books in China as well as numerous articles and book chapters in China, the United States, Japan, Germany, South Korea, Singapore, and India.

INDEX